BODY/STATE

Gender in a Global/Local World

Series Editors: Jane Parpart, Pauline Gardiner Barber
and Marianne H. Marchand

Gender in a Global/Local World critically explores the uneven and often contradictory ways in which global processes and local identities come together. Much has been and is being written about globalization and responses to it but rarely from a critical, historical, gendered perspective. Yet, these processes are profoundly gendered albeit in different ways in particular contexts and times. The changes in social, cultural, economic and political institutions and practices alter the conditions under which women and men make and remake their lives. New spaces have been created – economic, political, social – and previously silent voices are being heard. North-South dichotomies are being undermined as increasing numbers of people and communities are exposed to international processes through migration, travel, and communication, even as marginalization and poverty intensify for many in all parts of the world. The series features monographs and collections which explore the tensions in a 'global/local world', and includes contributions from all disciplines in recognition that no single approach can capture these complex processes.

Previous titles are listed at the back of the book

Body/State

Edited by

ANGUS CAMERON
University of Leicester, UK

JEN DICKINSON
University of Leicester, UK

NICOLA SMITH
University of Birmingham, UK

R Routledge
Taylor & Francis Group

LONDON AND NEW YORK

First published 2013 by Ashgate Publishing

2 Park Square, Milton Park, Abingdon, Oxon OX14 4RN

711 Third Avenue, New York, NY 10017, USA

Routledge is an imprint of the Taylor & Francis Group, an informa business

First issued in paperback 2016

British Library Cataloguing in Publication Data
Body/State. – (Gender in a Global/Local World)
 1. Social ecology. 2. Social control. 3. Human body – Political aspects. 4. Human
 body – Social aspects. 5. Sex customs. I. Series II. Body and state III. Dickinson, Jen.
 IV. Cameron, Angus, 1965– V. Smith, Nicola.
 304–dc23

Library of Congress Cataloging-in-Publication Data
Body/State / [edited] by Angus Cameron, Jen Dickinson, and Nicola Smith.
 p. cm. – (Gender in a Global/Local World)
 Includes bibliographical references and index.
 1. Power (Social sciences) 2. Social control. 3. State, The – Social aspects.
 4. Human body – Political aspects. I. Cameron, Angus, 1965– II. Dickinson, Jen.
 III. Smith, Nicola Jo-Anne.
 JC330.B596 2012
 303.3'3–dc23   2012021694

ISBN 978-1-4094-2449-9 (hbk)
ISBN 978-1-138-25351-3 (pbk)

Contents

List of Figures

Notes on Contributors

Claudia Aradau is Senior Lecturer in International Relations in the Department of War Studies, King's College London. Her research interrogates the effects of security practices for political subjectivity and emancipation. She is the author of *Rethinking Trafficking in Women: Politics out of Security* (Palgrave, 2008) and co-author, with Rens van Munster, of *Politics of Catastrophe: Genealogies of the Unknown* (Routledge, 2011).

Tom Boellstorff is Professor in the Department of Anthropology at the University of California, Irvine. From 2007-12 he was Editor-in-Chief of *American Anthropologist*, the flagship journal of the American Anthropological Association. He is the author of many articles and the books *The Gay Archipelago: Sexuality and Nation in Indonesia* (Princeton University Press, 2005); *A Coincidence of Desires: Anthropology, Queer Studies, Indonesia* (Duke University Press, 2007); and *Coming of Age in Second Life: An Anthropologist Explores the Virtually Human* (Princeton University Press, 2008). He is also the co-author of *Ethnography and Virtual Worlds: A Handbook of Method* (Princeton University Press, 2012).

Gavin Brown joined the Non-Stop Picket of the South African Embassy during the summer of 1986, when he was 16. Over the next four years, he became increasingly involved with both the Picket and the running of the City of London Anti-Apartheid Group. His most regular shift on the Picket was 12 – 6pm on Saturday afternoons. Since 2007 he has been a Lecturer in Human Geography at the University of Leicester. He is principal investigator on the "Non-Stop Against Apartheid: spaces of transnational solidarity activism" research project funded by the Leverhulme Trust (see http://nonstopagainstapartheid.wordpress.com/). He has published widely on the geographies of sexualities and social movement activism.

Ian Bruff is Lecturer in International Relations in the Department of Politics, History and International Relations at Loughborough University. His research focuses on European varieties of capitalism, neoliberalism, and social (especially historical materialist) theory. He is the author of *Culture and Consensus in European Varieties of Capitalism* (Palgrave, 2008) and a co-editor of *Critical International Political Economy* (Palgrave, 2011). He is the Chair of the Critical Political Economy Research Network of the European Sociological Association.

Angus Cameron has a varied, not to say confused, professional history embracing journalism, art history, international political economy, international relations, geography, management and performance art. Throughout all this interdisciplinary meandering his core interests have, however, remained constant: identity, spatiality, power. He is currently playing around with, among other things, money, cartography, metaphoric islands, boundaries, devils, tricksters, fools, theories of exception, virtuality and, of course, bodies. He is co-author of *The Imagined Economies of Globalization* (with Ronen Palan, Sage, 2004) and *Placing the Social Economy* (with Ash Amin and Ray Hudson, Routledge, 2002) and co-editor of the *Sage International Political Economy Reader*, (with Anastasia Nesvetailova and Ronen Palan).

Jen Dickinson is a human geographer based at the University of Leicester. Her research is focused on migration, diasporas and organ transplantation, with an underlying interest in the ethics and responsibilities of care. Currently she is researching the lively biogeographies of Kenya's national parks under decolonization. Her work has appeared in the journals *Social and Cultural Geography*, *ACME*, *Political Geography* and *Transactions of the Institute of British Geographers,* amongst others

Emma A. Foster is Lecturer in the Department of Political Science and International Studies at the University of Birmingham. She teaches in the areas of Gender and Sexuality and Gender and International Development/Relations. Currently she is researching issues of Gender and Sexuality broadly in relation to (Queering) International Development and Sustainable Development.

goldin+senneby (since 2004) is a framework for collaboration set up by artists Simon Goldin and Jakob Senneby; exploring juridical, financial and spatial constructs through notions of the performative and the virtual. Their collaboration started with The Port (2004-06); acting in an emerging public sphere constructed through digital code. Since 2010 their work has focused on The Nordenskiöld Model, an experiment in theatrical finance. Solo exhibitions include: 'The Decapitation of Money', Kadist Art Foundation, Paris (2010); 'Headless. From the public record', Index, Stockholm (2009); 'Goldin+senneby: Headless', The Power Plant, Toronto (2008). Group exhibitions include: 'The End of Money', Witte de With, Rotterdam (2011); 'The Moderna Exhibition', Moderna Museet, Stockholm (2010); 'Uneven Geographies', Nottingham Contemporary (2010); 'In living contact', 28th Bienal de Sao Paulo (2008). Residencies include: Kadist, Paris (2010); Gasworks, London (2008); IASPIS, Stockholm (2007)

Peter Kraftl is a Senior Lecturer in Human Geography at the University of Leicester. He is the author of over forty journal articles and book chapters about childhood and youth, geographies of formal and informal education, and architecture. He has recently co-investigated projects looking at young people's experiences of school spaces and sustainable urban design. He is co-editor (with John Horton and Faith Tucker) of *Critical Geographies of Childhood and Youth*

(Policy Press, 2012). He has two forthcoming books on *Geographies of Alternative Education* and *Cultural Geographies*.

Katie Ledingham is an ESRC funded postgraduate research student in the Department of Geography at the University of Exeter. Her research interests lie at the intersection between law and geography and she is undertaking her PhD thesis on 'Establishing a Reconciliatory Legal Dialogue: Traversing Boundaries, Perspectives and Understandings of 'Nature'.

Ming Lim is based at the University of Leicester. Her research is focused on marketing, global branding, consumer culture, ethics, social enterprise and the intersections between philosophy and management. She has co-authored *Marketing: A Critical Text* (Routledge, 2010) and another book on *Global Branding: Critical Perspectives* is forthcoming (Routledge). Her work has appeared in *Business Ethics: A European Review, Journal of Industrial Marketing Management, Consumption, Markets and Culture* and many others.

Bill Maurer is Professor of Anthropology and Law, and the Director of the Institute for Money, Technology and Financial Inclusion, at the University of California, Irvine. He is a cultural anthropologist who studies law, money and finance, particularly new and experimental financial and currency forms and their legal implications. His research has been supported by grants from the National Science Foundation, the Russell Sage Foundation, and other sources. He is the editor of six collections, as well as the author of *Recharting the Caribbean: Land, Law and Citizenship in the British Virgin Islands* (1997), *Pious Property: Islamic Mortgages in the United States* (2006), and *Mutual Life, Limited: Islamic Banking, Alternative Currencies, Lateral Reason* (2005). The latter received the Victor Turner Prize in 2005.

Elham Mireshghi is a PhD candidate in the Department of Anthropology at the University of California, Irvine. She holds a degree in Electrical Engineering and Computer Science and also has experience in the intellectual property arena. Her research explores lived experiences of kidney donation and transplantation in Iran, the only country to have a regulated program for compensated kidney donation. She is broadly interested in anthropology of the body, public policy, and concepts of gifting and value exchange. Her research has been supported by grants from the National Science Foundation and the Wenner Gren Foundation for Anthropological Research.

Mark Neocleous is Professor of the Critique of Political Economy at Brunel University, UK, and a member of the Editorial Collective of *Radical Philosophy*. His most recent book is *Critique of Security* (2008). His current project is a work of counter-strategic theory, centred on the concept of pacification.

Reecia Orzeck is Assistant Professor of Geography at Illinois State University. She writes on the international law, the Israeli-Palestinian conflict, and the body in academic and geopolitical discourses. Her previous work on the body includes the article, "What does not kill you: Historical Materialism and the body" *Environment and Planning D: Society and Space* 25:496-514.

Heather Palmer is a primary school teacher and freelance writer with an interest in the artistic representation of selfhood and material reality.

Nicola Smith is Senior Lecturer at the Department of Political Science and International Studies, University of Birmingham. Her publications include *Showcasing Globalisation? The Political Economy of the Irish Republic* (Manchester University Press, 2005) and *Global Social Justice* (Routledge, 2011), co-edited with Heather Widdows. Nicola recently completed a Leverhulme Trust-funded project on the political economy of male and transgender sex work in the UK and the Netherlands and is currently preparing a monograph for Palgrave on this theme.

Series Editors' Preface

States, powerful and contested, continue to exert power over the bodies of citizens, but the modalities of state disciplining and intervention are changing. So too, embodied responses to expressions of state power are adaptive, out of necessity and sometimes for revolutionary purposes. In this exciting new volume, *Body/State*, edited by Angus Cameron, Jen Dickinson, and Nicola Smith, questions are posed about the relationship between citizen body/ies and nation state(s). Has the meaning of the state changed relative to gendered bodies given the power of new media and digital technologies? On the one hand, states have gained the capacity to become even more intrusive into and beyond the 'private sphere', linking body/state in increasingly complex articulations. And yet, new media have also enabled citizenry to mobilize against state power in unprecedented and sometimes confusing ways. How, then, should we theorize such complexity within the gendered contemporary body politic? What are the biopolitics of particular cases? And, ultimately, has the meaning of the state changed? Such puzzles animate this truly interdisciplinary collection whose authors have backgrounds in geography, international relations, anthropology, politics and political economy, marketing, activism, and the arts.

The editors commence with a provocative introduction outlining the volume's purpose and promise; theoretical, empirical, and political. Each of the book's five sections encapsulates the varied engagements between bodies, embodiment, and states, whether in terms of regulation, surveillance and sovereignty, or resistance and escape from state power. What captured our attention in selecting this book for our series is its remarkable breadth and innovation. We believe it will appeal to scholars concerned with bodies and states to encourage new cross-disciplinary dialogues and bring new voices to the debate. Collections such as this one, examining state power, politics, and international relations alongside representations of edgy cultural performance, are relatively infrequent. But *Body/State* illustrates how complimentary modes of enquiry applied across a broad swath of subjects can expand our understanding of state power in an increasingly mediatized, digitalized world and bring new perspectives to both feminist scholarship and political studies. We are pleased to introduce these essays to a wide readership interested in our *Gender in a Global/Local World* thematic. We look forward to continuing the debates provoked by this collection.

Pauline Gardiner Barber
Marianne Marchand
Jane Parpart

Acknowledgements

This book began life as a chance encounter with a whiteboard. Jen Dickinson was teaching in a room recently vacated by one of Angus Cameron's classes, and thus was bequeathed the task of wiping the random scribble off the whiteboard that he had helpfully left behind. The class in question had been considering - at the request of the students themselves the previous week - the body as a state space, and the board was duly covered in stuff relating to monarchy, smoking, diet, police baton use, blood donation, organ transplantation, money and bodily metaphors of various kinds. Jen's shared interest in these things led to a conversation about bodies, which very quickly led to the kernel of the book. Further chance encounters led us to Nicki Smith's work on feminist political economy and, therefore, to the third co-editor. Even more happy accidents brought us into contact with several of the authors that have kindly contributed to this collection. The moral of this tale is: never clean your own whiteboard.

Our first and warmest thanks must go to the authors that have allowed us to publish their work as part of this collection. They have all been generous with their time (and occasionally with ours, for which we happily forgive them), but above all with their erudition without we could have done very little. We would like to thank colleagues in the School of Management and Department of Geography (Leicester) and the Department of Political Science and International Studies (Birmingham), for their support for our work and for this project. To the one or two individuals who tried to dissuade us from completing this book, because it wouldn't 'count' for some research audit or other, we offer nothing but pity.

We would very much like to thank Jane Parpart, Pauline Gardiner Barber and Marianne Marchand and the team at Ashgate (and particularly Kirstin Howgate) for making this project possible and for ensuring that the process throughout ran so smoothly. Nicki would also like to express her gratitude to the Leverhulme Trust for supporting her work on body politics, which includes this collaborative project. In addition, we must thank our students, not least the several generations who participated in and helped shape Angus' course 'Spatialities of the Contemporary State'. Without their inspiration, the whiteboard would never have been scribbled on in quite the way that it was, and this book might never have happened. Finally, we are all (as always) indebted to our friends and families.

For Agnes, Irene, Albert, Billy and Tom

Chapter 1

Bodies, States and Body-States

Angus Cameron, Jen Dickinson and Nicola Smith

In late November 2011, a young Egyptian activist, secularist and feminist, Aliaa Magda Elmahdy, posted nude photographs of herself on her blog. In the context of an ongoing domestic revolution in Egypt that had claimed hundreds of lives and witnessed appalling acts of police and military violence against civilians, this would not have seemed the most shocking act of protest. Even less so at a time when the combination of digital photography and increasingly global internet access make such images almost ubiquitous. The Egyptian revolution was, after all, purportedly the first to be mediated through social networking sites, and it is hard to imagine that none of those tweeting about events in Tahrir Square were not also sampling the Internet's 'other' content. Yet Ms. Elmahdy's act stirred up a storm of outrage not just from all parts of Egyptian society (the main opposition groups occupying Tahrir Square publicly denounced her), but from across the Arab world. At a time when Egypt was in a state of violent fragmentation, the image of a single woman's body managed to galvanise a degree of repressive social solidarity one might have thought impossible.

At one level Elmahdy's pictures can be read as simply a deliberate provocation to Egypt's Islamic groups. Whilst the outrage from the more conservative elements was entirely predictable, the degree of wider condemnation was more surprising. Although nudity was the headline cause for this, the Elmahdy case also exposed much deeper issues concerning, among other things, changing modalities of body representation, the nature and power of new media, the (in)visibility of women (primarily in Islamic societies, but far beyond them) and the power of state and society to discipline bodies. In short, and to a degree she probably never imagined, Elmahdy questioned the state and status of the body in a rapidly changing world.

In recent decades, as a consequence of intertwined processes of technological innovation (the Internet and related digital technologies above all), changing social and political attitudes (for example towards gender difference and sexual preference, to pornography, etc.) and greater direct access to power (the increasing, if uneven, reach of women into board-rooms and government, for example), the ways that bodies of all kinds are present/absent, represented, managed, shaped, disciplined and/or excluded are changing. While there is, perhaps nothing new in this – from its inception the 'social body' (Poovey 1995) has always been a constructed and emergent entity – the disruption of the relatively stable conceptual relationship between the citizen body and the nation state in its various forms is producing new potentialities and actualities to which bodies are having to adapt or be adapted. This is perhaps most strikingly illustrated by (but cannot be reduced to) the fact that the capacity of nation-states to intervene in body-states (of their own and others' citizens) has altered dramatically. This does not necessarily mean that such interventions have diminished, but that the nature of those interventions, the context in which they are and can be made, and the groups targeted by them are all changing. This not only raises questions over the nature of embodiment – where, for example, are the body's boundaries in the context of digital technologies? – but questions the meaning of the state itself. Aliaa Magda Elmahdy, after all, managed to elicit a state-like reaction from a socio-political context in which the formal institutions of the Egyptian state were barely functioning. Ironically, Egypt's emergent, mediatised, revolutionary crypto-state seems to be articulated through the same technologies that were hailed for their role in the occupation of Tahrir Square and by Ms. Elmahdy herself for her act of bodily defiance.

This book brings together a series of chapters that start, in various ways, to work round and through emergent body states. Although very different in style and content, all of the contributions are intended as accessible, relatively informal interventions that open up debate on issues important to all of us. It does not claim to be, and nor is it intended to be, comprehensive of the full range of possible body states – that would be far beyond the scope of any single volume. Rather, it is intended to create a space for a consideration of the theoretical, empirical and political implications they raise. This book has come into being because, as the case of Aliaa Magda Elmahdy above reveals, there has been a proliferation of ideas, insights and knowledge surrounding the biopolitics of bodies across an ever-widening range of social, political and academic concerns and thus warrants concentrated attention. In this introductory chapter, we lay out the groundwork for understanding these developments and contextualise the papers that follow.

Body Politics, Gendered States

States and bodies exist in different realms – or so it seems. The state is often seen as synonymous with the 'public' sphere of politics – a world of government, power and collectivity – whereas the body is frequently imagined to reside in the 'private' sphere – a world of intimacy, selfhood and individuality. Because of this, feminist scholars have long sought to highlight how the supposedly straightforward division between states and bodies is also deeply gendered and, as such, steeped in and reproductive of power relations. Central to feminist theory and political practice, therefore, has been a desire to expose and interrogate how states and bodies cannot and should not be separated so easily – if indeed they can be separated at all. At its most prosaic level, the bodies of most of those who sit in positions of power in the world's governments have traditionally been male (and even where not excusively male, nevertheless categorised as such) and, despite many years of effort towards female emancipation and participation, this is still largely the case. Even where this imbalance has begun to be redressed, accounts of women in parliaments have been concerned with the achievement of equal political representation with men in order that gender-based experiences and concerns might be more effectively advanced through the conceptualisation and implementation of equality of opportunities and rights. These efforts often explicitly revolve around the nature, status and security of women's bodies, through issues such as maternity rights, domestic violence, access to public space, and so on – (cf. Kantola 2006). The recent global trend of using gender quotas in order to increase women's political representation in formal politics demonstrates the continued existence of structural discrimination in women's access to the formal sphere of political decision-making.

Perhaps more importantly for our purposes here, feminist scholarship has sought to expose how the state itself is often coded as masculine: that is, it is associated with the public realm of political power and decision-making and, as such, with masculine influence and identity (Youngs 2000). The body, in contrast, is frequently coded as feminine in its multiple associations with nature, emotions, sexuality, vulnerability, reproduction and the family (Hooper, 2000). It is no surprise, then, that issues surrounding embodiment – not least with respect to the 'body politic' itself – have emerged as principal preoccupations for feminist thought and practice. For, as Wendy Harcourt (2009: 23) writes, the body can be regarded as:

> a place for political mobilization interconnected with other sites of resistance and political action … bodies are not external to political processes but firmly enmeshed in them, even if they are not necessarily the defining site for action. The lived experience of the body, the identity and definitions attached to bodies, inform and are connected to all political struggles.

These developments in our understandings of political subjectivities make the rigid public–private split between bodies and states untenable. It paves the way for a reconfigured understanding of often-abstracted political processes into a form that is literally seen and felt in the realities of the flesh. The perpetration of state-sanctioned gender violence is one example of how political processes are often experienced in highly embodied ways. Dibyesh Anand (2007) for example, has reflected upon the active complicity of the state in the sexualised stereotyping of Muslim masculinity by Hindutva leaders, which legitimised violence as a defence of the Hindu body politic. Similarly, Reecia Orzeck (this volume) explores the force-feeding of detainees at Guantanamo Bay by the US Department of Defense, which was justified in terms of the need to preserve life and yet can also be read as an attempt to silence the voices of the incarcerated men and, as such, as the violent reproduction of state sovereignty through bodily control.

There are deeper issues, too, regarding the realisation of bodies – and these relate to the complex ways in which bodies become invisible, denied and erased. Feminist thought and practice has long sought to expose and challenge how women have been '"left-out" of history: it is men who have been the subjects in history (his-story as opposed to her-story)' (Zalewski 2004: 37). In so doing, feminists have confronted how the body has so often been assumed to be that of a 'normal', heterosexual male, in part by seeking to render visible the embodied lives and experiences both of women and of stigmatised and minority men (Pettman 2000: 52). But feminists have also sought to highlight the 'problem of the missing body' in social and political discourse at a more fundamental level (Youngs 2000: 1). Charlotte Hooper (2000: 39), for instance, has explored how bourgeois rational masculinity is organised around a series of gendered dualisms (including public/ private, mind/body, and inside/outside) that include a 'fantasy of disembodiment' which 'depends upon the apparent invisibility or absence of bodies in social discourse, so that masculine reason could be separate from and untainted from the body'. Writing about the bodies of the missing, marginal or marginalized can open up new critical perspectives on taken-for-granted practices and processes, as Nicola Smith's chapter on male sex work (this volume) explores. In some cases this 'invisibility' of the body seems to extend equally to all bodies – as suggested by Angus Cameron's analysis of the disembodied 'faceless map' (this volume). However, even here the assumption is that the body standing behind the viewspace of the empty, scientific spaces of cartography is one characterised implicitly by a rationalist, masculinist, technological relationship to the mapped landscape.

Considerations of the ways in which states regulate bodies also point to the ways that state norms and practices are not fixed but are continually challenged and renegotiated. Indeed, a central concern of feminist thought and action is that the diffusion of state norms and practice into everyday corporeal experiences is too simplistic to capture how people engage with political processes and how emotions, subjectivities and bodily practices feed into these engagements (Pain 2009). Thus, even as states seek to discipline bodies, bodies can have a transformative power of their own, shaping the practices and progress of politics at different scales. Individual bodies may be weak relative to the instituted power of the state – but the weak have weapons too (Scott 1987).

All of the chapters in this book deal with the nature and meaning of the contemporary body, although they do so in multiple and overlapping ways: some directly, some obliquely, some from a particular political or theoretical perspective, others leave it to the reader to decide on their implications. Although the book as a whole has a gendered focus, not all of the chapters that follow address this explicitly. To have limited our selection only to those writers engaging directly with feminist and/or gendered theory and politics would have produced a very different book – and no doubt a worthy one – but not perhaps one that captured the breadth of debate about the changing nature of the body that first stimulated this collection. As important as we feel that the individual contributions are, therefore, our hope is that the book as a whole will both stimulate debate and, because of its variety, defy easy answers. This is not because we want to confound the possibility of solutions to the many and troubling issues raised by these contributions, but because the environment in which such solutions might be found is complex and evolving. Here we wish to give some shape to the debates we see emerging from these particular contributions, as a first pass pointing to other interpretations and combinations (rather than as a definitive categorization). Hence there are sections dealing with, among other things, physical changes to the body (Part I), the economic/monetary body (Part II), embodied political and social deviance (Part III), surveillance (Part IV) and the growing importance of virtuality (Part V). Before outlining the overall structure of the book, we shall draw out some of the overarching themes that bring these disparate chapters together as a whole. These are, in no particular order: *representation, intervention, commodification, discipline* and *materiality.* Here we examine each in turn.

Representation

In one way or another all of the chapters in this collection are concerned with issues of bodily representation. This includes the way particular categories of body come to be actively represented in and through institutional and judicial processes (Ledingham, Aradou, Brown, Kraftl, Neocleous, Bruff, Dickinson & Sothern), evolving representations of gender and sexuality (Lim, Sothern, Foster, Smith) artistic representations of bodies (Palmer, goldin+senneby), and various other functional mode of embodied representation via technology (Boellstorff), money (Maurer & Mireshghi) and maps (Cameron). In all cases the ways in which bodies are constituted and institutionalised in and through various forms of representation – and the way certain modes of resistance are also centrally concerned with body representation – is central to their ontological status. Whilst one can argue that the relationship between 'real' bodies and their multiple representations (as citizens, threats, objects, resources, etc.) has been intense for a very long time, and certainly since the parameters of the 'social', 'medical', 'hygienic', 'economic' and 'psychoanalytic' body (Poovey 1995, Freud *et seq*) emerged in the 19th century, new representational possibilities and dynamics are emerging. As Boellstorff argues, for example, the simultaneous emergence of online socio-economic spaces, highly mobile moneys and consumer markets and the normalisation of the multiple body not only proliferates the represented body (particularly in the form of the avatar), but alters the ontological hierarchies between them. Visual and other analogues of bodies have existed for many centuries in the form of portraits and statues of various kinds, but however powerful these have been, there has never been any doubt about the primacy of the living subject. With the increasing use of electronic representations of the body – numerical, visual, narrative, etc. – that primacy starts to break down to an unprecedented degree as more and more aspects of lived 'life' is mediated through supplemental bodies and bodily forms. A new language is needed for these phenomena because the 'digital', which Boellstorff extends far beyond its usual association with computer technologies to embrace its arithmetical and relational meanings, opens up new modes of corporeal subjectivity that expand the locational and identitary possibilities of bodies.

Although Boellstorff's 'cyphergs' embrace these possibilities actively and reflexively, such representational bodily extensions and replications appear everywhere. Most importantly, attempts, knowing or otherwise by state institutions to define and repackage the bodies of particular citizens for various purposes appear throughout. Between the physical and 'legal' disabled bodies in Ledingham's chapter, for example, which is the more powerful and more affectively 'real'? Similarly, Sothern's analysis of state responses to HIV in the form of health campaigns, reveals the ways in which disease is bound up with other constitutions of body and gender difference. Health campaigns aimed at *Fa'afafine* men – boys raised 'in the way of a woman' – understood to be particularly at risk of infection, combine traditional Polynesian representations of gay male bodies, with post-colonial, epidemiological and social representations. Brought together as the 'Greatest Treasures of The Pacific', these health campaigns, for all their attempts to produce positive images of gay Polynesian cultures, neverthless reproduce the tensions of 'orientalist' colonial identities. Approaching institutional representations of gender difference from a different perspective, Nicola Smith critiques discourses of commercial sex work in which dominant understandings of supply and demand close off multiple and contested understandings of bodies and sexualities.

Entering what might at first sight appear the more conventional representational territory of the visual arts, both Heather Palmer and goldin+senneby, in very different ways, explore the complexities bodily representation and identity. Palmer draws us into the often shocking world of Joel-Peter Witkin's photography. Witkin's imagery often includes corpses, sometimes whole, sometimes dismembered, sometimes actively manipulated by the photographer himself, to meditate on the nature of the body, self, death, the erotic and, in Palmer's terms echoing Bataille and Merleau-Ponty, the *"I"*. Palmer carefully peels back the layers of Witkin's imagery both in its parallel interest in photographic method and image surface, and in the longer history of representations of dismembered and/or mutilated bodies. Witkin's images are shocking not because such images are unusual – they appear in all recorded visual cultures throughout history – but because images of bodies, particularly poor, ugly, distorted and abject bodies, are often concealed, hidden away, taboo. Those taboos are in part, of course, imposed by states and media companies that censor, for reasons that are rather vague, the visibility of dead and destroyed bodies.

Swedish performance artists goldin+senneby also address the issue of decapitation and the body, though in a very different way. "Act 3, Chapter 12, Authority" is one product of their project 'Headless' – a long-term exploration of the complex relationships between money, art, agency and capitalism through an 'investigation' into offshore-registered company 'Headless Ltd.' The chapter presented here is drawn from the novelised version of this project – presented in the form of a spy thriller – in which many of the people drawn into the project, and the events in which they have participated, are (re-) presented in (semi-)fictional form. "Act 3, Chapter 12, Authority" is the climax of the novel, focusing on the mental disintegration of one of its core characters – the project's 'spokesperson/ emissary', Angus Cameron. Standing at the point when the disparate and fragmented strands of the novel are finally brought crashing together – decapitation (again, after Bataille), money, spatiality, power, identity, risk, threat, secrecy, etc –

the (semi-) fictional Cameron's self-identity unravels in front of a public audience and a group of Macaques in a cage in London Zoo. The strange location alludes to an epiphany Georges Bataille claimed to have had there in the 1920s, where the monkeys inspired one of his most (in)famous writings – *The Solar Anus* – which is concerned with themes of corporeality, putrefaction, excrement and death. It's faintly ridiculous portrayal of someone confronting the limits of both mental and physical capacity – not least because by the time he gets to the Zoo he has been re-embodied many times over both in reality and in fiction – highlights the contingency and fragility of our corporeal selves. goldin+senneby's version of Cameron does violence to the fictional person, but also explodes aspects of embodiment vested in such concepts as authorship, personhood, agency, publicity and sovereignty. And it does this against the implied context of a state society in which, as all of the chapters included here illustrate in one way or another, the state's contingent and evolving relationship with the body as both practice and concept. Neither goldin+senneby, nor any of the other authors here try to resolve the contradictions inherent in such a relationship – the necessity of attempting to govern the ungovernable and indefinable physicality of the body – but open, often in graphic, visceral terms some of what it means to try to be a wholly embodied person in the societies in which we live.

If all of the above deal in one way or another with representational inclusions (i.e. representing the *present* body in various ways), Cameron's essay addresses a particular instance of the body's structured, representational *absence*. Specifically, he considers the process by which the body becomes completely invisible as it is removed progressively from the 'viewspace' constructed by evolving cartographic methods. The disappearance of the body from most conventional maps is accentuated by its partial, and problematic, reappearance in Google's 'Street View' which includes the bodies of those who happen to be on the streets it captures, but whose faces, and therefore identities, are then digitally removed. Cameron thus examines the relationship between the body and complex representational world of cartography. Far from depicting the world as it 'really' appears, maps are increasingly acknowledged as representing a discursive terrain upon which the social world is imagined and constituted.

Intervention

A second, and recurring, theme in the book is that of intervention – not just in terms of the reach of states *into* bodies but also through the transformation *of* bodily states. For Emma Foster and Jen Dickinson and Matt Sothern, for example, the transformation is literal – both are concerned with direct surgical interventions in the body and their consequences. For Reecia Orzeck, no surgery is involved, but we see the state – in this case in the form of the United States military – directly intervening in, and defining, the 'body resource' of its prisoners in Guantanamo Bay. The transformations chronicled in these chapters are, therefore, motivated by very different dynamics. Foster's account of the role of the state in, depending on your perspective, female mutilation and/or beautification addresses the conflicting social, moral, gender and political dilemmas arising from the state's, and our individual unease with the status of women's sexualised bodies. Focusing on female genital surgery, Foster compares and contrasts discourses surrounding surgery in Western and non-Western states, which she argues 'work to define difference and justify power imbalance between states' and thus hinder the emergence of new forms of solidarity and alliance.

The bodily interventions for Dickinson and Sothern are, on the surface at least, much simpler to reconcile – organ transplants save lives, after all – but in practice raise difficult moral and psychological issues. Organ 'transfer', they argue, does not neatly resolve the problems faced by the recipient of such 'gifts of life', but produces a set of real or perceived social and personal obligations, in addition to ongoing medical conditions and interventions. Orzeck's hunger strikers raise similarly ambiguous issues – they are being kept alive by the US state so that they can be punished according to the precepts of a legal regime they do not recognize. This is being done in the name of their 'rights'. Orzeck interprets the state's use of involuntary feeding and its distorted readings of transnational rights legislation as a form of biopolitical regulation for the silencing of detainee's speech and the co-production of nationalistic feelings and sentiments. Not only have the prisoners been deprived of their freedom to move, but their capacity to manage, regulate and, as they have chosen, destroy their own bodies has been taken from them.

Commodification

The chapters by Dickinson and Sothern and Foster in particular highlight a further theme to run throughout the book: that of commodification. Can and should bodies and body parts be used as commodities to be altered and 'enhanced' (as in the case of genital surgery), exchanged and even traded in capitalist markets (as in the sale of body parts)? The question of the body's 'value' – its problematic expression in terms of money – is addressed in Bill Maurer's and Elham Mireshghi's chapter. The monetization of bodies and body parts is far from new: with a history embracing ancient practices of 'bridewealth' dowries, the trade in cadavers and, latterly, 'live' body-parts and actuarial constructions of bodies through health insurance processes. Both through a range of historical and literary examples and through the particular case of the two systems of valuing body parts under contemporary Iranian sharia law – *arsh* and *diyeh* – Maurer and Mireshghi present an account of what they call the 'bricolage of body-worlds underwritten by law, state and money'. Through interlinked, and sometimes competing systems of metaphorisation, legalisation and valuation, the natural bodies are rendered in these 'body-worlds' as historically and spatially contingent assemblages thoroughly intertwined with evolving constructions of money.

Ming Lim approaches the commodification of bodies from a rather different direction, examining the changing constructions and self-definitions of women's bodies in the context of neo-Confucian bio-political regimes in East Asia. Conditions produced through capitalist globalisation are enabling East Asian women to renegotiate and reconstitute their identities with respect to childbearing, gender roles and familial ties. Lim connects these processes to postmodern and feminist analyses of the ways in which the state's constitution of individual bodies takes place within the ongoing formulation of personal and collective histories and identities. Most importantly, she reveals ways in which women are beginning to regain control of their identities despite the efforts of patriarchal state ideologies. In direct contrast to Lim's contribution, Ian Bruff takes issue with postmodern and post-structuralist accounts of bodily commodification by drawing on the rich tradition of historical materialist thought that, above all, emphasises 'the compulsion to sell our bodies on the labour market in order to live'. Noting how the human body has increasingly come to be conceptualised not as a biologically determined, 'natural' entity but rather as multifarious, pluralized, fluid and malleable, Bruff argues for greater recognition of the 'living, breathing, corporeal materiality of the body' in social and political theory, including with respect to the analysis of the relationship between body and state. While Nicola Smith's research with male sex workers in San Francisco also shows how bodily materiality figures into their decisions to enter into the commercial sex industry, she nonetheless challenges understandings that corporeal commercial transactions can be reduced to rational economic calculations. Rather, she argues, the sales of bodies are deeply entwined with social and emotionally situated understandings of freedom, intimacy and discovery.

Discipline

The social and cultural embeddedness of the ways in which bodies are experienced, understood and articulated is of enormous significance to the theme of discipline. All of the authors present the social, economic and cultural positioning of the relationships between states and bodies as contingent across time and place, in order to draw out some of the complexities of power, agency and resistance. Mark Neocleous explores the extension of the 'olfactory state' particularly through the use of police sniffer dogs and more generally, through the expanded use of smell in the technologies and practices of state surveillance. This is a form of state power that has no 'frontline', he argues, and as such the power of the state over bodies is becoming part of the mundane ordering and suppression of deviancy. It is also a means by which the regulatory and forensic potential of the physical body is being extended far beyond our immediate body-space by state agencies.

Claudia Aradau is also concerned with state surveillance, exploring the contradictory ways in which anti-trafficking discourses depict migrant women. On the one hand, these women are presented as vulnerable bodies in need of protection. On the other, they are also deemed potentially dangerous to state and society and must therefore be 'rehabilitated' and, ultimately, returned to their country of origin. Drawing on both feminist and postmodernist theory, and on the literature on the 'politics of pity', Aradau traces the interwoven discourses of risk, danger, victimhood, trauma, sexuality, offending and security as the state tries to 'make sense' of the status of these women's bodies both to understand them but also then to categorise them for purposes of control.

The bodies Gavin Brown examines are, by contrast with the above, deliberately 'undisciplined'. Using the 1986 non-stop picket of the South African embassy in London as an example, he opens up space for questions about the formation of cultures of solidarity against the state. He attends to the everyday forms of conviviality generated and the use of unruly bodies to push the boundaries of political and social convention which, he argues, offers embodied learning opportunities for protesters to think and act critically about the British state. Nevertheless, the bodily coherence of state opposition is also highly contingent, taking place against individuals' terrain of risk. In the context of increasing incidences of street protest and revolution throughout the Middle East and many parts of Europe, remembering the ways in which bodies as sites of opposition and autonomy can be constituted, is very timely.

Whilst Brown examines incidents of overt, public and sometimes violent conflict between state and body, Peter Kraftl's contribution explores ways in which similar tensions can be articulated within domestic, familial settings. Using the concept of the 'moment of withdrawal' from the state, he argues that homeschooling mother's decision to withdraw their children from school takes place in particular temporal intersections between the culminations of their own bodily praxis and feelings as mothers on one hand, and the practices of the state on the other. Together, the co-constitution of bodies and states takes place against the backdrop of the emotional demands of both mothers and their children.

Materiality

For all their many differences, something that runs through all of the chapters here is a renewed focus on the *materiality* of the body. This is in part a product of the fact that most of the chapters here are based on various kinds of empirical research – recording and reflecting on the concrete, lived experiences of bodies and processes of embodiment. In two cases this affects the authors themselves directly. Unusually, perhaps (though we can't know for certain because in other collections this might not be seen as pertinent and thus not alluded to) two of the authors here are transplant recipients – directly sharing the materiality of other bodies. It may, of course, be this very fact that prompts them to think and write about bodies in the ways that they do, but it may also be simply a product of the fact that significant material transfers between bodies are now possible to an unprecedented degree. Even beyond these two, however, the engagement with the physical realities of bodies runs through all of the chapters. Indeed, one of the key points of tension in many of the contributions lies precisely at the intersection between various social, legal and narrative constructions of bodies (by states, theorists, religions, courts, medics, etc) and the actual bodies that variously resist these constructions or simply don't, or can't conform to them. Many of the bodies described in this book, therefore, are here because they are unable easily to occupy the various normative spaces expected of them in the ways that most of us do. These are the bodies that, for whatever reason find or put themselves, in some sense 'beyond the pale' often precisely because of their material physicality.

So, for example, the disabled bodies in Ledingham's chapter find themselves caught between legal constructions and lived experiences that do not match up. The physicality of the transplant process means that the recipients of Dickinson's 'gift of life' can't necessarily feel quite as grateful as they ought to. By contrast, many of the sex workers in Smith's chapter stubbornly refuse to conform to stereotypes of victimhood and exploitation, but revel in the physical pleasure of their chosen profession. Indeed, many of them have explicitly rejected lives where the exploration of physical sexuality was prohibited, condemned and/or concealed. The extraordinary physicality of Joel-Peter Witkin's photographs, both because of the dismembered bodies they record and because of the physicality of the images themselves, achieved, as Palmer describes it, through the transformation and mutilation of the film negatives themselves, re-emphasises the physicality both of the subjects and the viewer – in often very uncomfortable ways. In a rather different sense, the legal/ conceptual dismemberment of the body in the complex Iranian compensation laws described by Maurer and Mireshghi also stands as a stark reminder of the physicality of the body – even at the intersection of law and economy.

What all this points to, in various ways, is that the physical body itself is vastly more complex than is recognised either by states, by legal systems, by police forces and armies, by the medical profession or, indeed, by academics. And this partly explains a strand of argument laid out most explicitly by Ian Bruff below, but present throughout, that is critical of the many efforts to 'theorise' the body – if not to ignore the physicality of the body, then to subordinate it to complex social constructions. Bruff's critique of much post-structural thought in his call to refocus on the 'natural' body, particularly the natural body in the context of a capitalism that continues to consume living bodies even in the 'digital age'. As Apple Inc. discovered with their much-reported problems of worker suicide at the Shenzhen i-Pad factory, just because workers are making the machines that enable the apparently disembodied digital age, doesn't make them immune to the physical and mental stresses of the real world.

As the chapters below argue in many different ways, physical, natural, material bodies constitute an irreducible problem for those trying to organise the social world. As James C Scott noted (1998: 136), because states of all kinds and scales have historically been very bad at designing or legislating for complexity, they tend to impose order by categorising and rationalising their subjects and territories. This often involves attempting to impose constraints on 'natural' bodies (as described here by Orzeck, Aradau, Neocleous and others), but even this can never reduce their materiality to a simple, malleable form.

The Structure of the Book

With these overarching and overlapping themes running throughout the book, the chapters are structured as follows. Part I, 'Bodies Modified and Divided', considers how the production, regulation, policing and maintenance of borders (physical, social, sexual, political, religious, etc.) are used to enable or constrain the physical (re)shaping of the body. The three chapters in this section, by Emma Foster, Reecia Orzeck, and Jen Dickinson and Matt Sothern respectively, all address ways in which bodies are physically transformed and, in so doing, explore the status of the body as a bordered object – in the sense both that borders run through bodies and that bodies define borders – produces indeterminate and contingent outcomes – both for the bodies in question and for those attempting to impose order upon them. Part II, 'Capital Bodies', extends the state's concern with the flows of bodies that make up the nation to consider how they are enrolled in the complex structures of capitalist exchange that forming the basis for maintaining and contesting a set of relationships between states and markets. The chapters by Ian Bruff, Bill Maurer and Elham Mireshghi, Nicola Smith, and Ming Lim, all consider the complex intersections between bodies, states and markets. Part III, 'Deviance and Resistance', examines both how states seek to discipline 'non-normal' bodies and appreciates the capacity of changes in the socio-cultural meaning and nature of bodies to resist and/or escape states. The four chapters by Kate Ledingham, Gavin Brown, Peter Kraftl, and Matt Sothern each illustrate in different ways the frictions between to the corporate state and bodies that are constituted and/or which constitute themselves 'differently'. Seeing like a state, as James C Scott pointed out some years ago often involves a process of simplification – of stripping out the 'noise' from the domain to be governed so that the state can be seen (in other words, can see itself) more clearly. In all these cases, embodied identities other than those of the normalising state are variously 'discovered' (Sothern), 'constructed' (Ledingham) or 'self-actualised' (Brown and Kraftl) in a constant process of negotiation and enactment. Part IV, 'Surveillance and Sovereignty' consists of chapters by Claudia Aradau, Mark Neocleus, and Angus Cameron and develops themes of deviancy and resistance by considering the impact of new technologies both on the intimate regulatory reach of states into and across bodies and on the nature of embodiment itself. Finally, Part V, 'The Body Virtual' consists of three very different takes by Tom Boellstorff, Heather Palmer, and goldin+senneby on the more explicitly 'represented' body in cinema, online worlds and the visual and performing arts. In so doing, it examines the impact of new technologies and online spaces both on the intimate regulatory reach of states into and across bodies and on the nature of embodiment itself.

References

Anand, D. 2007. Anxious Sexualities: Masculinity, Nationalism and Violence. *British Journal of Politics and International Relations*, 9(2): 257–69.

Harcourt, W. 2009. *Body Politics in Development: Critical Debates in Gender and Development.* London: Zed.

Hooper, C. 2000. Disembodiment, Embodiment and the Construction of Hegemonic Masculinity. In: Gillian Youngs (ed) *Political Economy, Power and the Body.* Basingstoke: Palgrave.

Kantola, J. 2006. *Feminists Theorise the State.* Basingstoke: Palgrave.

Pain, R. 2009. Globalized Fear? Towards An Emotional Geopolitics. *Progress in Human Geography*, 33 (4), 466–486.

Pettman, JJ. 2000. Writing the Body: Transnational Sex. In: Gillian Youngs (ed) *Political Economy, Power and the Body.* Basingstoke: Palgrave.

Scott, JC, 1987, *Weapons of the Weak: Everyday Forms of Peasant Resistance*, Yale University Press.

———— 1998, *Seeing Like a State: How Certain Schemes to Improve the Human Condition Have Failed*, New Haven, Yale University Press.

Youngs, G. 2000. Embodied Political Economy Or An Escape From Disembodied Knowledge. In: Gillian Youngs (ed) *Political Economy, Power and the Body.* Basingstoke: Palgrave.

Zalewski, M. 2004. *Feminism after Postmodernism.* London: Routledge.

PART I
Bodies Modified and Divided

Chapter 2

Female Circumcision vs. Designer Vaginas: Surgical Genital Practices and the Discursive Reproduction of State Boundaries

Emma A. Foster

Introduction

100 to 140 million women and girls worldwide have undergone some form of circumcision (WHO 2009). This is of major concern to international institutions, such as the UN and WHO, and is generally considered a problematic practice which perpetuates gender inequalities. Officially, many international institutions, particularly the UN, have included female circumcision (FC), otherwise known as female genital mutilation (FGM), onto their human rights, women's rights and health agendas (Toubia 1995: 225). Throughout these agendas FC/FGM is considered a marker of female oppressionand, as previously mentioned, is considered a human rights/women's rights abuse. On the other hand, in 'developed' countries, female genital cosmetic surgery (FGCS), although far from reaching figures comparable to FC/FGM, is rapidly on the increase marking FGCS's legitimate status in the 'developed' countries where it is practiced. Indeed, finding accurate figures on FGSC is difficult. However, there is considerable data from plastic surgeons that the demand for FGCS is significantly on the increase. For example, the number of women requesting FGCS in the UK doubled between 2000 and 2005 to reach over 800 operations per year and in the US there was a 30% increase in FGCS procedures between 2005 and 2006 (2008, New View Campaign).

The practices of FC/FGM in the 'developing world' are often presented as evidence of female powerlessness (see Toubia 1995: 232) whereas practices of cosmetic surgery in the 'developed world' have been used as a marker of 'liberated' female sexuality through the claim that it results in 'sexual enhancement' (Braun 2005: 412). Indeed, FGCS is often wrapped in the contemporary medico-psychological discourse that it in fact increases female sexual pleasure and that it has female sexuality and enjoyment supposedly at its heart (*ibid.:* 408, also see Davis 2002). However, Wilson (2002) argues that although the practices of FC/FGM and cosmetic surgery (breast augmentation in this case) are narrated in very different ways the outcome of said practices are both characterized through systems of gender stratification whereby women are subordinated to men. She argues that:

[P]atriarchy and the 'cult of virginity'... and phallocentrism and 'liberated' female sexuality... lead to similar processes of female subordination to male interests, however differently these interests may be defined (496).

Although insightful, Wilson's work fails to recognize a multidirectional and multifaceted view of power. In contrast, I argue that discourses of gender inequality are used to (re)produce unequal power relations between 'developed' and 'developing' states. Furthermore, I demonstrate how the narratives of sexual empowerment related to FGCS in 'developed' states work to inhibit *solidarities across difference* (McRobbie 2009: 27) and how notions of empowerment and freedom, driven by the zeitgeist of postfeminism, work to blinker (although not blind) those culturally intelligible as women of problematic gender practices within what they would consider their own cultures. As Angela McRobbie notes:

[M]edia reportage on women who are deemed to be less fortunate... disarticulates possible affiliations which would be based on Western feminist postcolonialist critique of how Western sexual freedoms are strategically deployed so as to support notions of civilization and superiority, and by preventing such a possibility, it displaces possible solidarities, with a reinstated hierarchy of civilization and modernity, and a discourse which celebrates the freedoms of fashion conscious "thong wearing" Western girls in contrast to those young women who, for example, wear the veil (ibid.)

In order to show the racial/geographical double standard, articulated through gendered discourses, this chapter examines the practices of FC/FGM and FGCS. Indeed, there are a number of feminist texts, influenced by postcolonialism, that draw on how the nation-state, and subsequently nationalism, is constructed and reinforced through bodily practices (for a good example of this see McClintock, ed. 1997). Further, said literature notes how non-Western (gendered and sexualized) bodies are defined as deviant in order to sustain notions of the superiority of western states (see Nagel, 1998) and to promote forms of interventionism into the affairs of 'developing' states (see Chowdhury, 1995).

Through an attempt to draw parallels between the practices of FGCS and FC/FGM (not to suggest that different cultural norms and social rules are necessarily equivalent) this chapter demonstrates the contestability, or mythic status, of incommensurable boundaries between 'developed' and 'developing' states. Echoing questions raised by post-colonial theorists and feminists like Trinh Minh Ha, such as: '[W]ho would dispute the fact that Western influence should be challenged in its global domination? But again, who never hesitates to take the license what is Western and what is Eastern in this context?' (Minh-Ha 1991: 161), this chapter case studies female genital surgical practices to blur state boundaries between the 'developed' and the 'developing' whilst also arguing that these mythic boundaries are discursively (re)produced through the ethnocentric rhetoric of those considered 'developed'; those that consider themselves able to speak for everyone else. Ultimately, the chapter highlights potential affinities, across (creative) difference both within and between defined, although not definitive, cultures, which can be drawn through an evaluation of these (multiple) genital surgical practices. Overall, this chapter contends that surgical genital practices work to define antagonistic differences and justify power imbalances between states and, further, it argues that if this connect between states and practices were eroded within discourses new, more helpful, forms of alliance and solidarity, which transcend national boundaries, could be developed.

Difference and Affinity

The comparison between FC/FGM and cosmetic surgery to enhance desirability has been made by a variety of authors (see Toubia 1995, Walker and Palmer 1996, Sheldon and Wilkinson 1998, Dustin 2010, and, in relation to breast augmentation specifically, Tamar Wilson 2002, Chambers 2004, and in relation to FGCS specifically, Davis 2002). On the whole, these authors contend that both the cosmetic surgical practices that occur in most 'developed' states and the practice of FC/FGM are comparable and that they, by and large, represent two different orders or models of male domination. For example, Tamar Diana Wilson (2002), comparing breast augmentation to FC/FGM, argues that these two practices are products of two systems of male domination, namely patriarchy and phallocentric capitalism. However, this puts a development lineage on these two, dichotomized types of oppression. The implicit sentiment of this work is that women in 'developing' states are oppressed through systems of patriarchy (an oppression considered overcome or at least intellectually passé and defunct in the West), whilst women in 'developed' states, the arguably post-feminist world, are manipulated within a new, modern form of male domination, namely the system of phallocentric capitalism. This type of theorizing, although going some way to demonstrate an affinity between women across national and regional difference, problematically offers a teleological account of oppressions which fits neatly with radicalized notions of developed and developing; modern and traditional; linear progress.

Arguably, a circumnavigation of the binary of Western women and non-Western women (whereby the former are problematically considered more liberated and empowered), which is indicative of wider power relations between 'developed' and 'developing' states (where the former (re)produces knowledge and value systems thereby maintaining and (re)producing unequal power relations) is necessary for two reasons. Firstly, at the bodily level of opening up dialogue and subsequent reflective action relating to genital practices which could be considered politically and ethically problematic and secondly, to somewhat diminish the unequal power relations between 'developed' and 'developing' states whereby the situation of women is often used as a 'benchmark of development' (see Runyan 1996). As such, informed by theorists such as Donna Haraway and Trinh Minh-Ha, I suggest that coalition based on affinity between peoples across geographical state boundaries and cultures (seeking creativity in difference and solidarity in affinity) would assist in facilitating both these outcomes. Indeed, a number of authors have also sought to highlight the potential in acknowledging affinity politics for issues such as climate change and as a driver of transnational feminist movements (see Collins 2010, 13; Dean, 1996). This would work to help to overcome Western 'arrogance' (or perceptions thereof) and the subsequent resentment felt by non-Western women who recognize intervention as being patronizing and possibly colonizing. It is from this mutual understanding or affinities that issues of female genital surgeries can be tackled. As Nahid Toubia notes:

> To understand why many women defend a practice that risks their health and damages their sexuality, we have to understand that even the most highly educated individuals become defensive when they feel their culture and personal identity are being attacked... Africans who love and cherish the positive aspects of their cultures and have been wounded by colonialism fear that actions against FGM will be used as another excuse to invade and humiliate them (1995: 232).

Toubia clearly identifies the problems of what could be deemed as Western interference and non-Western resistance over the matter of FC/FGM as a cultural practice. However, she goes on to suggest that; '[w]e must, therefore, identify FGM as part of the global subordination of women' (*ibid.*) and in so doing calls for global action. This, however, is universalizing and ignores differences between multiply identified and multiply oppressed peoples.

Instead difference needs to be recognized as a creative force, not something to be papered over through notions of women's global subordination. In line with affirmative post-colonial feminist theory what is necessary in order to include a sensitive, whilst critically potent, analysis of female genital surgeries is a re-evaluation of difference. Positions of strategic universalization in order to facilitate coalition, disregard notions of difference whereas positions which recognize difference often do so in an over-simplistic, antagonistic and negative way. Many feminists sympathetic to a post-structural approach argue that differences should be celebrated and should act as a starting point for political action (Fraser and Nicholson 1990, Hennessy 1993). For many reflective feminist theorists difference does not negate the possibility of political action or solidarity but rather formulates fluid and contextually specific political actions that can potentially transcend problematic binary formations (Minh-Ha 1997, Haraway 1991) such as developed/developing. As Trinh Minh-Ha eloquently states:

> Difference. does not necessarily give rise to separatism. One can further say that difference is not what makes conflict. This is where confusion often arises and where the challenge can be issued. Many of us still hold on to the concept of difference not as a tool of creativity to question multiple forms of repression but as a tool of segregation used to exert power on the basis of racial and sexual essences. The apartheid type of difference (Minh-Ha 1997: 416).

Minh-Ha's conceptual re-evaluation of difference to counter what she terms the *'apartheid type of difference'* could work to rectify problematic power relations with regard to the FC/FGM debate, and the developed/developing debate more broadly.

Alongside this notion of creative difference, international dialogue strategies to inform policy on genital surgeries need to be operational through acknowledging that affinities may exist between women cross culturally. For example, there may be more variation between the practices that are positioned under the umbrella term FGCS than there are between particular FGCS and FC/FGM practices. In other words, two women who reside in the UK and have undergone different forms of FGCS may well find the procedure more comparable to Sudanese woman's experience than to each other's. This potential affinity should be acknowledged in order to erode the geographical boundaries that produce the power relations between the 'developed world' and the 'developing world'. It is important to bear in mind here that shared affinity is a term that is particularly useful as it opens up the possibility of a shared empathy between people who may well not share what have been previously considered an identity, geographically organized or otherwise. As Donna Haraway has noted in her seminal piece *Simians, Cyborgs and Women* (1991: 155), '... there has... been a growing recognition of another response through coalition – affinity, not identity'. Therefore, affinity as a concept of potential relations opens up a temporary space for solidarity and coalition between people with shared knowledge rather than through shared (and problematically naturalized) identities. Indeed, affinity is not identity politics as the latter supposes a permanent and essentialized set of oppressions and experiences. This is a particularly important point considering the problems associated with essentialism highlighted by many contemporary feminists (see Witt 1995 for a good summary of anti-essentialist feminist philosophy).

Issues of Consent: The Negative Construction of Non-Western Women

Age and issues of consent exhibit a marked difference between the two practices of FC/FGM and FGCS. Unless deemed medically necessary FGCS can only be undergone by women over the age of 18 in most 'developed' countries. On the other hand, however, FC/FGM is more often than not carried out upon very young girls (dependant on culture and geographical location). This is undoubtedly an area of international concern.

Neither FC/FGM nor FGCS can be undergone by under 18s in the UK and other 'developed' countries. However, FGCS is an option for over 18s due, in part, to notions that adult women can make that choice – in other words they have the ability to consent. However, it remains illegal for adult women in the UK, the US and other 'developed' countries to undergo FC/FGM (Davis 2006: 68) and international efforts have gone into stopping the procedure of FC/FGM in the 'developing' countries where it is practiced (Toubia 1995: 225). This highlights the assumption that women in Western liberal states can validly consent to these operations whereas those women in (or connected to, in that they may domicile in the 'developed' countries) 'developing' states cannot validly consent to what are similar procedures. This further exemplifies the construction of Western women as liberated and knowledgeable whilst their counterparts in 'developing' countries are constructed as backward and ignorant of their own minds and oppressions (for example see Mohanty 1988, Choudhry: 1995).

Indeed, Soraya Mire, a Somali filmmaker who has undergone FC, notes in Inga Muscio's (wo)manifesto, *Cunt: A Declaration of Independence* that:

> [Western women] come into conversations waving the American flag, forever projecting the idea that they are more intelligent than I am. I've learned that American women look at women like me to hide from their own pain. In America, women pay the money that is theirs and no one else's to go to a doctor who cuts them up so they can create or sustain an image men want. Men are the mirror. Western women cut themselves up voluntarily (cited in Davis 2002).

Similarly Sheldon and Wilkinson (1998) highlight the double standard and inconsistencies of this assumption based around liberated Western women and disempowered non-Western women:

> The people of the countries where female genital mutilation is practiced resent references to 'barbaric practices imposed on women by male-dominated primitive societies', especially when they look at the Western world and see women undergoing their own feminization rites intended to increase sexual desirability (Sheldon and Wilkinson 1998: 263).

This point highlights that many women who belong to countries where FC/FGM is practiced, far from being ignorant, recognize that similar practices are going on in the Western countries for similar reasons. This is hardly representative of 'ignorance' or insularity.

Furthermore, there is evidence that women who identify with FC/FGM cultures and who have not undergone circumcision resent their parents for not putting them through the procedure. Indeed many of these women seek the procedure as adults (who when negating the radicalized assumptions highlighted above are just as capable of 'consenting' as women from the West). For example, a study undertaken by Walley (1997) showed that adolescent girls in Western Kenya, where FC/FGM takes place between the ages of 14-16, 'look forward enthusiastically to their initiation ceremony' (Wilson 2002, also see Conroy 2006). These girls are on the verge of adulthood in Western terms (where consent is something they are almost graced with) and rather than fearing FC/FGM, which is narrated as abuse in the international arena, they actually demonstrate enthusiasm for the procedure.

As I have highlighted the issues of consent and choice are central to the conception of difference between FC/FGM and FGCS practices. This conception of difference assumes that Western genital surgeries are legitimate whereas cultures that practice FC/FGM are supporting human and women's rights abuses. This, I argue, works to retard and obscure the dialogue regarding genital surgical practices and therefore is not particularly effective in terms of modifying potentially dangerous and problematic genital anxieties and practices cross culturally. Rather, for this dialogue to be effective, difference and affinity need to be reconsidered.

Comparing FGCS and FC/FGM Practices

This section of the chapter, then, seeks to identify similarities between the practices of FC/FGM and FCGS to offer a counter-narrative to the underlying notion that the practices of genital surgeries which occur in 'developing' states are oppressive and recognizable as human rights abuses whilst the genital surgeries undergone in 'developed' states are tied to choice and sexual empowerment. Indeed, I am not suggesting that the narrative of similarity that I am drawing here represents the reality surrounding genital surgeries, rather I am putting forward a case to show similarities in order to demonstrate how *affinity* between people can be drawn cross culturally and to demonstrate the contestability of the boundaries between 'developed' and 'developing' states and the cultural practices within said states. As is aforementioned, by comparing the similarities, a more open discussion can be derived across cultural difference. Suggesting that the practices of genital surgery can be compared and that similarity can be drawn undermines the mind-set of a superior West working to at best patronize, and at worst colonize, 'developing' states. Moreover it undermines the construction of women in the 'developing world' as ignorant victims of oppression, in need of saving. Arguably, as outlined above, it is this mind-set which prevents useful discussion on this issue.

One key difference between the two practices of FC/FGM and FGCS relates to the different types of women or female sexuality that are being sought through the procedures. In societies that practice FC/FGM, the desired outcome is to shape women around socio-sexual expectations such as chastity, fidelity, tamed sexuality and motherhood (see Toubia 1995, Rahman and Toubia 2000, Wilson 2002). In societies that permit FGCS the ideal women is represented as sexually liberated, neatly put together aesthetically and 'constantly', or at least easily, orgasmic (Braun 2005). Although different in emphasis, genital modifications cross culturally are designed to 'rectify' and 'treat' supposed female inadequacies. With regard to FC/FGM, a woman is considered both manly (as she has externally visible genitalia) and not marriageable if she has not undergone the procedure (Wilson 2002: 501). With regard to FGCS women's genitalia are constructed as deficient in that, pre-operatively, women's enjoyment of sex is pathologized as sub-par with surgical 'enhancement' being the process to rectify this 'dysfunction' (Braun 2005: 418). Cross culturally then it could be said that female genital modifications are procedures; 'of designing bodies to fit certain sexual practices, rather than designing sexual practices to fit bodies' (*ibid*).

Related to the above point, another difference which is often cited is that FGCS is conducted, and works to, enhance female sexual pleasure whereas FC/FGM is designed to limit and tame female sexuality in favour of female honour (for example see Johnson in Goodman *et al.* 2007: 271). In most cases FC/FGM is indeed designed to limit or completely eradicate female sexual pleasure, however, some FGCS surgery practices can also limit female sexual pleasure in favour of 'aesthetic genital modification'. Writing in the *British Medical Journal*, gynecologist Sarah Creighton and clinical psychologist Lih Mei Liao contend that 'incision to any part of the genitalia could compromise sensitivity – an important aspect of sexual experience' (2007).

With regard to the actual shaping of matter or bodies FC/FGM and FGCS practices both work to emphasize or construct gender dimorphism and parallels can be drawn between the outcomes of the procedures. FC/FGM procedures are indeed varied across cultures. Similarly there are a variety of different surgeries which fall under the banner of FGCS[1]. The most extreme form is that of pharaonic circumcision / infibulation which is the removal of all external female genitalia with the remaining flesh being sutured together leaving only a very small urethral and vaginal opening (15% of women who have undergone FC/FGM have had this extreme form). However, not all FC/FGM is this extreme. The mildest form of FC/FGM is called the sunna circumcision which is the removal of the skin around the clitoris (see Rymer, 2003 for a medical based description of different types of FC/FGM). Arguably the end result of the sunna circumcision would not be too dissimilar from some cosmetic surgery alterations, such as clitoral hood reductions.

Another procedure where there are direct comparisons between forms of FC/FGM and FGCS concerns genital modifications made after childbirth. In countries that practice the most extreme forms of FC/FGM women after childbirth often go through a reinfibulation procedure – this is the sewing shut of scars post childbirth. This practice is done to tighten the vagina in order to increase male stimulation through intercourse (Gruenbaum 1997) and, as a byproduct, in some societies to prevent the husband from taking another wife (Lightfoot-Klein 1980: 99). Although considerably less severe, similar practices occur in 'developed' countries; where women request surgery, post child-birth, with the desired effect of vaginal tightening. These procedures include the imaginatively entitled 'husband stitch' or fat injections (Braun 2005: 417). Like reinfibulation, the rationale for vaginal tightening procedures in 'developed' countries is tied to increasing male pleasure during intercourse (Jahoda 1995), although in the West it is also linked to increased female sensation during intercourse as well.

Accepting that some of the FC/FGM practices are comparable to some FGCS practices may invoke the response that a key difference between the collective

---

1   Practices of FGCS range from labia minora reductions and augmentations, vaginal tightening, clitoral hood reductions, clitoral repositioning, G-Spot amplification and hymen reconstruction.

procedures is that FGCS is done in a clean medical environment with the use of anesthetic whilst FC/FGM is done in unsterile environments, with unsterile equipment such as knives and shards of glass, by poorly trained traditional midwives without the use of anesthesia. Although there are many horrific stories of the practice of FC/FGM that confirm this view, it is important to note that it is not always the case. In some Sudanese urban areas (Toubia 1995) and in parts of Guinea, female circumcision has been performed by medical practitioners with the use of anesthetic (Wilson 2002: 497). This shows that the ritual / cultural practice of FC/FGM can potentially be, and have been in a few instances, medicalized drawing it closer to FGCS practices. Indeed, as Conroy (2006) has noted '[t]here are encouraging signs that the cultures which practice female genital mutilation are responding to the concerns about the health consequences while trying to maintain their cultural values' (106).

FC/FGM is justified in certain cultures through a belief system that female virginity is of the utmost importance before marriage (Wilson, 2002, 501). FC/FGM protects the virginal state of the female body, as with the most extreme forms of FC/FGM a woman cannot be penetrated without obvious surgical intervention. Furthermore, FC/FGM is meant to deter women from having extra-marital affairs and engaging in homosexual behavior. This is because in most cases the clitoris is removed – this means that the organ most related to sexual pleasure is removed leaving only the vagina – responsible for reproduction. This practice is arguably, then, concerned with controlling female sexuality and reducing the female body to a reproductive (monogamous and heterosexual) instrument. This is very important in patriarchal societies as it provides a security about the paternity of offspring. Although this emphasis on virginity and deterring homosexuality is not so obviously apparent in Western female genital modification practices (as they are based around narratives of liberating female sexuality) at closer investigation we can definitely draw some parallels. For instance, one FGCS procedure is hymen reconstruction which restores the appearance of virginity, and although not so much protecting a female's virginity to secure paternity it does adhere to the cult or fetishization of virginity. Similarly, moreover, FGCS adheres to traditional gendered, heterosexualized stereotypes whereby the gaze is 'heterosexual male' and the aesthetic stimulus is classed as female. Moreover, images from which women choose their new vaginas are, according to the plastic surgeons involved in these procedures, more often than not the heterosexualized (and airbrushed) images of women in pornographic magazines aimed at a heterosexual male readership, such as Playboy (Braun 2005).

Finally, to demonstrate a direct comparison between FC/FGM and FGCS you only need to look as far as the World Health Organization's information of the subject. It is important to note that WHO are firmly against the practice of FC/FGM, suggesting that; '[i]t has no health benefits and harms girls and women in many ways' (WHO 2009). However, WHO's definition of FGM does not exclude FGCS procedures and can easily be extended to FGCS practices:

> Female genital mutilation comprises all procedures involving partial or total removal of the external female genitalia or other injury to the female genital organs for non-medical reasons (WHO 2009).

Although not acknowledged by WHO, this definition would suggest that FGCS practices are no different to practices that international institutions see as the mutilation and abuse of the female body; as markers of female disempowerment in some parts of the 'developing world'.

What Now?

Although the definition of FGM outlined by international organizations such as WHO could include Western practices of FGCS, the general international consensus is to prohibit the FC/FGM practices based in ethno-cultural traditions whilst FGCS remains unscrutinized in these arenas. International organizations have been involved in producing policy initiatives which target states which allow the practice of FC/FGM in an effort to prevent its continuation. For example, the United Nations Children's Fund (UNICEF), the United Nations Population Fund (UNFPA) and WHO issued a joint statement in 1997 opposing FC/FGM practices. This statement was re-issued in 2008 taking a firmer stance regarding the abandonment of FC/FGM (WHO 2009). There have been a series of initiatives put in place from the international community to eradicate the practice of FC/FGM in 'developing' countries. These initiatives tend to target FC/FGM in Africa, and include the dissemination of education and information about the risks related to the practice, strategies to 'empower' women and the persuasion of national legal and political institutions and other important authority and community actors within states that practice FC/FGM to work towards eliminating the practices through a legalistic and policy framework (WHO 2011: 48-55). In other words, the international community is seeking to eliminate the practices of FC/FGM through the soft policy of gaining support from local and national bodies to reflect on and reject the practices. However, to reiterate, there is no reflection regarding the similar practices that are associated with 'developed' countries and consumer lifestyles.

On the other hand, feminist and gender scholars who recognize the comparison between the practices of FC/FGM and FGCS tend to call for the prohibition of all unnecessary female genital surgeries. For example, Sheldon and Wilkinson (1998) argue, from a legal perspective, that if FC/FGM is considered an illegal practice then many forms of FGCS should also be outlawed (also see Davis 2006). Indeed feminist scholarship is correct in highlighting that the two practices are comparable but I argue that the language of outright prohibition is problematic. This prohibition of all practices relating to unnecessary genital surgeries ignores the differences between genital surgeries and the possible personalized feelings of empowerment that may be the consequence of some medical genital modifications (see Goodman *et. al.* 2007). Moreover, the focus on genital surgery tends to dualize the anatomy suggesting that some parts of the body can be surgically changed while others cannot. For instance a face lift, although likely to be unnecessary and also working to adhere to the cultural norms of gender dimorphism, would probably remain unchallenged whereas surgery on genitalia would be forbidden. This negates personal ownership over this particular part of the female body and works in itself to reproduce problematic taboos regarding female genitalia (for example see Braun and Wilkinson 2001: 17).

Conclusion: What Next?

Given the associated problems with either prohibiting genital surgeries that are not identified as Western cosmetic surgery (as the international community advocates) or prohibiting genital surgeries altogether as some feminist scholars suggest, I argue that what is necessary is an open dialogue between people across nations about issues of genital anxiety and genital surgery. This dialogue should be based on an understanding of affinity (Haraway 1991) and creative difference (Minh-Ha 1997). This framework recognizes that there are similarities and differences between all genital modification practices. As such, this framework allows for a better climate for an open, less stratified dialogue to develop between people in 'developing' countries and people in 'developed' countries due to the acknowledgment of affinity (or similarity) whilst not universalizing or essentializing the experiences of women (within and between cultures) through the acknowledgement of (creative) difference. This would work to improve the quality of dialogues about the subject of genital modifications and, thus, would also better inform policy making on all types of genital surgeries.

References

Braun, V. 2005. In Search of (better) Sexual Pleasure: Female Genital Cosmetic Surgery. *Sexualities*, 8(4), 407-424.

Chambers, C. 2004. Are breast implants better than female genital mutilation? Autonomy, gender equality and Nussbaum's political liberalism. *Critical Review of International Social and Political Philosophy*, 7(3), 1-33.

Chowdhry, G. 1995. Engendering Development? Women in Development (WID), in *International Development Regimes*, edited by M. H. Marchand, and J. L. Parpart, Feminism, Postmodernism, Development, London: Routledge.

Collins, P. H. 2010. The new politics of community, *American Sociological Review*, 75(1), 7-30.

Conroy, M. 2006. Female Genital Mutilation: Whose Problem? Whose Solution?. *British Medical Journal*, 333(7559), 106-7.

Davis, S. W. 2002. Loose Lips Sink Ships. *Feminist Studies*, 28(1), 7-35.

Dean, J. 1996. *Solidarity of Strangers: feminism after identity politics,* California: University of California Press.

Dustin, M. 2010. Female Genital Mutilation / Cutting in the UK. *The European Journal of Women's Studies,* 17(1), 7-24.

Fraser, N. and Nicholson, L. 1993. Social Criticism without Philosophy: An Encounter between Feminism and Postmodernism, in *Postmodernism: A Reader,* edited by T. Docherty. London: Longman.

Gruenbaum, E. 1997. The movement against clitorodectomy and infibulations in Sudan in *Gender in Cross Cultural Perspective,* edited by C. B. Brettell and C. F. Sargent. New Jersey: Prentice Hall.

Goodman, M. P. (*et. al.*) 2007. Is Elective Vulvar Plastic Surgery Ever Warranted, and What Screening Should Be Conducted Preoperatively?. *Journal of Sexual Medicine,* 4, 269 – 276.

Haraway, D. 1991 *Simians, Cyborgs, and Women: The Re-invention of Nature.* London: Free Association Books.

Hennesy, R. 1993. *Materialist Feminism and the Politics of Discourse.* New York: Routledge.

Jahoda, S. 1995. Theatres of Madness, in *Deviant Bodies: Critical perspectives on difference in science and popular culture,* edited by J. Terry and J. Urla. Bloomington: Indiana University Press.

Kitzinger, S. 1994. *The Year after Childbirth: Surviving and enjoying the first year of motherhood.* Toronto: Harper Collins.

Liao, L. M. and Creighton S. 2007. Requests for cosmetic genitoplasty: how should healthcare providers respond?. *British Medical Journal,* 334(7603), 1090-1092.

Lightfoot-Klein, H. 1989. *Prisoners of Ritual: An odyssey into female circumcision in Africa.* New York: Harrington Park.

McClintock, A. ed. 1997. *Dangerous Liaisons: Gender, nation and postcolonial perspectives,* Minneapolis: University of Minnesota Press.

McRobbie, A. 2009. *The Aftermath of Feminism: Gender, Culture and Social Change.* London: Sage.

Minh-ha, T. 1991. *When the Moon Waxes Red.* London: Routledge.

———— 1997. Not You / Like You: Postcolonial Women and the Interlocking Questions of Identity and Difference, in *Dangerous Liasons: Gender, Nation and Postcolonial Perspectives,* edited by A. McClintock et al. Minneapolis: University of Minnesota Press.

Mohanty, C. T. 1988. Under Western Eyes: Feminist Scholarship and Colonial Discourses. *Feminist Review,* 30 (Autumn), 61-88.

Nagel, J. 1998. Masculinity and nationalism: gender and sexuality in the making of nations. *Ethnic and Racial Studies,* 21(2), 242-269.

New View Campaign, 2008. *Challenging the Medicalization of Sex.* [online]. Available at: www.newviewcampaign.org, [accessed: 11 April 2011].

Sheldon, S. and S. Wilkinson 1998. Female Genital Mutilation and Cosmetic Surgery: Regulating Non-Therapeutic Body Modification. *Bioethics,* 12(4), 263-285.

Rahman, A. and Toubia N. 2000. *Female Genital Mutliation: A Practical Guide to Worldwide Laws and Policies.* London: Zed Books.

Rymer, J. 2003. Female Genital Mutilation. *Current Obstetrics and Gynecology,* 13(3), 185-190.

Toubia, N. 1995. *Female Genital Mutilation: A Call for Global Action.* New York: Women Ink.

Walker, A, and Palmar P. 1996. *Warrior Marks: Female genital mutilation and the sexual blinding of women.* New York: Harcourt Brace.

Walley, C. J. 1997. Searching for Voices: Feminsim, anthropology and the global debate over female genital operations. *Cultural Anthropology,* 12, 405-438.

WHO, 2009. *Female genital mutilation.* [online]. Available at: http://www.who. int/mediacentre/factsheets/fs241/en/index.html, [accessed: 28 March 2011].

———, 2011. Female genital mutilation. [online]. Available at: http://www.who. int/topics/female_genital_mutilation/en/, [accessed: 29 March 2011].

Wilson, T. D. 2002. Pharaonic Circumcision Under Patriarchy and Breast Augmentation Under Phallocentric Capitalism. *Violence Against Women,* 8(4), 495-521.

Witt, C. 1995. Anti- Essentialism in Feminist Theory. *Philosophical Topics,* 23(2), 321-344.

Chapter 3

Hunger Strike: The Body as Resource

Reecia Orzeck

We have a policy that is to preserve life. That policy is an ethical policy. It's in the best interests of the individual who is a hunger striker, for his life to be preserved, in our judgment (Winkenwerder 2006).

Introduction

The first coordinated hunger strike at the Guantánamo Bay detention facility began in February of 2002, and the last of these strikers were the first to be fed against their will by the United States Department of Defense (Dao 2002). During the June/July 2005 strike, approximately 50 of the 52 to 200 detainees on strike were fed intravenously (Gutierrez 2005: 9, 11). When the strike recommenced in August as many as 20 of its 76 to 210 participants were being kept at the camp hospital and being fed intravenously and through nasal tubes. According to camp spokesman Major Jeffrey J. Weir, the hospitalized strikers were not generally strapped to their beds and gurneys, but were in handcuffs and leg restraints (see Lewis 2005b, Gutierrez 2005). In December 2005, restraint chairs arrived at the camp (Golden 2006b) and their use saw the number of strikers drop from 84 in January of 2006 to 4 by February of that year (Golden 2006a). Numbers rose briefly to 86 in May 2006. A new strike began at the start of 2007, and in April most of the then 17 participants were being force-fed (Golden 2007a, Goldenberg 2007). At the start of the Obama presidency, between 40 and 70 of the 245 remaining detainees were on strike, and 35 of these strikers were being force-fed (Reid 2009, Rosenberg 2009). As of at least August 2010, the Department of Defense no longer reveals the precise number of detainees being force-fed at Guantánamo Bay (Rosenberg 2010).

Like others prisoners before them, the War on Terror detainees at Guantánamo Bay have used hunger strikes as a way of challenging the material and legal conditions of their detention. While the strikes have often been triggered by particular events—a camp guard removing a makeshift turban from a praying detainee, the beating of a young detainee, the transfer of detainees to Camp 6, a maximum security complex—they have lasted because of the more general demands that animate them: better medical care, greater respect for the Koran, an end to the hierarchy of detainee privileges, an end to the indefinite nature of the detainees' detention, and the application of the Geneva Conventions to the camp. The United States Department of Defense has responded to these strikes, as the chronology above makes clear, by feeding the detainees against their will. It has defended this practice by insisting that it is motivated in its actions by the desire to protect the lives of the detainees, and by arguing that the practice of force-feeding is consistent with existing professional and legal guidelines, in particular, the World Medical Association's (WMA) Malta Declaration and Title 28 of the US Code of Federal Regulations (CFR).

This chapter critically examines the Department of Defense's justifications of its force-feeding practices, and uses the Department of Defense's representations of the detainees and the strikes to suggest an alternative, unstated, motivation for this practice. In the first half of this chapter, I assess whether the force-feeding practices at Guantánamo Bay are indeed consistent with the relevant World Medical Association declarations and the US Code of Federal Regulations. I argue that these practices are not consistent with either of the relevant World Medical Association declarations—Malta or Tokyo. While the Code of Federal Regulations is more permissive than these declarations, it does not give authorities a free hand in deciding when to begin a force-feeding regimen. Unfortunately, the Code does not specify when and after what kinds of efforts force-feeding becomes acceptable. The vagueness of the Code, coupled with the absence of public information about the Department of Defense's actual force-feeding practices at Guantánamo Bay, make it difficult to assess with certainty whether these practices are consistent with the spirit of the Code. Evidence exists, however, that suggests that the Department of Defense is interpreting the Code of Federal Regulations liberally. The questionable nature of the Department of Defense's compliance with both the World Medical Association guidelines and the Code of Federal Regulations suggests that its primary interest is in using these documents as justifications for its practices rather than as guides to action.

If this assessment is correct, a subsequent question presents itself: *why* is the Department of Defense so invested in the force-feeding of hunger striking detainees that it is willing to skirt existing professional and legal guidelines to do so? I begin the second half of this chapter by suggesting some of the limitations of answering this question through the lens of biopolitical theory. While the management of biological life has been widely accepted as the *modus operandi* of the modern state, I suggest that a too-complete acceptance of the theory of biopolitics—particularly as it appears in the writings of Giorgio Agamben—may blind us to motivations at work other than the state's desire to reproduce its own authority over matters of life and death. In the balance of the chaper I examine both the Department of Defense's practice of force-feeding and its representations of the strikers; I argue that the force-feeding should be understood not only as an attempt to preserve detainee lives, but as part of a multi-pronged effort to silence detainee speech. Silencing detainee speech matters not only because the US state wants to avoid domestic and international criticism, but because detainee speech disrupts the state's own ability to represent the detainees as it will, and thus to use their silent bodies as inputs for the achievement of particular domestic gepolitical ends.

Justifying Force-Feeding at Guantánamo Bay

Until the United States Supreme Court granted detainees at the Guantánamo Bay detention facility the right to counsel in 2004, the Department of Defense enjoyed near-complete control over what the public knew about what was taking place at the camp. While knowledge remains imperfect about a place that so few civilians have visited (none unguided by camp authorities), our picture of the strikes and of the Department of Defense's response to them has improved as lawyers have gained access to the detainees, and as journalists and health care practitioners have gained access to the site and its official representatives. What little outcry there has been about the Department of Defense's treatment of the hunger strikers—most prominently in two letters published in the British medical journal, *The Lancet*, each with over 250 signatures (Nicholl *et al.* 2006, Nicholl *et al.* 2007)—came after detainee accounts of the feeding regimen surfaced.[1] Detainees and their counsel argued that the Department of Defense was using force-feeding as a form of torture: restraining even those who were willing to accept enteral (tube) feeding; feeding detainees so much that they became ill; inserting the nasal tubes roughly; inserting them anew with every feeding rather than allowing the detainees to keep them in between feedings; and using the same tubes for multiple detainees (for some of these accounts, see Lewis 2005a, Savage 2005, Lewis 2006, Denbeaux and Hafetz 2009: 265–280).

While some camp officials admitted that rough force-feeding techniques represented a strike-breaking strategy (see Schmitt and Golden 2006, White 2006), others defended these techniques as having become necessary once camp personnel became convinced that the strikers were intent on committing suicide (see Potter 2006). The restraints, some camp authorities argued, were needed to keep detainees from removing needles from their arms and from purging what they had been fed (see Smith 2005, Golden 2006b, Schmitt and Golden 2006, Winkenwerder 2006). Others suggested that the restraints were for the protection of the medical staff in addition to that of the detainees (see Winkenwerder 2006, Golden 2007a, see also US Department of Defense 2009: 57).

In addition to defending the particular methods used to force-feed the detainees, the Department of Defense has had to defend the very practice of feeding detainees against their will. This it has done by asserting its commitment to the preservation of detainee lives (Winkenwerder 2006, see also Golden 2006b), and by claiming that its practices are consistent with the World Medical Association's Malta Declaration and Title 28 of the Code of Federal Regulations. A close examination of these and other relevant documents, however, calls this claim into doubt. The Department

---

1   Condemnations came from other sources as well: see Physicians for Human Rights 2005, 2006, Crosby et al. 2007, Dakwar 2009. On the role and responsibilities of health practitioners involved in the War on Terror more generally, see, inter alia, Miles 2004, Bloche and Marks 2005a, 2005b, Okie 2005, Physicians for Human Rights 2005, Annas 2006, Rubenstein and Annas 2009, American Psychiatric Association 2006.

of Defense's elevation of life-saving above other principles—in particular, the principle of detainee autonomy or self-determination—requires a distorted reading of the Malta Declaration and a complete disregard of the World Medical Association's no less relevant Tokyo Declaration. Moreover, while Department of Defense policy regarding the treatment of hunger-striking detainees may be consistent with Title 28 of the Code of Federal Regulations in letter, the Title is vague enough to permit an interpretation of it that would arguably amount to non-compliance with its spirit. Without more complete knowledge of Department of Defense practices, we cannot pronounce on this question with certainty. We can, however, conclude with some confidence that the Department of Defense is more deeply committed to its practice of force-feeding than it is to compliance with existing standards governing the treatment of incarcerated hunger strikers.

The World Medical Association's Declarations

The Department of Defense's compliance with the Malta Declaration was asserted on several occasions by the former Assistant Secretary of Defense for Health Affairs, Dr. William Winkenwerder Jr., including at a roundtable with the press held on the occasion of the Department's publication of Department of Defense Instruction 2310.08E (hereafter, DoDI 2310.08E or the Instruction) in the summer of 2006. A general set of medical guidelines, the Instruction codified the Department of Defense's policies regarding the feeding of hunger-striking detainees at Guantánamo Bay.[2] Noting that there had been some discussion of the Malta Declaration by critics of the Department of Defense's force-feeding practices, Winkenwerder explained to the press why he and his colleagues saw their practices as consistent with the Declaration:

> We view what we are doing as largely consistent with [the Malta] declaration. The Malta Declaration notes that when there is a conflict appearing with a hunger striker that the moral obligation urges the doctor to resuscitate that patient, even though it's against the patient's wishes. That's in the Malta document.

Winkenwerder went on to note that the doctor's intervention should take place once a hunger striker "has lapsed into coma and is impaired and unable to make a decision." He then defended the Department of Defense's early application of this principle. "It's our view," Winkenwerder stated,

---

2   As Winkenwerder Jr. made clear to the press, DoDI 2310.08E did not alter but reaffirmed and clarified existing Department practices regarding the treatment of hunger strikers.

that we're basically along the same ethical tenets, same ethical line of thinking; we just don't want to have someone get to death or near death before we seek to save them. And that only just makes good sense.[3]

Winkenwerder's argument does not withstand scrutiny. At issue is not only whether one can indeed apply the Declaration *earlier*, as Winkenwerder claims that the Department of Defense is doing, and still be compliant with it, but whether the Department of Defense is working with a correct understanding of the World Medical Association's position regarding the treatment of even comatose hunger strikers. We deal with the latter first. While Winkenwerder does mention the competing principles of beneficence and autonomy that must be considered in the treatment of hunger strikers, he misrepresents the weight that the Malta Declaration gives to each of these, cultivating the incorrect impression that the Malta Declaration allows beneficence to take precedence over autonomy. Consider Winkenwerder's account of the physician's conflict (the first quotation in this section) alongside the complete reference to which he is referring:

> [The doctor's] conflict is apparent where a hunger striker who has issued clear instructions not to be resuscitated lapses into a coma and is about to die. Moral obligation urges the doctor to resuscitate the patient even though it is against the patient's wishes. On the other hand, duty urges the doctor to respect the autonomy of the patient (1992 version, preamble point 2).[4]

As this excerpt suggests, the Malta Declaration is not as "pro-life" as Winkenwerder implies. In fact, while the Declaration does acknowledge the ethical difficulties that hunger strikes may pose for some doctors, it *does not* suggest that these difficulties may compromise a competent patient's right to self-determination. The Declaration is written so that a doctor who for reasons of conscience cannot abstain from resuscitating an unconscious striker will not have to, but neither will a striker have to accept the care of such a doctor. The Declaration instructs the doctor to "clearly state to the patient whether or not he is able to accept the patient's decision to refuse treatment or, in case of coma, artificial feeding." If the doctor cannot accept the patient's decision, the Declaration goes on, the striker is

---

3   Speaking to Harper's Magazine's Luke Mitchell, Winkenwerder makes the same point: "We would prefer not to have people lapse into a coma or to be near death when we make that decision . . . In other words, if we're there to protect and sustain someone's life, why would we actually go to the point of putting that person's life at risk before we act? So I think we're operating on a very similar set of ethical reasoning, but it's applied at an earlier stage" (quoted in Mitchell 2006: 10).

4   The Malta Declaration was first adopted in 1991; it was revised in 1992 and in 2006. The 2006 revision was deemed necessary given the "erroneous interpretations" of the Declaration in circulation (World Medical Association 2006).

"entitled to be attended by another physician" (1992 version, preamble point 4; 2006 version, guideline 15).

The document further states that "the ultimate decision" as to whether a physician should intervene or not lies with the doctor "without the intervention of third parties whose primary interest is not the patient's welfare" (1992 version, preamble point 4 and guideline 4; 2006 version, principle 6 and guideline 18), and that the doctor, in making this decision, should respect the wishes expressed by the striker when he or she was well. This last point appears in both the 1992 and 2006 versions of the Declaration. The 1992 version states that the doctor can administer the treatment that he or she deems in the best interest of a comatose patient, "always taking into account the decision he has arrived at during his preceding care of the patient during his hunger strike" (guideline 4). The 2006 version is even clearer: it states that, if made by competent patients, "advance instructions can only generally be overridden if they become invalid because the situation in which the decision was made has changed radically since the individual lost competence" (guideline 17).

No independent doctors have been allowed to treat or meet with the hunger strikers at Guantánamo Bay, and the Department of Defense screens potential camp doctors to ensure that they are comfortable with the force-feeding regimen (Okie 2005). Clearly, the Guantánamo Bay strikers do not have the access to the independent doctor who is willing to respect their wishes that the Malta Declaration requires. Even if the Guantánamo Bay strikers were only being force-fed once they had lapsed into a coma, the Department of Defense would still fall short of compliance with the Malta Declaration.

Insofar as the Department of Defense applies Malta "at an earlier stage" (Winkenwerder, quoted in Mitchell 2006, see *supra* note 3), it is also in violation of the World Medical Association's guidelines. The Malta Declaration speaks mainly to cases where a striker can no longer make his or her wishes known. About the feeding of *competent* detainees, the 1992 version states: "[a] doctor requires informed consent from his patients before applying any of his skills to assist them, unless emergency circumstances have arisen…" (1992 version, preamble 1.2; see also guideline 2.3). Once again, the 2006 version does away with all ambiguity. It states that:

> Hunger strikers should not be forcibly given treatment they refuse. Forced feeding contrary to an informed and voluntary refusal is unjustifiable (2006 version, principle 3; see also 2006 version, guideline 21).

The 2006 version also clarifies that beneficence does not necessarily mean "prolonging life at all costs, irrespective of other values." Rather, benefitting a patient "includes respecting individuals' wishes as well as promoting their welfare," and avoiding causing a patient harm "means not only minimizing damage to health but also not forcing treatment upon competent people" (2006 version, principle 4). Finally, the 2006 version confirms the ethicality of allowing a "determined hunger striker to die in dignity" rather than submitting them to "repeated interventions against his or her will" (2006 version, guideline 19).

In addition to the Malta Declaration, however, the World Medical Association has another, older, declaration that speaks to the force-feeding of *competent* detainees, along with other issues relating to the medical care of incarcerated patients. Point 5 of the 1975 Tokyo Declaration (point 6 in the 2006 version of that document) states clearly that, as long as they are deemed competent, hunger-striking prisoners "shall not be fed artificially." Given the existence of a World Medical Association declaration that speaks directly to the feeding of conscious hunger strikers—and given that both the Malta and Tokyo Declarations were cited by critics of Department of Defense practices (Nicholl *et al.* 2006, Cady 2006)—it is difficult to see the Department of Defense's claim of compliance with its own interpretation of the Malta Declaration as anything but a diversion from the reality of its non-compliance with the World Medical Association's guidelines, guidelines intelligible to anyone willing to engage in a good faith reading of both of the relevant declarations.

In order for the Department of Defense to be compliant with the World Medical Association's guidelines, it would have to respect the rights of competent detainees to engage in hunger strikes. According to the World Medical Association's declarations, the Department of Defense's stated interest in preserving detainee lives does not supersede the detainees' rights to self-determination, whatever the consequences of the exercise of those rights.

Title 28 of the Code of Federal Regulations

The Department of Defense's compliance with the Code of Federal Regulations has been asserted both orally, like its compliance with the Malta Declaration, and in official documents regarding the Guantánamo Bay detention facility. DoDI 2310.08E, mentioned above, states that, while health care is generally provided with detainee consent, "[i]n the case of a hunger strike, attempted suicide, or other attempted serious self-harm, medical treatment or intervention may be directed without the consent of the detainee to prevent death or serious harm" (4.7.1). It goes on to note that "procedures for dealing with cases in which involuntary treatment may be necessary to prevent death or serious harm shall be developed with consideration of procedures established by Title 28, Code of Federal Regulations, Part 549" (4.7.3). The Code of Federal Regulations is also mentioned in the Department of Defense's "Review of Department Compliance with President's Executive Order on Detainee Conditions of Confinement" (hereafter, the Walsh report), published in 2009. Ordered by President Obama within days of his inauguration, the purpose of the Walsh report was to describe current Department of Defense policies and practices at Guantánamo Bay, pronounce on their compliance with all applicable laws governing confinement by the US state (including Common Article 3 of the Geneva Conventions) and issue recommendations where appropriate. The report notes that Department of Defense policy regarding the treatment of hunger-striking detainees "is similar to that used by the Bureau of Prisons, as authorized in Title 28, Code of Federal Regulations, Part 549" (56).

While the Code of Federal Regulations is more permissive than the Tokyo and Malta Declarations, it remains a cautious document—one that makes infringements upon inmate self-determination conditional upon a determination of medical necessity. Title 28's section on inmate hunger strikers' "refusal to accept treatment" begins by noting that when "a physician determines that the inmate's life or health will be threatened if treatment is not initiated immediately, the physician *shall give consideration* to forced medical treatment of the inmate" (CFR, 549.65.a, my emphasis). "Reasonable efforts" shall then be made to convince the inmate to accept treatment voluntarily. After such efforts have been made, physicians may order treatment without the consent of the inmate once "a medical necessity for immediate treatment of a life or health threatening situation exists" (CFR, 549.65.b and c).

Assessing whether the Department of Defense practices are consistent with the Code of Federal Regulations is difficult given both the vagueness of the Code's guidelines (what are "reasonable efforts"? What constitutes "a medical necessity"?) and the lack of public information about Department of Defense practices regarding the treatment of hunger-striking detainees Guantánamo Bay. DoDI 2310.08E and the Walsh Report both suggest that the requirement in the Code of Federal Regulations that force-feeding take place only once the detainee's health is at risk is being respected. DoDI 2310.08E states that, while detainee consent to intervention is not necessary in cases of hunger strikes, the intervention "must be based on a medical determination that *immediate treatment or intervention is necessary to prevent death or serious harm*" (4.7.1, my emphasis). Similarly, according to the Walsh report's description of practices at Guantánamo Bay, intervention without consent is only considered once the detainee's "medical condition deteriorates to a point, which in the judgment of the attending physician, would present *a significant threat to life or health* if the fasting were to continue" (56, my emphasis).

But at what point does a hunger strike begin to present a threat to the health of the striker? As medical professionals know, the body begins to react to the absence of food and drink almost immediately (Crosby *et al.* 2007). In principle, then, the Department of Defense could begin a force-feeding regimen at any point and still insist that the practice was consistent with Code of Federal Regulations. Because we do not know when, according to what criteria, and after what kinds of efforts, doctors and other authorities at Guantánamo Bay are deciding to begin force-feeding the hunger-striking detainees,[5] we cannot accurately assess the consistency of Department of Defense practices with the restrained spirit of Title 28 of the Code

---

5   This information—as well as information on the "procedures for dealing with cases in which involuntary treatment may be necessary" that DoDI 2310.08E says would be developed "with consideration of procedures established by Title 28" (4.7.3)—was

of Federal Regulations. That said, Winkenwerder's rhetoric above—in particular his failure to link the early application of the Malta Declaration to situations of medical necessity—as well as the fact that the feeding of detainees requires their being physically restrained suggests that the criteria of the existence of a "threat to life or health" is being interpreted very liberally at Guantánamo Bay.[6]

Moreover, the Guantánamo Bay physicians' lack of independence also casts doubt on Department of Defense compliance with the Code of Federal Regulations. As George Annas has noted, "only a physician (not the warden) is permitted to make treatment decisions on the basis of [the Code of Federal Regulations]" (2006: 1379). If other military personnel are making decisions about force-feeding the hunger strikers at Guantánamo Bay, "the rules of the Bureau of Prisons are not being followed" (2006: 1380).

A further point bears mentioning. US courts have very often found in favor of penal authorities in legal contests over the treatment of hunger-striking prisoners, but this has not uniformly been the case. Several courts, including the Supreme Court of Georgia and the California Supreme Court, have upheld the right of competent prisoners to strike to death, in some cases directly rejecting the state's stated interest in preserving the inmates' lives. Moreover, Mara Silver (2005) has persuasively suggested that holdings that find against hunger-striking prisoners may be inconsistent with recent US Supreme Court decisions. The Supreme Court's rulings in *Cruzan v. Director, Missouri Department of Health* and *Washington v. Glucksberg* affirm the individual's right to refuse medical treatment. Given that the Supreme Court has also found, in *Turner v. Safley*, that prisoners retain those rights that are not inconsistent with their status as prisoners or with penological objectives, it is not clear to Silver why the state's interest in life-preservation should prevail over prisoners' rights to expression and privacy. As she (2005: 645) puts it:

> In cases where a nonprisoner wishes to refuse treatment, the preservation of life is subrogated to the individual's right to self-determination. There is simply no reason why the same outcome should not prevail in the case of prison inmates, unless the state has a stronger interest in preserving the life of a prisoner than a nonprisoner.

To the extent that it is life preservation, rather than prison order, that provides the occasion for force-feeding in the Code of Federal Regulations, the Code itself may eventually be discovered to be inconsistent with these Supreme Court rulings.

---

formally requested from Defense Press Operations in February 2011. As of this writing, I have not received a response.

6   Note also the comment of camp spokesperson Lt. Col. Jeremy Martin who, in October 2005, said that the suggestion that the hunger strikers were near death was "absolutely false" (quoted in White 2005).

Detainee Bodies as Geopolitical Resources

As the foregoing discussion suggests, the Department of Defense is arguably less interested in strict compliance with professional and legal guidelines regarding the treatment of hunger-striking prisoners than it is in using references to these guidelines to justify its force-feeding regimen. What remains to be explored is why the Department of Defense—or, more broadly, the US state—is so invested in force-feeding the striking detainees. One explanation is that the commitment to feeding the detainees is a function of the biopolitical nature of the modern state—its preoccupation with its own authority over the terrain of life and death. This is the argument offered by Patrick Anderson, one of the few social scientists or humanists to have attempted to make sense of the Department of Defence's force-feeding of the detainees. According to Anderson, "[w]hat terrorizes the state" about hunger strikes "is its inability to assert its sovereignty in these matters of life and death" (2009: 1733), matters over which the state has claimed jurisdiction ever since "[t]he ancient right to kill and to let live" gave way to a biopolitical model in which the state, or the sovereign, *makes live and lets die*" (Agamben 1999: 82, cited in Anderson 2010: 148, 2009: 1735, see also Foucault 2003: 241). For Anderson, the strikes subvert the US state's "insistent, embittered reproduction of sovereignty" and reveal "the desperation with which this state has deployed and intertwined its institutions to stage and seize 'bare life'" (2009: 1736).

While Anderson is one of only a few scholars to have examined the hunger strikes, there has been no shortage of scholars examining the Guantánamo Bay detention facility (and the War on Terror more generally). Many of these scholars, moreover, have—like Anderson—done this work with the help of Agamben's writings on biopolitics, sovereignty, bare life and the space of exception (see, *inter alia*, Agamben 2005, Minca 2005, Gregory 2006, Hannah 2006, Elden 2007). And indeed, Agamben's work seems ideally suited to the analysis of Guantánamo Bay. In insisting that neither US law nor the laws of war applied to the "enemy combatants" at Guantánamo Bay, President George W. Bush seemed to provide a perfect illustration of several of Agamben's major theses, among them: that the sovereign's power is the power to decide the exception—to decide who will be subject to his discretion rather than to law; that sovereign power reproduces itself, as Anderson suggests above, on the backs of the residents of this state of exception; and that the once-hidden and local operations that undergird sovereignty have now become overt and general, with the state of exception "today [reaching] its maximum worldwide deployment" (Agamben 2005: 87).

Others have refrained from using an Agambenian frame, pointing out the weaknesses of Agamben's account itself (Neocleous 2006) or its inapplicability to Guantánamo Bay and the War on Terror (Johns 2005).[7] Two considerations inform my own reservations about viewing the Department of Defense's response

---

7   It should be noted that not all of the scholars who find Agamben's work useful adopt it uncritically.

to the hunger strikes at Guantánamo Bay through the lens of Agambenian theory, and in particular, through the lens of Agamben's understanding of biopolitics. First, like all theoretical apparatuses, Agamben's account of biopolitics tends to illuminate some practices and objects better than others. The risk of being seduced by the apparent fit between Agamben's theses and the events at Guantánamo Bay is that we will see most clearly what the theory best illuminates, mistaking the vividness that is an effect of the theory for a property of the practice or object itself. Because Agamben's theories are oriented towards life-and-death issues, they tempt us to take the Department of Defense at its word when it claims that the purpose of the force-feeding of the detainees is the preservation of their lives.[8] The Department of Defense's stated explanation—"[w]e have a policy that is to preserve life" (Winkenwerder 2006)—is perfectly coincident with Agamben's theory of biopolitics. But what if life-preservation if not the reason, or not the only reason, for the practice of force-feeding?

Second, and relatedly, not only does Agamben's theory of biopolitics illuminate particular practices or objects at the expense of others, but it provides a ready explanation for the existence of those practices or objects. Not only do we tend to see what the theory invites us to see, then, but so too do we tend to accept the theory's explanation for what we are seeing. Translated into the particulars of our case: an Agambenian frame encourages an understanding of the force-feeding as indeed about life-preservation, and it provides a ready explanation for *why* life-preservation is a goal of the US state—control over life and death is what the modern state wants. Agamben's confidence in his own narrative about the historical ascendence of biopolitics and about the location of its teleological destiny in the present make specific questions about the Department of Defense's response to the Guantánamo Bay hunger strikes redundant in advance. There is no reason to ask why the US state might be force-feeding the detainees: it is written into the modern state's DNA.[9]

As I will suggest below, the Department of Defense has a motivation for force-feeding the detainees that we cannot see if we have already accepted the motivation of life-preservation provided to us by both the Department of Defense

8 For an argument that demonstrates the limitations of Agamben's exclusive focus on the life and death binary, see Hannah 2006.

9 While this chapter cannot accommodate a substantive critique of Agamben's treatment of biopolitics, it might also be added that Agamben's account of biopolitics has been critiqued for its ahistoricism, among other things. As Andreas Kalyvas has observed, Agamben's account lacks any discussion of the "reasons, forces, interests, struggles, movements, strategies, and actors that were and still are involved in the unfolding of bio-sovereign politics" (2005: 112, see also Bernstein 2004), and it is undisturbed by events as varied as "the birth of the ancient-Greek democratic city, the institution of isonomia, the emergence of commercial capitalism, the modern discovery of rights, the invention of constitutionalism, the democratic revolutions of the late eighteenth century, and the entry of the laboring masses into politics," all of which, for Agamben, merely contribute to the "inexorable historical unfolding" of biopolitics (2005: 111).

and by Agamben's account of biopolitics: this is the motivation to silence detainee speech. Acknowledging this motivation opens the door towards a fuller understanding of the US state's interest in the Guantánamo Bay detainees. In what follows, I first establish that silencing political speech was an important reason for the force-feeding of the hunger strikers at Guantánamo Bay. I then argue that the state's interest in thwarting detainee self-representation in this way is a function of its desire to use the detainees as resources for domestic geopolitical ends.

Silencing Detainee Speech

It has long been acknowledged that hunger-striking is a form of political speech, one often adopted by those denied ordinary or formal avenues of communication, such as, for example, the right to speak before court. As former Guantánamo Bay detainee Mundah Habib stated, the hunger strike was the only way to "send a message to the public outside to know what's going on" (quoted in Doctors attack US over Guantanamo 2006). Although the emaciated body may appear as "a radical negation of the other," self-starvation is in fact a deeply social act, a performance utterly dependent on its spectator (Ellman 1993: 17). By refusing to eat, the striker takes his or her protest inside, but this internal ordeal transforms the body's surface, turning it into a legible text, a "living dossier" of discontents both biological and political (1993: 17). That the bodies of incarcerated hunger strikers often cannot be seen by those to whom the speech of their strike is addressed renders all the more evident the desperate nature of this act.

That the goal of the Department of Defense's force-feeding regimen is to silence the speech that the hunger strikes represent is amply suggested by camp authorities' representations of the strikers as either suicidal or disingenuous. To the extent that they are persuasive, these representations of the strikers neutralize the communicative potential of the strikes. By representing the strikers as suicidal (see Potter 2006, Winkenwerder 2006), camp officials effectively deny that the strikes are speech at all. While some detainees have admitted to hoping for death, and while suicides have been attempted and have occurred at the camp (some explicitly planned as a form of protest, see Gutierrez 2005, Worthington 2007), to characterize most of the Guantánamo Bay hunger strikers as suicidal is to efface the distinction between a detainee who wants to die and one who wants to protest but is willing to die while doing so. As should be obvious in a country where "give me liberty or give me death" is a celebrated slogan, a hunger striker may consider death an acceptable outcome of his or her strike without having death as his or her goal. As the World Medical Association notes, hunger strikers can be divided into two groups: those that "fast to gain publicity to achieve their goal, but have no intention of permanently damaging their health," and those who are willing to "risk their health or their lives for a cause" (WMA Declaration of Malta: a background paper on the ethical management of hunger strikes 2006: 37). Surely, it is into the latter category, rather than into the category of someone suicidal, that falls someone like detainee Binyam Mohammed, who stated in 2005 that he would not stop his fast "until I either die or we are respected" (quoted in Gillan 2005).

When camp officials have not denied that the strikes are a form of speech, they have often represented this speech as disingenuous and the strikers themselves as manipulative. In 2005, Lt. Col. Jeremy Martin, a spokesperson for the detention facility, suggested that hunger-striking was a technique "consistent with the al Qaeda training," and that it reflected "the detainees' attempts to elicit media attention and bring pressure on the United States government" (quoted in White 2005). When stories emerged in 2006 about the military using the feeding to inflict pain on the strikers, military spokespersons responded by saying that "the prisoners are for the most part terrorists, trained by Al Qaeda (sic) to use false stories as propaganda" (quoted in Schmitt and Golden 2006). In 2007, when detainees began striking to protest the conditions at a new maximum security complex at the camp, camp spokesperson Cmdr. Robert Durand called the strikes "propaganda," and suggested that they were part of an effort by detainees and their counsel to "discredit the detention mission" (quoted in Golden 2007b, see also Glaberson 2007). Finally, when hunger striker Sami al-Haj produced sketches depicting his condition, camp spokesperson, Navy Cmdr. Rick Haupt, stated that "al Qaeda trains its operatives to allege inhumane treatment" (quoted in Guantanamo force-feeding sketch censored 2008).

As an aside, it is worth noting that a similar strategy has been used to characterize the detainees that have attempted, or successfully committed, suicide. The military began characterizing suicide itself as "manipulative self-injurious behaviour" early on (Smith 2005), and the suicides of 2006 were described by Rear Adm. Harry B. Harris Jr. as, not "an act of desperation, but an act of asymmetrical warfare against us," committed by individuals who have "no regard for human life, neither ours nor their own" (quoted in Glaberson and Williams 2009). State Department official Colleen Graffy referred to these suicides as a "good PR move" and "a tactic to further the jihadi cause," and Lieutenant Commander Jeffrey Gordon characterized the dead as "fanatics like the Nazis, Hitlerites, or the Ku Klux Klan, the people they tried at Nuremberg" (quoted in Rose 2006).

Putting Detainee Bodies to Work

Clearly, the Department of Defense's interest is not only in preserving lives but in silencing detainee speech. Why? As some commentators have observed, quite apart from the intelligence they may or may not possess, the detainees seem to have been intended to serve a particular symbolic purpose. It is not only that the captured detainees help to stage a "reversal of national humiliation" (Butler 2004: 77–78). They also help to create, among Americans, "the belief that the homeland is secure" (Ahmad 2009: 1695). As Susan Willis notes, commenting on the "security ideology" that the American public consumes:

> The suffering and mental breakdown of the tortured detainees is traded against
> the wellbeing of Middle America: they must stay there in order to preserve the
> peace and prosperity of the citizenry (2006: 125).

The detainees, then, are an input: a resource set to work inside a machine—
Guantánamo Bay—that works to confirm domestic fears about the existence of
an enemy; to produce a sense of national vindication; and to locate responsibility
for that vindication in a heroic state and its representatives (on the simultaneous
production of security and threat, see Katz 2007). What must the detainees be,
to be this kind of input? Importantly, they need *not* be subjects with intelligence
to impart. This helps to explain the otherwise mysterious fact that so many of
the detainees were effectively purchased—handed over to US authorities by
Pakistan or the Northern Alliance at a time when "the United States offered
large bounties for capture of suspected enemies" (Denbeaux and Denbeaux
2006: 3)—rather than carefully selected for the intelligence they possessed (see
Golden and Van Natta 2004).[10]

To perform their symbolic duty, the detainees need only be screens onto which
the US state can project the representation that it prefers. The technologies of
race and sex no doubt go a long way toward corroborating, in the eyes of the
American public, the state's story that these men are the worst of the worst—
that they are veritable *biohazards*, as is suggested by the widely circulated early
pictures of the orange-clad detainees (for an insightful reading of the photographic
representations of Guantánamo Bay and its detainees, see Van Veeren 2010).
As an ideological apparatus, the Guantánamo Bay detention facility both relies
upon and reproduces the discursive construction of Muslim and Arab men as
uncivilized and violent (Said 1978, 1997, Shaheen 1991, Puar and Rai 2002).[11]
But if race and sex go a long way towards ensuring that the American public
will be receptive to perceiving these bodies in the manner that the state presents
them, these technologies cannot be relied upon exclusively. They are bolstered
by a moratorium on any representations that might compete with the state's
representation of the detainees. The brown and male bodies at Guantánamo
Bay must also be *silent* bodies. What makes the detainees risky as resources

---

10   According to Laurel E. Fletcher and Eric Storver (2009: 20), more than a third of
the 62 former detainees interviewed by their team "said they knew, either from personal
observation or being told by U.S or Pakistani officials, they had been sold to the United
States." Interestingly, in my survey of newspaper articles about the force-feeding regimen,
I came across no arguments by any US officials that suggested that the detainees needed to
be kept alive because of the intelligence they possessed.

11   We can venture that this construction goes some way towards explaining how little
outcry there has been about the force-feeding of the Guantánamo Bay detainees in the
United States: if 9/11 was an emasculating event, force-feeding—an experience that has
been likened to rape—can be seen as a small part of the United States' remasculinization
effort, a micro-scale staging of the drama of vindication (on the War on Terror as a process
of remasculinization, see Puar and Rai 2002).

is that they consist of more than bodies. Like the capitalist who must employ workers—his gravediggers—if he is to exploit labor power, a state that wants to make symbolic use of living human bodies must contend with the fact that these bodies are also human subjects, capable of representing themselves. When they do represent themselves, their status as a resource that can be deployed by the state is compromised; they cease to be representational vacuums. Hence the imperative that the state disrupt the communicative potential of what little self-representation is able to make it out of the camp.

Another illustration of the Department of Defense's efforts at disrupting the ability of the detainees to communicate is its unwillingness to allow the public to see the faces of the detainees. According to Department of Defense policy, photographs of detainees may be out of focus, taken from behind, or cropped so that the face is not visible (though the beard—that reminder of the detainees' exoticness—may be) (Rosenberg 2008). While US officials have suggested that this policy was adopted with the Geneva Conventions' proscription against humiliation in mind, Elspeth Van Veeren observes that the policy keeps the detainees "from turning their eyes and therefore their gaze back at the viewer" (2010: 1733). As such the detainees' "ability to communicate with the viewer is limited" (1734), as is the possibility that the viewer will have an "empathetic encounter" with the objects of the photographs (1735).

As this example makes plain, in addition to being a potential resource for the US state, the bodies of the detainees are also resources for the detainees themselves. We need our bodies to communicate: to speak, to act, to gaze. Denied the ability to communicate in these ordinary ways, we can recruit our bodies to perform more unorthodox tasks. The Department of Defense's denial that the strikes represent sincere speech can be read as an attempt to deny the detainees the use of their own bodies as resources. At stake for the Department of Defense is more than the possibility that the detainees' speech—whatever form it takes—will challenge the state's authority over matters of life and death. At stake is more than the possibility that the speech will draw attention to the detainees' mistreatment at the hands of the US state. At stake is also the US state's ability to use the bodies of these detainees as resources of its own. Through the speech of the strike, the detainees threaten to deprive their captors of the use of their (detainee) bodies as silent screens onto which the state's representations can be projected. In attempting to silence detainee speech, then, the Department of Defense has been attempting not only to guard the state's sovereign power, not only to protect the state's name, but to preserve the state's investment.

Conclusion

My goal in this chapter has been, first, to assess whether the Department of Defense's practice of force-feeding hunger-striking detainees at the Guantánamo Bay detention facility is consistent, as the Department of Defense claims, with the World Medical Association's guidelines and with Title 28 of the Code of Federal Regulations. My argument here has been that the Department of Defense's practices are not consistent with either of the World Medical Association declarations relevant to the treatment of hunger striking detainees. Because of both the vagueness of Title 28 of the Code of Federal Regulations and our lack of information about the protocols governing the treatment of hunger-striking detainees at Guantánamo Bay, it is impossible to state with certainty whether the Department of Defense's force-feeding practices are consistent with Title 28. It is clear, however, that the Department of Defense is committed to its practice of feeding the detainees against their will. The second goal of this chapter has been to inquire into the reasons for the state's commitment to this practice. Whatever the feeding of the detainees may have to do with life preservation—a point made by the Department of Defense and echoed by Agambenian biopolitical theory—I argue that it is also motivated by a desire to deprive the detainees of the use of their bodies as vehicles for speech. Silencing detainee speech is imperative if the state is to use the detainees' bodies for its own representational purposes.

What counts as a resource changes over time and across space, depending on our stage of development and our particular social goals (Harvey 1974, 1996). The use of detainee bodies as resources is no less contingent. President Obama campaigned on a promise to close the Guantánamo Bay detention facility that the George W. Bush Administration had found so useful. At least at the start of his presidency, it was the proper disposal of these bodies that occupied Obama's attention. Ultimately, however, Senate opposition to funding the closing of the detention facility, and widespread right-wing rhetoric (including in the Senate and in Congress) about the dangers of allowing Guantánamo Bay detainees—even those deemed innocent—onto American soil, altered Obama's plans. The state's representation of the detainees as the worst of the worst, and its struggle to silence detainee self-representation, have borne fruit in the form of a nation unable to see the detainees as anything but the threats they've been presented as. The risk for the detainees is that Guantánamo Bay, the machine for which they have been inputs, will be transformed into the container in which they—like radioactive waste—are stored *in perpetuum*.

Acknowledgments

Thanks to Angus Cameron, Jen Dickinson, and Nicola Smith for inviting me to contribute to this collection and for providing excellent feedback along the way. Carol Rosenberg of *The Miami Herald* answered many questions and pointed me in the direction of useful resources. Thanks also to Ian Bruff, Matt Hannah, Steve Herbert, Matt Himley, Maria Meindl, Bob Ross and two anonymous reviewers for their comments and critiques.

References

Agamben, G. 1999. *Remnants of Auschwitz: The Witness and the Archive.* New York: Zone.

————. 2005. *State of Exception.* Chicago: University of Chicago Press.

Ahmad, M. I. 2009. Resisting Guantanamo: rights at the brink of dehumanization. *Northwestern University Law Review,* 103(4), 1683–1763.

American Psychiatric Association. 2006. APA passes position statement barring psychiatric participation in interrogation of detainees.

Anderson, P. 2009. There will be no Bobby Sands in Guantánamo Bay. *PMLA,* 124(5), 1729–1736.

————. 2010. *So Much Wasted: Hunger, Performance, and the Morbidity of Resistance.* Durham: Duke University Press.

Annas, G. J. 2006. Hunger strikes at Guantanamo: medical ethics and human rights in a "Legal Black Hole." *New England Journal of Medicine,* 355(13), 1377–1382.

Bernstein, J. M. 2004. Bare Life, bearing witness: Auschwitz and the pornography of horror.

Parallax, 10(1), 2–16.

Bloche, M. G., and Marks, J. H. 2005a. Doctors and interrogators at Guantanamo Bay. *New England Journal of Medicine,* 353(1), 6–8.

————. 2005b. When doctors go to war. *New England Journal of Medicine,* 352(1), 3–6.

Butler, J. 2004. *Precarious Life: The Powers of Mourning and Violence.* New York: Verso.

Cady, D. 2006. AMA reiterates opposition to feeding individuals against their will: American Medical Association.

Crosby, S. S., Apovian, C. M., and Grodin, M. A. 2007. Hunger strikes, force-feeding, and physicians' responsibilities. *JAMA: Journal of the American Medical Association,* 298(5), 563–566.

Dakwar, J. 2009. ACLU letter to Defense Secretary Gates in response to force-feeding of Guantánamo detainees: ACLU.

Dao, J. 2002. Navy doctors force-feeding 2 prisoners. *The New York Times,* April 2.

Denbeaux, M., and Denbeaux, J. 2006. Report on Guantanamo Detainees: A Profile of 517 Detainees through Analysis of Department of Defense Data.

Denbeaux, M. P., and Hafetz, J. eds. 2009. *The Guantánamo Lawyers: Inside a Prison Outside the Law.* New York: New York University Press.

Doctors attack US over Guantanamo. 2006. *BBC News,* March 10.

Elden, S. 2007. Terror and territory. *Antipode,* 39(5), 821–845.

Ellman, M. 1993. *The Hunger Artists: Starving, Writing, and Imprisonment.* Cambridge, Massachusetts: Harvard University Press.

Fletcher, L. E., and Stover, E. 2009. *The Guantánamo Effect: Exposing the Consequences of US Detention and Interrogation Practices.* Berkeley: University of California Press.

Foucault, M. 2003. *'Society Must Be Defended': Lectures at the Collège de France 1975–76*. New York: Picador.

Gillan, A. 2005. Hunger strikers pledge to die in Guantánamo. *The Guardian*, September 9.

Glaberson, W. 2007. Guantanamo prisoner cuts his throat with fingernail. *The New York Times*, December 4:A27(L).

Glaberson, W., and Williams, M. 2009. Officials report suicide of Guantanamo detainee. *The New York Times*, June 3.

Golden, T. 2006a. The battle for Guantánamo. *New York Times*, September 17.

———. 2006b. Tough US steps in hunger strike at camp in Cuba. *The New York Times*, February 9.

———. 2007a. Guantanamo detainees stage hunger strike despite force-feeding policy. *The New York Times*, April 9.

———. 2007b. Hunger strike breaks out at Guantánamo. *The New York Times*, April 8.

Golden, T., and Van Natta, Don J. 2004. US said to overestimate value of Guantánamo detainees. *New York Times*, June 21.

Goldenberg, S. 2007. Guantánamo bay inmates in mass hunger strike over new solitary cells. *The Guardian*, April 10.

Gregory, D. 2006. The black flag: Guantanamo Bay and the space of exception. *Geografiska Annaler: Series B, Human Geography*, 88(4), 405–427.

Guantanamo force-feeding sketch censored. 2008. *Associated Press*, March 17.

Gutierrez, G. 2005. The Guantánamo prisoner hunger strikes and protests: February 2002–August 2005. New York: Center for Constitutional Rights.

Hannah, M. 2006. Torture and the ticking bomb: The War on Terrorism as a geographical imagination of Power/Knowledge. *Annals of the Association of American Geographers*, 96(3), 622–640.

Harvey, D. 1974. Population, resources, and the ideology of science. *Economic Geography* 50 (3):256–277.

———. 1996. *Justice, Nature and the Geography of Difference*. Oxford: Blackwell.

Johns, F. 2005. Guantánamo Bay and the annihilation of the exception. *The European Journal of International Law*, 16(4), 613–635.

Kalyvas, A. 2005. The sovereign weaver: beyond the camp. In *Politics, Metaphysics, and Death: Essays on Girogio Agamben's Homo Sacer*, ed. A. Norris, 107–134. Durham: Duke University Press.

Katz, C. 2007. Banal terrorism: spatial fetishism and everyday insecurity. In *Violent Geographies: Fear, Terror, and Political Violence*, eds. D. Gregory and A. Pred, 349–361. New York: Routledge.

Lewis, N. A. 2005a. Guantanamo detainees gain in ruling. *The New York Times*, October 27:A22(L).

———. 2005b. Widespread hunger strike at Guantanamo. *The New York Times*, September 18.

———. 2006. Guantanamo detainee seeks court action. *The New York Times*, March 3:A16(L).

Miles, S. H. 2004. Abu Ghraib: its legacy for military medicine. *The Lancet* 364:725–729.

Minca, C. 2005. The return of the camp. *Progress in Human Geography*, 29(4), 405–412.

Mitchell, L. 2006. God mode. *Harper's Magazine*, August.

Neocleous, M. 2006. The problem with normality: Taking exception to "Permanent Emergency."*Alternatives*, 31(2), 191–213.

Nicholl, D. J., Atkinson, H. G., Kalk, J., Hopkins, W., Elias, E., Siddiqui, A., Cronfrod, R. E., and Sacks, O. 2006. Forcefeeding and restraint of Guantanamo Bay hunger strikers. *The Lancet*, 367(9513), 811.

Nicholl, D. J., Jenkins, T., Miles, S. H., Siddiqui, A., and Boulton, F. 2007. Biko to Guantanamo: 30 years of medical involvement in torture. *The Lancet*, 370(9590), 823.

Okie, S. 2005. Glimpses of Guantanamo – medical ethics and the War on Terror. *New England Journal of Medicine*, 353(24), 2529–2534.

Physicians for Human Rights. 2005. Forced feeding of Gitmo detainees violates international medical codes of ethics.

———. 2006. Physicians for Human Rights denounces new Pentagon instructions on medical support for interrogation.

Potter, C. J. 2006. Drastic force-feeding measures push Gitmo hunger strike to lowest point. *Paper Chase*, February 9.

Puar, J. K., and Rai, A. S. 2002. Monster, terrorist, fag: the war on terrorism and the production of docile patriots. *Social Text*, 20 (3 72), 117–148.

Reid, T. 2009. Hunger strike by Guantanamo inmates aims to grab new President's attention. *The Times*, January 15.

Rose, D. 2006. How US hid the suicide secrets of Guantanamo. *The Observer*, June 18.

Rosenberg, C. 2008. Guantánamo photos reverberate around the world. *The Miami Herald*, January 12.

———. 2009. Judge OK's use of Guantanamo forced-feeding chair. *The Miami Herald*, February 11.

———. 2010. Ramadan at Guantánamo includes nightly force-feedings. *The Miami Herald*, August 24.

Rubenstein, L. S., and G. J. Annas. 2009. Medical ethics at Guantanamo Bay Detention Centre and in the US military: a time for reform. *The Lancet*, 374(9686), 353–355.

Said, E. W. 1978. *Orientalism*. New York: Pantheon Books.

———. 1997. *Covering Islam: How the Media and the Experts Determine How we See the Rest of the World*. Revised Edition ed. New York: Vintage Books.

Savage, C. 2005. Guantanamo medics accused of abusive force-feeding. *Boston Globe*, October 15.

Schmitt, E. and Golden, T. 2006. Force-feeding at Guantanamo is now acknowledged. *The New York Times*, February 22.

Shaheen, J. G. 2001. *Reel Bad Arabs: How Hollywood Villifies a People*. New York: Olive Branch Press.

Silver, M. 2005. Testing Cruzan: prisoners and the constitutional question of self-starvation. *Stanford Law Review*, 58(2), 631–662.

Smith, C. S. 2005. Gitmo's hunger strikers. *The Nation*, October 17.

US Department of Defense. 2009. Review of Department Compliance with President's Executive Order on Detainee Conditions of Confinement. Washington, D.C.: US Department of Defense.

Veeren, E. V. 2011. Captured by the camera's eye: Guantánamo and the shifting frame of the Global War on Terror. *Review of International Studies*, 37(4), 1721–1749.

White, J. 2005. Guantanamo desperation seen in suicide attempts. *The Washington Post*, November 1.

———. 2006. Guantanamo force-feeding tactics are called torture. *The Washington Post*, March 1.

Willis, S. 2006. Guantánamo's symbolic economy. *New Left Review*, 39, 123–131.

Winkenwerder, W. 2006. Media roundtable with Assistant Secretary Winkenwerder, ed. US Department of Defense

WMA Declaration of Malta: a background paper on the ethical management of hunger strikes. 2006. *World Medical Journal*, 52(2), 36–43.

World Medical Association. 2006. WMA condemns all forced feeding: World Medical Association.

Worthington, A. 2007. *The Guantánamo Files: The Stories of the 774 Detainees in America's Illegal Prison*. London: Pluto Press.

Chapter 4

Organ Transplantation: The Debt of Life?[1]

Jen Dickinson and Matthew Sothern

Introduction

In 2009, 2,552 organs from deceased donors were transplanted in the UK, yet more than 10,500 people remain on the UK solid organ transplant waiting lists (NHS Blood and Transplant 2009). Tragically, more than 1,000 people die each year waiting for the so-called 'gift of life' or because they become too ill whilst waiting to remain viable list candidates. Given the difficulty of resolving the supply and demand tension that organ waiting lists index, promotion of organ transplantation usually centres on increasing the number of organs available for transplant by encouraging voluntary registration as an organ donor (Morgan, Mayblin and Jones 2008; Bird and Harris 2010). These efforts at increasing the supply of organs from deceased donors are organised through the potent metaphor of the 'gift of life'. This metaphor positions organ transplantation as a supererogatory gift, where donors' altruism leads them to literally give corporeal fragments of themselves to save the life (usually) of an unknown stranger. Framing transplant surgery itself as the end point to the problem of the recipient's diseased organ the 'gift of life' obliges us to join the 'NHS Organ Donor Register [which] means that [we] could save 15 lives after [we] die' (www.nhs.uk/live well/donation).

Despite the framing of organ donation as purely altruistic act, this kind of corporeal giving is more complex. As Titmuss (1970) has argued, donation of blood rests upon a sense of intercorporeal connection with others and on an understanding of the vulnerability of ourselves and/or our loved ones . As with blood donation, reluctance to join the organ donor register is extolled as a failure both of general social obligation and particular potential need. Injunctions urging us to 'give' our blood and organs foreground the agency of donor, but in doing so they also obfuscate the fact that in the vast majority of cases 'donor[s] participate in the actual gift exchange not as a knowing giver, but as a gift object' (Siminoff and Chillag 1999: 35). If there is a 'donor', with respect to cadaveric donation, it should not be understood as synonymous with the person in whose body the organs were once housed. Instead, organ transplantation is the result of permission from the donor's (grieving) family, by the policies of the hospital, the decisions

1   Adapted by permission of Taylor and Francis from the journal article 'Repaying the gift of life: self-help, organ transfer and the debt of care', in Social and Cultural Geography volume 12, issue 8, pp. 889–903. Copyright © 2011

of the doctors, psychologists, and the work of the algorithms which assist tissue matching. Even more fundamentally, much of the luck of getting an organ rests on the accident of geographical and temporal proximity between the donor who has to die in the right way and those who may eventually receive their organs.

This chapter examines the sharp asymmetries between the ways in which the 'gifting' assemblage (donor, family, medics) are constituted and that of the recipient's treatment. Although, as Davies (2006) has argued, the ethical position of organ recipients is critically important, the multiple ways in which they are constructed through the narratives and practices of the donation process is neglected. Here we use anthropologist Lesley Sharp's (2006) redefinition of 'organ trans*plant*' as 'organ trans*fer*' to draw out the necessary chain of connection between donation, procurement, transplantation surgery and the 'life' that is lived once one becomes a recipient. The focus on the recipient of the organ is important because surgery does not return the body to some pre-illness pristine health, but exchanges a terminal condition—say, chronic liver failure—for a chronic condition, that of a liver transplant recipient. The recipient is not a passive receiver of the gifted organ, but rather one who must carefully construct their post-transplant life to ensure that these rare 'gifts' are not 'wasted'.

Using self-help and autobiographical texts we demonstrate that recipients' practices of self-care are strongly tied to obligations of care for the others who made that organ transfer possible: donors, other potential recipients, medical staff and the metaphor of the 'gift of life' itself. These texts are useful because they are more than a simple witnessing of the extraordinary practices of organ transfer. Rather, as Arthur Frank's (1998) work on illness narratives explains, they are yet another 'technology of the self'. In other words, whilst illness stories tell of the struggle to carve out a sense of self in the face of radically new forms of embodiment, they also observe the broader systems of knowledge power through which caring for the self is narrated. Autobiography and self-help are, therefore, forms of story- telling, where the medical, practical and emotional advice offered by and to organ recipients is aimed both at interpolating a normative recipient (e.g. Sothern 2007) and at constructing careful relationships with the wider assemblage of organ transfer.

Organ Transfer and the Spatialities of the Body

The removal of organs from one body and their transplantation into another is the spectacular culmination of biomedical progress. It is a technological achievement of both surgical technique and pharmacological treatment (Sharp 2006). As practice, it requires a whole host of scientific, cultural and socio-legal transformations. Together, such transformations have refigured the composition and integrity of the body-spaces as well as a redrawing of the phenomenological distinction between self/other (Abrahamsson and Simpson 2011). Whilst most accounts of organ recipients' struggle to adjust to their new organ are organised around the binary between donor and recipient (Shildrick *et al* 2009), we complicate this distinction between self and other by mapping the multiple Others involved in organ transfer.

The piercing of the 'dermal boundary' (Delaney 2003) and the deconstruction of the contents therein has revealed the body to be an assemblage of systems, pathways, tubes, pumps and filters (Stafford 1993). Modern biomedicine distributed across departments devoted to ophthalmology, hepatobiliary, cardiothoracic and renal medicine has remapped the body away from a radical, 'impeachable individual specificity [and onto] wide open interchangability' (Palumbo-Liu 2002: 88). The diagnosis of the failure of an organ, its removal and the transplantation of a new one provides 'a particularly dramatic reminder of the divisibility of the individual' (O'Byrne 2002: 169). The loss of a sense of wholeness is a wound through which strangeness—a sense of alienation from one's body, dialysis machines, pacemakers and constant pharmacological interventions—intrude. Organ transplantation as treatment encourages us to make distinctions between the useless parts of our bodies and the recycling of valuable ones (Squier 2004). In this way, organ transfer rests upon the Cartesian mind/body distinction, on an understanding that there is a distance between the self and the body in which that self is housed.

As most organs are transplanted from cadaveric donors, the movement of organs from one body to another has also required an intricate system of distinguishing life from death. Organ transfer re-maps life away from the body (specifically the heart) and onto consciousness and the brain (but not the brain stem) to ensure the harvesting of organs from a cadaver that is still breathing (Lock 2002). In this way, organ transfer can be seen as occasioning two deaths—the first the declaration of 'brain death' and the second the ceasing of vital systems with the surgical removal of organs themselves. Organ transfer, widely understood as 'the 'gift of life', demands a parallel gift—the 'gift of death', the giving over of a life before its normally recognized time' (Nancy Scheper-Hughes 2000: 201).

Numerous studies have suggested that the barriers to increased organ donation have more to do with the failure to adopt this mechanistic understanding of the body (Lock and Crowley-Makota 2008). Similarly, for recipients these clear distinctions between life/death and self/other necessary for the framing of an Organ as an interchangeable spare part may not be so straightforward. Whilst the juxtaposition of sickness and death to health and life that is common to the imagery of the 'gift of life' promises a powerful vision of the ailing body restored to wholeness once the wires, tubes, and external machines that pump, filter, excrete and oxygenate fluids have been removed.

Nevertheless, for those fortunate to receive an organ, the picture is not always too rosy. A new organ is not the same as a new steel hip; the organ always remains a corporeal fragment of an Other that will never be fully assimilated. The regular ingestion of immunosuppressants (necessary to prevent the rejection of the new Organ) work to blind the immune system to internal difference. But immunosuppressants cannot remove these distinctions altogether nor can they secure vulnerability as they provoke changes in body morphology, cancers and increased susceptibility to infection. Cyclosporine and other anti-rejection drugs may be 'the chemical of tolerance [that works to] "quell xenophobia"' (Palumbo-Liu 2002: 88) but they nonetheless ensure the wound to embodied coherence remains open. The body of the transplant recipient cannot be described as natural but must be understood as intercorporeal: the body of the recipient mixes original tissue with the tissue of the recipient, framed by the chemical suppression of the immune system.

Transplant patients who are successful in carefully maintaining the delicate balance between Self and Other, despite the physical and psychological problems they may face, are less likely to suffer episodes of organ rejection and are thus more likely to embody the promise of the 'gift of life'. Put another way, it is the vigilant chemical maintenance of the dialectic between Self and Other, not its resolution as promised in the imagery that often accompanies 'the gift of life,' on which the possibility of life post- transplant depends. For Christopher Fynsk (2002: 27-30), whilst the transformation of the body that the transplant recipient undergoes is certainly quite physical, [...] it is suffered in a 'meta-physical' manner inasmuch as it entails a radical dispossession or disappropriation from which the 'I' speaks.

The 'I' into which the foreign organ has been inserted is thus one whose existence is marked by something like a chronic phenomenological intimacy with otherness itself. The post-transplant body is a site of multiple intercorporeal connections, one in which the distinction between the self and the non-self is better conceptualised in terms of boundary crossings. In this way, the skin of the post-transplant body, even after the dialysis tubes, monitors and other external signs of organ failure have been removed, cannot be the border that secures the subject. It is to how autobiographical and self- help texts prescribe how recipients should care for this complex intercorporeal self that we now turn.

Practising an Intercorporeal Spatiality of Care

Acknowledging that the failure of an organ disrupts the integrity of the body-subject (cf. Merleau-Ponty 1962) is a key starting point for transplant self-help literature. Most of these texts begin with descriptions of the common causes of organ failure, what symptoms the reader may experience and explain possible treatments. The overt purpose is to educate and empower the recipient by marking their body as an object of close scrutiny and attention. Readers should advise their medical teams immediately of changes and should learn carefully the meaning of their blood results. On the one hand, this is a practical advice on the self-management of organ failure, where the potential organ recipient plays key role by giving up alcohol, drugs, eating well, watching their fluid intake, exercising moderately, and observing carefully the routine of medications, treatments and observational visits. On the other hand, these texts are explicit that these everyday care-of- the-self practices connect to a wider project of managing medical expectation of what constitutes a good recipient. Advice on how to perform the 'good recipient', both before and after transplantation surgery, is the key theme running through many of these texts. Houlihan (1988: 25) advises her reader that the good patient is necessary because whilst medical criteria appear to be objective 'subjectivity enters into the decision making when the committee consisting of doctors (both internists and surgeons), nurses, social workers and psychologists, tries to evaluate the patients chance of success'. Liver recipient Elizabeth Parr (Parr and Parr Mize: 20–22) is clear that those still waiting for a transplant must consciously manage this subjectivity:

> The most important thing to remember when talking with any member of the transplant team is to sell yourself to them. You must let them know why it is important that you receive a transplant and that you are committed to that decision .. In a way, the purpose of the evaluation is to rule out any medical or technical reason that you should not undergo transplant, but also to see what you do with direction ..[a patient] who does not follow instructions given to him or her may be perceived by the team as not being dependable.

By specifically highlighting their qualities of commitment and reliability, transplant candidates must signal their capability to effectively respond to long-term biomedical instruction. Drawing on interviews with transplant surgical teams, Robert Finn (2000: 26–27) in his step-by-step guide to organ transplantation, is even more explicit that prospective recipients need to the careful about how they present themselves to medical teams:

> We look at every patient with the thought in the back of our heads: It this the place to put one of these rare organs? Would it have a good chance of working based on what we know about the person? Is this someone who follows through with things he starts? Is he a rule follower, or is he the type of person who has never followed a rule in his life?.. Because transplant teams have a great deal of experience with non-compliance ... take special care during the interviews to demonstrate a high level of personal responsibility.

Matching organs to recipients is always more than an assessment of the biological compatibility between organ and recipient— it involves an assessment of the recipient's ability to adjust to the rigours of living with a new organ. Patient attitudes towards and compliance with routines of self-care before transplant are carefully monitored by nurses, physicians, physiotherapists, technicians and dieticians since these are seen as the best evidence of their ability to care for the self post-transplant. Because it ultimately falls on the recipient to have a good outcome to transplantation (through diet, exercise, guarding against infection and drug compliance), the locus of these care practices is the corporeal space of the recipients' body. What is clear from these two quotes, however, is that this is more than a biopolitical project of interpolating the self- regulating patient under the gaze of biomedicine (although it certainly is this).

Two elements stand out. The first point is that this advice encourages the conscious manipulation of the recipients presentation to the biomedical gaze, in so doing these texts facilitate a gaze back into the medical professions rendering the power of the biomedical gaze contingent to the performance of the recipient. The second feature of these texts is the insistence on the overriding context of organ scarcity, caring for the organ is not simply about conforming to biomedical expectation. Instead, caring for the organ is something owed by the recipient and medical professionals both to the donor and to those who will not be so lucky to receive the rare 'gift of life'.

Repaying the Debt of Life

Richard Titmuss's (1970) classic text *The Gift Relationship* remains the touchstone for most work on the gifting of blood, organs, and other bodily material. The study compares ideological, institutional and cultural frameworks through which gifts of blood are made and distributed. Distinguishing, primarily, between those systems where donors were paid for their blood and those organised around notions of obligation, Titmuss argued that systems where the giving was not subject to direct financial reward led to a safer and more sustainable blood supply. Blood donation is often held up as the purest example of altruism because it is non- reciprocal and remains anonymous. However, Titmuss showed that blood donation was motivated by more than simply disinterested altruism and was instead founded on 'some sense of obligation, approval and interest; some feeling of 'inclusion' in society; some awareness of the need and the purposes of the gift' (238). In other words, donation is a form of recognition of the incompleteness and vulnerability of an unknown recipient and an understanding that you or your loved ones may need the gifts of others.

It is this same sense of vulnerability of both recipient and donor around which the injunctions to give the 'gift of life' are organised. Rather than a purely altruistic behaviour, then, both blood and organ donation should be conceived of as a form of beneficent exchange because 'where there is giving there is also getting' (Lamanna 1997; Ferguson, *et al* 2008). Silk (2004) argues that blood donation establishes a symmetric relationship between donor and recipient where blood marks the contours of national belonging. Yet, for all its reliance on the gift theory derived from the work of Mauss (2001) much of the discussion of blood and organ donation remains focused on the donor and the role of the recipient remains secondary (there are obvious exceptions for non-cadaveric donation; see Gill and Lowes 2008). This is somewhat surprising given that at the core of Mauss's ideas is an insistence that gift exchange is organised around obligations to give, receive and reciprocate. Gifts always carried with them traces of the giver and they thus bind together giver and receiver. Much of his work, consequently, focused on the obligation of reciprocity where the recipient's social standing rested upon finding appropriate ways to repay the gift. Gifting establishes a normative relationship between giver and receiver.

Organs are 'powerfully binding' (Murray 1987: 33) but unlike gifts of the potlatch, the giving of an organ is a radically singular gift, it can only be given once, it cannot be re-given, it cannot be given back. Even more importantly, within cadaveric transplantation the giving of an organ cannot easily be repaid to the donor (at least insofar as the donor is understood to be the person whose organs have been transplanted). How, then, does the organ recipient re-pay a donor who is no longer there? These self-help and autobiographical texts construct a duty of reciprocity as an obligation beyond individual 'donor'; instead, they argue that the organ recipient has an obligation to the systems through which organ transfer is organised. For example, speaking of his heart transplant, Cal Stoll insists that recipients are duty-bound to accept and be proactive about maintaining an ongoing relationship with the practices of biomedical care:

> The sooner you take control of your life after transplantation, the better chance you have of a quality of life. But if you lie around feeling sorry for yourself, you're in trouble. You don't get something for nothing in this world. We traded death for a lifetime of medical management. Living with an attitude of compliance, I'll live forever. (Helmberger 1992: 111)

Stoll's insistence that 'you don't get something for nothing' positions his compliance with medical surveillance as a response to debt. Further, his use of pronoun 'we' implies that this debt is not wholly his own but is rather shared with other recipients who he expects to respond in the same way. Ronald Jensh (2001) in his autobiographical account of his heart transplant makes a similar observation:

> As recipient of this precious jewel, one has agreed to take on a commitment; a guardian role. That role must be consciously fulfilled to the best of one's ability.. With unpleasant memories, I enter the hospital on a regular basis for check-ups and biopsies. The smell of disinfectant, the sterile atmosphere, the reminder that I must always rely on medications and physicians in order to lead a 'normal' life.. I approach each visit with trepidation and anxiously await the results. Knowing how well I feel in general, it would be so much nicer to put off these visits. But my responsibility is to my new heart, the donor, his family, my family, the physicians who performed the miracle, and the patient who might have received this organ had I not been fortunate enough to be selected.

Jensh sketches a wide range of known and unknown, living and dead others to whom he owes an ongoing debt; these include to his new heart, to the donor, the donor's family, the hospital, the surgeon, and those others still waiting for a new heart. Mindful of these debts, Jensh urges his readers, whom he has earlier identified as organ recipients and their families, to view the transplant as a need of constant repayment through careful guardianship lest he squander the gifts of these multiple others. It is clear from this guidance that the development of caring relationships with a range of others is scripted as one way in which transplant recipients can reciprocate for the 'gift' they have received. These are reinforced in the advice offered by transplant professionals who, though perhaps rather more abruptly, approach transplant patients' duty of reciprocity through the trope of organ scarcity. Consider the National Kidney Federations' and the Lancashire Teaching Hospitals' patient guides, which view patients' failure to adequately recognise the 'gift of life' through appropriate practices of self-care as a failure in their obligations both to oneself and those others with whom the organ may have been placed:

> Whether you have received a kidney transplant from a deceased donor or as a living donor transplant: Try to regard it as a unique gift and treat it with respect. There is a shortage of transplants and patients have to wait so do not waste your transplant. (Lancashire Teaching Hospitals 2007)

> Looking after your transplanted kidney for the long term is just as important as looking after it in the early days. Make a real effort every day, no matter whether it's the 5th or 15th anniversary of your kidney … not all patients are lucky enough to get a transplant. (Stein et al. 2008)

This advice is not simply about complying with regimes of medical self-care for the recipients' own sake; rather there is an explicit construction of care as reciprocity for the gift of the life others have not been so fortunate to receive. In both the instructions given by medical professionals and in the autobiography of recipients, it is through living well that recipients are encouraged to acknowledge and repay these multiple debts. These texts are replete with scenes of both spectacular and quiet triumph: whether it is the heart and lung recipient whose new lung 'Tina' allowed her the miracle of just getting up the stairs (Jewett 2003) or the competition in-line skater whose new kidney helped him to place fourth in a world competition (Noworyta 2006):

> Cal Stoll is a transplant program's dream. Although he was past the average age for such a procedure, the doctors found he possessed the criteria they were looking for … His new lifestyle, while not without difficulties, is a constant source of joy for him. He carries that joy wherever he goes and the people he meets finds it contagious. That's perhaps his greatest gift to prospective or new transplant recipients. He serves as a role model who exemplifies the new quality of life an organ recipient can attain. (Helmberger 1992: 113)

Cal's exemplification of life afforded by the 'gift of life' gives donation a purpose and meaning, in many ways proof of the good we are all asked to do as potential donors. At the same time, Cal's story is supposed to provide inspiration and support for those prospective and new transplant recipients who are going through the real traumas of waiting for and adjusting to living with a transplanted organ. That Cal's very life is now described as 'a gift' that he can give to prospective and new transplant patients in response to the gift of the organ he has received goes some way to addressing the question of exchange at the centre of Mauss's gift theory. Individuals are compelled to return the gift of the organ by living as the good recipient, because this is the promised outcome of 'gift of life'. Coping with an Organ Transplant, written by liver recipient Elizabeth Parr and transplant coordinator Janet Mize, is even more explicit about the centrality of the performance of the recipient to the promise of organ transfer:

> The recipient gives an 'Organ Recital', talking about the experience anytime he or she can. People will view the recipient as unique, at least for a while, and ask questions. These questions can easily foster a dissertation that goes on and on . . . The recipient is in a position to do a lot of good for the transplant cause, talking up donation and representing success. Unfortunately, one can also reverse ones impact by becoming self-promoting. We all have to guard against this imposition on others. Really, all we have to do is think a little about even what we are calling 'recipient'. We have been given a gift. Just as with our original gift of life, we have not done anything to merit it. (Parr and Mize 2001: 112)

In our view, this advice from Parr and Mize is both essential and problematic. It is essential because the idea that we can do good and alleviate the suffering of others by allowing the use of our organs (and those of our loved ones) is the central message of the 'gift of life' narrative—it is a powerful story that compels what has come to be called generosity and sustains the system of organ transfer. Nonetheless, it is also problematic because getting the organ recital right by 'performing' the good organ recipient can obfuscate the very real difficulties of adjusting to the grafted organ. As heart recipient Ardelle laments 'they stare at my chest and I feel like a freak. I know they're thinking about me having someone else's heart' (Helmberger 1992: 56). Even though it is some time since her transplant, and the new heart is functioning well, the rigours of living with the intercorporeal fragment of the Other do not go away. Whilst these self-help texts advocate a way of responding to the receipt of an organ that helps to ensure the reproduction of the gifting system, there are aspects of scripting the good recipient that are deeply prescriptive concerning what types of lives are most appropriately lived as witness to the 'gift of life'. The debate, from both the public and medical professions, that sometimes surrounds the placing of livers with alcoholics is a reminder that normative assumptions about which recipients are most deserving are intimately related to the celebration of the 'gift of life' and index the danger that recipients will be blamed if the transplant is unsuccessful (see Thornton 2009; Sharkey and Gilliam 2010).

Conclusion

Projects of interpolating the careful and purposeful use of the organ are clearly vital to ensuring the success of organ transfer. We have tried to tease out the complex set of obligations, responses and responsibilities engendered in response to the receiving of an organ as they are described in texts written by and for transplant recipients. The organ recipient is expected to bear living witness to the miracle of the 'gift of life', where this witnessing—in both spectacular and everyday acts—is always over-determined by the spectre of just how lucky one is to receive this gift. Whilst the relationship between the donor and the recipient is usually at the heart of the debates around transplant patients' self-care, this chapter has shown that recipients' obligations for their new intercorporeal self are articulated to a wide range of others. Organ transfer thus emerges as a 'social ontology of connection . . . foregrounding social relationships of mutuality and trust (rather than dependence)' (Lawson 2007: 3). However, organ transfer is also framed as a system of giving where the burden for reciprocity falls heavily on the recipient. Autobiographical and self-help texts argue that those waiting for and those who have received a new organ must sustain a web of care that connects their new organ to the wider transplant community and the framework of institutions, knowledges and values that make organ transfer possible. As such, we should also view self-help texts as themselves entangled in these frameworks of knowledge power that prescribe what transplants patients' mutualities of care should look like. In these texts, organ transfer as what Rose and Navos (2003) call a biosocial community, foregrounds a dominant understanding of recipient defined through their caring relation- ships with the spatialities of organ transfer. There is a danger that in foregrounding duties of care, this closes off the multitude of responses that individuals have to living with a transplant, some of which may be overwhelmingly negative, others simply ambivalent and which can emerge as such at different times and at different places. Fox and Swazey (2002) assert that there is a 'tyranny' inherent in receiving a gifted organ: organ transplantation exerts a powerful influence over the recipients' lives because of the degree of ethical responsibility placed on the recipient to have a successful outcome to the transplant. We do worry, therefore, that the normative construct of what constitutes an appropriate ethical response to the gift of life is too narrow. Whilst the autobiographical texts we use tell of the centrality of the struggle to carve out a sense of self in the face of the radically new forms of embodiment they also gloss over these contradictory responses. Indeed, the cultural and spatial complexities of both the ethics of donation (Davies 2006) and of the meaning of the nature of the relationship with the other (Lock 2002) means that recipients' ethical responses can never be captured by the simplistic notion that there is a 'right' way to care for the 'gift of life' as we see articulated in these texts. Thus, rather than approaching 'care' through the framework of organ transfer, we think a more effective approach would be to begin with recipients' struggle to carve out a sense of self as they live with their new organs within the multiple environments they inhabit.

Notes

In this paper, we refer exclusively to cadaveric donation. Issues surrounding the ethical complexities of living donation and its reciprocity are beyond the scope of this paper, but nevertheless provide an interesting and comparative set of debates (see, for example, Hippen and Taylor 2007)

References

Abrahamsson, S. and Simpson, P. (2011) The limits of the body: boundaries, capacities and thresholds, *Social & Cultural Gepography* 12(4): 331–338.

Bersani, L. and Philips, A. (2008) *Intimacies*. Chicago: Chicago University Press.

Bird, S. and Harris, J. (2010) A time to move to presumed consent for organ donation, *British Medical Journal* 340: 1010–1012.

Bondi, L. and Fewell, J. (2003) 'Unlocking the cage door': the spatiality of counselling, *Social & Cultural Geography* 4(4): 527–547.

Brown, M. (2003) Hospice and the spatial paradoxes of terminal care, *Environment and Planning* D 35(5): 833–851.

Burt, R. (2002) *Death Is That Man Taking Names*. Berkeley: University of California Press.

Conradson, D. (2003) Geographies of care: spaces, practices, experiences, *Social & Cultural Geography* 4(4): 451–454.

Davidson, J. and Milligan, M. (2004) Embodying emotion sensing space: introducing emotional geographies, *Social & Cultural Geography* 5(4): 523–532.

Davies, G. (2006) Patterning the geographies of organ transplantation: corporeality, generosity and justice, *Transactions of the Institute of British Geographers* 31(3): 257–271.

Delaney, D. (2003) *Law and Nature*. Cambridge: Cambridge University Press.

Ferguson, E., Farrell, K. and Lawrence, C. (2008) Blood donation is an act of benevolence rather than altruism, *Health Psychology* 27(3): 327–336.

Fielder, L. (1996) *The Tyranny of the Normal*. Lincoln, MA: David R. Goodine.

Finn, R. (2000) *Organ Transplants*. Cambridge: O'Reily.

Fox, R.C. and Swazey, J.P. (1992) *Spare Parts*. New York: Oxford University Press.

———. (2002) *The Courage to Fail: A Social View of Organ Transplants and Dialysis*. New Brunswick: Transaction Publishers.

Frank, A. (1998) Stories of illness as care of the self, *Health* 2: 329–348.

Fynsk, C. (2002) L'Irreconciliable, CR: *The New Centennial Review* 2(3): 23–36.

Gill, P. and Lowes, L. (2008) Gift exchange and organ donation: Donor and recipient experiences of live related kidney transplantation, *International Journal of Nursing Studies* 45: 1607–1617.

Greenhough, B. (2010) Citizenship, care and companion- ship: Approaching geographies of health and bioscience, *Progress in Human Geography* 32(5): 153–171.

Hazeldine, R. (2003) Love yourself: the relationship of the self with itself in popular self-help texts, *Journal of Sociology* 39(4): 413–428.

Helmberger, P.S. (1992) *Transplants*. Minneapolis: Chronimed Publishing.

Hippen, B.E. and Taylor, J.S. (2007) In defense of transplantation, American *Journal of Transplantation* 7: 1695–1697.

Houlihan, P.J. (1988) *Life Without End: The Transplant Story*. Toronto: NC Press.

Hoystad, O. (2007) *A History of the Heart*. London: Reaktion Books.

Jensh, R. (2001) *Lifelines*. Bloomington: Xlibris.

Jewett, S. (2003) *I Call My New Lung Tina*. Camarillo, CA: Water Signs Publishers.

Lai, A.L., Dermody, J. and Hanmer-Lloyd, S. (2007) Exploring cadaveric organ donation, *Journal of Marketing Management* 23: 557–558.

Lamanna, M.A. (1997) Giving and getting: altruism and exchange in organ transplantation, *Journal of Medical Humanities* 18(3): 169–192.

Lancashire Teaching Hospitals (2007) 10 Do's and Don'ts for the Kidney Transplant Patient. Lancaster: Lancashire Teaching Hospitals NHS Foundation Trust.

Lawson, V. (2007) Geographies of care and responsibility, *Annals of the Association of American Geographers* 97(1): 1–11.

Lock, M. (2002) *Twice Dead*. Berkeley: University of California Press.

—————— and Crowley-Makota, M. (2008) Situating the practice of organ donation in familial, cultural, and political context, *Transplant Review* 22(3): 154–157.

Mauss, M. (2001) *The Gift*, 2nd ed. New York: Routledge.

McDowell, L. (2004) Work, workfare, work/life balance and an ethic of care, *Progress in Human Geography* 28(2): 145–163.

Moss, A.H. and Siegler, M. (1991) Should alcoholic's compete equally for liver transplantation? *Journal of the American Medical Association* 265(10): 1295–1298.

Murray, T.H. (1987) Gifts of the body and the needs of strangers, *Hastings Center Report* 17(2): 30–38.

Merleau-Ponty, M. (1962) *The Phenomenology of Perception*. London: Routledge.

Misje, A.H., Bosnes, V., Gasdal, O. and Heier, H.E. (2005) Motivation, recruitment and retention of voluntary non-remunerated blood donors: a survey-based questionnaire study, *Vox Sang* 89(4): 236–244.

Milligan, C. (2003) Location or Dislocation? Towards a conceptualization of people and place in a care-giving experience, *Social & Cultural Geography* 4(4): 455–470.

—————— and Wiles, J. (2010) Landscapes of care, *Progress in Human Geography* 34(6): 736–754.

—————— and Power, A. (2010) The changing geography of care, in Brown, T., McLafferty, S. and Moon, G. (eds) *A Companion to Health and Medical Geography*. Oxford: Wiley-Blackwell, pp. 567–586.

Morgan, M., Mayblin, M. and Jones, R. (2008) Ethnicity and registration as a kidney donor, Social *Science and Medicine* 66(1): 147–158.

Nancy, J.-L. (2000) *Being Singular Plural*. Stanford: Stanford University Press.

——————. (2002) L'Intrus, *CR: Centennial Review* 2(3): 1–14.

NHS Blood and Transplant (2009) UK Transplant Activity Report 2008–2009, Available at http://www.uktranspla nt.org (accessed 31 July 2010).

Noworyta, P. (2006) *Transplant to Handplant*. Lincoln, NV: iUniverse.

O'Byrne, A. (2002) The politics of intrusion, *CR* 2(3): 169 – 187.

O'Neill, R. (2006) Frankenstein to Futurism, *Transplantation Reviews* 20(2): 222–230.

Palumbo-Liu, D. (2002) The operative heart, *CR* 2(3): 87–108.

Parr, E. and Mize, J. (2001) *Coping with an Organ Transplant*. New York: Avery.

Rose, N. and Navos, C. (2003) Biological citizenship, in Ong, A. and Collier, S. (eds) *Global Assemblages: Technology, Politics, and Ethics as Anthropological Problems*. Oxford: Blackwell Publishing, pp. 439–463.

Rosengarten, M. (2001) A pig's tale: porcine viruses and species boundaries, in Bashford, A. and Hooker, C. (eds) *Contagion: Historical and Cultural Studies*.2. 2. London/New York: Routledge, pp. 168–182.

Royal College of Physicians (2010) *Thank You for Life: Letters from Transplant Recipients to Donors' Families*. London: Royal College of Physicians.

Scheper-Hughes, N. (2000) Global traffic in human organs, *Current Anthropology* 41(2): 191–224.

Sharkey, K. and Gilliam, L. (2010) Should patients with self-inflicted illness receive lower priority in access to healthcare resources? Mapping out the debate, *Journal of Medical Ethics* 36: 661–665.

Sharp, L. (1995) Organ transplantation as a transformative experience, *Medical Anthropology Quarterly* 9(3): 357 – 389.

———. (2006) *Strange Harvest*. Berkeley: University of California Press.

Shildrick, M., McKeever, P., Abbey, S., Poole, J. and Ross, H. (2009) Troubling dimensions of heart transplantation, *Medical Humanities* 35: 35–38.

Silk, J. (2004) Caring at a distance: gift theory, aid chains, and social movements, *Social & Cultural Geography* 5(2): 229–251.

Siminoff, L.A. and Chillag, K. (1999) The fallacy of the 'Gift of Life', *Hastings Center Report* 29(6): 34–41.

Sojka, B.N. and Sojka, P. (2003) The blood-donation experience: perceived physical, psychological and social impact of blood donation on the donor, *Vox Sang* 84(2): 120 – 128.

Sothern, M. (2007) You could truly be yourself if you just weren't you: sexuality, disabled body-space and the (neo)liberal politics of self-help, *Environment and Planning* D 25: 144–159.

Squier, S. (2004) *Liminal Lives*. Durham, NC: Duke University Press.

Stafford, B. (1993) *Body Criticism*. Cambridge, MA: MIT Press.

Stein, A., Higgins, R. and Wilde, J. (2008) *Kidney Transplants Explained*. London: Class Publishing.

Thornton, V. (2009) Who gets the liver transplant? The use of responsibility as the tie breaker, *Journal of Medical Ethics* 35: 739–742.

Titmuss, R. (1970) *The Gift Relationship*. London: New Press.

Waldby, C. (2002) Biomedicine, tissue transfer and intercorporeality, *Feminist Theory* 3(3): 239–254.

Williams, A. (2002) Changing geographies of care: employing the concept of therapeutic landscapes as a framework in examining home space, *Social Science and Medicine* 55(1): 141–154.

PART II
Capital Bodies

Chapter 5

The Body in Capitalist Conditions of Existence: A Foundational Materialist Approach

Ian Bruff

Introduction

This chapter argues for the continued relevance of the *natural* body to analyses of the relationships between bodies and states. That is, human needs may well be elastic and prone to some manipulation, but the living, physical materiality of the human body cannot be neglected or ignored. In consequence, it is impossible to argue for the *wholly* open-ended and contingent nature of human existence: there is a clear directedness to the evolution of the societies in which we live (past, present or future), because of the corporeal foundations upon which such societies are built. To put it another way, there is nothing outside the thoughts we have about the world, but there are inevitable asymmetries, repetitions and tendencies *within* these thoughts towards our need for food, water, shelter and so on. This must be taken into account when considering the relationships between bodies and states.

This notion of a *foundational materialism* has two key aspects, which taken together unite the foundations of our lives with the foundations of the knowledge we construct about the world (see also Bruff 2011a). *One*, the physical materiality of the human body makes production a necessity, forming in the process the foundation for how human life is sustained; *two*, and consequently, in our research we should be clear that the satisfaction of human needs is 'the steady ground atop of which all change takes place: the transhistorical basis of human history.' (Orzeck 2007: 508). This approach serves us better than the various recent attempts to 'rematerialize' discussions of contemporary capitalist societies,[1] because these contributions (intentionally or not) concede too much ground to the dominant poststructuralist perspectives which this chapter critiques. In contrast, my argument is rooted in perhaps *the* fundamental tenet of historical materialism – the rich and diverse tradition within which I situate my work – namely the corporeal basis for labour's double freedom in capitalist conditions of existence

---

1 Most obviously Hardt and Negri's trilogy, but also the more general upsurge in work inspired by inter alia Foucault's later writings, Deleuze and Guattari, Latour and more recently Bennett.

(Bruff 2009a: 345–7; 2009b). This starting point enables us to account much more satisfactorily for how capitalism was founded on the backs of bodies, and how it is reproduced through them.[2] To put it more viscerally, capitalism's emergence and perpetuation is founded upon transhistorical human needs that must be satisfied in order to survive, and this manifests itself on an everyday basis in the compulsion to sell our bodies on the labour market in order to live.

My approach stands in contrast to the predominant view of the body since the rise of poststructuralist and anti-humanist perspectives from the 1960s onwards. There has been a laudable desire to critique the notion that there is an inherent, 'pre-social', human being, with all of the attendant biological determinisms. Many have sought to deconstruct, and thereby render fluid and contingent, the view of human subjectivity which stressed the universal characteristics of human cognition and meaning-making. This, perhaps inevitably, entailed not only a rejection of the mind-body dualisms which tended to assume that human thought and action were relatively natural and universal, but also the naturalness of bodies themselves. As a result, the human body has come to be conceptualized in a much more varied, contingent, open-ended, and ultimately pluralized and malleable way.

This does not mean, of course, that the human body necessarily *appears* in such a manner: the relationships between bodies and states (plus other institutional mechanisms) can (and often do) produce a narrow and constrained set of bodily practices which are patterned according to prevailing cartographies of knowledge that are inscribed into technologies of power and governance operative across societies. As such, although we should be clear that *potentially* human bodies are pluralized, varied and open-ended, it is also the case that this potential is frequently not exploited; at least on a macro level. This means, in turn, that we need to remain aware of the localized acts of resistance and difference which challenge societal norms about 'normal' bodily practices, and thus expose the artificial and arbitrary nature of more dominant assumptions about the body.

Central to the development and popularization of these points have been scholars such as Michel Foucault and Judith Butler. A key interest of both has been the regulation of sexual practices according to received notions of 'normality' and the materialization of sex in and through gendered identities. In essence, they argue that everyday practices, and the 'truths' that such practices embody, produce effects *on* bodies so that those bodies come to represent (and are the vehicle for) these 'truths'. In consequence, bodily practices are reiteratively constituted in and through discursive construals of 'normality'. This means that it is not just acts of sex which are of importance, but also the notion of sex itself. As such, these contributions go considerably further than, for example, radical feminism, for they argue that – in addition to the latter's focus on gender and how such connotations categorize women in certain ways – 'normal' sexual practices and the classifications of biological sex themselves are arbitrary constructions. This does not mean that 'the materiality of bodies is simply and only a linguistic effect',

---

2   Many thanks to Reecia Orzeck for this point.

but that it is impossible to separate the body from discourses about it (Butler 1993: 30). As such, *everything* is material, but not in the traditional, pre-social, biologically deterministic way.

In many respects I concur with the desire to overcome false dualisms and to enquire constantly into what we may otherwise take for granted. However, a key weakness of this scholarship is that – despite the apparent emphasis on the body – the dominant focus is on the discourses which constitute its practices. The very real corporeality of the human body is neglected to the point of ignorance. Therefore, the explicit *presence* of bodies in the contributions of poststructuralist and/or poststructuralist feminist authors, because bodies 'matter', is the condition for their *absence*. More specifically, it is only through taking the body for granted that one can focus so relentlessly on discourses about the body. However, this is fundamentally flawed and unsatisfactory, and I will argue that the body's physical materiality is a spectre haunting this scholarship, to the extent that it forces us to think anew about these issues.

The rest of this chapter will: (i) critique the above positions in greater depth; (ii) offer my foundational materialist alternative; (iii) relate this alternative to historically specific capitalist conditions of existence; and (iv) conclude on the wider relevance of my argument. The key underlying theme is that it is simply impossible to ignore the physical materiality of the body, which has crucial consequences for how we analyse relationships between bodies and (capitalist) states.

The Performative Absence of the Body

Paul Rabinow and Nikolas Rose (2006: 208), in one of the first issues of the journal *BioSocieties*, remark that '[f]or Foucault, sexuality was crucial, in part, because [it] was the hinge that linked an anatamopolitics of the human body with a biopolitics of the population.' In other words, bodily practices at the micro, everyday level, are intimately connected to the social body and thus the investment of 'truths' about sexual practices in governing practices, technologies and regulations. This is founded upon a view of power not as repressive and limiting but in fact, through the multiple human relationships that together permeate and constitute the social body, as productive. That is, power is not conceived as a 'thing' in the possession of one person, group or institution (such as the state), but instead as a multiplicity of social relationships (some of which could be viewed as state-like but not of the state). Indeed, a frequent claim was that 'every human relation is to some degree a power relation' (Foucault 1988: 168). Therefore, '[p]ower is everywhere..because it comes from everywhere' (Foucault 1979: 93), and it 'produces reality...domains of objects and rituals of truth. The individual and the knowledge that may be gained from him [*sic* as throughout] belong to this production' (Foucault 1977: 194).

Foucault's later work on biopower and subjectification brought together these different conceptual developments (for example, see Foucault 2007, 2008). Here we find that a gradual transformation occurred as societies approached modernity, with the traditional prerogative of sovereigns to adjudicate on whether someone should live or die being replaced by governmental capacities which sought to manage populations in the name of fostering certain styles and modes of living. As a result, the body increasingly became an object of *both* institutional and individual practices:

> Foucault conceptualizes the governmental target of the population as a new collective focus of biopolitics, representing a 'political object' insofar [as] the population is that on which and towards which the acts of government are directed, but also a 'political subject' insofar as it is the population that is called upon to conduct itself in a particular way. (Gudmand-Høyer and Horth 2009: 106).

This means that power is exercised through the way in which action, or conduct, is brought to bear on other actions/conducts. It manifests itself in the rules governing human conduct and the self-regulation of conduct by humans, and we govern ourselves in multiple ways across all forms of human practices (Foucault 1982; Rose 1996). As such, we do not possess our *bodies* but our *selves*: the body is both the object and subject of the 'truths' about it. For this reason bodies can be produced as both docile, in conformity with prevailing practices and norms about them, and in struggle against the same practices and rituals of 'truth'. For Kate Nash (2000: 25) this means that power 'represents the potential fluidity of social relations', for 'as soon as there is a power relation, there is a possibility of resistance..there are no relations of power without resistances' (Foucault 1982: 123; Foucault 1980: 142).

It is the contemporaneous reproduction and subversion of dominant social norms, as expressed through everyday bodily practices, which Butler extends to the notion of sex itself. She argues that 'gender' is not just a social construction regarding 'naturally' different men and women – the pre-given, and binary, sexual categories – but instead should be viewed as 'the very apparatus of production whereby the sexes themselves are established' (Butler 1990: 10). As Stern and Zalewski (2009: 624) have recently commented, keeping this in mind is essential if we are not to 'forget again how bodies become sexed through gender'. In other words, we become 'human' only once our sex has been rendered intelligible by presumptions about gender and sexuality – in turn, we become sexed and gendered only through presumptions about what it means to be human. Therefore, Butler's theory of performativity, whereby gender performance and gender identity are each other's constitution and expression (Butler 1990: 25), makes it possible for us to argue that sex itself, and not just sex as part of the wider body, must come under critical scrutiny.

This, for her, is of crucial political importance because it enables us to acknowledge which zones of social life are populated by those bodies whose existence is deemed 'unlivable' by way of their culturally illegible and 'impossible' practices, as can be witnessed in how such views are frequently embodied in the law (Butler 1993: 1–4 especially). This demonstrates how human/subhuman distinctions can be drawn in accordance with a whole range of norms – for instance, Butler discusses exclusions on the grounds of heteronormative assumptions about 'natural' sex and 'natural' bodily manifestations of sex, which affect negatively those bodies engaged in homosexual practices and/or in sex reassignment processes (of course, there are others) (for example, see Butler 2004). However, as with Foucault on resistance, it immediately alerts us to how there could be ways in which we are able to subvert and render discontinuous apparently static and fixed social structures through new forms of repetitional practices which confound previous assumptions and norms (Butler 1997: 19–20). This means that 'we can only rearticulate or resignify the basic categories of ontology, of being human, of being gendered, of being recognizably sexual, to the extent that we submit ourselves to a process of cultural translation.' (Butler 2004: 38). Again, our bodies are the objects and subjects of social norms, meaning that they are always open to change and cannot be fixed or rendered impermeable.

Totalizing the body

The above approaches are not without their problems, and this can be observed with recourse to their totalizing ontologies (see also Bruff 2009a). Although these works portray themselves as critiques of ontology, for it is from the notion that there is 'an' ontology that objectifying categories are derived, it is impossible to escape the need to posit which aspects of the world are more important than others in order to write *anything*. Put more simply, 'some kind of assumptions (as to what we are thinking *about*) must be made before we can even begin to think' (Thompson 1995: 48; original emphasis). It is impossible to escape the need to, even if implicitly, posit which aspects of the world are more important than others. This means that 'some degree of essentialism is unavoidable. The disputes are usually over *which* essences we should accept as important' (McLennan 1996: 67; original emphasis) – whether, I might add, this is acknowledged explicitly or not. Therefore, the necessary specificity of any scholar's perspective on the world – who is able to capture the whole of the world in all of its complexity and spatio-temporal variability? – is the ontological basis for the construction of analyses and critiques. An excellent illustration of this can be found in Butler's (1993: 9–10; original emphasis) explicit connection of her work with Foucault's:

> [We need to] return to the notion of matter, not as site or surface, but as *a process of materialization that stabilizes over time to produce the effect of boundary, fixity, and surface we call matter*. That matter is always materialized has, I think, to be thought in relation to the productive and, indeed, materializing effects of regulatory power in the Foucaultian sense. Thus, the question is no longer, How is gender constituted as and through a certain interpretation of sex? (a question that leaves the 'matter' of sex untheorized), but rather, Through what regulatory norms is sex itself materialized? And how is it that treating the materiality of sex as a given presupposes and consolidates the normative conditions of its own emergence?

There is an underlying assumption that human social practices, in all of their richness and diversity, are constituted by productive power/knowledge relations which are the *singular* constitutive source of these practices. In the above quote, Butler conceptualizes 'matter' as the materialization of regulatory power, which in turn produces appearances of fixity and stasis when it comes to social norms about sex. However, the regulatory power itself is taken as a given, because in this scholarship multiple forms of power relations 'entertain complex and *circular* relations with other forms' (Foucault 1982: 213; emphasis added). Therefore, it is of no consequence where one is in the circular and ongoing process of materialization and rematerialization, because nothing is external to the power/ knowledge relations which constitute this process. To put it another way, the human body is forever constituted by the power/knowledge relations which are taken to be the essential productive basis for human social practices. Even as a 'subject' – via resistances (Foucault) and/or reiterations (Butler) – bodily practices are founded upon what already and always is constituting their conduct and movement. The body itself, despite its apparently central presence in these texts, is therefore produced as absent.

Throughout Foucault's and Butler's writings the body is ephemeral and hollow: they do not deny that there is a materiality that can be *observed* as 'a body' – the body as a referent – but there is no satisfactory discussion of why it should be conceptualized in this way. For instance, Foucault (1977: 170) discusses how the very definition of discipline – central to his work on the Panopticon and surveillance – is that individuals are both its instruments and objects. This prepared the ground for his subsequent work on governmentality and conduct upon conduct, because the creation of 'docile bodies' (the centerpiece of *Discipline and Punish*) in the prison could be extrapolated to society as a whole through the *management* rather than circumscription of human conduct. Thus the state is comprised of a series of governmental practices which exercise self-restraint, focusing not on repressive technologies of power but instead producing and reproducing 'rules of the game' which ensure that bodies are always in movement yet also exercising self-restraint upon themselves in the name of continuing to live. This means that populations securitize themselves in non-coercive ways against perceived risks to their survival (Foucault 2007), which also makes it possible to develop 'differential modes of treatment of populations, which aim to maximize the returns on doing what is profitable and to marginalize the unprofitable…to assign different social destinies to individuals in line with their varying capacity to live up to the requirements of competitiveness and profitability.' (Foucault 2008: 261).

This is a banal and highly selective account of the horrors attendant to processes of primitive accumulation which have been taking place ever since the emergence of capitalism. Marx (1976: 899) described this particularly memorably, and much more appropriately: '[t]hus were the agricultural folk first forcibly expropriated from the soil, driven from their homes, turned into vagabonds, and then whipped, branded and tortured by grotesquely terroristic laws into accepting the discipline necessary for the system of wage-labour.' However, we should not expect any more from Foucault, for his anti-humanism *necessarily* entailed the focus on the theories of biopower that he read into various versions of economic liberalism (Behrent 2009). This has been lauded in recent years for its ability to account for '[t]he emergence of a set of de facto obligations for populations to perform as *Homo oeconomicus* [which] bespeaks the pre-eminence of a radically self-governing subjectivity in contemporary capitalism.' (Kiersey 2009: 386). Yet these arguments ignore the *physical* materiality inherent to the constitution and daily reproduction of social relationships which require our body to be sold on the labour market in order to receive an income and thus survive; that is, the *compulsion* to be a commodity.

Later in the chapter I will consider this issue in greater depth, but it is sufficient for now to assert that, for Foucault, the body is – whether one is discussing his archaeological, genealogical or subjectification phases, or his more concrete works on discipline, governmentality or sexuality – produced by the power/knowledge relations which are the singular constitutive source of human social practices more generally. The very means by which it is consistently *present* in the writings is to render it *absent*: it is always the expression of something else. Moreover, one can say *precisely the same thing* about Butler's work. This can be most clearly observed in her more recent writings on mourning and violence, which connect her earlier work on 'livable' gender identities with Foucault's and Agamben's discussions of biopower. Take for instance her claim – in many respects quite astonishing – that she is now working with 'a more general conception of the human…one in which we are, from the start…*by virtue of bodily requirements*, given over to some set of primary others' (Butler 2006: 31; emphasis added). However, the implications of this are immediately denied, for she claims that the source of our 'common human vulnerability' cannot be recovered (ibid.). Thus, as with Foucault, the physical materiality of the body is simultaneously invoked and rejected, and in consequence the productive power/knowledge relations remain intact as the essence of human existence.

More damagingly, it seems that Butler herself 'knows' what the source of our common vulnerability is. A few pages earlier she claims that '[t]he body implies mortality, vulnerability, agency' (ibid.: 26), and in the preface she makes this declaration: '[t]hat we can be injured, that others can be injured, that we are subject to death at the whim of another, are all reasons for both fear and grief.' (ibid.: xii). That she does not go any further than this, exploring instead the discourses of fear and grief and the violence that they may well constitute (see also Butler 2009), highlights the connection between this and her earlier work.[3] For example, if we return to the above discussion of materiality, then we find that although Butler (1993: 10) concedes that 'sexually differentiated parts, activities, capacities,

---

3   In consequence, it means that Catharine MacKinnon's (2006: 53; original emphasis) sarcastic remark – originally made in 2000 – still holds: '[i]nconveniently, the fact of death is a universal – approaching 100 percent…[Moreover] life and death is even basically a binary distinction – and not a very nuanced one either, especially from the dead side of the line'.

hormonal and chromosomal differences' exist, she is clear that sex materializes through discursive performativity and thus is an effect of gender performance. The physical materiality of the body is given, and then it is taken away.

This explains Butler's tacit alliance with Giorgio Agamben's work when it comes to the post-2001 world and what many view as an era characterized by state exceptionalism. This enables her – as Agamben does (for example, Agamben 1998) – to focus almost exclusively on the *production* of bare life rather than explore how this production process is predicated on knowledge of how a minimal existence for 'non-humans' can be achieved, i.e. of how the body functions. Apparently the body's natural limits exert no influence on what it takes to render a human life 'bare':[4] instead, the body is *only* the target and constituted outcome of biopolitical strategies, for it has no constitutive role to play. This means that, for instance, the reason why some forms of torture are more effective and popular than others – they must have a physical effect if they are to have any constitutive power – are glossed over in favour of anodyne descriptions of what it means for human life to be 'bare' and the 'exceptional'/'indefinite' regulatory power which the 'sovereign' state arrogates to itself in order to manage such bareness (cf. Orzeck, this volume).

It has been necessary to engage in a deep and lengthy discussion of Foucault and Butler, for their huge influence has rendered much poststructuralist social science, feminist or otherwise, rather unreflexive. As Salem (2011) and Smith (2011, 2012) point out with regard to prostitution and male sex workers, this has resulted in much of the literature being decidedly *un*critical about the unspoken assumptions present within poststructuralism. This is ironic, for a major strength of such scholarship has been the exposure of artificial binaries, exclusionary categorizations, universalistic assumptions, and so on. However, with recourse to my argument that, for *all* humans, it is impossible to escape the need to (even if implicitly) posit which aspects of the world are more important than others, we can put the spotlight back on these writings.

As such, the above critique suggests that there is a wider malaise within poststructuralist scholarship: it is impossible to prevent the living, breathing, corporeal materiality of the body from sneaking back into the text, yet the significance of these instances is denied on the grounds of anti-essentialism. For example, Butler (1993: 12) claims that the critics of *Gender Trouble* 'presuppose a set of metaphysical oppositions between materialism and idealism embedded in received grammar', tarnishing all with the same brush in consequence. The irony here is that a scholar dedicated to overcoming false binaries constructs her own artificial dualism in order to categorize her critics in a universalistic manner. This means that there is an inability in the literature to acknowledge how 'reflexive, interrogative capacities morph *out of* corporeality, [and nor is there] any conception of a situated body with active, agentic capacities' (Coole 2007:

---

4   Many thanks to Reecia Orzeck for this point. See also her chapter for more on the limits of an Agambenian approach.

231; emphasis added). As a result, such scholarship 'surrenders an investigation of or engagement with experience to an analysis of discourse (or representation).' (ibid.: 104).

To conclude this section, the body is continuously *present* in the work of Foucault, Butler and others, yet the way in which it is discussed renders bodily practices a mere expression of, and vehicle for, something else. That something else is the power/knowledge relations which are the essential basis for human existence and thus the constitutive force in/of society. As a result, the body is in fact *absent* from this scholarship because it is always being produced by the social norms about it. Herein lies the crux of the problem, for it is through the repetitional and citational practices within and across poststructuralist texts that we can appreciate just how dominant this approach to the body is. In other words, a literature interested in performative bodily practices is itself performative, because it is through observing the widespread, ritualized and stylized references to the body that we can note the empty and hollow conceptualization of the flesh. In consequence, *the body is produced as absent; it is performatively absent; it does not 'matter'; it is the expression of essences of human existence that are non-corporeal.*

Yet, the way in which its physical materiality leaks into these writings (through statements which are not substantiated) suggests that the real, living, breathing, corporeal body is a spectre which haunts these works. However, this is a fundamentally flawed and unsatisfactory state of affairs, because it is only through taking the body for granted that one can focus so relentlessly on discourses about the body. Therefore, the task for the rest of the chapter is to outline a foundational, materialist alternative which takes the body seriously.

Towards a Foundational Materialism

As argued in the introduction, in both our own lives and in our research we should be clear that the satisfaction of human needs is 'the steady ground atop of which all change takes place: the transhistorical basis of human history.' (Orzeck 2007: 508). This of course constitutes a fundamental challenge to the work critiqued in the previous section, because this invokes the physical materiality of the human body. If a consideration of the natural body is viewed as a step too far – and many poststructuralists would claim that this is – then Joseph Fracchia's (2005: 51) challenge needs answering. He argues:

> [It is true that] the cultural determination, for example, of what properly satisfies hunger and of what is considered too disgusting to eat can result in a situation that a starving person in need of food will not eat some form of nourishment because of cultural taboos. We may admire the power of culture to elevate mind over body, but we should not forget that rejection of food because of cultural taboos will ultimately lead to the pyrrhic victory of the body over mind – death.

Therefore, human needs 'may be remarkably elastic, they may vary enormously through time and across space, but our bodies can never get used to certain types of privation and exposure. Can it be that there are no implications of this?' (Orzeck 2007: 511). Surely there are, and it makes it necessary for us to acknowledge that '[t]o understand the social practices and cultural products of any time and place, we need to know something about [the] conditions of survival and social reproduction, something about the specific ways in which people gain access to the material conditions of life.' (Wood 2008: 12). To put it another way, there are inevitable asymmetries, repetitions and tendencies *within* our thoughts about the world towards our need for food, water, shelter, etc. As a result, there is a clear directedness to the evolution of the societies in which we live (past, present or future) – there cannot be full contingency because of the foundations upon which human existence is built.

Therefore, poststructuralist approaches are based on a false pretext which takes the body for granted and thus eliminates it from consideration, because the body is dissolved into discourse. However, as Fracchia (2005: 43) argues, we should be discussing not embodied minds but thinking bodies, because it is 'the set of corporeal constraints, the needs and limits embedded in human corporeal organisation, that prevents humans from making their histories as they please, that imposes limits on the variability of human cultures and on human malleability.' Hence, and in contrast to Butler's claims about those who disagree with her, there is no mind-body dualism because the mind is 'one of the many indispensable human bodily instruments' and not merely constitutive of the hollow body (ibid.: 47; see also Sayer 2011: 98–142).

Antonio Gramsci's writings on 'common sense' are of relevance here, for it helps us arrive at a considerably more satisfactory account of materiality than Foucault or Butler. For instance, take his (1971: 357) observation that 'the only "philosophy" is history in action, that is, life itself'. This rejection of the thought/ action dichotomy enables us to see that our thoughts about the world are embodied in all aspects of human activity: the conceptions we hold thus provide 'a point of reference for [both] thought and action' (Green and Ives 2009: 14). Therefore, these conceptions – which together form our version of 'common sense' and thus the basis for how we make sense of the world – are embodied in all human social practices (for example, see Gramsci 1971: 323–31, 419–23).

This may, at first glance, appear little different to what was critiqued in the previous section. However, Gramsci's notes on human nature (for example, 1971: 351–60) are an exemplary illustration of how to avoid separating the corporeal and the ideal while also refraining from attempting to posit the precise and unchanging weighting of one over the other. Hence his point that the logical conclusion of overly naturalistic arguments is that 'the determining matrix of history would be the kitchen' (ibid.: 354), and belief that the opposite position has 'a utopistic basis' because of its reduction of life to the realm of ideas (ibid.: 356). Nevertheless, he clearly seeks to avoid a merely 'pragmatic' solution to the issue, whereby everything is more or less an amalgam of everything else:

> That the objective possibilities exist for people not to die of hunger and that people do die of hunger, has its importance, or so one would have thought. But the existence of objective conditions, of possibilities or of freedom is not yet enough: it is necessary to 'know' them, and know how to use them. And to want to use them. (ibid.: 360).

Therefore, unlike Butler in her writings on precarious life and violence, and in contrast to Foucault's bland discussions of human self-regulation in modern (capitalist) societies, Gramsci makes it clear that ideas are material social processes *through*, not in isolation from or when dominant over, the body. Hence, it is *not* power/knowledge relations which are productive of human social practices, but the generative capacities of human corporeality itself (Fracchia 2005; Coole 2007). The ideas we hold about the world are immanent to the flesh. As such, the content of our thoughts about the world can neither be predicted nor fixed across space and time, but it is the case that our '[m]aterial circumstances are the net of constraints, the "conditions of existence" for potential thought and calculation about society' (Stuart Hall 1996: 44). The profound inequalities that are characteristic of capitalist societies are predicated upon this fundamental point, because capitalism is a historically specific form taken by the productive activities necessary for the sustaining of human life. This is the topic of the next section.

Bodies in Capitalism

As Marx and Engels (1998: 47) argue in *The German Ideology*, 'the production of means to satisfy [human] needs, the production of material life itself…[is] a fundamental condition of all history, which today, as thousands of years ago, must daily and hourly be fulfilled merely in order to sustain human life.' This means that for social enquiry to be persuasive it must be clear that '[w]hatever the social form of the production process, it has to be continuous' (Marx 1976: 711). Therefore, capitalism may be a *historically specific* mode of production, but its emergence and perpetuation is founded upon *transhistorical* human needs that must be satisfied in order to survive (cf. Fracchia 2004).

To put it more bluntly, workers are – through having little alternative – compelled to sell their bodies on the labour market in exchange for payment and thus a means of living. This is enforced through state regulations and injunctions guaranteeing labour's 'double freedom', which in effect means that labour is 'free' both to earn a living and to starve. At the same time, however, the owners of the means of production also need access to the labour market in order to purchase and thence employ the labour deemed necessary for production-for-profit to take place (Wood 2002: 2–3). Hence both capital and labour depend on the market and thus on each other; yet there is a profound inequality between those in possession of, and those without, ownership of the means of production. Dependence on the market for *survival* is considerably more visceral and compelling an experience than dependence on the market for *profit*. In consequence, the relationship between capital and labour is simultaneously mutually dependent and, through the nature of this reliance upon each other, intrinsically unequal (see Bruff 2011b on the implications for institutional practices). As Orzeck (2007: 511) argues:

> Why is the labourer, after all, trapped in the wage relation? The gradual erasure
> of other modes of subsistence is only part of the answer. In fact, if the labourer
> did not have to meet certain needs for his or her own reproduction, his or her
> 'freedom' to sell his or her labour power would not be an ironic freedom at all.

Therefore, capitalism is not just a historically specific means of organizing production; it is also 'a mode of exploitation [and] a relationship of power.' (Wood 1981: 19). This means that those who do not possess or own the means of production are caught between a rock and a hard place, for capitalist production is both an inherently unequal process and also the basis for survival. As Stuart Hall (1996: 38; original emphasis) argues, we should consequently not be surprised that, over time, this comes to be taken for granted and viewed as somehow 'natural', for 'the "market" experience is *the* most immediate, daily and universal experience of the economic system for everyone.' This is not to say that these arrangements come to be viewed positively; more that no other way of subsisting is deemed a realistic option.

   All of this means that the real, living, breathing, corporeality of the human body cannot be explained away through simple references to how such corporeality is managed and self-managed via a range of governmental techniques. This fundamentally misunderstands how and why the body's physical materiality is the condition for the effectiveness of the various techniques which seek to manage it. Instead it is taken for granted, with Foucault (1979: 141) blandly asserting that capitalism 'would not have been possible without the controlled insertion of bodies into the machinery of production and the adjustment of the phenomena of population to economic processes.' While this is *descriptively* accurate, it gives us little analytical purchase. Instead, we should acknowledge how 'the pressures and limits of what can ultimately be seen as a specific economic, political, and cultural system [i.e. capitalism] seem to most of us the pressures and limits of simple experience and common sense.' (Williams 1977: 110). This is a very different, and much more sophisticated, view of 'determinism' than is usually offered when invoking 'determinism' to critique an (often historical materialist) opponent. Moreover, such an approach to human social practices is:

> derived from the observation of historical eventuation *over time*. This observation
> is not of discrete facts *seriatim* but of *sets* of facts with their own regularities:
> of the repetition of certain kinds of event: of the congruence of certain kinds
> of behaviour within differing contexts: in short, of the evidences of systematic
> social formations and of a common logic of process…[Furthermore] even within
> each seemingly-static [historical moment] there will be found contradictions and

liaisons, dominant and subordinate elements, declining or ascending energies. (Thompson 1995: 64; original emphases).

This, as with Gramsci on common sense, does not appear at first glance to be too distinct from the poststructuralist argument that we are the objects and subjects of social norms. However, and again with Gramsci, we have arrived at this point equipped with a significantly more appropriate conceptualization of *how* and *why* certain repetitions and regularities will be both more significant and also more enduring than others (see also Thompson 1967). Intriguingly, this moves us towards the terrain occupied (critically) by Foucault and Butler – both have positioned their work in relation to the phenomenology literature – for when Thompson (1995: 235; original emphasis) argues that 'consciousness is *lived* as much as it is *known*', it is through an invocation of Maurice Merleau-Ponty against Louis Althusser. This is instructive, for although Thompson did not discuss the body as such, it reminds us that 'Foucault's antipathy towards phenomenology means he is unable to investigate normalized existence as it is experienced.' (Coole 2007: 117). Moreover, it demonstrates, *contra* Butler, that 'although bodies can be differentiated from one another with the help of sexual, racial, or other hierarchies they can also be differentiated *simply by virtue of their being condemned to exist* in space and scale.' (Orzeck 2007: 504; emphasis added).

Of course, this final point can be made in a general sense, but in capitalism bodies are condemned to historically specific modes of existence in space and scale, and this can be adequately understood only from a foundational materialist perspective on such existences. Therefore, the essential basis for human survival – that is, the need for food, water, shelter, etc. – must be the means by which we understand how bodies are the basis for the profoundly unequal social relations which exist in capitalist societies. Following on from this, the centrality of the human condition to our outlook gives us insights into what kind of emancipatory politics could be built from such a starting point. More specifically, and in contrast to the poststructuralist emphasis on a pseudo-metaphysical ethics which is disconnected from the realities of living, we ought to show how values such as equality, dignity and social justice should be pursued *in and through* the satisfaction of human needs, not in abstraction from them. We will always need to produce in order to live, but the organization of production need not be along the exploitative lines characteristic of capitalist societies. Recognizing this is an essential prerequisite for, in a post-capitalist world, the maximizing of the potential for human possibilities to become human freedom (cf. Gramsci 1971: 360).

Conclusion

So where could we go from here? Space permits little more than a few suggestions; however, a quote from a recent Butler monograph (Butler 2004: 31; emphases added) helps illuminate the broader aims of this chapter:

Possibility is an aspiration, something we might hope will be equitably distributed, something that might be socially secured, something that cannot be taken for granted, *especially if it is apprehended phenomenologically*...The normative aspiration at work here has to do with *the ability to live and breathe and move* and would no doubt belong somewhere in what is called a philosophy of freedom.

For Butler, this entails a critique which 'is understood as an interrogation of the terms by which life is constrained in order to open up the possibility of different modes of living' (ibid.: 4). However, the openings provided by her allusions to phenomenology and modes of living are closed down again, because she maintains that we are nevertheless 'always constituted by *norms* not of [our] making'. (ibid.: 15; emphasis added). This suggests that if we are to overcome the shortcomings associated with poststructuralism, then we need to move decisively beyond it. For example, Diana Coole (2007: 175–6) argues:

an entire corporeal subtext of lived meanings is always interwoven with cognition and discursive exchanges...[Moreover] power relations can also readily proliferate on this somatic level, where dynamics of exclusion or competence are communicated via body language, gestures, and performances, which usually escape analysis yet which weave their effects in potent ways of which participants are rarely explicitly aware...[The body] weaves meanings that have visceral, intercorporeal significance, where intellectual activities and communications remain anchored in more sensuous processes. This dimension of intercorporeality is never outrun.

Therefore, a renewed phenomenology of our lived, corporeal experiences as situated in capitalist conditions of existence is a potentially very fruitful area of conceptual and empirical exploration. This would build on the claims already made for a post-antihumanist phenomenology (Crossley 2001) and an updated materialist feminism (Young 2005), while also connecting with the resurgence of interest in historical materialism during the current times of capitalist crisis (Harvey 2010). Furthermore, it would bring into view the alternative geographical-philosophical traditions which could contribute positively to such an endeavour (cf. Sauer and Wöhl 2011); 'continental European philosophy' should *not* be restricted, or equated, to French poststructuralism (cf. Timon 2011). Most importantly, though, such an enterprise should be clear that to take the body for granted, to produce it as absent, to render it the expression of something else, is to overlook the rich traditions across the decades in critical social theory on the human condition.

Acknowledgements

I am indebted to Nicola Smith and especially Reecia Orzeck for numerous conversations over the years on the themes covered in this chapter. More recent discussions with Kirsty Alexander, Harriet Salem, Sean Timon and Stefanie Wöhl have also been of considerable help, as were conversations several years ago with Vicky Warner. Finally, I would like to thank the editors of this volume, and the anonymous referee of an earlier draft of this chapter, for comments and advice.

References

Agamben G. 1998. *Homo Sacer: Sovereign Power and Bare Life*. California: Stanford University Press.

Behrent, M. C. 2009. Liberalism without humanism: Michel Foucault and the free-market creed, 1976–1979. *Modern Intellectual History*, 6(3), 539–68.

Bruff, I. 2009a. The totalisation of human social practice: Open Marxists and capitalist social relations, Foucauldians and power relations. *British Journal of Politics & International Relations*, 11(2), 332–51.

———. 2009b. Assertions, conflations and human nature: a reply to Werner Bonefeld. *British Journal of Politics & International Relations*, 11(3), 554–6.

———. 2011a. The case for a foundational materialism: going beyond historical materialist IPE in order to strengthen it. *Journal of International Relations and Development*, 14(3), 391–9.

———. 2011b. What about the elephant in the room? Varieties of capitalism, varieties in capitalism. *New Political Economy*, 16(4), 481–500.

Butler, J. 1990. *Gender Trouble: Feminism and the Subversion of Identity*. New York: Routledge.

———. 1993. *Bodies That Matter: On the Discursive Limits of Sex*. New York: Routledge.

———. 1997. *Excitable Speech: A Politics of the Performance*. New York: Routledge.

———. 2004. *Undoing Gender*. New York: Routledge.

———. 2006. *Precarious Life: The Powers of Mourning and Violence*. London: Verso.

———. 2009. *Frames of War: When is Life Grievable?* London: Verso.

Coole, D. 2007. *Merleau-Ponty and Modern Politics after Anti-humanism*. Lanham, MD.: Rowman & Littlefield.

Crossley, N. 2001. The phenomenological habitus and its construction. *Theory and Society*, 30(1), 81–120.

Foucault, M. 1977. *Discipline and Punish: The Birth of the Prison*, translated by A.Sheridan. London: Allen Lane.

———. 1979. *The History of Sexuality. Vol.1: An Introduction*, translated by R. Hurley. London: Allen Lane.

————. 1980. *Power/Knowledge: Selected Interviews and other Writings, 1972–1977*, edited by C. Gordon, translated by C. Gordon et al. Brighton: Harvester.

————. 1982. The subject and power, in *Michel Foucault: Beyond Structuralism and Hermeneutics*, edited by H. L. Dreyfus and P. Rabinow. Chicago: University of Chicago Press, 208–26.

————. 1988. *Politics, Philosophy, Culture: Interviews and other Writings, 1977–1984*, edited by L. Kritzman, translated by A. Sheridan et al. London: Routledge.

————. 2007. *Security, Territory, Population: Lectures at the Collège de France, 1977–78*, translated by G. Burchell. New York: Palgrave Macmillan.

————. 2008. *The Birth of Biopolitics: Lectures at the Collège de France, 1978–1979*, translated by G. Burchell. New York: Palgrave Macmillan.

Fracchia, J. 2004. On transhistorical abstractions and the intersection of historical theory and social critique. *Historical Materialism*, 12(3), 125–46.

————. 2005. Beyond the human-nature debate: human corporeal organisation as the 'first fact' of historical materialism. *Historical Materialism*, 13(1), 33–61.

Gramsci, A. 1971. *Selections from the Prison Notebooks*, edited and translated by Q. Hoare and G. Nowell-Smith. London: Lawrence and Wishart.

Green, M. and Ives, P. 2009. Subalternity and language: overcoming the fragmentation of common sense. *Historical Materialism*, 17(1), 3–30.

Gudmand-Høyer. M. and Horth, T. L. 2009. Liberal politics reborn. *Foucault Studies*, 7, 99–130.

Harvey, D. 2010. *The Enigma of Capital: And the Crises of Capitalism*. London: Profile.

Hall, S. 1996. The problem of ideology: Marxism without guarantees, in *Stuart Hall: Critical Dialogues in Cultural Studies*, edited by D. Morley and K.-H. Chen. London: Routledge, 25–46.

Kiersey, N. J. 2009. Neoliberal political economy and the subjectivity of crisis: why governmentality is not hollow. *Global Society*, 23(4), 363–86.

MacKinnon, C. A. 2006. Postmodernism and human rights, in C. A. MacKinnon, *Are Women Human? And Other International Dialogues*. Cambridge, MA: Cambridge University Press, 44–63.

Marx, K. 1976. *Capital: A Critique of Political Economy. Vol. I*, translated by B. Fowkes. London: Penguin in Association with New Left Review.

————. and Engels, F. 1998. The German ideology, in K. Marx (with F. Engels), *The German Ideology (including Theses on Feuerbach and Introduction to the Critique of Political Economy)*. Amherst, NY.: Prometheus, 27–568.

McLennan, G. 1996. Post-Marxism and the 'four sins' of modernist theorizing. *New Left Review*, 1(218), 53–74.

Nash, K. 2000. *Contemporary Political Sociology: Globalization, Politics and Power*. Oxford: Blackwell.

Orzeck, R. 2007. What does not kill you: historical materialism and the body. *Environment and Planning D: Society and Space*, 25(3), 496–514.

Rabinow, P. and Rose, N. 2006. Biopower today. *BioSocieties*, 1(2), 195–217.

Rose, N. 1996. *Inventing Our Selves: Psychology, Power, and Personhood.* Cambridge: Cambridge University Press.

Salem, H. 2011. What does it mean to argue that International Relations is complicit in the production of the world of international relations? *Unpublished manuscript.*

Sauer, B. and Wöhl, S. 2011. Feminist perspectives on the internationalization of the state. *Antipode*, 43(1), 108–28.

Sayer, A. 2011. *Why Things Matter to People: Social Science, Values and Ethical Life.* Cambridge: Cambridge University Press.

Smith, N. J. 2011. The international political economy of commercial sex. *Review of International Political Economy*, 18(4), 530–49.

———. 2012. Body issues: the political economy of male sex work. *Sexualities*, 15(5-6), 586-603.

Stern, M. and Zalewski, M. 2009. Feminist fatigue(s): reflections on feminism and familiar fables of militarisation. *Review of International Studies*, 35(3), 611–30.

Thompson, E. P. 1967. Time, work-discipline and industrial capitalism. *Past & Present*, 38(1), 56–97.

———. 1995. *The Poverty of Theory: or an Orrery of Errors.* New Edition. London: Merlin Press.

Timon, S. 2011. Applications and opportunities: towards foundational phenomenological methodologies in International Relations. *Unpublished manuscript.*

Williams, R. 1977. *Marxism and Literature.* Oxford: Oxford University Press.

Wood, E. M. 1981. The separation of the economic and political in capitalism. *New Left Review*, 1(127), 66–95.

Wood, E. M. 2002. *The Origin of Capitalism: A Longer View.* London: Verso.

———. 2008. *Citizens to Lords: A Social History of Political Thought from Classical Antiquity to the Late Middle Ages.* London: Verso.

Young, I. M. 2005. *On Female Body Experience: 'Throwing Like a Girl' and Other Essays.* Oxford: Oxford University Press.

Chapter 6

Money Bodies

Bill Maurer and Elham Mireshghi

What judgment shall I dread, doing no wrong?
You have among you many a purchased slave,
Which, like your asses and your dogs and mules,
You use in abject and in slavish parts,
Because you bought them: shall I say to you,
Let them be free, marry them to your heirs?
… You will answer
'The slaves are ours': so do I answer you:
The pound of flesh, which I demand of him,
Is dearly bought; 'tis mine and I will have it.
If you deny me, fie upon your law!

The Merchant of Venice, IV.i

Introduction

Outwitted by fair Portia, who challenges him to extract his pound of flesh without spilling one drop of blood, the blood not being explicitly named in the original contract, Shylock remains the literary figure in English most associated with the dense metaphorical and practical linkages between the human body and filthy lucre, and the repugnance – at least on the surface – of attempting to reduce all things, even human flesh, to money. And yet, Shylock in *The Merchant of Venice* is also a morally-motivated character, the one who recalls everyone's common humanity, Jew or Gentile. Portia's clever legal maneuver is, in contrast, an act of exclusion. Denying him blood, she refuses Shylock kinship with his Catholic compatriots who, presumably, all drink from the cup of the blood of Jesus Christ. It is as if the response to Shylock's famous question, 'If you prick us, do we not bleed?' is, from Portia, 'No. As you do not partake of the blood of our Savior, so you do not share in the blood of spiritual kinship, of our policy, of humankind itself.'

Shylock challenges the law's hypocrisy: do not express horror at my attempted extraction of a pound of flesh when you, Christian Venetians, keep slaves as you keep chattel and dogs. In joining human slavery and animal bondage Shylock echoes the etymology of capital – money that reproduces, which so horrified Aristotle because it is contrary to nature for inanimate objects to become fecund like the beasts. The word 'capital' derives from heads of cattle, livestock serving as measure of wealth, store of value and medium of exchange for ancient and contemporary pastoralists. And while the equation of human bodies with money, the putting of a price on human beings, may remain abhorrent to us today, we live in a world where health insurance companies receive payments based on 'capitation' formulas, measuring out human life and receiving compensation for care 'by the head.' We should not begrudge poor Shylock when monetary calculations of human life and its constituent parts are as commonplace as cash and coin.

Death

Shylock helps us better to see two intertwined histories linking money and body, and the connections between money, bodies, and states. We can think, first, of actual brokers in bodies: from slave economies to the trade in body parts, the body has functioned and continues to carry value as currency. Kevin Bales, author of *Modern Slavery*, estimates there are 27 million enslaved people in the world today (Bales, Trodd and Williamson 2009). Prices for slaves range from US$40–90 for a bonded labourer to almost $2,000 for a sex slave. And the initial outlay turns out to be a sound investment, global profits from slavery accounting for an estimated $91 billion in 2007 (Kara 2008), with a return on investment for a sex slave of over 500%.[1]

One need not trade in the body entire, however. There are lucrative markets in parts. Now, if rendered down to its constituent elements, the human body is only worth $5–10 on the market. Chopped up into more valuable bits – internal organs, arms, skin, cornea – you can fetch a nice sum if done 'legitimately' through medical organizations and nonprofits that assist in organ and tissue donation, or, according to *Wired Magazine* (2003) around $45 million if done entirely on the international black markets (see also Cheney 2007; Scheper-Hughes and Wacquant 2002).

To profit from the body, you need not go into human trafficking, trading in whole bodies or specializing in specific parts. There are numerous experiments going on around the world that seek to employ the body as a form of currency. Since money is a mere sign, a convention set by the social contract or the state, depending on one's philosophy, people could come to an agreement to use specific signs made by the body to index value kept in a vault somewhere or recorded electronically in the ether of interconnected computer databases. Biometric currencies can link an identifiable person and his parts (retinas, fingerprints) to his bank account. Pay by pressing your finger on a point-of-sale terminal. Withdraw by getting your eye scanned. Technologists and interaction designers come up with science fiction-like ideas for sign-language moneys (Maurer 2010) while state governments deploy biometrically encoded smart cards for banking transactions (for one such experiment in Ghana, see Breckenridge 2010). The Government of India is in the

---

1   This estimate is based on Kara's calculations for income generated by a sex slave, and the assumption that the slave's room and board is equivalent to 10% of her yearly earnings.

process of creating a Universal ID for its 1.25 billion people. Each will receive a biometric smart card. Among its other intended functions, the scheme will solve, it is hoped, financial institutions' and banks' need to verify their clients' identities and thus provide financial access to millions who currently cannot open an account due to their lack of identity documents (UIDAI 2010).

Besides brokers in bodies and the use of the body in brokering, Shylock's fate points to another history of money's embodiments. In 1278 there was a massacre of Jews in London accused of being coin-clippers, debasing the King's currency by adulterating its metallic content (Prestwich 1988). Many were killed and Jews throughout England were rounded up and imprisoned. Though the accusations were the product of political hysteria, the punishment was not an unusual one for counterfeiters or debasers, Jewish or otherwise.

The English literary canon, especially in the Elizabethan era, is full of references to clipped coins, often yoking money (debased or not) to sovereign power (legitimate or not). Christopher Marlow's *Doctor Faustus*, first performed in 1604, contains a memorable scene in which Wagner secures the servitude of the Clown, first by offering him money. The Clown refuses, believing guilders to be 'girdirons,' the shackles worn by the condemned in Hell (and about to be metaphorically thrust upon the Clown after he is terrorized by the demons Wagner summons). Wagner then offers him French crowns, which the Clown mocks as worthless tokens, as the coins were associated with counterfeits and debased currencies in Elizabethan England. French crowns figure in Shakespeare, too: he often employed the French crown in puns linking them to venereal disease and impotence (e.g., *Measure for Measure*, Act I, scene 2). The French currency was doubly dangerous: either it was debased, and thus worth less than its putative value, or it was a mark of French power in a sovereign England. Thus royal decrees at the time urged the English to bore holes in the French coins in order to reduce their circulation and their threat to the body of state.

Corporal and capital punishment frequently befell counterfeiters and debasers. The American Coinage Act of 1792 levied the death penalty on debasers who would take from the body of the coin any fraction of its intended weight of gold or silver. Populists and revolutionaries exercised the flip-side of this punishment, tarring and feathering the tax collector or excise man, as in the Boston Tea Party. Though not fatal it was still a torturous punishment effected upon the body of the agents of state revenue collection. Both counterfeiters and tax collectors have from time to time been branded by mobs bearing hot irons tipped with metal coins, their bodies being stamped with the mark of their offence, or their desire.

Life

Branding with coins is a live practice even today, but for different purposes. From the late 1980s through the early 2000s, doctors and nurses in the Boston area and around Orange County, California, noticed that patients brought into the doctor's office or emergency room for unrelated ailments were seen to have been scraped or branded with coins. (We doubt anyone assumed they had been visited this punishment for counterfeiting). They were mainly recent Vietnamese or Cambodian immigrants. It turned out that they were not victims of abuse but rather had been treated with a traditional healing practice called *cạo gió* in Vietnamese and *kor kchoal* in Khmer which is believed to draw illness from the body (see, e.g., Ready 2001). Public health officials today provide cultural sensitivity training to hospital staff on this and similar traditional therapies.

Coins and money on the body for life or health is a recurrent theme in the world's monetary cultures. Women frequently adorn themselves with objects that serve as a store of wealth – gold jewellery, precious stones, silver – often bequeathed to them by their kin or provided by the family of their groom at the time of marriage. There is a lucrative market in gold jewellery in every South and Southeast Asian immigrant community, primarily for weddings as well as remittances to the home country. If faith forbids the wearing of gold by men (as with Islam in many parts of the world), then women can become the bearers of this commodity. Such practices hark to longstanding traditions of exchange at marriage: bridewealth, whereby the groom's family gives gifts to the bride's family; dowry, whereby the bride's family makes prestations to the groom's; or brideservice, whereby the groom contributes labor to the bride's family for a period of time before the marriage (see Collier 1988).

Such marriage exchanges point toward the larger issue of 'wealth in people' frequently noted in the anthropological literature as at the origins of state formation and/or in contradistinction to liberal capitalist states. In contrast to the institutions of slavery, in which humans are commodified as chattel, wealth in people refers to 'the accumulation of social relations' frequently figured as a gathering of social debts, kinship, or religious or political clientelism (Guyer 1995: 86). From Melanesian 'big men' who accrue fame and followers by giving things away, to African chiefs whose power is consolidated through transactions at the interface of people and things, wealth in people indexes a world of multiple and overlapping currencies and their diverse articulations to the mechanisms of power and state. The complexity itself can be staggering. Guyer provides an example:

> In Southern Cameroun *akuma* – conventionally translated as wealth – consisted primarily of wives, indigenous currencies and livestock, while *biem* – currently meaning 'things' – covered trade goods, including both the ivory traded out and the imported goods brought in. Items we think of as things, in the sense of being inanimate, fell into both categories (Guyer 1995: 88).

While it may sound exotic to contemporary Western industrialized or post-industrial ears, the concept is not alien and the law is rife with examples where the interface between wealth in people, wealth in goods and wealth in money becomes a fraught zone of regulatory, moral and economic conflict. Much of what international non-governmental organizations and multilateral bodies consider 'corruption' would fall under the heading of the traffic between wealth in people and capital accumulation. Transparency International's definition of corruption as the 'abuse of entrusted power for private gain' (http://www.transparency.org/news_room/faq/corruption_faq) begs the question of how and by whom such power has been entrusted, what the boundaries of the private might be, and how to measure gain. Political favoritism and graft, when mapped onto kinship, chart the shifting lives of social relationships, wealth in people mapped onto the networks of power constituting the modern state and its interstices.

Bribery, extortion, political corruption, 'money politics:' this returns us to the question of the lifeblood of society, the body of state, the spiritual community, the substance denied Shylock by Portia. Blood money is restitution for a life taken, but it is also a term used to refer to the hit-man's pay. When Judas brought his blood money to the temple, the priests purchased with it the potter's field, the place for the poor and foreign who die outside society's orthodoxy, thus, according to some, bringing the outsiders into the light of salvation. Civic authorities in the United States and elsewhere today maintain 'potter's fields' for the burial of the indigent and unclaimed, bringing them in their final resting place into the kinship of the state, a final citizenship.

Blood money like kinship itself thus awkwardly unifies both death and life, and, if anything, extends life through the presumption of durability and extensibility of kin, citizenry and state into the indefinite future. Life and health insurance proceed from similar logics, and likewise awkwardly straddle the line between commodification of the human body, its life-force, and a membership-making compensation, at once guarding family and loved ones against loss as well as creating and acknowledging common membership in a polity. The ideologically pitched debates in the United States at the start of President Barack Obama's administration over universal health insurance and the populist horror fantasy of 'death panels' – bureaucrats making life or death decisions over the care of the aged and incapacitated – were struggles over the definition of the citizenry and the obligations of the state to its people, specifically, the demarcation of the boundaries of peopleness.

Ironically, perhaps, despite the death panel moral panic, the standard insurance practice of capitation endures in many parts of the Anglo-American world, and is likely to continue. Payment 'by the head' rather than by the cost of care governs medical insurance's money transfers, incentivizing fewer medical interventions and rationing healthcare. Where 19th century reformers worried that insurance would commodify personhood, gambling against death and usurping the role of God in providing divine protection (Zelizer 1983: 73), few in the early 21st century remark on the fact that capitation reflects a wager based on the law of large numbers and the gospel of economic efficiency.

Compensation

Elsewhere, of course, states figure bodies through different monetary practices and logics. The Islamic Republic of Iran provides a case of a no less bureaucratized, no less formalized, but differently monetized configuration of bodies, specifically, for the compensation required for bodies damaged. Mandated by the Iranian Islamic Penal Code, *diyeh* is the financial compensation a person must pay when he or she inadvertently causes physical injury to another.[2] If the bodily damage was premeditated, the injured person may request diyeh instead of corporal retribution (i.e. an eye for an eye), as can the kin of the murdered victim, in lieu of execution. Diyeh, which is often translated as 'blood money,' predates Islam, but was inscribed with Islamic legitimacy by the Quran and the Prophet Mohammad's endorsement. Surah Nisa of the Quran says:

> Never should a believer kill a believer; but (if it so happens) by mistake (compensation is due): if one (so) kills a believer, it is ordained that he should free a believing slave, and pay *diyeh* to the deceased's family, unless they remit it freely... (Chapter 4, Verse 92)

It has been reported that the Prophet Mohammad said to his son-in-law. 'Ali ibn 'Abi Talib:Oh 'Ali, verily 'Abd al-Muttaleb established five traditions during the 'jahiliya'[3] that Allah continued in Islam...he established the tradition of 100 camels for murder and Allah continued that in Islam (Ḥurr al-'Amili1982, cited in Heydari 2004: 169).

The consensus among Shi'i and Sunni jurists is that 100 camels is the proper *whole diyeh* ('diyeh-e kamel') mandated in the case of homicide, though several other hadith suggest equivalents in other livestock, as well as inanimate commodities (Karimi 1999). These traditions have been literally realized in the Iranian Islamic Penal Code. Article 297 stipulates six forms of compensation from among which the culprit can theoretically choose:[4]

1. 100 healthy, flawless and not too lean camels
2. 200 healthy, flawless and not too lean cows
3. 1000 healthy, flawless and not too lean sheep
4. 200 articles of clothing made from the 'helleh' of Yemen
5. 1000 flawless, pure gold coin dinars, where every dinar is one 'mesqal' weighing 18 'nokhod'[5]

---

2 Islamic Penal Code, Book Four 'Diyat,' Part One, Articles 294-296.

3 Jahiliya or the 'state of ignorance' refers to the condition of pre-Islamic Arabiya.

4 From the official web journal of the Judiciary Branch of the Islamic Republic of Iran, www.dastour.ir

5 One mesqal is equivalent to 4.608 grams.

6. 10,000 flawless, pure silver coin dirhams, where every dirham weighs 12.6 nokhod

Whether or not originally intended to avoid commensurating the body with a singular thing ('Abedi et al. 2007: 21), or easing payment for the cow and sheep herder or for the merchant devoid of camels, diyeh in contemporary Iran is paid in cash. Based on the market value, and the opinion of 'experts,' the Justice Ministry announces specific values for 100 camels, 200 cows and 1000 sheep that escalate with inflation. For the year 2010 (solar hejri year 1389), the amounts were announced respectively as, 450, 550, and 900 million rials[6] (approximately US$43,000, $53,000 and $86,000, respectively).

The Islamic diyeh system does more than determine a payment for slaying; a host of rulings lay out the compensation for particular parts, arms, legs, ear lobes, eye-lashes, nipples; even the right testicle is differentiated from the left.[7] The decreed amounts vary according to severity and are calculated in terms of proportions to the whole diyeh (for the whole body). Injury is based on both functionality and 'cosmetic wholeness' (Sachedina 2009). One might not fathom eyebrows to hold any necessary bodily function, but as an ornament of the face, their ruin can warrant up to half a whole diyeh.

Classical jurists agree that body parts are roughly divided into four different types: 1-those that are unique (such as the tongue, nose, penis, and bladder), 2-those that come in pairs (such as ears, eyes, eyebrows, arms, legs, feet, and lips), 3-parts that come in more than pairs (such as fingers, eyelids, toes, and teeth), and 4- non-countable parts (such as skin and hair) (ibid, see also Haji-Dehabadi 2004). In addition to the hierarchy of parts, a hierarchy of gender and religion differentiates the diyeh due to a woman and a man, and a Muslim from a non-Muslim. The whole diyeh of 100 camels halves for women (Article 300), and only a fraction is due to the non-Muslim (though in 2004 the Iranian Islamic Penal Code was modified to match the diyeh of recognized religious minorities[8] with that of Muslims).

Two rationalities of calculating compensation, however, based on two different understandings of the body are conjoined in the contemporary Iranian diyeh system. In Sharia-inspired diyeh calculations inscribed in the Penal Code, one unique body part metonymically stands in for the entire body. In this way of figuring compensation, if a unique body part loses its functionality, for example a tongue is severed, or the capacity to speak is lost, the diyeh amount is equivalent

---

6   Sazman Qazayi Niroohay-e Mosallah [Judicial Organization of the Armed Forces] www.Imj.ir http://www.imj.ir/index.php?option=com_content&view=article&id=1268:---1389&catid=284:-1389&Itemid=469

7   The diyeh for the left testicle is 2/3 of the whole body, while the diyeh for the right one is 1/3 (Iranian Islamic Penal Code, Article 435).

8   Iran recognizes Zoroastrians, Jews, and Christians as religious minorities. Bahai's are notably excluded and receive no compensation.

to the whole body, not just the whole tongue. Similarly, if an arm is severed or severely harmed, so as to lose its functionality, the diyeh is equal to half the body, as is the case for other body parts that come in pairs (such as eyes, ears, legs). The diyeh for a single finger is one-tenth the whole body, given the victim originally possessed all ten digits. Also, removal of a man's beard, such that it permanently halts its growth entails the full diyeh, and if it grows back, one-third the full-body diyeh, and the removal of a man or woman's head-hair entails full-body diyeh, if it leads to permanent baldness (Iranian Islamic Penal Codes, Arts. 294–301).

Now, the Islamic edicts detail only a limited number of physical harms, which do not include those less visible to the eye, such as lacerations on the diaphragm (1% of the full diyeh), epiphora of the eye (excessive tear-production) (2%), or mental illness. Wherever the diyeh system is silent, there is the *arsh* system, the particulars of which are devised in part by forensic scientists and medical practitioners. A key reference, *Pajuheshi dar naqs-e ozvi va arsh* (*An Investigation of Physical Impairment and Arsh)* (Abedi et al. 2007) explains that permanent injuries consisting of anatomical damage, functional damage, or damage to beautifying structures, as well as temporary injury (such as bruising on the skin) are assessed individually and separately and summed up for a final diyeh amount to be determined. It is possible for this amount to exceed one full diyeh. There are complicated mathematical formulae and indices to determine the extent of physiological trauma and probability of survival, including methods first promulgated by the American Association for Advancement of Automotive Medicine.

The *arsh* system elaborated by medical professionals and forensic scientists is thus based on a severity scale of harm to health (anatomical, physiological and mental), whereas the *diyeh* system in the Penal Code is based on a conception of the body as containing microcosms of itself within it. In *arsh*, the body is treated as a collection of individual parts operating cooperatively to sustain life. In portions of the Penal Code directly applying Shari'a rulings, on the other hand, the *diyeh* system takes the body as a whole comprising of whole functions and whole 'beauty aspects,' which are each partible into externally visible segments: ten fingers are considered to comprise a whole, damage to which would warrant a full *diyeh*; damage to a single finger would warrant 1/10 of the full *diyeh*. Damage to a single digital bone in the thumb (a phalanx) warrants 1/20th compensation (since the thumb only has two phalanges), where as for any other finger of the hand which has three digital bones, damage to one would warrant a 1/30th compensation of the full *diyeh*. Whereas the *arsh* system starts from the presumption of the corporeal and functional wholeness of a body entire, the *diyeh* system figures the body as a set of distinct wholes, each of which is a metonym for the entire body. Put together, the two systems create a bricolage of body-worlds underwritten by law, state, and money.

Weight

The question of compensation brings us back to where we started, with the pound of flesh. Compensation for body parts, as illustrated in the diyeh/arsh bricolage, opens up the question of how we conceptualize the human body itself. Is it a unified whole? Always? What makes it so? Is it the iteration of a series of wholes, each repeated at a different level of scale, such that the hand is to the arm as the two arms are to the whole person, or a similar logic (for a New Guinea example along these lines, see Mimica 1988)? Can that pound of flesh be separated, literally or figuratively, from the blood and sinew and fat that accompanies it, seemingly inseparable from it? This series of questions, in turn, calls forth the mind/body problem: is the body the seat of the mind, or is the mind transcendent, more than the sum of the bloody parts? Is the person properly speaking coterminous with the mind, while the body is merely matter absent that spark of consciousness?

It is significant that many philosophers have asked the same questions of money: Is money a convention of consciousness, or a material valuable in itself? Fiat currencies, created by the state, are worthless paper until the breath of the state animates them with the spark of value. Only then will they circulate from hand to hand in a community of believers, the citizenry of a polity.

The anthropologist Keith Hart (1986) has famously remarked that money is simultaneously both 'heads' and 'tails.' Animated by the head of state, the sovereign, it is a token of political authority and an abstraction accepted by convention and political decree. Yet it is also a commodity measured in units of value, often linked to the weight or tale of precious metals. £1 flesh, 1lb flesh. The person as token and tale. Money as capital and currency. Both sides of the coin welded together make money, money. Money is both an idea and an object, Hart reminds us. So, too, the human body, and the body of state. That pound of flesh is dearly bought indeed.

References

Abedi, M-H., Ranjbaran, R., Mahdavi, A-H. and Nateqifard, F. 2007. *Pajuheshi dar naqs-e ozvi va arsh [An Investigation of Physical Impairment and Arsh].* Tehran: Turan.

Bales, K., Trodd, Z., and Williamson, A. K. 2009. *Modern Slavery: The Secret World of 27 Million People.* Oxford: Oneworld Publications.

Breckenridge, K. 2010. The World's First Biometric Money: Ghana's e-Zwich and the Contemporary Influence of South African Biometrics. *Africa: The Journal of the International African Institute,* 80(4), 642–662.

Cheney, A. 2007. *Body Brokers: Inside America's Underground Trade in Human Remains.* New York: Broadway.

Collier, J. 1988. *Marriage and Inequality in Classless Societies.* Stanford: Stanford University Press.

Guyer, J. I. 1995. Wealth in People, Wealth in Things: Introduction. *Journal of African History*, 36(1), 83–90.

Haji-Dehabadi, Ahmad. 2004. Qa'edey-e diyeh-e a'za dar fiqh-e imamiyyeh va ahl-e sunnat [The Principle of Diyeh of (body) Parts in Imami (Shi'i) and Sunni Jurisprudence]. *Fiqh va Hoquq [Jurisprudence and Law]* 2: 137–168.

Hart, K. 1986. Heads or Tails? Two Sides of the Coin. *Man*, 21(4), 637–656.

Heydari, A .2004. Mahiat-e Hoquqi-e Diyeh [The Legal Character of Diyeh]. *Fiqh* 40: 165–190.

Ḥurr al-'Amili, Muḥammad ibn al-Ḥasan.1982. Wasa'il al-Shi'ah ila taḥṣil masa'il al-shari'ah. In *Kitab al-diyat*. Beirut: Dar ehya al-torath al-arabi.

Kara, S. 2010. *Sex Trafficking: Inside the Business of Modern Slavery*. New York: Columbia University Press.

Karimi, H. 1999. Maqadeer-e diyeh-e kameleh [Amounts of the Full Diyeh]. *Majalay-e pajuhesh-e falsafi-kalami [Journal of Philosophical-Theological Research]*1: 64–75.

Maurer, B. 2010. Finger counting money. *Anthropological Theory*, 10(1), 1–7.

Mimica, J. 1988. *Intimations of Infinity: The Cultural Meanings of the Iqwaye Counting and Number System*. Oxford: Berg.

Prestwich, P. M. 1988. *Edward I (The English Monarchs Series)*. New Haven: Yale University Press.

Ready, Tinker. 2001. Healing Traditions: Americans Have Only Recently Begun to Experiment with Body Work, Herbs, Acupuncture, and Other Forms of Oriental Medicine. Cambodians have been doing it forever. *The Boston Phoenix*, June 21–28.Available at: http://www.bostonphoenix.com/boston/news_features/other_stories/multipage/documents/01683418.htm

Sachedina, A. 2009. *Islamic Biomedical Ethics*. Oxford University Press.

Scheper-Hughes, N., and Wacquant, L., eds. 2002. *Commodifying Bodies*. Thousand Oaks, CA: Sage Publications Ltd.

UAIDI. 2010. From Exclusion to Inclusion with Micropayments. *Unique Identification Authority of India Planning Commission Report*. Available at: http://uidai.gov.in/.

Zelizer, V. 1983. *Morals and Markets: The Development of Life Insurance in the United States*. New Brunswick, NJ: Transaction Publishers.

Chapter 7

Corporeal Capitalism: Invisible Male Bodies in the Global Sexual Economy

Nicola Smith

Introduction

The analysis of global sexual economies has emerged as an important part of a wider feminist project to re-imagine the boundaries of what constitutes the 'inside' and 'outside' of globalisation and capitalism. Emphasising the importance of such an agenda, the chapter argues that continued understandings of commercial sex as 'women's work' place male and transgender bodies on the outside rather than the inside of the analysis of global sexual economies. Highlighting the need to address this gap in contemporary theorising and empirical analysis, I offer an illustration of research into male sex work through discussion of fieldwork with male escorts in San Francisco. In so doing, I draw upon and situate myself within feminist scholarship that seeks to 'embody' the study of political economy by grounding it in real human experience: that is, to locate economic and political processes in contextually specific times and places by exploring how real, living human-beings (in this case, male sex workers) try to make sense of the structured contexts in which they find themselves (Youngs 2000a).

The Body in IPE

Given that the body has long represented a central site of enquiry across the social sciences and humanities, it is notable that scholarship within that most 'material' of disciplines (Hooper 2000: 31), International Political Economy, has not historically preoccupied itself with such messy matters of embodiment. As Charlotte Hooper (ibid.) notes, it is 'supremely ironic' that a field so concerned with issues of inequality and poverty – and, as such, with the fulfilment of the material needs of physical bodies – should have been built around abstractions from, not explorations of, embodied social contexts. In particular, as Matthew Watson (2005) has observed, despite its superficial heterodoxy, IPE scholarship has all too often been disciplin*ed* by questions about 'states' and 'markets' in which both are divorced from any kind of social setting. As Gillian Youngs (2000: 25) similarly notes, this separation of 'states' and 'markets' from their social context has produced a disembodied picture of the world in which the 'lives and experiences of people, the basics of social relations of power' have largely been left unacknowledged and unexplored.

Feminist scholarship by no means has a monopoly on bodies, but nevertheless it has been at the forefront of attempts to take issues of embodiment seriously within IPE. Feminist political economists have highlighted how globalisation and capitalism are not 'out there' phenomena that are materially or analytically separable from actually-existing human lives but, quite the contrary, they 'impact directly and often violently on the bodies of actual people' (Pettman 2000: 52). Feminists have thus sought to 'make visible something of the mess, pain, pleasure and pressure of everyday life' (Pettman 2003: 158) by exploring how global processes are inscribed, imprinted and circulated on bodies (Penttinen 2008). In so doing, they have emphasised the need to explore how differences such as gender, ethnicity and sexuality are not natural essences *of* bodies but rather are written *on* bodies, so that embodied experiences and identities are intimately intertwined with uneven relations of power. As Wendy Harcourt (2009: 22) puts it, feminist analysis has drawn attention to bodies as 'sites of contestation in a series of economic, political, sexual and intellectual struggles … [in] which the play of powers, knowledges and resistances are worked out'.

In positioning bodies at the centre rather than the margins of international political economy, feminists have challenged IPE's disciplinary boundaries by exposing how those boundaries depend upon a number of tacit dualisms. These do not just include states/markets, politics/economics and national/international (all of which share the common status of being treated as internal to IPE) but also deeper dichotomies relating to what constitutes the 'inside' and 'outside' of IPE in the first place. In particular, feminists have pointed to a clear division between the 'public' realm (e.g. of government, of work) and the 'private' realm (e.g. of home, of family) – a move that has enabled personal, domestic and familial relations to be bracketed off and treated as external to the discipline (Steans 2006; Waylen 2006). This separation is, moreover, deeply gendered, for the public boundary serves to define 'the world of political and economic power, of decision-making and influence, to which masculine influence and identity are primarily attached', whereas the private boundary defines 'the world of social reproduction, of home and family, to which feminine influence and identity are primarily attached' (Youngs 2000: 19).[1] Such boundaries thus operate as hierarchies associated with the privileging of the masculine over the feminine (Griffin 2009; Peterson 2010), with the former linked to public space/rationality/culture/the mind and the latter with private space/emotions/nature/the body (Pettman 2000; Hooper 2001). In this sense, while the body has been 'missing' in IPE, the discipline has also 'colluded

---

1   Of course, neo-Gramscian and other 'critical' IPE scholars have also generated a wealth of invaluable insights into 'everyday life', but here I wish to focus on how feminist work in particular has highlighted the way(s) in which bodies are 'inscribed with differences that matter' in terms of gender, race and sexuality (Pettman, 1997: 94; see also Steans and Tepe 2010).

with the displacement of both body and sex onto women', with bodies/sexuality/ femininity all relegated to the private realm and thus erased from disciplinary concern (Pettman 1997: 97).[2]

Sexual Labour As 'Women's Work'?

While feminist IPE has therefore sought to *de*construct the (implicit) valorisation of masculinity/the masculine, so too it has offered a *re*constructive project in which 'feminised' bodies, identities and activities are no longer marginalized but are instead placed centre-stage (Youngs 2004; Peterson 2005). Vital to this project has been a concern with, and interrogation of, the informal and private sphere of emotional, domestic, caring and sexual labour (or 'reproductive economy'), as distinguished from the formal sphere of primary, secondary and tertiary production (or 'productive economy') (Peterson 2010: 209-11). Within this context, the commercial sexual sector has emerged as an important focal-point of analysis within feminist IPE. Building on a long tradition of feminist thought that has sought to reveal how sex and sexuality – those most 'private' and 'intimate' aspects of identity – are in fact deeply political (Youngs 2000a), feminist IPE has highlighted the intersections between sexuality and economy, too (see for instance Charusheela 2008; Griffin 2009; Cabezas 2009). Sexuality is seen as 'embodied and embedded in the logic and structuring of globalising capitalism' (Gottfried 2004: 10),[3] serving to reflect, reinforce and reproduce global structural inequalities. The international political economy of commercial sex, it is argued, can be understood in terms of structural hierarchies between men and women, between rich and poor, and between the first and third worlds (Pettman 1996; Bertone 1999; Enloe 2001; Peterson 2003; Jeffreys 2008; Penttinen 2008). As with other sectors of the economy, the sex industry operates in terms of supply and demand: the supply of women from developing countries whose limited economic opportunities lead them to sell sex; and the demand for exotic Others by men from affluent countries who can afford their sexual services (ibid.). As Agathangelou (2005: 8) contends, the commercial sex industry should be viewed in terms of 'the asymmetric sexual division of labour based on racialised sex and the institutionalisation of desire with millions of women, primarily, paying the price of such exploitation with their labour and their bodies'.

Such accounts have certainly not gone unchallenged, however – indeed, there is long-standing debate within and outside feminist IPE about the political,

---

2 This is, of course, not to deny the significant contestation amongst feminist political economists – not least with respect to tensions between the materiality and construction of bodies – but rather to highlight the profound and distinctive contribution that feminist scholarship has made to IPE more broadly.

3 I have paraphrased Gottfried here, for the original quotation refers to gender rather than sexuality.

economic and social implications of the global sex industry, and especially whether the sale of sex can ever represent a site of resistance to (as opposed to oppression under) gendered, classed and racialised power relations (cf. Kempadoo and Doezema 1998; Jeffreys 2008). Despite this contestation, though – and as enormously valuable as scholarship on global sexual economies has undoubtedly been – it is not without its own gaps and blind-spots (as feminist IPE scholars would be the very first to acknowledge).[4] Particularly notable is the way in which feminist IPE – along with the bulk of literature on commercial sex more broadly – focuses almost exclusively on the experiences and status of female sex workers. Given both the desire to make women's lives more visible in IPE and the fact that sexual labour has been historically and culturally been constructed as something that 'women' do, this is certainly understandable. But it also reflects something of a conceptual leap in which the sex industry is not only explored as a femin*ised* sphere of work – i.e. as marginalised and denigrated due to its association with the private realm of erotic/affective life – but is also directly attached to female bodies[5] – i.e. as labour that is not just discursively constructed as 'women's work' but that is, in reality, 'women's work' (Smith 2011). In this sense, commercial sex is, in effect, 'displaced' on to women's bodies in IPE scholarship, with male and transgender bodies consequently erased from the analysis.

While not wishing to imply for one moment that feminist IPE's empirical focus on women has been anything other than an 'indispensable' project (Peterson 2005: 517), I am nevertheless conscious that the lack of attention to/acknowledgement of male and transgender sex work has its own empirical, conceptual and normative implications. In empirical terms, the focus on women tends to be justified (if it is justified at all) on the grounds that the 'vast majority' of sex workers are female; indeed, a huge amount of theoretical weight rests upon the shoulders of this empirical assertion and yet it is never really interrogated empirically. (Rather, the phrase 'vast majority' is uttered and, like a rabbit in a hat, all the male and transgender sex workers magically disappear). As a result, and despite the enormous

---

4   As Sandra Whitworth (1996: 6) notes, feminist scholarship has tended to be highly self-critical and reflexive – although 'it is difficult to [be so] in an intellectual and political environment in which any attempt to theorise and explore women or gender is an improvement over the silences which proceeded it'.

5   Although I do not use scare-quotes when referring to 'female' and 'male' in this essay, I fully embrace Judith Butler's (1999) argument that the binary between 'male' and 'female' is itself discursive rather than a natural biological 'fact'. I am grateful to one commentator for raising the issue of how I can bring in the bodies of male and transgender sex workers without essentialising them (given that I want to dismiss the essentialisation of identities)? This is obviously a very tricky and complex issue that I could not begin to do justice to here, but as Kath Browne has put it (following Butler): 'While I wish to contest the boundaries of gender and sex, I also seek to be intelligible' (Browne, 2004: 443). In order to make sense of participants' narratives (who referred to themselves as 'women' in Browne's study, and 'men' in mine) it is 'necessary to use these sexed terms' whilst also acknowledging their fluidity and instability (ibid.).

amount of ink that has been spilt on the global sex trade, little political economic scholarship exists on male sex work (although notable exceptions include Collins 2007; Padilla 2007). In conceptual terms, the focus on 'women and girls' means that commercial sex and its gendered implications are, in effect, situated within a 'heterosexual matrix' (Butler 1999: 45) in which the buyers of sex are assumed to be heterosexual men. This means that (arguably) the very hetero-normative gender logics that are in need of disruption end up being reinforced, with male demand/female supply discourses feeding into dominant understandings of an essential (if not biologically-determined) gender order in which sexual objectification is tied to female bodies and sexual subjectivity is tied to male ones.

Finally, in normative terms, the 'disappearing' of male and transgender sex workers (Agustin, 2006) not only means that their subjectivities and potential for political agency are denied, but also cannot be separated from the gender politics surrounding the status of female sex workers. As Shannon Bell (1994: 40-1) notes, in modernist discourse, the prostitute body has been 'marked out and defined' as a 'distinct female body', with the category of 'prostitute' thus contained within the category of 'woman'. This has allowed oppositions between wife/prostitute, virgin/whore, good girl/bad girl, and so on, to be treated as internal to (rather than as written *on* to) the category of 'woman'. While feminist discourse has sought to unpack and challenge such dichotomies, it has also served to reinforce them (ibid.). For instance, Jo Doezema (2010) highlights how the image of the suffering and degraded third world prostitute has been used as a powerful tool to promote particular feminist agendas that claim to 'speak for' (but do not necessarily reflect) the interests of third world sex workers themselves. The 'injured body' of the third world prostitute is not only deployed as a symbol of women's universal sexual subordination but also allows Western feminists to present the third world prostitute as Other, by contrasting her with 'emancipated' women. First world sex worker organisations, too, have reinforced the dichotomy between 'free' and 'forced' prostitution by insisting that 'free' sex workers should be afforded legal rights whilst accepting that 'forced' prostitutes need saving (2005: 71-2). Such narratives, Doezema argues, imagine the 'free' Western sex worker as independent and autonomous and the 'forced'/trafficked third world prostitute as naïve and passive (1998: 42). More than this, they also reproduce the distinction between 'good' and 'bad' women (i.e. between innocent/forced and guilty/voluntary prostitutes), which bolsters the notion that 'women who transgress sexual norms deserve to be punished' and encourages the pursuit of abolitionist policy agendas in the name of 'saving' the innocent (ibid.). As I have argued elsewhere (Smith 2011), it is no accident that the image of the 'injured prostitute' is that of a female prostitute, for it is an image that depends upon and sustains discourses surrounding gender violence that would lose their political purchase (and, indeed, their discursive intelligibility) if framed in terms of the 'sexually exploited men' and 'sexually predatory women'. In other words, the fact that male and transgender bodies have historically been (and continue to be) placed on the outside of the category 'prostitute' is central to – not incidental to – the perpetuation of women-as-victim discourses that many feminists (including myself) would wish to normatively oppose.

Exploring Male Sex Work Empirically

The above discussion highlights how the study of male and transgender sex work warrants closer attention not only on its own terms but also as a means to re-contextualise the meanings, practices and politics surrounding commercial sex more broadly. The remainder of this paper offers an empirical illustration of research into this under-explored area through discussion of fieldwork I undertook in 2008 with male escorts based in San Francisco. My fieldwork was very much inspired by the kind of feminist IPE I have outlined above, i.e. that which seeks to 'embody' the study of political economy by grounding it in actually-existing human experience (Youngs 2000a). As Gillian Youngs writes, such an approach aims to render people *present* within contextually-specific times and places (i.e. rather than as 'hidden by the statistics of disembodied frameworks') by treating them as '*living* and *actual* subjects engaging with structural forces and negotiating them [original emphases]' (ibid: 21). Importantly, moreover, I do not wish to locate or interrogate the 'essence' of male sex work, for example by considering whether or not it is inherently oppressive. Rather, I proceed from an understanding of commercial sex as both historically and culturally contingent and also socially and politically contested; that is, as a set of meanings and practices that possess no inherent 'truth' to be uncovered. In so doing, I draw on the growing body of sex-radical, poststructuralist and postcolonial feminist scholarship (see for instance Vance 1992; Bell 1994; Califia 1994; Zatz 1997; Kempadoo 1998; Egan, Frank et al. 2006; Agustin 2007) that views commercial sex as implicated *in* but not determined *by* social structures, so that it can simultaneously reinforce, destabilise and disrupt power relations (Chapkis 2002). This allows me explicitly to allow for the ontological and empirical possibility that commercial sex may be experienced, understood and articulated in a multiplicity of different, ambiguous and contested ways. At the same time, I see these potentially divergent experiences, understandings and articulations not as isolated and atomised but rather as always-already grounded in their social context and produced by/productive of broader political, economic and cultural processes. As such, I am interested to explore how the people engaged in commercial sex 'make sense of' it (Phoenix 2001) and I do so within the context of an understanding of commercial sex as underpinned and reproduced by a 'diversity of sexual-economic exchanges and ... complexity of power relations' (O'Connell Davidson and Sanchez Taylor, 2005: 1).

With these theoretical issues in mind, the rest of this chapter explores male sex work in San Francisco empirically. As mentioned above, there is now a considerable literature within and outside IPE on sex tourism to, and sex trafficking from, poorer countries (including some studies of female and gay sex tourism, which have focused most notably on the Caribbean – see for instance Ryan and

Hall 2001; Phillips 2002; Sanchez Taylor 2006; Padilla 2007). This scholarship has quite rightly pointed to the significance of global power inequalities in creating the conditions for increasing numbers of disadvantaged people to be drawn into the sex industry world-wide. However, comparatively little attention has been devoted to the expansion and diversification of sexual economies in the post-industrial cities of the West, where more and people from the higher socio-economic strata are joining the sex industry as sellers (rather than just consumers) of sexual services (Bernstein 2007a). As a highly prosperous post-industrial city in which there is a thriving sex industry, San Francisco offers a particularly interesting location from which to explore male sex work. This is not least because the city has become widely-known as one of the 'gay capitals' of the world; indeed, it is reported to have the largest gay, lesbian and bisexual 'population' (as a percentage of the overall 'population') in the United States (Gates 2006). While the sale of sex is officially criminalised in San Francisco, male and transgender sex work is relatively organised in political terms and visible in cultural terms (for example, the city hosted one of the world's first art festivals for male sex workers in June 2009).

The discussion that follows draws on in-depth interviews with twelve San Francisco-based male escorts, which were undertaken in March-April 2008.[6] As noted above, the aim of this research was not to discover what 'type' of person becomes a male escort, nor to uncover some kind of underlying and essential 'reality' of the male sex industry. I was not motivated, therefore, by the desire to find out whether male sex workers are 'just as exploited' as female ones, for this arguably rests upon the assumption that there *is* a sovereign subject of the female sex worker to be identified as exploited and who can, in turn, be compared with the sovereign subject of a male sex worker (and, for that matter, the sovereign subject of a San Francisco male sex worker). Yet there is a long-standing tendency in academic and policy debates to treat sex workers as defined by, or reduced to, the sale of sex (as in the claim that prostitutes sell 'themselves') or, alternatively, as atomised, autonomous and rational decision-makers (for a review see Scoular 2004). In contrast, my research was informed by an understanding of sex workers as multiply constructed subjects who are 'socially constituted within complex

---

6 Respondents were identified via openly-accessible online male escorting sites, with just under one third agreeing to be interviewed. The interviews lasted between one and five hours and were tape-recorded and then transcribed (with the exception of one, as consent was withheld for this). Interviews took place either face-to-face in restaurants and bars in San Francisco's city centre and 'gay quarter' or over the telephone, and took the form of relaxed, informal and two-way conversations that were loosely structured in order to create as much space as possible for interviewees to elaborate on their motivations, experiences and understandings of commercial sex. The content of each interview varied, but common themes included participants' reasons for entering the industry, their perceptions of its benefits and drawbacks, and their views on the appropriateness of current policy frameworks with respect to commercial sex. All interviewees have been guaranteed complete confidentiality with respect to their identities, with all names and certain other identifying details altered accordingly.

social webs' along 'many (often contradictory) axes … [that] may involve not only gender identities, but also a full range of complex social relations and subject positions including ethnic, cultural, subcultural, sexual, regional, national, and other identities' (Barvosa-Carter 2001: 127). As such, I was interested in speaking *with* male sex workers (rather than *for* them, as some kind of unified and stable category), and I did so from multiple standpoints with the desire to capture a diversity of context-specific meanings (see O'Neill 2000: 67). I therefore see these accounts of lived experiences 'as texts and discourses through which subjects constitute themselves with identities, goals, interests and desires' (Hansen 2010: 24) whilst also fully recognising my own role as an active participant in (rather than a detached observer of) the construction of meaning(s).

Male Sex Work in San Francisco

> I – like everyone else who went into this business – went into it because I chose to go into it. I have a lot of different options, I have two college degrees. I was practicing as a lawyer – and I hated it. Sitting in an office researching all day, all night, I had no life whatsoever, and I chose to get out of that and to do something else … [Now] I work from my home: I brush my teeth, I sit on my computer, I can be wearing nothing, I can be wearing whatever I want, dealing with email all day, and I meet one or two persons a day. And I do it in my own time, I'm my own boss, I don't have to deal with all of the office politics, if I want to go out of town I don't have to ask HR for permission, I just do it. That's pretty nice. And the added benefit is: oh, I'm being paid to have sex. Hello! I don't find that a tough job (Josh, early thirties).

The work of Elizabeth Bernstein (2007a; 2007b) has drawn attention to the growing participation of middle-class, white professionals in the commercial sex sector in post-industrial cities of the West, including San Francisco. As she outlines, in recent years modern-industrial street prostitution in San Francisco has progressively been replaced with new, diverse and spatially dispersed forms. This has been made possible by a combination of local developments – including sustained campaigns by the police to crack down on street work – and large-scale ones – such as the reorientation away from productive labour and towards services and consumption in urban centres. For example, the dot-com boom of the 1990s led to an influx of young professionals into San Francisco, and they have been 'at the forefront of a new economy in sexual services, both by creating a demand for them and by facilitating new conditions of production' (2007b: 38). In particular, Bernstein identifies a discernible shift in the practice(s) of commercial sex both in social terms (i.e. from street-based communities to individually-based and technologically-mediated encounters) and in spatial terms (i.e. from outdoor to indoor work) (ibid.: 69). She links such changes, moreover, to the emergence of a new 'postindustrial paradigm of sexual commerce' (ibid.: 175) in which the emotional meaning(s) attached to commercial sex are being redefined. Whereas Western sexuality has traditionally been constructed in terms of a 'relational' sexual ethic predicated on marital/durable relationships, Bernstein points to the rise of a 'recreational' sexual ethic[7] that 'derives its primary meaning from the depth of physical sensation and from emotionally bounded erotic exchange' (ibid.: 6). Crucially, although relational sexuality has been positioned explicitly in ideological opposition to market activity, recreational sexuality 'is available for sale and purchase as readily as any other form of commercially packaged leisure activity' (ibid.: 7).

While Bernstein's work has been criticised on the grounds that she draws overly-generalised conclusions about global sexual economies based on her analysis of just three cities (San Francisco, Amsterdam and Stockholm) (Weitzer 2010), I nevertheless found that the concept of a 'recreational sexual ethic' chimed with me a great deal when undertaking my own fieldwork in San Francisco. In particular, I was struck by the ways in which many of the men I spoke to appealed to discourses surrounding the sale of sex as a form of sexual exploration, self-expression and even spiritual discovery. To illustrate this with a 'living' example: Dennis was in his mid-forties and had been escorting for many years. Previously, he had been an academic and as part of that he had started reading about sexuality, which (as he put it) became something that he wanted to explore not just through the mind but also through the body. As Dennis explained, escorting was for him less about the money (as he had left what he considered to be a well-paying job to do it) and more about the exploration of sexuality for both him and his clients. Emphasising how fulfilling he finds escorting to be, Dennis talked about the very real and positive impact that he feels he has on people's lives, considering sexual therapy to be an important part of his job. Although he could not share any specific stories due to the desire to respect his client's confidentiality, he saw his work as equally (if not more) effective than 'talking therapies' with respect to helping clients who had experienced sexual abuse, for instance. While Dennis expressed surprise that, at his age, he was still able to escort full-time, he also anticipated moving on to something else in a few years on the grounds that he has found it so rewarding to have a 'life change' and wants to experience as much as he can before he dies. As Dennis articulated, sex work above all represented, for him, a form of embodied critique of the social norms and stigmas surrounding sexuality.

Tony, who was in his early fifties and had specialised in BDSM[8] for several years, also took pains to emphasise how escorting represents a celebration of sex based upon the recognition of 'its therapeutic value, its intrinsic value, its necessary value'. As he explained, he had been brought up in a 'right-wing, fundamentalist Republican' family who considered his homosexuality to be 'wrong and other than acceptable' (he was no longer in contact with them). The sale of sexual services, he argued, offered a way through which he could re-envision (and thus reclaim)

---

7   Here she explicitly draws on the work of Edward Laumann et al. (1994).

8   BDSM is an acronym referring to bondage, discipline, sadism and masochism.

spirituality from the 'religiosity' he had been brought up with: 'there's a word that I like that refers to what I do – it's called "sacred intimate". And it literally confers the idea that what you do has a sacred quality about it because of it connecting with the spirit of the person that you are interchanging with'. Escorting thus offered both a means of sexual exploration and a means to resist 'Puritanical' societal norms, for 'our background here [the US] has made sex like the most wrong thing you could possibly think of'. As he concluded: 'I'm very, very lucky – I consider myself one of the luckiest men in the world, to do what I do and to be able to do it with the people I do … it's all wonderful and it's all experimental'.

When listening to and engaging with such narratives, I was conscious of how the sex-positive and sex-radical discourses they invoked have so often been dismissed on the grounds that they are 'unrepresentative' of prostitution experiences more broadly (see for instance Jeffreys 1997; O'Connell Davidson 1998). Certainly sex-positive and sex-radical accounts (such as Chapkis 1989; Bell 1994; Paglia 1994) tend to privilege the voices of sex workers who occupy positions of relative structural advantage (i.e. they are Western, white, middle-class, and so on) and, as such, can be criticised for overlooking how uneven power relations impact upon the ability of more-marginalised sex workers to 'mount discursive challenges' (Scoular 2004: 348). The majority of the men I interviewed did indeed consider themselves to be middle-class professionals (for example, two had worked as classically-trained musicians, one had been in bio-technology, and all but two were university-educated), with every one also claiming to be making an extremely good living from sex work (as much as ten thousand dollars a month). While I did not regard the people I interviewed to be somehow 'representative' of San Francisco sex workers[9], I was also constantly mindful of the 'culturally and historically contingent quality of global sex [commerce] as it unfolds in local cultural contexts' (Padilla 2007: 6) when undertaking my fieldwork. As Bernstein (2007b) outlines, the position of relative socio-economic advantage that many of the city's sex workers seem to occupy can be related to San Francisco's broader political-economic context, including its participation in the global knowledge-economy. For example, two-thirds of San Francisco's formal workforce are engaged in knowledge-related positions (*San Francisco Business Times*, 22 May 2009) and, while 11.2 per cent of the county's population are below the US Census poverty line (US Census Bureau 2010), it has been ranked both as America's fourth most expensive city (Mercer 2009) and as its second 'greediest' city in terms of the proportion of the population who were classified as 'super-rich' (*Forbes*, 3 December 2007).

As participants in, and beneficiaries of, San Francisco's prosperous post-industrial economy, the male escorts I interviewed were therefore situated in a position of relative socio-economic privilege compared to many other sex workers in the global sexual economy (and, to some extent, the local one; a small number of

---

9 The people who accepted my interview request were also more likely to have been the very same people who felt the most comfortable with, and positive about, their work.

street-workers still operated on the Castro, for instance). That having been said, it was not so much the state of San Francisco's economy but rather its socio-cultural climate that interviews emphasised when talking about their own experiences of sex work. In particular, they pointed to San Francisco's long history of offering a relatively accepting and tolerant social context within which divergent sexualities could be practiced and expressed. Since the 1970s, San Francisco has become known as a 'gay cultural Mecca' (Armstrong 2002: 115), with key developments including the rapid rise of gay identity organisations (from just one in 1970 to over three hundred less than two decades later), the creation of the first dedicated gay neighbourhood (Castro) in the United States, the increased size and visibility of the annual Freedom Day Parade, and the growth of gay migration to the city (see ibid. and D'Emilio 1989 for detailed social histories of San Francisco's gay movement). As Tony, for instance, outlined: 'There's something about San Francisco, in general, that is more liberal than any other place in the country ... So divergent people – people of divergent lifestyles and opinions – seem to gravitate here'.

Indeed, if any kind of 'shared' narrative of experience emerged from most (if not all) of the interviews, it was that male escorting could be regarded as a form of resistance to – and, in some cases, outright rebellion against – the perceived cultural norms of American society-at-large. More specifically, the sale of sex was frequently constructed as an open challenge to what Adrienne Rich (1980: 631) has famously termed 'compulsory heterosexuality'. In the words of Josh, for instance:

> Everyone in their lives feels controlled – particularly sexually. And the idea that there is this group of people out there who aren't part of this system of control makes all of us who are part of the system of control feel very uncomfortable ... And part of the discomfort that the rest of society feels towards those who are homosexual is that they do blur those lines ... But whether someone is trying to create a law about homosexual sex, about prostitution, about drug-use, about bigamy – all of those things are always somebody else imposing their views, usually from religion, on to us.

Yet, as much as San Francisco was praised for offering a fairly progressive sexual environment, many of the men I spoke to also pointed to the lack of official sanctioning of prostitution there. Prostitution remains illegal in San Francisco following the defeat of Proposition K on 4 November 2008 (which would have banned police from using public resources to investigate or prosecute people engaged in prostitution) (San Francisco Department of Elections 2008). The lack of legal legitimacy was, in turn, seen to exacerbate the social stigmas surrounding prostitution – including, crucially, amongst the gay community itself. Indeed, although escorting was constructed as a form of resistance to heterosexuality, so too a number of interviewees cautioned against conflating gay culture with sexual libertarianism and, more specifically, with social tolerance towards sex work. In particular, several of the men I spoke to remarked of a double-standard within and beyond San Francisco's gay community, with the *purchase* of sex deemed to be fairly acceptable (indeed, it was seen to be commonly practiced) but the *sale* of sex attracting considerable social stigma. (As Ben – who was in his mid-twenties and worked as an artist, film director and part-time escort – articulated: 'A lot of gay men look down on escorting – they're kind of able to move that line over just enough to accept themselves being gay, but not escorts').[10] Indeed, most of the men I spoke to said that they did not feel able to tell their friends (whether gay or straight) – let alone their families – about their work for fear of being judged. (For instance, Simon – who was in his early thirties and had escorted for a year – reported that he had already lost two close friends 'because I don't feel that comfortable telling them'). This was something that I discussed at length with several of the interviewees, although we focused less on the psychological impact of stigma management (an issue that has received quite a bit of attention in the extant literature on male sex work – see for instance Koken, Bimbi et al. 2004; Morrison and Whitehead 2007) and more on the societal norms underpinning sex work's lack of cultural legitimacy, even within the gay community. As a feminist scholar, I was especially interested by the way in which Josh made sense of this in explicitly gendered terms (although admittedly this was within the context of an earlier conversation about feminism that I had instigated). Pointing to the 'anti-female' values of Western society (which he attributed to the influence of Judeo-Christian-Islamic culture), Josh argued that for the gay community, too: 'We still devalue things that are feminine' – hence, he suggested, why sex work retained its social stigma (i.e. as a 'feminine' occupation). Simon, too, pointed to the maintenance of gender hierarchies as a means to make sense of sex work's persistent stigma within and outside San Francisco's gay community. As he noted, for instance, there remains a clear demarcation between 'tops' and 'bottoms' (i.e. between those who perfect 'active' and 'passive' roles in commercial and other sexual transactions) along gendered lines, so that as he explained: 'If you're a top, you're still a man. But if you're a bottom, well …'.

At the same time, however, I found that interviewees also frequently appealed to dualistic gender logics when making sense of their own individual experiences – not least when distancing such experiences from those of 'other' sex workers. A common theme in the interviews was how the concepts of 'free choice' and 'consent' could be applied fairly unproblematically to their own working lives, and every single person I spoke to robustly dismissed the notion that the sale of sex is by definition exploitative. But frequent distinctions between sex workers were also drawn along gendered and racialised lines, with 'sex slaves' and 'trafficked women' constructed in direct opposition to the interviewees' own experiences and identities (interestingly, when I asked about this further I was informed that such

---

10   A contrasting account was put forward by Ethan, who was in his early twenties and had done quite a bit of pornography as part of his sex working career. As he put it: 'It's very, very accepting here [in San Francisco] – in fact it's looked on in a very positive light, it's like I'm kind of celebrity here for gay people. People look up to you in a way. That's probably what helps me do it'.

ideas about 'sex slaves' and 'trafficked women' were principally informed by news reports and films such as *Lilya 4-Ever*). In addition, binaries in terms of sexuality were sometimes appealed to, as well – although this was not always in order to highlight the interviewees' own sense of freedom. For instance, Adam – who was in his early twenties and had come to San Francisco from Eastern Europe several years ago – identified two types of escorts: those who are straight (like himself) and motivated primarily/purely by financial incentives, and those who are gay and find pleasure/enjoyment in their work due to the 'natural' fit between their sexuality and occupation. As Adam told me: 'the reason why I changed [became an escort] was because of the money. Even though I'm straight. I have to tell you that I'm one hundred per cent straight. I don't like doing this at all'. Adam therefore described his own experiences of escorting as 'hard to handle, it's kind of disturbing' due to his (hetero)sexuality (although he also explained that escorting with women was 'kind of terrible – worse than what I do now').[11] At the same time, however, he also insisted that he was 'absolutely not' being exploited, for 'lots of people do their jobs and they don't like it' whereas 'I'm satisfied with my life because I know I have a future'. (His dream was to get rich, go home, find a wife, have children and run a property empire with the money he had made as an escort).

Adam's story brought to mind Dennis Altman's (1999: xiv) identification of two dominant narratives with respect to male sex work. The first narrative sees sex workers as not "really' homosexual and instead emphasises economic necessity as the key motivation for male sex work. As Davies and Feldman (1997: 32) write, the male sex worker/rent-boy is imagined as 'a young heterosexual male, suborned against his will into the lowest and vilest of practices, existing in a relationship of economic dependency and emotional antagonism with his despised but necessary clients'. The second narrative, by contrast, is more 'far more romantic' and depicts the sex worker as '"really" homosexual, who uses the sale of his body as a form of legitimation for what is otherwise unacknowledgeable' (Altman 1999: xiv). While such narratives have rarely been articulated in explicit dialogue with feminist theory, they nevertheless mirror what Bell (1994: 137) calls 'the dichotomisation of the prostitute body into an abused body and an empowered body' in feminist and modernist discourse. I was intrigued, therefore, to meet Michael, who framed his own life story in terms of an explicit rejection of such binaries. Now in his mid-thirties, Michael said that he had sold sex since becoming a street hustler in his teens in order to fund a serious drug addict. At that time, Michael – who noted how he had been abused as a child and had also struggled with his sexuality – found that selling sex reinforced a sense of self-hatred: 'People would pay me to have sex with me, and I didn't realise the value of what I was giving to them, and I didn't realise the value of what I was doing'. Several years ago, however, he had both kicked the drugs and become close friends with a female escort who told him

---

11 As he explained: 'You know, if I do oral with a guy, with condoms, you don't feel that much. But with a woman who is two hundred pounds and you can hardly get closer and you have to work on her for two hours and she's hiring for half the money – that's terrible'.

about the therapeutic and spiritual value of sex work: 'I kind of had a spiritual awakening in my life ... [Now]I totally believe in my heart that this is what I'm supposed to be doing right now'. In particular, Michael was keen to emphasise that what he offers is, above all, skills, caring and intimacy: for example, he found it particularly rewarding to help clients who felt unattractive to feel desirable, because he 'knows what it feels like to hate your body'.

Yet, just as many of the men I spoke to emphasised the (positive) social value of commercial sex, so too they appealed to the 'right' to engage in sex work in terms of (negative) social freedoms. For, while the sale of sex was presented as a direct expression of resistance to dominant hetero-normative gender models, equally such resistance was often articulated through straightforward appeals to neo-liberal free-market ideology (such as in claims that it is 'just business' or that it represents little more than a 'choice ... to go to someone and make money and profit off of it'). In this sense, the expansion of capitalist markets into the sexual realm was seen not only as a logical extension of the economic sphere but also as an important means of securing personal freedoms. Within this context, I was not surprised that although the need for the removal of legal constraints on commercial sex was consistently stressed by interviewees, this was not seen to translate into the need for social and labour rights too. (Quite the contrary: the strong sense was that government should 'keep its hands off our bodies' and the idea of having to formally register as 'legitimate' workers – including having to pay taxation as such – was not regarded as a welcome one). While this faith in unregulated markets jarred somewhat with my own normative commitments – indeed, a common criticism of sex worker activist discourse is that it reproduces rather than challenges neo-liberal market ideology (see for instance Dickinson 2006; Penttinen 2008) – I was also fascinated by the way in which commodification was itself articulated as a form of resistance in this way. For, as Noah Zatz (1997: 277) reminds us, commercial sex can be read as subversive precisely because of its 'open challenge both to the identification of sex acts with acts of desire and to the opposition between erotic/affective activity and economic life'. In Euro-American culture in particular, the association of labour with the public realm and intimacy/ desire with the private realm means that sexuality is viewed as something that should not be 'bought'; money and sexuality are 'thought of as things that cannot, do not, and/or should not mix' (ibid.: 294). Seen in these terms, commercial sex represents a space in which the boundary between the (public) sphere of work and the (private) sphere of sexuality is 'constantly transgressed' – hence its lack of cultural and institutional legitimacy (ibid.: 298-9). This was something that Ben, for instance, articulated very clearly. As he said: 'We, as a culture, we place shame on our body. The idea that you're commodifying your body – people consider it very degrading'.

Above all, I found that – although the men I spoke to clearly regarded themselves as transgressive – they also appealed to dominant gender logics (and, for that matter, neo-liberal discourse) as a means to make sense of their working lives. To bring the discussion back to Elizabeth Bernstein's work, I certainly found that the sale of sex was 'subjectively normalised' (2007b: 7) in terms of how many of the interviewees spoke of their own attitudes towards the work. But what the concept of a 'recreational sexual ethic' does not capture so well, perhaps, is the complexity of layered meanings that emerged in these narratives (or, at least, in my reading of these narratives, which is what I have been able to offer here). Rather than attempting to impose some kind of resolution and uniformity on to these tensions and contradictions, I have instead been reminded of Carole Vance's (1992: 3) famous claim that the 'hallmark of sexuality is its complexity: its multiple meanings, sensations, and connections'. Yet it is precisely this potential for complexity – that is, for multiple, divergent and contested experiences and understandings of commercial sex – that is/are so often closed off in academic and policy debates, which instead 'enclose the prostitute body within a theorised totality' (Bell 1994: 187). In presenting these (necessarily partial) fragments and stories, my aim has not been to posit an opposing and overarching 'truth' of commercial sex as a means to somehow 'disprove' prevailing interpretations that it is an industry consisting essentially of sexually exploited, forced and trafficked female bodies. But I have nevertheless sought to render a little more visible how male bodies, too, are far from 'absent' in the global sexual economy (Pettman 1997: 95), whilst also attempting to contribute towards a broader feminist political economy agenda of making actually-existing human lives a central part of the story I have told.

Conclusion

Central to feminist political economy is the desire to interrogate the 'lower circuits' of capital relations – that is, domestic labour, janitorial/custodial work, tourism and sex work – as opposed to (exclusively) the 'upper circuits' of capital relations – that is, trade, financial markets, capital flows (Agathangelou 2005: 7). Within this context, the analysis of global sexual economies has emerged not only as an important area of enquiry in its own right but also as part of a broader feminist agenda to re-map the conceptual and empirical terrain of International Political Economy as a field of study. Emphasising the profound importance of this literature, I have nevertheless noted how much scholarship on commercial sex remains predicated (whether explicitly or explicitly) on an imagined ideal-type of female worker and male client, so that the sex industry is not only only explored as a femin*ised* sphere of work but is also directly tied to female bodies. Emphasising the need to address this gap in contemporary theorising and empirical analysis, I have then offered an illustration of research into male sex work through discussion of how male escorts in San Francisco negotiate the complex meanings and practices surrounding gender, sexuality and political economy.

Acknowledgements

This chapter represents a considerably revised and extended version of an earlier article, 'Body Issues: The Political Economy of Male Sex Work', *Sexualities,* 2012, 15: 5, 586-603, http://sexualities.sagepub.com. I would very much like to thank the Leverhulme Trust for their support for my research into male and transgender sex work (Project Grant RCEJI4969).

References

Acker, J. 1990. Hierarchies, Jobs, Bodies: A Theory of Gendered Organisations, *Gender and Society*, 4(2), 139–58.

Agathangelou, A. M. 2005. *The Global Political Economy of Sex: Desire, Violence and Insecurity in Mediterranean Nation States*, Basingstoke: Palgrave.

———. and Ling, L. H. M. 2003. Desire Industries: Sex Trafficking, UN Peace-Keeping and the Neo-Liberal World Order, *Brown Journal of World Affairs*, 10(1), 133–48.

Altman, D. 1999. Foreword, *Men Who Sell Sex*, in P. Aggleton (ed.) London: UCL Press, xiii-xix.

Armstrong, E. 2002. *Forging Gay Identities: Organising Sexuality in San Francisco, 1950–94*, Chicago: University of Chicago Press.

Barry, K. L. 1995. *The Prostitution of Sexuality: The Global Exploitation of Women*, New York: NYU Press.

Barvosa-Carter, E. 2001. Strange Tempest: Agency, Poststructuralism, and the Shape of Feminist Politics to Come, *International Journal of Sexuality and Gender Studies*, 6(1–2), 123–37.

Bell, S. 1994. *Reading, Writing and Rewriting the Prostitute Body*, Indianapolis: Indiana University Press.

Beneria, L. 2003. *Gender, Development and Globalisation: Economics as If All People Mattered*, London: Routledge.

Bernstein, E. 2007a. Sex Work for the Middle Classes, *Sexualities*, 10(4), 473–88.

———. 2007b. *Temporarily Yours: Intimacy, Authenticity and the Commerce of Sex*, Chicago: University of Chicago Press.

Browne, K. 2004. Genderism and the Bathroom Problem: (Re)Materialising Sexed Sites, (Re)Creating Sexed Bodies, *Gender, Place & Culture*, 11(3), 331–46.

Bryman, A. 2008. *Social Research Methods*, Oxford: Oxford University Press.

Butler, J. 1999. *Gender Trouble: Feminism and the Subversion of Identity*, London: Routledge.

Cabezas, A. 2009. *Economies of desire: sex and tourism in Cuba and the Dominican Republic*. Philadelphia, Temple University Press.

Chapkis, W. (1989) *Live Sex Acts: Women Performing Erotic Labour*, New York: Routledge.

————. 2002. The Meaning of Sex, *Sexuality and Gender*, in C. L. Williams and A. Stein (eds.) London: Blackwell, 207–20.

Charusheela, S. 2008. Labor Activism, Sweatshops, Slavery, and the Categories of Class Analysis, *Rethinking Marxism*.

Chow, E. N.-l. C. 2003. Gender Matters: Studying Globalisation and Social Change in the 21st Century, *International Sociology*, 18(3), 443–60.

Collins, D. 2007. When Sex Work Isn't "Work": Hospitality, Gay Life, and the Production of Desiring Labour, *Tourist Studies*, 7(2), 115–39.

D'Emilio, J. 1989. Gay Politics and Community in San Francisco since World War Ii, *Hidden from History: Reclaiming the Gay and Lesbian Past*, in B. Duberman, M. Vicinus and G. Chaucey (eds.) New York: New American Library, 456–73.

Davies, P. and Feldman, R. 1997. Prostitute Men Now, *Rethinking Prostitution: Purchasing Sex in the 1990s*, in G. Scrambler and A. Scrambler (eds.) London: Routledge, 29–53.

Dickinson, D. 2006. Philosophical Assumptions and Presumptions About Trafficking for Prostitution, *Trafficking and Women's Rights*, in C. van den Anker and J. Doomernick (eds.) Basingstoke: Palgrave, 43–53.

Doezema, J. 1998. Forced to Choose: Beyond the Voluntary V. Forced Prostitution Dichotomy, *Global Sex Workers: Rights, Resistance and Definition*, in K. Kempadoo and J. Doezema (eds.) London: Routledge, 34–50.

————. 2005. Now You See Her, Now You Don't: Sex Workers at the UN Trafficking Protocol Negotiations, *Social and Legal Studies*, 14(1), 61–89.

————. 2010. *Sex Slaves and Discourse Masters: The Construction of Trafficking*. London, Zed.

Dworkin, A. 1992. Prostitution and Male Supremacy, *Prostitution: From Academia to Activism*. University of Michigan Law School.

Enloe, C. H. 2001. *Bananas, Beaches and Bases: Making Feminist Sense of International Politics*: University of California Press.

Fawcett, B. 2000. *Practice and Research in Social Work*, London: Routledge.

Gates, G. J. 2006. Same-Sex Couples and the Gay, Lesbian, Bisexual Population: New Estimates from the American Community Survey. Los Angeles: The Williams Insitute, UCLA.

Gottfried, H. 2004. Gendering Globalisation Discourses, *Critical Sociology*, 30(1), 9–15.

Griffin, P. 2009. *Gendering the World Bank: Neoliberalism and the Gendered Foundations of Global Governance*. Basingstoke: Palgrave.

Hansen, L. 2010. Ontologies, Epistemologies, Methodologies, *Gender Matters in Global Politics: A Feminist Introduction to International Relations*, in L. Shepherd (ed.) London: Routledge, 17–27.

Harcourt, W. 2009. *Body Politics in Development: Critical Debates in Gender and Development*, London: Zed Books.

Hooper, C. 2000. Disembodiment, Embodiment and the Construction of Hegemonic Masculinity, *Political Economy, Power and the Body*, in G. Youngs (ed.) Basingstoke: Palgrave, 31–51.

———. 2001. *Manly States: Masculinities, International Relations and Gender Politics*, New York: Columbia University Press.

Jeffreys, S. 1997. *The Idea of Prostitution*, North Melbourne: Spinifex Press.

———. 2008. *The Industrial Vagina: The Political Economy of the Global Sex Trade*, London: Routledge.

Kempadoo, K. and Doezema, J. eds. 1998. *Global Sex Workers: Rights, Resistance and Definition*, London: Routledge.

Koken, J. A., Bimbi, D. S., et al. 2004. The Experience of Stigma and the Lives of Male Internet Escorts, *Journal of Psychology & Human Sexuality*, 16(1), 13–32.

Laumann, E. O., Gagnon, J. H., et al. 1994. *The Social Organisation of Sexuality: Sexual Practices in the United States*, Chicago: University of Chicago Press.

Mercer. 2009. Worldwide Cost of Living Survey 2009 – City Ranking.

Morrison, T. G. and Whitehead, B. W. 2007. "Nobody's Ever Going to Make a Fag Pretty Woman": Stigma Awareness and the Putative Effects of Stigma among a Sample of Canadian Male Sex Workers, *Journal of Homosexuality*, 53(1–2), 201–17.

O'Connell Davidson, J. 1998. *Prostitution, Power and Freedom*, Michigan: University of Michigan Press.

———. and Sanchez Taylor, J. 2005. The Informal Tourist Economy in the Caribbean: Gender, Race and Age: ESRC Final Report R000237625: ESRC.

O'Neill, M. 2000. *Prostitution and Feminism: Towards a Politics of Feeling*, Cambridge: Polity Press.

Ozbay, C. 2010. Nocturnal Queers: Rent Boys' Masculinity in Istanbul, *Sexualities*, 13(5), 645–63.

Padilla, M. 2007. *Caribbean Pleasure Industry: Tourism, Sexuality and AIDS in the Dominican Republic*, Chicago: University of Chicago Press.

Paglia, C. 1994. *Vamps and Tramps: New Essays*, London: Penguin.

Pateman, C. 1988. *The Sexual Contract*, Stanford: Stanford University Press.

Penttinen, E. 2008. *Globalisation, Prostitution and Sex Trafficking: Corporeal Politics*, London: Routledge.

Peterson, V. S. 2003. *A Critical Rewriting of Global Political Economy: Integrating Reproductive, Productive and Virtual Economies*, London: Routledge.

———. 2005. How (the Meaning of) Gender Matters in Political Economy, *New Political Economy*, 10(4), 499–521.

———. 2010. International/Global Political Economy, *Gender Matters in Global Politics: A Feminist Introduction to International Relations*, in L. Shepherd (ed.) London: Routledge, 204–17.

Pettman, J. J. 1996. *Worlding Women: A Feminist International Politics*, London: Routledge.

————. 1997. Body Politics: International Sex Tourism, *Third World Quarterly*, 18(1), 93–108.

————. 2000. Writing the Body: Transnational Sex, *Political Economy, Power and the Body*, in G. Youngs (ed.) Basingstoke: Palgrave, 52–71.

————. 2003. International Sex and Service, *Globalisation: Theory and Practice*, in E. Kofman and G. Youngs (eds.) London: Continuum, 157–73.

Phoenix, J. 2001. *Making Sense of Prostitution*, Basingstoke: Palgrave.

Rich, A. 1980. Compulsory Heterosexuality and Lesbian Existence, *Signs*, 5(4), 631–60.

San Francisco Department of Elections (2008) City and County of San Francisco Consolidated Presidential General Election, 4 November 2008: Election Summary.

Scoular, J. 2004. The "Subject" Of Prostitution: Interpreting the Discursive, Symbolic and Material Position of Sex/Work in Feminist Theory, *Feminist Theory*, 5: 3, 343–55.

Smith, N. J.-A. 2011. The International Political Economy of Commercial Sex, *Review of International Political Economy*, 18(4), 530–49.

Steans, J. 2006. *Gender and International Relations*, Cambridge: Polity.

————. and D. Tepe. 2010. Social reproduction in the international political economy: theoretical insights and international, transnational and local sitings. *Review of International Political Economy* 17(5), 807–815.

US Census Bureau. 2010. State and County Quickfacts: San Francisco County, California, http://quickfacts.census.gov/qfd/states/06/06075.html.

van der Veen, M. 2001. Rethinking Commodification and Prostitution: An Effort at Peacemaking in the Battles over Prostitution, *Rethinking Marxism*, 13(2), 30–51.

Vance, C. S. 1992. Pleasure and Danger: Towards a Politics of Sexuality, *Pleasure and Danger: Exploring Female Sexuality*, in C. Vance (ed.) London: Pandora, 1–27.

Watson, M. 2005. *Foundations of International Political Economy*, Basingstoke: Palgrave.

Waylen, G. 2006. You Still Don't Understand: Why Troubled Engagements Continue between Feminists and (Critical) IPE, *Review of International Studies*, 32, 145–64.

Weitzer, R. 2010. Book Review: "Temporarily Yours: Intimacy, Authenticity and the Commerce of Sex" By Elizabeth Bernstein, *Gender & Society*, 24(1), 135–7.

Whitworth, S. 1996. *Feminism in International Relations: Towards a Political Economy of Gender in Interstate and Non-Governmental Institutions*, London: Macmillan.

Youngs, G. 2000a. Embodied Political Economy or an Escape from Disembodied Knowledge, *Political Economy, Power and the Body*, in G. Youngs (ed.) Basingstoke: Palgrave, 11–30.

————. 2000b. Introduction, *Political Economy, Power and the Body*, in G. Youngs (ed.) Basingstoke: Palgrave, 1–8.

————. 2004. Feminist International Relations: A Contradiction in Terms? Or: Why Women and Gender Are Essential to Understanding the World 'We' Live In, *International Affairs*, 80 (1), 75–87.

Zatz, N. D. 1997 Sex Work/Sex Act: Law, Labour and Desire in Constructions of Prostitution, *Signs*, 22 (2), 277–308.

Chapter 8

Asian Bodies/Western States (of Mind): A Postmodern Feminist Reading of Reproduction in East Asian Cultures

Ming Lim

Introduction

What is the status of the female body/subject in East Asian societies today? In this paper, I consider this question, among others, through a double lens: the postmodern constructions of the female subject and subjectivity (Hekman, 1991), and sociologies of global risk and 'compressed modernity' that have disrupted (and continues to disrupt) age-old practices of consumption, production and reproduction in Neo-Confucian societies (Beck and Beck-Gernsheim, 2001; Beck and Grande, 2010).

This double perspective is both intimidating and potentially revealing. Debates around female subjectivity are historically, epistemologically and ontologically situated in ways which make easy assertions impossible; at the same time, post-industrial nations in East Asian (South Korea, Taiwan, Hong Kong and Singapore) pose immensely complex challenges for gender studies. These cultures have been influenced by, and also transform, Western modes of feminist theory and practice in ways which generate complex modifications of gender relations (Truong, 1999).

As noted by Tu (1996: 17), there can be no simple "fusion of horizons" between the realities of East Asian development trajectories and the Confucian heritage of these societies. The dynamic interplay of intellectual, social, political, and economic currents in Japan and the Four Mini-Dragons (South Korea, Taiwan, Hong Kong, and Singapore), may be shaped by Confucianism but the highly compressed pace of modernization and Westernization in these countries calls for a reassessment of how such age-old cultures of authority, ideology and hierarchy are changing gender relations and gender studies. These changes offer an exciting opportunity for feminists, East and West, to debate these issues from a critical, transcultural and multidiscplinary perspective. As Klimenkova (1992: 283) observes, the plurality and diversity of women's experiences in the global economy today sharpens the need for feminists "to take into account not only the experience of past epochs, but also the diversified experience (woman's experience in this case) in different strata: the experience of women not only in the West but also in other parts of the world".

This chapter, therefore, aims to examine the female body in these societies in terms of "the interrelationship of gender and the circuits of consumption, distribution, production and reproduction" (Brah and Coombes, 1997) from perspectives inspired by postmodernism. Specifically, I wish to explore the implications of current debates for the female body in East Asian cultures and its status as subject in such debates. Drawing upon both Western as well as Eastern perspectives, I argue that such an exploration is urgently needed in the field of feminist scholarship for several reasons. First and foremost, it can illuminate the vital question of what kinds of political agency are being exercised through women's embodied practices. If, as Hekman (1991: 44) contends, "political agency is vital to the formulation of a feminist politics," then an understanding of how political conditions shape women's choices in East Asia is crucial to understanding the emergence of feminist politics in that context. But we can still go further than this. By understanding the political contexts and practices of East Asian women, we enrich our understanding not only of the politics of feminism but the politics of the *bodily* choices women make. The female body, in other words, has *its* development trajectory. Second, East Asian feminist studies, I argue, problematizes and illuminates postmodern critiques of the subject that have shaped Western debates around the female body/subject and its agency and/ or passivity. Third, and more broadly speaking, there is increasing evidence that East Asian women are radically renegotiating the complex and shifting contract between the body and the state. Postmodernist perspectives on gender, with their emphasis on the culturally-mediated otherness of Asian, African and Middle Eastern cultures, provide a means of understanding how East Asian women's bodies traverse the boundaries between autonomy and control.

One problem, however (among others), is the issue of translation. Terms like 'gender', 'the body' and 'feminism' carry different connotations and cultural nuances in different languages and have an ideological and ontological charge which differs across the cultures in question.

These issues notwithstanding, a standard narrative of East Asian womanhood and her body persists in the literature. For decades, it has been possible (and, indeed, common) for researchers to point to the oppressive and discriminatory nature of Confucian culture upon women's bodies. The notion of subjectivity in East Asian feminist studies is complicated by the neo-Confucian theme which exercises governmental power over family, gender relations and the female position in the cosmic hierarchy. Women's bodies were both valorized and also subjected to a range of disciplinary norms. Above all, women's bodies were to be cared for and unaltered because they were the vehicle for carrying a child and heir. She was a subject insofar as she carried an 'other' subject, the sex of which would have profound consequences for her familial and social position. Scholars are now beginning to re-examine this standard narrative in terms of its 20th and 21st century socio-economic and cultural manifestations (Beck and Beck-Gernsheim, 2002; Chang, 2009; Chang, 1997).

The question of female bodies and female subjectivity can thus be seen, in more recent discussions, as a problematic which needs to acknowledge the nuanced and diverse meanings of the 'subject'. The caveats between postmodernism and feminism, in other words, now become particularly relevant in the East Asian context because it is precisely the constitution of the 'subject' that is changing in these societies. It is these caveats, and how they are refracted through a consideration of East Asian female subjectivity, that forms the focus of my paper. I argue that a postmodern construction of the East Asian body/subject can, and should, be undertaken in order to illuminate the changing dynamics of female resistance to neo-Confucian biopolitics.

The 'postmodern,' of course, remains a highly contested category of thought and set of discourses but let us allow, for the moment, a notion of postmodern thinking, as a means of acknowledging and understanding heterogeneity, displacement and a search for new meanings in practical ways. It has to be noted, however, that feminists have had, for several decades now, a fractious relationship with key tenets of postmodernism (I touch upon some of the features of this relationship in the next section), but I maintain that postmodernist theorizations of the subject can still enliven and illuminate contexts of great change or even crisis, situations where consumers either entertain, or embody, a sense of possibility, of adventure, of choice and alternativity in the midst of difficult circumstances. Indeed, certain features of postmodernism, as I see it, allows us to take a step forward to a moment when, as Susan Bordo insightfully argues, "the significance and vitality of those 'other truths' (the truths made available through *non-European* cultural traditions, through gendered experience, through histories of subordination) would be culturally recognized" (1993:282, my emphasis). Postmodern constructions of 'othernesses', therefore, become possible and are vindicated by studying cultural traditions touched profoundly by Confucianism, Buddhism and other strands of spiritual humanism.

A key thread in these arguments on risk derives from the work of sociologists concerned with the impacts of historical transformation upon everyday life and how individuals construct choices in the context of 'second modernity' and 'reflexive modernization' (Beck and Grande, 2010; Beck and Beck-Gernsheim, 2001). This work builds upon notions of global risk and its implications for individuals and societies (Beck, Giddens and Lash, 1995). Very recently, East Asian scholars have taken on their theories and greatly expanded on them in terms of their applicability to East Asian cultures (Han and Shim, 2010; Chang, 2010). It is noted that the scale and speed of compressed modernization has resulted in "high consequential risks in East Asian countries whose complexities, heterogeneities, and intensities seem to surpass those experienced in Western countries" (Han and Shim, 2010: 474). Perceived risks based on public opinion run the gamut from ecological destruction to traffic jams and real estate prices.

The key questions which inform this paper are, therefore: 'What are the emerging constructions of the female body in East Asian societies and the regulatory/political contexts through which women exercise agency? What are the interanimations, the confluences, the fault lines in this shifting contract between states and the individual vis-à-vis the body? And, last but not least, how can we theorize the existing and emerging sites of resistance for women in how the gendered body is produced and consumed by the state and societal actors?

This chapter begins with a brief summary of the neo-Confucian context to the modern East Asian body. Drawing upon postmodernism, I then proceed to examine the politico-social regulation of the female body, focusing specifically on the status of its subjectivity and concomitant issues related to how bodies interact with forces of societal risk and personal calculations of those risks. Of particular interest for my paper is the biopolitical choices displayed by women's bodies with regard to pregnancy, childbirth, reproduction. The implications of such choices are re-examined through a new take on postmodern feminism. Finally, I conclude with some thoughts for future research.

Context: The Neo-Confucian Body/Subject in East Asian Societies

For over 500 years, the precepts of Neo-Confucianism have prevailed in Korea, Japan and China, anchoring men, women, children, families and society in a schema and set of hierarchies which, up until the 20th century, governed women's bodies according to strict codes of morality. That Confucian precepts have played a governing role in relations between the state and the family, between the family and its members and between men and women for centuries is beyond question. Its key tenets are still pervasive in East Asia today. These societies may have transformed themselves economically and politically but culturally, Confucian ideas have, until recently, at least, continued to exercise a powerful hold on the collective consciousness of their people: duty to family, state, society and Heaven, filial piety and cultivation of the moral self. The centrality of the family unit in Confucian thought has directly influenced the position of women in society and also the function and status of her body as a near-sacred vessel of *ki*, a material and spiritual force which flows through all things and bodies and which unites every particle in the universe (Lee, 1993; DeBary et al., 1960). *Ki* cannot be destroyed and has to be nurtured as well as passed on through the generations. The *ki* of one's ancestors flow continuously and powerfully through the ages; one's body was thus part of the body of the family, the community, the state and, ultimately, of the great universe itself.

The Neo-Confucian exhortations to cultivate self, wisdom and self-knowledge, however, extended only to men. Women were not supposed to strive explicitly for such self-understanding and self-transcendence; instead, they had the role of *instantiating* the body of the family, of making it corporeal so that future generations could survive. Yet, far from being an active, generative, creative force for life, her body was conceived of as a passive receptacle for *ki*, the male force (Yoon, 1990). Bearing sons, therefore, was infinitely better than producing daughters. The overwhelming focus on the woman's body as bearer of life rather than as an autonomous subject meant that they were regarded as *"subjectless bodies*" (Kim, 2003: 101). While she was supposed to exercise great care over her body during pregnancy, making sure it was covered and, indeed, veiled at all times while outside the house (Deuchler, 1992), she was not supposed to alter or try to improve her bodily form in any way. Her body was to be invisible.

This attitude to the female body in Neo-Confucianism is troubling to a number of Asian feminist philosophers. Lai (2000: 127), for instance, questions the long-standing criticism of Confucian thought as one which "does not provide avenues for women to succeed beyond the domestic context". The Confucian emphasis on the woman's body as the vessel and carrier of reproductive labour has, over the last four to five decades, come under strain as East Asia embarked upon rapid industrialization, modernization and Western-style capitalism. At the same time, the structural and political constraints of neo-Confucian theories of the woman's body *have not entirely vanished*.

Female Bodies: States of Mind and the Mind of the State

In more recent times, the intersections between the female body and the state's rules, regulations, norms and constraints have taken on both new, and familiar, forms. It has been noted by anthropologists, political scientists and sociologists that although the state's dominion might have appeared to have conceded ground in the wake of neoliberalism the rise of transnational corporations and the globalisation of both trade and labour, its grip on individuals remains pervasive and unlocatable (Foucault, 1991; Taussig, 1997). The chosen site for state machinations is the individual's body, where, as Agamben (1998) notes, the latter's 'bare life' becomes both the subject and the object of the state's conflict. Modern politics conflates the subjectivity of individuals and their participation in public life and thus conjoins the law and violence. The state is now everywhere and in every body: "Bare life is no longer confined to a particular place or a definite category. It now dwells in the biological body of every living being." (Agamben, 1998, 139-140). In its extreme phase, the modern Western state integrates techniques of subjective surveillance with procedures of objective totalization (through penal, civil and juridical institutions), creating what Foucault (1994) identifies as a real "political" *double bind*, constituted by individualization and the simultaneous totalization of structures of modern power. In states torn apart by war, genocide and terrorism, bodies are traded as goods in place of any kind of sovereignty. Even the most intimate places where bodies live are subsumed by the state so that everyday life itself becomes "a central domain for the production and reproduction of the state" (Navaro-Yashin, 2002, p. 135).

Empirically, conceptualizations of the state's power over women's bodies are richly mined for analysing the interrelationships between the body and the state, through global networks of labour, employment and trade which survive on women's labour. This literature is vast and diverse and, almost without exception, makes for deeply troubling reading. The interventions of the state in, and through, women's bodies, especially, touches all races, ethnicities, geographies, ages and nationalities in hostile, often brutal ways: deep accounts of the lives of women across the globe, from South America to Southeast Asia, from Eastern Europe to Africa, Australasia and the Caribbean can be found across a multidisciplinary spectrum (e.g. Zheng, 2011; Fregoso and Bejarano, 2010; Lim, 1998; Kempadoo and Doezema, 1998; Shannon, 1995). The conceptual focus of these studies is equally diverse, although the vast majority document the obvious and subtle ways in which women's labour is used, consumed and governed by the state through circuits of power in which women are paid virtually nothing (see Saskia, 2000, Lucas, 2007).

A clear thread in such narratives is the conviction that the state is very far from retreating from citizens' lives and that, contrary to the proclamations of its demise by some commentators (e.g. Appadurai, 1996; Kearney 1995; Tsing 2000), its grip, especially in neo-liberal democracies, is greater than ever (Aretxaga, 2003). The state, in other words, is deeply gendered: state institutions, policies and frameworks profoundly influence how women live their lives and even how they die. The implications for how women think about their subjectivity, their bodies and their agency will have to be discussed at this point.

Feminism and Postmodernism: Implications for Female Subjectivity

In the West, a fundamental shift in the notion of the subject has been developing since the 70s and 80s. In their different ways, some of the West's most influential exponents of post-structuralist thinking --- Lacan, Derrida and Foucault – have drawn attention to the political, linguistic, cultural and psychic forces that makes subjects of human beings and have thus, severally, taken apart the discursive and psychological unity of the transcendental 'self'. Powerful, ubiquitous socio-cultural and economic forces traverse, contaminate and alter the human subject and its condition which render its erasure virtually inevitable. That is, as Hekman (1991: 45) puts it, "subjectification entails subjection". With the death of the subject, however, feminism is dealt a blow the modernist feminist did not have to address: while modernist feminists were able to attack the "masculine subjectivity of modernity" (Hekman, 1991: 46), how are postmodern feminists going to deal with the wholly determined subject which postmodernism has, accidentally, carelessly or otherwise, left to us?

In the late 1980s and 1990s, feminists continued to wrestle with this dilemma: what is supposed to replace the opposition between the transcendental, self-determining transcendental subject and the determined, constituted subject? One solution could be to de-polarize the woman as either constituted or constituting subject, to allow the two binaries to dissolve. A postmodernist twist to this dialectical construction is to posit subjectivity as a property of discourse rather than as something externally constituted to the self. Thus, subjects in postmodernism are constituted within, and by, discursive mechanisms.

Many feminists, however, have criticized this abstract solution as flawed, not least because the subject in postmodernism is now somehow devoid of agency (Braidotti, 1987; de Lauretis, 1984). An early phase of the 'second wave' of feminism focused on reintroducing agency into the debate on women's subjectivity: for a number of them, it was clear that women's experiences and natures were somehow – and essentially -- different from those of men's. Women had a distinctive "inner world" (de Lauretis, 1986: 182) that she could graft onto (and thus influence) the "outer world" of codes and social norms. Thus, women could exercise considerable agency while also always already enmeshed in "the practices, discourses and institutions that lend significance…to the events of the world (de Lauretis, 1984: 159). Women's subjectivity was formed out of this dialectical engagement between her inner and outer worlds (Lauretis, 1986; see Alcoff, 1988). Thus, women's personal experiences could interweave with the political, economic and cultural realities she encountered in everyday life.

Attractive as this dialectical concept of female subjectivity seems, however, it has been criticized on the grounds that it perpetuates precisely the same unhelpful dichotomy between the constituting and constituted subject it was designed to resolve (Hekman, 1991). There is, however, a further, and arguably more serious, weakness in the argument. This relates to the implicit "notion of a unified subject" (Mack-Canty, 2004: 158) which was presumed to apply across different cultures, practices and experiences. A more radical phase of feminism followed which questioned the universality of this "unified subject".

Today, ecofeminists and third wave feminists point to the logic of beginning with the woman's embodied perspective. Where second wave feminists had argued that "the personal is political," third wave feminists ask: '*Which* person? *Whose* politics?' They call for renewed study of the embodied particularity of women's voices and experiences – black, lesbian, African, Asian, Caribbean, the aging and aged, socially and economically excluded, the poor and so on and so forth – and the diversity of voices in globalised and globalizing economies (Arneil, 1999).

Over the last decade or so, feminism has gathered considerable conceptual and empirical force from embracing a plethora of different voices around the globe. So-called 'third wave' feminists are, interestingly, mirroring many of the values of postmodernism: dispersion, multiplicity, reflexivity. Two movements, in particular, are significant in pushing forward global agendas to tackle poverty, inequality, environmental destruction and social injustice: postcolonial feminism and ecofeminism. Also an understanding that women's subjectivity is inextricably tied to her choices about children, reproduction and the family raise new questions about the role of the state, her use of bodily power and, thus and thereby, her sense of agency in those contexts.

These issues take on a new complexion when we consider the phenomenon of 'compressed modernity' (Chang and Song, 2010) which has, very recently, been articulated as a set of macroeconomic and cultural conditions in which East Asian societies like South Korea, Japan and Singapore have achieved huge gains in GDP, exports, foreign direct investment and trade surpluses within an extremely short space of time. Although women have gained economically from these developments, the consequences upon their bodies are only now beginning to emerge in the sociological literature.

Compressed Modernity and Its Gendered Discontents

While it is generally acknowledged that the rise of global cities around the world over the last few decades has generated profound socio-economic and cultural changes for their citizens, the effects of compressed globalization on women are still not well-understood. As a result, the implications of these changes for gender studies have not been clearly nor rigorously studied (Brooks, 2006). Sassen (1998), for instance, notes that conventional accounts of globalization continue to be legitimized "in male gendered terms" (82). Even highly sophisticated accounts of 'global modernities' (Featherstone, Lash and Robertson, 1995) hardly touch upon gender, even though, as Brooks (2006) notes, the interactions of gender with the praxis of "'nation' and 'society'" surely deserve as much theoretical attention as "overarching" processes of control and "social relations over time and space" (Brooks, 2006, p. 16; see Massey, 2005).

Some notable exceptions to this trend in globalization studies exist, however, particularly in reference to the processes of 'compressed modernity' (Chang, 1999). It is noted in this strand of literature (much of it preoccupied with East Asian changes in gender-related behaviour) that societies which have undergone extremely rapid processes of economic modernization and transformation are now witnessing dramatic changes in how gender roles are changing, in line with workers' "intense actions for self-protection and collective survival" (Chang, 2009: 42). This argument is persuasive, not least because the author has experienced the effects of compressed modernity first-hand and has also, in this context, observed a trajectory of changing behaviours on the part of other women as a result of those effects. The role of the state in alleviating these effects in the name of a healthy birth rate, growing the pool of talent, and so on and so forth is still being debated by writers, not least because the refusal of women to reproduce is due, in no small part, to the state's political confusion in the face of the human, moral and cultural implications of compressed modernity.

These impacts of conditions of 'compressed modernity' on women's biological choices (indistinguishable in some ways from their socio-economic choices, I might add) gives the interrelationship between the state and the body a somewhat different complexion from the conditions in other apparently similar cultural and political contexts. Although scholars have clearly identified the links between gender, patriarchy, economies and reproduction (Salzinger, 2003; Acker, 2004; Gottfried, 2004), much of this literature is focused upon labour rights in emerging economies where social mobility and economic freedom for women remain challenging to achieve. The image of the female labourer as "dexterous, docile, tolerant, and cheap" (Salzinger, 2003), although changing quickly in these contexts, may still be said to be a stereotype which hinders women's emancipation in countries like the Philippines, Mexico and Brazil. This image, however, is far from global. The characterizations of female workers presented by a number of experts in the field do not apply to countries like South Korea, Japan, Singapore and Hong Kong, widely acknowledged by economists as having achieved some of the highest rates of per capita income and productivity in the world. Women in these countries have benefitted from rapidly expanding economies. A large class of highly-education, professional women have emerged to take their places on company boards, in academia, government ministries and in global institutions like the World Bank and the World Health Organization. Yet, their responses to globalization are, as I have emphasized, under-explored in the literature on globalization, gender and the body.

While it may be argued that countries which have undergone rapid industrialization have also witnessed falling birth rates and changes in reproductive behaviour, the conditions in East Asia (and Singapore) are still unique. In these countries, the speed of industrialization and modernization has been so rapid the state has had little time to prepare its institutions for the choices of women; as a result, unanticipated tensions and dilemmas have arisen for how their governments will cope with a shrinking tax base, the need for a large influx of migrant workers (a problem Japan has famously refused to confront) and how a Confucian society founded upon the centrality of the family will be sustained. Further, numerous and persistent exhortations by the governments of these countries to women to 'do their national duty' have fallen on deaf ears. In this sense, the ways in which women choose to exercise agency requires further analysis.

Taking all these debates into account sheds new light upon Foucault's identification of state power as a field of multiple forces; women under conditions of 'compressed modernity' show that these forces are in the bodies of women, subject to their subjectivity. Further, the bodies of women, rather than the state, have become the new battleground for political and economic struggles between the state and its citizens (Foucault 1978, 1979, 1991). Women, in this instance, have actually begun to reposition the question of the state in relation to the meaning of the body's sovereignty (Aretxaga, 2003). If, as Aretxaga notes, "the question of desire as well as fear becomes most crucial in rethinking the kind of reality the state might be acquiring at this moment of globalization, not only of capital, services, and culture but also of security operations and states of emergency," then we may ask ourselves: what do women desire and fear in states where prosperity and political stability prevail, at least for large numbers of women? The question of their subjectivity emerges in interesting ways if, as I shall go on to show, their bodies' resistance to the state occurs at the intersection between their bodies and their minds.

Anti-Reproduction as Resistance: Individualization, Individualism and the Female Body/Subject

Another quiet revolution has been occurring in the status of the female subject in some East Asian societies since the 1990s. The behaviour of women in Japan, Taiwan, South Korea, and Singapore over the last two decades has showed a startling – an unprecedented – reversal from neo-Confucian norms associated with marriage, childbearing, gender roles and familial ties (Chang and Song, 2010). While this demographic shift is by no means restricted to East Asian economies – all developed economies are dealing with this issue, even the U.S. – the confluence of compressed modernity, a deeply chauvinistic capitalism and the Confucian heritage in East Asia make women's subjectivity and agency in these contexts rather more complicated.

Within only two or three decades of having achieved economic success, South Korea, Japan and Singapore, especially, have witnessed plunging birth rates, dramatic shifts in the status and rate of biological as well as social reproduction and in the political contract between individuals and the state. These developments, exacerbated by trends in globalization, rising economic volatility for both households and individuals and the increasing influence of Western neoliberal pressures which favour a reduced role for state welfare, have combined to produce what Asian scholars call "stranded individualizers" (Chang and Song, 2010: 539). These are individuals caught between the vestiges of a neo-Confucian ethics of care for family and the continuity of generations, on the one hand, and the constellation of forces which make biological reproduction unacceptably risky for both men and women in these societies today.

Chang, citing Beck's theory of 'second modernity' (1999), notes that "other institutions of modernity, such as the state, industrial economy, firms, unions, schools, and welfare systems, have become increasingly ineffective in helping to alleviate such (gender-based) familial burdens and dilemmas" (Chang, 2010: 539). Recent economic crises and the increasingly weakened structures of labour unions in Korea have hardened women's resistance to making further concessions to the neo-Confucian ethic of putting body before selfhood; they were, in other words, "staging offensives against their country's chauvinist capitalist modernity" (ibid., 540).

The state's failure to support the woman's body in the reproductive realm had to be resisted. And so, in a quiet, but utterly critical, act of reproductive sabotage (Chang and Song, 2010), Korean women have, over the last two decades, responded to hostile institutional and political realities by voting with their bodies:

> By radically deferring, foregoing or ending marriages, by sternly refusing to produce more than one or two offspring (or to procreate at all), or by courageously rejecting family relations beyond the nuclear unit, South Korean women have taken their society – and, to some extent, the world – by surprise. (Chang and Song, 2010: 340)

This apparent choice is strikingly replicated in Singapore, Taiwan, Hong Kong and Japan. The birth rates in all these countries are among the lowest in the world and have become a point of intense national debate among policymakers and a headache for their governments. The Singapore experiment in demographic control, in particular, shows how closely governmental regimes based on capital accumulation interacts with women's choices over their bodies and reproduction.

In the 1960s, the Singapore government instituted a 'Stop at Two' policy in order to persuade women to curb their reproduction in the interests of economic growth. The policy was almost wholly successful, to the extent that birth rates continued to plunge well into the 80s and 90s. Today, Singapore women (more highly-educated than ever) are stubbornly refusing to have children. In the absence of a comprehensive welfare policy for mothers, the government was obliged, after much debate in Parliament, to offer mothers willing to have more children a cash bonus. Yet, birth rates continue to stay among the lowest in the developed world. At a replacement rate of 1.2 (the number of children each woman has), the fertility rate is well below what is required to sustain Singapore's economic growth (Kotkin, 2010). In recent years, the government has looked to selective immigration to address this issue but new problems of overcrowding, Singaporeans' resentment over new immigrants' rights and privileges and the rising cost of living have emerged as a result.

Other neo-Confucian societies such as Hong Kong and Taiwan pose equally fascinating issues for both feminists and postmodernists. What accounts for the fact that women's rates of reproduction in all these societies are among the lowest in the world?

Spaces/Sites of Resistance: New Spaces for Women's Agency?

Global modernities have created an apparent plethora of choices for women in all these societies. Consumer culture has taken on the complexion of Western modes of fashion and consumption, but also, perhaps more menacingly, in powerful mechanisms of control which cannot be precisely located in *either* capitalism *or* neo-Confucian morality but in a jarring intersection of the two regimes. In certain cultures, the global and the local intermingle and women appear to make choices over their sexualities and bodies in ways which defy governmental diktat but which come with conditions attached for their bodies and fertility.

The biopolitics of reproduction in these contexts offers feminists a new kind of juxtaposition: the woman's biology *serving* her destiny: pushing against the constraints of state and familial expectations and, perhaps, even against her desire for children. Further empirical research will need to be done in order to ascertain some of the complex reasons for why, and how, women in East Asian societies are voting with their wombs on issues of gender equality and gender rights. Such research is urgently needed not because it serves the state, but because women's resistance to procreation throws up profound cultural, political and economic challenges for how they *position themselves and their bodies* in society. While Western 'feminisms' have tended to focus almost exclusively on the female body as a cultural construction – for valid reasons – we are reminded that women's bodies (as biological agents of reproduction) in other contexts are also changing in response to complex religious and familial structures.

A Body of One's Own: Western States of Mind?

We have now arrived at a conundrum for feminist readings of the body: how far can women's bodies take on the State? Are East Asian women's individual choices over the body a way of expressing 'Western' trends towards individualization or a means of public communication about what she wants for herself in societies caught between neo-Confucian values and postmodern subjectivity? The individualization of a woman in these contexts raises new questions for feminist readings of the body because a new kind of agency is being activated: a radical refusal, a radical deferral, a silent revolution that *others* the body to the state so that it cannot be used for national duty, for reproductive service. Women in these contexts are not choosing the paths of single motherhood or abortion commonly seen in developed Western economies today: the far less generous social welfare systems in Asia do not make such choices economically feasible for many women. Instead, they demonstrate what it is to be postmodern in the most extreme sense: to take the political *into* their own bodies, literally transforming female subjectivity into an act of radical socio-political sabotage. The state is helpless before this refusal. It can do nothing.

Through the actions of such women, a fresh understanding of that established feminist maxim, 'A Body of One's Own,' emerges. A body of one's own is a clear signal of political praxis and agency which goes beyond the body-subject to trouble the status quo. If this interpretation sounds too triumphalist, let us be reminded that the individualization of one's body has long been the golden vision for Western feminists' articulations of what it means to be a woman. In a pioneering study of young women in East London, for instance, Woollett and Marshall (1997) discovered that a typical notion among them was that "one's body was one's own" (29). "Young women," they concluded, "resisted ideas of collective moralities and ideologies such as those which recognize the viewpoints of others and the rights of others to influence they use or make decisions about their bodies" (ibid.). According to Chang and Song (2010), this act of resistance raises issues of how South Korean women were exercising their individualism.

What now, of the future for East Asian women? Which 'feminism' will do? Or, rather, which construction of feminism would allow women in cultures of 'compressed modernity' to exercise a politics of agency which remain under-theorized in the literature? Neither 'Third World feminism' nor 'eco-feminism' nor any of the various waves of feminism I have outlined in this paper appear to fit the bill exactly. The story is still unfolding in a number of these societies and the territorial ground between women, bodies and their control of the state continues to pose fascinating risks as well as opportunities for women's rights in East Asia.

Conclusion

I began this paper by raising some issues related to the emergence of new practices of women's bodies in East Asia. It has not been feasible to provide a comprehensive overview of the politics of reproduction in these societies, but it has been my aim to chart, even summarily, the antecedents and consequences of compressed modernity upon women's bodily choices, with specific regard to their reproductive choices. In the process, I hope I have been able to bring to bear various phases of feminism upon this important, yet under-explored, context.

The female body in some East Asian societies, one may conclude, is politicized in ways which renegotiate the changing pressures of compressed modernity and post-industrialization. Changing and intense labour processes, combined with huge shifts in how women now choose to live out their lives within and outside the home have facilitated and accelerated latent demands in these societies for greater acknowledgement by the state and institutional 'others' of the immense threats to women's agency under these circumstances. How women's resistance to both culture and the age-old body of culture will continue to change is a fascinating question for researchers to investigate. Annandale (2003) has pointed out, rightly, that capitalism 'shapes biology in its own image, [and] . . . that image is one of an increasingly flexible body ever attuned to the consumption needs of patriarchal capitalism' (p. 93). Observable changes in how women can be seen in the rise of what has been called a 'global capitalist' body (Kim, 2003) should continue to exercise feminist researchers for years to come.

My paper has reviewed feminist scholarship on the political regulation of the female body and its emerging interanimations with developed East and Southeast Asian economies like Singapore, Korea and Taiwan. In the process, I had wanted to develop notions of female autonomy in the context of the specific religious, cultural and political structures in these societies. While a comprehensive analysis of the subject would not be feasible within the scope of this paper, it was hoped that a comparative perspective on the body will further extend our understanding of the consumption of an increasingly body-conscious culture in postmodern societies.

I have argued that the shifting relationship between the state and the body of East Asian women (very broadly speaking), on the other hand, remains uncharted territory. The experiences of certain Asian cultures with "compressed modernity" (Beck and Beck-Gernsheim, 2001) have led to a multiplicity of choices for women in terms of health, beauty, bodily modification and enhancements of all kinds, some of which surpass what is available in the West. Yet, the ontological grounding of such consumer choices in age-old religious and cultural practices surely require deeper scrutiny. The question of how a Confucian ethics of the 'self' and the 'body' (Zhang, 2002) is modified and transformed through consumer consciousness as well as state boundaries of control and legitimacy, in particular, is significant.

In the process, I hope I have shed some new empirical light upon the established – and still largely Western -- debates between feminism and postmodernism. Similarly, my argument has also, hopefully, brought a new theoretical perspective to bear upon the pragmatic and physiological choices women in East Asian cultures are making in the 21st century.

Any visitor to Singapore, Seoul, Tokyo, Hong Kong and Taipei today has to be struck by the tremendous faith in capitalism exhibited by their governments and people. Urgent industrialisation has created prosperous societies in these cultures and, in the process, new needs and demands for women's rights and equality. A new generation has a far more shadowy memory of those initial pressures which led previous generations to abandon age-old beliefs and practices in politically unsettling times, creating socially and culturally radical transformations that have mostly gone unrecorded in the West. Is there not an intellectual *rapprochement* between the Eastern body and the Western mind, however? How can it be voiced? As a thoughtful feminist philosopher reminds us:

> The contemporary Western world can no longer tread along its beaten track. It
> has to abandon it, and the whole point is how well-equipped a human being will
> be to meet this change in "cultural paradigms," how thoroughly, in intellectual
> terms, this change will be articulated by the parties involved in these processes"
> (Klimenkova, 1992: 285).

If my paper proves anything, it is that the East, too, has, for a while now, felt its grip on old certainties slip away; the change now needs to be articulated as well as enacted. Such a political move carries risks perhaps even more profound than those encountered by, and in, the body in its resistance to the state but it makes the theorization of such resistance possible in the first place. By doing this, woman speaks out her conditions, her body and her understanding of how her body is produced and consumed by the state and others. In this way, she forges a new path out of the 'beaten track' which *all* feminisms have bequeathed to us.

References

Acker, J. (2004) 'Gender, capitalism and globalization', *Critical Sociology*, Jan, 30: 17–41.

Annandale, E. (2003) 'Gender and health status: does biology matter?', in S.J. Williams, L. Arneil, B. 1999. *Politics and Feminism*, Oxford: Blackwell.

Agamben G. (1998) *Homo Sacer: Sovereign Power and Bare Life.* Stanford, CA: Stanford University Press.

Appadurai A. (1996) *Modernity at Large: Cultural Dimensions of Globalization.* Minneapolis: University of Minnesota Press.

Aretxaga, B. (2003) 'Maddening states', *Annual Review of Anthropology*, 32: 393–410.

Beck, U. and Grande, E. (2010) 'Varieties of Second Modernity: the Cosmopolitan Turn in
Social and Political Theory and Research', *British Journal of Sociology*, 61(3): 409–43.

———. and Beck-Gernsheim, E. (2001) *Individualization:Institutionalised Individualism and its Social and Political Consequences*. London: Sage.

———., Giddens, A. and Lash, S. (1995) *Reflexive Modernization*, Cambridge: Polity.

Brooks, A. (2006) *Gendered Work in Asian Cities: The New Economy and Changing Labour Markets*, Aldershot, Hampshire: Ashgate.

Bordo, S. (1993) *Unbearable Weight: Feminism, Western Culture and the Body*. London: University of California Press.

Chang, K-S. (2009) 'Compressed Modernity and its Discontents: South Korean Society in Transition', *Economy and Society*, 28 (1): 30–55.

Gottfried, H. (2004) 'Gendering globalization discourses', *Critical Sociology*, 30 (1): 9–15.

Featherstone, M. and Lash, S. 'Globalization, Modernity and the Spatialization of Social Theory: An Introduction', in Featherstone, M, Lash, S. and Robertson, R. (eds). 1995. *Global Modernities*, London: Sage, 1–24.

Foucault, M. (1978) *The History of Sexuality*. New York: Vintage Books

———. (1979) *Discipline and Punish: The Birth of a Prison*. New York: Random House.

———. (1991) 'Governmentality'. In G Burchell, C. Gordon and P. Miller, *The Foucault Effect: Studies in Governmentality* (Eds), 87–104. Chicago: The University of Chicago Press.

———. (1994) *Dits et Ecrits*, Paris: Gallimard, 1994; 4 vols., 229–32.

Fregoso, R-L. and Bejarano, C. (2010) *Terrorizing Women: Feminicide in the Américas*. Duke: Duke University Press.

Giddens, A. (1991) *Modernity and Self-Identity. Self and Society in the Late Modern Age.* Cambridge: Polity Press.

Han, S-J and Shim, Y-H. (2010) 'Redefining Second Modernity for East Asia: A Critical Assessment', *The British Journal of Sociology*, 61 (3), 465–488.

Hekman, S. (1991) 'Reconstituting the Subject: Feminism, Modernism and Postmodernism', *Hypatia*, 6 (2), 44–63.

Joy, A. and Venkatesh, A. (1994) 'Postmodernism, Feminism, and the Body: The Visible and the Invisible in Consumer Research', *International Journal of Research in Marketing*, 11 (4): 333–357.

Kearney M. 1995. 'The local and the global: the anthropology of globalization and transna- tionalism', *Annual Review of Anthropology*, 24:547–65.

Kempadoo, K. and Doezema, J. (1998) *Global sex works: rights, resistance and redefinitions*, London: Routledge.

Klimenkova, T.A. (1992) 'Feminism and postmodernism', *Philosophy East and West*, 42 (2): 277–285.

Kotkin, J. (2010) 'Singapore's demographic winter', 07/06/10. Available at: http://www.forbes.com/2010/07/06/singapore-population-economy-opinions-columnists-joel-kotkin.html. Accessed 11 August 2011.

Lazar, Michelle M. 2001. For the good of the nation: 'strategic egalitarianism' in the Singapore context', *Nations and Nationalism*, 7 (1): 59–74.

Lim, L. (1998) *The sex sector: the economic and social bases of prostitution in Southeast Asia*, International Labour Office, Geneva.

Lucas, L. (ed.), 'Unpacking globalization', in L. Lucas (ed.) *Unpacking globalization: Markets, Gender and Work*. Lanham, MD: Lexington Books, 1–12.

Mack-Canty, C. 2004. *'Third wave feminism and the need to reweave the nature/ culture duality'*, *NWSA Journal*, 16(3), 154–179.

Montserrat, D. (ed). 1998. *Changing Bodies, Changing Meanings: Studies of the Human Body in Antiquity*. London and New York: Routledge.

Moskowitz, Marc L. 2008. "Multiple virginity and other contested realities in Taipei's foreign club culture", *Sexualities*, 11: 327–351.

Navaro-Yashin, Y. (2002) *Faces of the State: Secularism and Public Life in Turkey*. Princeton, NJ: Princeton University Press.

Salzinger, L. (2003) *Genders in Production: Making Workers in Mexico's Global Factories*, Berkeley: University of California Press.

Sassen, S. (1998) *Globalization and Its discontents*, New York: The Free Press.

———. (2000) 'Women's burden: counter-geographies and the feminization of women's survival'. *Journal of International Affairs;* Spring, 53 (2): 503–524.

Shannon, S. (1995) 'The global sex trade: humans as the ultimate commodity', *Crime and Justice International*, pp. 5–35.

Suleiman, Susan (ed). (1986) *The Female Body in Western culture*. Cambridge: Harvard University Press.

Taussig M. (1997) *The Magic of the State*. New York: Routledge.

Truong, T-D. (1999) 'The Underbelly of the Tiger: Gender and the Demystification of the Asian Miracle', *Review of International Political Economy*, 6 (2): 133–165.

Tsing, A. (2000) 'The global situation', *Cultural Anthropology*, 15:327–60.

Tu, W-M. 'Introduction' in Tu, W-M. (1996) (ed). *Confucian Traditions in East Asian Modernity:Moral Education and Economic Culture in Japan and the Four Mini-Dragons*, American Academy of Arts and Sciences, 1–10.

Woollett, A. and Marshall, H. (2007) 'Reading the Body: Young Women's Accounts of their Bodies in Relation to Autonomy and Independence', in K. Davis (ed.) *Embodied Practices: Feminist Perspectives on the Body*, London: Sage, pp. 27–40.

Zhang, E. (2002) 'The Neo-Confucian Concept of Body and its Ethical Sensibility', *Philosophy and Medicine*, 61 (1), 45–65.

Zheng, T. (2009) *Red Lights: the Lives of Sex Workers in Postsocialist China*, Minneapolis and London: University of Minnesota Press.

PART III
Deviance and Resistance

Chapter 9

Bodies of the State: On the Legal Entrenchment of (Dis)Ability

Katie Ledingham

Introduction

Despite the passing of the Disability Discrimination Act (1995) and its subsequent amendments, most recently the Equality Act of 2010, there is growing evidence to suggest that disabled individuals are not only facing increasing socio-economic inequality, but are also having to restructure their lives in order to avoid the risk of harassment and abuse. Yet, regardless of the evidence of such injustices, disability studies continue to be characterised by their marginality at international conferences and by their distinctly insular and fragmented nature. Even more problematic, is that disability literatures have dangerously overlooked the role of state law in engendering both difference and disadvantage. Indeed, although the law has been criticised for its inclusion of the 'medical' model of disability, such criticism has been largely tangential and fails to consider the performative implications and privileged assumptions that the law entrenches in its understanding and defining of the disabled body. Whilst the law is not the only variable that can be implicated in the widening of the inequality gap between the 'disabled' and the 'abled' body, its effectiveness in conditioning our social imaginaries makes it a highly significant focus of academic endeavour. This chapter does not seek merely to foreground the repressive tendencies of law, but rather, to advance the movement towards the co-production of a legal process that is empowered, affirmative and excessive.

Through synthesising a deconstructive reading of the terms 'disability' and 'disabled,' as entrenched in the Disability Discrimination Act (1995), with the voices of those who have firsthand dealings in the law and in disability issues, this chapter engages in a creative exploration of how it is that the disabled body is constituted within the British legal system. In examining both the socio-spatial enactment and the socio-spatial implications of the legal constitution of the 'disabled' body, it unveils the role of state law in its instigating of a politics of 'othering,' and most contentiously, in inadvertently contributing to the recent rise in disability hate crime. By bringing to the fore the unsettling and contentious ramifications of the role of the legal system in facilitating the replication and assimilation of 'disability' into societal practice, it is intended that the reader is provoked into a persuasive realisation that things could, and should, be otherwise. Whilst the discussion that follows is both provocative and experimental, it does not however, propose that we just 'do away' with the legally entrenched terms of 'disability' and 'disabled.' As this chapter argues, the relationship between the 'law' and those that it categorises as being 'disabled' is intensely convoluted. Rather, the overarching aim of the discussion is to advocate the application of a critical and porous mode of thinking that is able to permeate and to thus challenge the pervasive influence of legally bounded ideology. There is much that legislative policy can learn from such a mode of thinking and instead of trying to maintain present ways of being, state legislation has a great deal to gain from redirecting its agenda away from that of preservation and security (attributes regarded to indicate the highest form of statecraft), and rather towards an innovative and transformational consideration of how things could be otherwise.

Disability Studies in Context: A Brief Overview

Debates relating to the study of disability proliferated following the emergence of the 'cultural turn' and a heightened sensitivity towards the role of representation and difference in the production of meaning. In order to retain a degree of coherency in a new found plurality of approaches, many studies within disability literatures focused on a particular strand of analysis, with key topics including that of gender, language and scale. For instance, where the work of Dyck (1998) explored the everyday, often unremarked geographies of disabled women within the home, Kitchin and Wilton (2003) rather considered the scales of activism adopted by disabled individuals, and Linley (2007) investigated the relationship between disability, social exclusion and public service provision. Though these studies and many others like them were clearly united in their attempts to link spatial practices with the (dis)empowerment of the 'disabled' body, their disparate nature can be in part implicated in contributing to the 'marginality' of disability issues at international conferences and within academic journals (Imrie and Edwards, 2007).

Disability studies have been further limited by a series of methodological constraints which stem from a continuing preference for disability research to engage in ethnography. The popularity of ethnography can be illustrated by pointing to the discussions of Leavitt (1992), Löfgren (2006) and Schneider (2010), who have all adopted variants of this participatory methodology in order to document localised experiences of 'disability.' Whilst this technique clearly has its merits, including a reduction in the distance between the 'researcher' and the 'researched,' it has, however, restricted the broader applicability of disability research in that it has predominately resulted in a narrative description of localised circumstance and has failed to consider the fundamental appropriateness of labelling certain sectors of society as 'disabled.' This omission is most clearly apparent in the seminal work of Golledge (1993) and his calling for the establishment of a geography both *of* and *for* disability. Indeed, as was once put by Kitchin and Hubbard (1999: 195) 'it seems that many social and cultural geographers are happy to survey (and 'map') the exclusionary landscape, but rarely do much to change that landscape.'

Due to this contextual structuring which has tended towards disparity and narrative description, disability studies across the disciplines have not surpassed in any notable form, the overarching yet deeply entwined contentions that 'disability' is either the result of a 'medical' condition intrinsic to the body of an individual, or, is a negative 'societal' infliction imposed by 'psychological beliefs in inherent superiority or inferiority' (Shakespeare, 2006: 14). This chapter thus extends the range of coverage adopted by disability studies through analysing the neglected and contentious relationship between the spatial praxis of 'disability' and legally entrenched discourse. In contrast to many writings on disability, whilst it recognises that author positionality is an important consideration, the chapter does not entertain the question of who should or shouldn't engage in disability research, and for this, it does not apologise. It is argued that all insight, regardless of its limitations, possesses an inherent value that may be utilised and built upon for transformational means. The chapter proposes that through thinking in a manner that aspires towards transformative outcomes, it becomes possible to broaden the imaginative horizons that govern the tangible and the lived experiences of the future.

Disability Discrimination Legislation: A Problematic Frame of Reference

Prior to the passing of the UK Disability Discrimination Act in 1995, there was no centralised institutional mechanism -through which disability discrimination could be effectively contested. In order to facilitate the identification of discriminatory practice, the DDA imposed a series of arbitrary categorisations relating to both the act of discrimination and the subject of discrimination. Widely perceived as being long overdue, the DDA opened by asserting that 'a person has a disability for the purpose of this Act if he has a physical or mental impairment which has a substantial and long term adverse effect on his ability to carry out normal day to day activities' (DDA, 1995: s1). Given that this defining framework was quick to receive criticism for premising itself upon the medical model of disability, it is surprising to find that as we approach two decades since its enactment, scant attention has been afforded to considering the implications of entrenching the terms 'disability' and 'disabled,' in addition to their linguistical semantic associations within state law. Indeed, we know from an extensive range of interdisciplinary sources that words are incredibly potent tools of expression. Words contribute to the ordering of human behaviour and influence the ways in which we rationalise our interactive relationships. As a case in point, the work of Lakoff and Johnson (1981) argues that the communicative use of metaphors has a critical impact in the shaping of our everyday realities. Lakoff and Johnson attest that through coming to correlate an 'argument' with the act of 'war,' the cognitive mind processes an 'argument' as an activity that needs to be 'won.'

In accordance with the DDA, we know that a person is regarded as having a disability if they are 'unable to effectively carry out normal day to day activities.' If we are to engage in the cognitive networking processes of deduction and inference which utilise the linguistical tools of synonyms and antonyms, then the defining framework of 'disability' as entrenched within the DDA, may be translated as follows; 'a person with a disability is ineffective and fundamentally subordinate to the norm.' Clearly, this is a very different statement in comparison to that which is entrenched within the DDA, but as contentious as this latter reading of the DDA may be, it often exhibits the greatest correlation with the lived experience of the 'disabled' body:

> it's astonishing how people will just turn strange.. even embarrassed.. when dealing with people with disabilities.. they will speak through the carer rather than to the disabled person.. they will speak at the wheelchair..they just assume that disabled people cannot interact for themselves (Care Worker: Interview, 02/10/10)

> people think they know things about us before they even know us.. if you know what I mean.. like what we can and can't do.. like they think that they have to talk to us louder and slower (User Led Local Support Organisation: Information Conference, 11/06/10).

Regardless of whether or not we understand meaning to be relational (see Saussure, 1959), inherently unstable (see Derrida, 1967), or a mixture of the two, it is apparent that not only do the terms 'disability' and 'disabled' delimit possibilities in understanding, but there is a distinct divergence between what Saussure (1959) would refer to as the 'signifier' (the legally entrenched term 'disability') and the 'signified' (the person who is regarded by the legal system as being 'disabled'). In short, legally enshrined phrases and terms such as 'adverse' and 'long term effect' on one's 'ability,' act in numerous instances as tools of deception and imprisonment; imprisoning not only for many disabled people, but also for non disabled people alike, whose minds have been colonised by a series of negative terms and negative associations that are dubiously reflective of what it actually means to be 'disabled.' In this sense, the legally entrenched term 'disability' may be regarded as an intensely problematic pillar of derivative cognitive social reference, that shapes the ways in which people with and without disabilities preconceive their interdependence with one another. Following his experience of being temporarily wheelchair bound and subsequently identified as 'disabled' by those who did not know him, it was similarly asserted by David Prosser (2009) of the Independent Newspaper; 'I'm pretty sure that, when I broke my pelvis, my brain wasn't injured at the same time, but I am being treated like a helpless child.'

This is not however, to discount that differences in bodily ability and functionality do indeed exist and that legally enshrined protection in some instances is a critical necessity. Take, for example, the case of a young woman who was left severely disabled after being administered the drug vinblastine intrathecally, when it should have been administered intravenously. Her carer noted that the accident 'impacted on every area of her life,' leaving her in need of 'total care'

(Care Worker: Interview, 02/02/10). Had there not been the legal mechanism in which this individual's reduction in bodily ability could be demonstrated in a court of law, then it is debatable whether she would have received an appropriate level of compensatory damages that would have provided for the level of care that she subsequently required. Nonetheless, placing the extremities temporarily aside, variance in terms of strength and ability is quite simply a fact of life and differences in 'ability,' whether they be physical, cognitive or social, are relevant to the entirety of the human population and operate along a congested, multi-directional continuum, as opposed to existing within the legally bounded, segregated and categorical dualism that separates an unstated grouping of the 'abled' from the 'disabled.' In this sense, the legally entrenched terms of 'disabled' and 'disability' invoke a process of 'othering' immanent to the syntax. For the legal system to perpetuate this semi-stated dualism is to disregard the assertion of Wolbring (2010) that disabled people do not view themselves as being a part of a distinct group, and to ignore the realisation that "just because you might be less able in one aspect of your life, does not mean that you are less able in all aspects of your life" (User Led Support Organisation: Information Conference, 11/06/10).

The Legal Constitution of 'Disability' and Socio-Spatial Action

In order to further highlight the significance of the law's understanding of and engagement with the 'disabled' body, it is imperative that its broader implications are brought to the fore. The section that follows thus links the legal, institutionalised abstraction of a particular idea, with the tangible and the lived experience, focusing in particular on employment and disability hate crime. Employment provides a crucial means for people to infuse their life with meaning and to self subsist within our neo-liberal economy. Yet, by legally defining the disabled person as 'impaired' and as with a diminished 'ability' to perform normal day to day tasks, the legal system is placing the 'disabled person' at odds with the capitalist notions of efficiency, performance and productivity that so frequently characterise the place of work and the space of the broader capitalist economy. If one is to take this dualistic opposition into account, then it is of little surprise to learn that only half of the disabled population in the UK are in employment, compared to a substantially higher 80% of the non-disabled population (Steventon and Sanchet, 2008). By extension, it is equally unsurprising to learn that the poverty rate for disabled people is substantially higher than it is for their non-disabled counterparts (Barnes and Mercer, 2010).

Beyond this, what these figures do not reveal, is that over one million unemployed disabled people of working age want to work and attest that despite their efforts, they have been unable to secure employment (Office for National Statistics, 2009). Although it is probable that there exists a series of complex and multifaceted reasons for this trend, including, for example, differences in qualifications and in the area of geographical location that employment is being sought, the act of assigning an individual with the demonstrably problematic label of being 'disabled,' can be regarded as a causative factor in the current widening of the inequality gap between the 'abled' and 'disabled' body. Indeed, it was recently documented in the Trailblazer's Employment Report (2010: 3) that '70 per cent of young disabled people believe their job applications have been rejected due to the perception of disability.'

In a related vein, the work of Alan Hyde (1997) has explored how the American legal system (re)constructs the body in varying ways, including as a 'commodity,' a 'property' and a 'machine.' Note here the linkage to the notions of bodily efficiency, performativity and consumption; the key ideals that are widely regarded to characterise the place of work and of the space of the capitalist economy. Although Hyde's writings provide a series of fascinating insights into the laws engagement of and with the human body, Hyde does not consider the broader implications of the body's portrayal within legalistic discourse. Such an omission substantiates the observation of Vayda (2009) that whilst there exists a wealth of works which describe, analyse and explain discourse, studies which consider the impacts of such discourse remain 'few and far between.' To consider the impacts of discourse is undoubtedly a risky exercise, not least because it exposes itself to the critique of being a tenuous and soft approach to study. Nonetheless, given that academia prides itself upon its alleged emancipatory potential, there is a real need for the academy as a whole to be more open in its embracing of methodological variety. It has long been recognised that it is much easier to 'observe in a general way that language and social life are inextricably linked than it is to develop this observation in a rigorous and compelling way' (Thompson, 1991: 1): this does not, however, mean that we should not try.

As alluded to previously, through identifying the disabled body as a 'problematic' and 'dysfunctional' entity, disabled individuals are subsequently construed within the societal imagination as different, and as a form of 'other.' The notion of the societal 'other' appears within an extensive range of philosophical literatures, where it has been asserted that group differentiated domination and oppression are defining characteristics of societal politics. When interviewing the disabled director of an international disability rights network, the interviewee remarked that "we live in society of extreme discrimination..people hate *us*" (Director, International Disability Rights Organisation: Interview, 21/04/10). The use of 'us' in this context is particularly illuminating because it hints at the role of disabled people themselves in creating a group identity. Nonetheless, the point of the matter is that whilst this interviewee's assertion is highly contentious, there is much evidence that would appear to support the remark. Certainly, the issue of disability hate crime was recently described by the then Chief Prosecutor Sir Ken Macdonald, QC, as 'a scar on the conscience' of the criminal justice system (CPS, 2008) and there is much evidence to suggest that it is increasing at an alarming rate (Martin, 2011). With hate crime often being premised upon a combination of both a misunderstanding of the hate subject and of a politics of 'othering,' the legal system can be implicated in contributing to the existence of such hateful activity, since, not only has it instituted the recognition of the disabled body as a form of 'other,' but its construction of the disabled body as a problematic and dysfunctional entity has been shown to be founded upon a decisive mix of considerable misunderstanding and generalisation. In relation to this apparent culture of condemnation, it is interesting to observe that within media discourses, constant coverage is afforded to the cases of individuals who have been exposed for exploiting the disability benefit system. What makes this particularly concerning, is that at the same time, there are a shocking numbers of cases whereby disabled individuals have been taunted, murdered and driven to suicide because of their 'disability' (Quarmby, 2008) and yet, these instances are sparsely documented by the mainstream media.

The Mutually Constitutive Nature of 'Disability'

Given the demonstrably significant implications of the legal construction of the 'disabled' body, how is it that the legal systems entrenchment of 'disability' has managed to avoid any substantive, interrogative examination from either academia or from disability rights organisations themselves? As Bourdieu suggests (1991: 113) 'the language of authority never governs without the collaboration of those it governs.' During the course of this investigation[1], it was interesting to observe that the terms 'disabled' and 'disability' were readily deployed by disabled and non-disabled people alike, with little consideration afforded to the deeper implications of using such terminology. By way of illustration, the following assertion was made by a representative of a regional disability network: 'In the Disabled People's movement we have adopted what is called the Social Model of Disability. In terms of language, we refer to ourselves as "Disabled People" (but as disabled by how society treats us)' (Regional Disability Network: Personal Correspondence, 12/03/10)

Similarly, during the conference run by the local user led support organisation (11/06/10), both the leaders and the participants frequently spoke of their desire to achieve full, equal rights "for all disabled people." Taking into account the negative semantic components that the legally entrenched term of 'disability' possesses, to describe oneself as disabled (either as disabled medically, or as disabled by societal attitudes) is inherently problematic in the movement towards achieving greater equality. Certainly, it has been noted in a range of linguistical studies that the frequent and assertive use of a term may act to enhance its perceived legitimacy, and it is suggested that this legitimising effect is further compounded

---

1 Entitled 'Contesting Theory, Challenging Practice: Legal Constructions of the Disabled Body and their Contribution to the Production and Maintenance of Geographies of Inequality,' the research project upon which this chapter is derived, combined semi structured interviews with observational analyses and a critical discourse analysis in order to creatively interrogate the relationship between the law and those that it recognises as being 'disabled.'

where it is 'disabled' people themselves utilising such terminology. Nonetheless, it is recognised that it is relatively easy for me, given my positionality as someone without a 'disability' (at least in the strictly legal sense of the term), to criticise others for defining themselves in such a manner. It is also recognised, that if a 'disabled' person is to receive state support, then they must place themselves within the bounded parameters of the legal definition of what constitutes a disability. Thus, a mutually constitutive relationship is produced, whereby an individual must pursue and align themselves with the legal definition of the 'disabled' body in order to reach particular outcomes. Undoubtedly, there are those who would argue that if disabled people are actively using the legal system in order to acquire support, then they must therefore be in need of this support, which, by extension, must be indicative of recognition on their part, that they are less able than others. However, it is quite apparent that in numerous instances, disabled people do not need state support because they are less 'able,' but because they are discriminated against on the grounds of their body's 'disabled' categorisation.

It was asserted in the introductory section of this chapter that much of the debate within the field of disability studies has failed to transcend the medical/social debate, whereby 'disability' is understood as primarily a medical condition intrinsic to the body of an individual, or, as an infliction of society, imposed by a combination of disabling attitudes and structures. This stagnation was also found to be evidenced in the field, with the local user led support organisation declaring that its "main motto or mission statement is to work on the social model of disability" (Local User Led Support Organisation: Information Conference, 11/06/10). In a similar vein, when discussing the social model of disability with the director of the international disability rights network, the interviewee remarked that this was getting "right to the heart of it [disability issues] straightaway" (Director International Disability Rights Network: Interview, 21/04/10). Disability rights activists and organisations are thus trying to highlight problematic societal attitudes towards disabled individuals in an attempt to remedy some of the many challenges faced by the disabled body within society. As part of this effort, they are participating in a range of initiatives such as the 'Roadmap to 2025' that aims to strengthen the disabled voice and to flesh out the legislation relating to key themes which have been identified by disabled people as being in need of improvement.

This continually expanding network of disability rights initiatives and organisations is not necessarily making the voices of disabled people 'stronger,' but rather acting as a hindrance in the movement towards achieving greater equality, not least because such initiatives are diverting attention away from a questioning of the fundamental legitimacy of labelling an individual as being 'disabled.' In order to substantiate this point further, it is interesting to note that despite the active nature of disability rights organisations, each of the subsequent amendments to the DDA has continued to retain the medical definition of disability, and, the Legal Aid, Sentencing and Punishment of Offenders Bill of 2011, entirely omitted disability hate crime issues, in spite of the government's prior pledge to reduce the disparity in sentencing between disability hate crime murders and other hate crime murders. Thus, as these initiatives of disability rights organisations develop and become more complex and interlinked, the voice which does question the fundamental fairness of the 'disability' label and its entrenchment within state law, becomes silenced amidst the multitude of other voices which are rather engaging with this convoluted network. This observation aligns itself with the work of Foucault (1972), who believed it to be the everyday mechanic domains of administrative organisation that make the governance of a particular idea possible; in this case, the law's very particular idea of 'disability.'

The Law and the Nurturing of Knowledge

The legal system has not only acted to entrench the problematic term 'disability,' but it has also acted to entrench what is essentially no more than a privileged understanding of the concept of 'disability.' This privileged understanding regards the 'disabled' individual as fundamentally different, as being in need of the law's protection and as unable to function in a normal, efficient and performative manner. Through constituting the disabled body in this way, the legal system has thus acted to institutionalise its very own value judgement that differentiates between the levels of 'ability' that it considers to be 'normal' and the level of ability that it considers to be subordinate to the 'norm.' What makes this significant is that the legal construction of the disabled body considerably diverges from what it actually *means* to have a 'disability,' and yet, in spite of this, the legal system continues to entrench its understanding of the 'disabled' body with very little resistance. Accordingly, it is apparent that all of the interests discussed in this chapter have been conditioned by the law into becoming active agents in facilitating the manifestation and the (re)production of the disabling system of 'disability.' As put by Derrida (2002: 233), 'there is no law without enforceability, and no applicability or enforceability of the law without force.' For this reason, these interests must therefore step aside from the conditioning force that is the law, and redirect their critical reflections not away from the law, but rather towards it. If they do not, there is a very real risk that these reproductive material spatial practices, in conjunction with our heavily conditioned social imaginaries, will continue to work in tandem until the potential for new possibilities of being is significantly diminished. It is recognised that many negative attitudes regarding 'disability' and the 'disabled,' have their own historical, temporal and even religious contexts, but it is the contention of this chapter that if the law can dispel the able/disabled categorical dualism that is inherent in its entrenchment and defining of 'disability,' and aspire instead to engage with the continuum of ability, this will play a key role in lessening the continued subjugation of the disabled body. The practical implications of such a continuum are discussed below.

Towards a Body Continuum

In spite of the above, it would be far too simplistic to propose that the law just 'does away' with its engagements with the 'disabled' body. Though the legal definition of the 'disabled' body acts in many instances to negatively condition the identity of the individual that is labelled as such, it also provides a channel of support for others. Thus, what is needed is a pushing of the categorical boundary between the 'abled' and the 'disabled.' In other words, instead of dealing in this bounded dualism, we should aspire to engage with the *continuum of ability*. In terms of how this could be achieved in a court of law, it would be interesting to explore the practical application of what Hyde refers to as a 'body fantasia,' which seeks to establish an empathetic *communion* between other bodies and by extension, is designed to weaken our ability to deny 'the significance of others' (1997: 263). Hyde attests that this communion could be achieved through the law developing a 'greater self-consciousness about its discursive construction of the body' (1997: 263). An application of Hyde's 'body fantasia,' in a specifically disability context, could thus help in the recognition that 'disabled people' are most fundamentally individual beings and are equally worthy of the "the same equality that everyone else takes for granted" (Local User Led Support Organisation: Information Conference, 11/06/10). Such an application would also limit the ability of the law to engender the mutually constitutive relationship which enables the law to hide behind its façade of rationality and reason. The practical application of this literal pushing of the dis/abled categorical boundary would by no means be an easy task, but given the proven gravity of the current implications of the legal constitution of the 'disabled' body, we should not acquiesce to the normative, comfortable assumption that the law exists to resist repression.

Amidst the evidence of increasing injustices faced by the disabled body, it is quite clear that change needs to happen very soon. This is particularly true when we take into account the new and contentious initiative of the Department for Education (2011), that encourages parents to formally label their child as 'disabled,' even though the policy itself recognises that disability is a highly 'subjective' experience and that 'it is not always easy to know whether a child is disabled.' The significance of the need for these changes can be further highlighted by reiterating that the victims of the legal constitution of the 'disabled' body are not just disabled people, but are also non disabled people alike, whose minds have been colonised by the borders and the limitations imposed by legally entrenched discourse. It is only through acquiring the realisation that we are all limited by the discourses that are available to us, that there can emerge a widespread impetus to challenge legally entrenched discourse and to thus bring about new possibilities of being. According to Capra (1996: 282), 'To be human is to exist in language. In language we coordinate our behaviour, and together in language we bring forth our world.' Yet, whilst we do to a significant extent exist in language, our language need not necessarily be one of acquiescence but one of aspiration and change.

References

Barnes, C and Mercer, G. 2010. *Exploring Disability.* Cambridge: Polity Press.

Bourdieu, P. 1991. *Language and Symbolic Power.* J.B. Thompson (ed.) Oxford: Polity Press.

Capra, F. 1996. *The Web of Being: A New Synthesis of Mind and Matter.* London: Harper Collins.

Crown Prosecution Service. 2008. Society Must Do Better On Disability Hate Crime Says DPP. Available at; www.cps.gov.uk/news/press_releases/161_08/; accessed 04/07/2010. Department for Education. 2011. Parent/Carer Questionnaire: Explanatory Notes. Available at www.northamptonshire.gov.uk/en/councilservices/EducationandLearning.aspx; accessed 20/01/2011.

Derrida, J. 1967. *Of Grammatology.* Trans. G.C. Spivak. Baltimore, MD: JHU Press.

————. 2002. Force of Law: "The Mystical Foundations of Authority." In: Derrida, J and Anidjar, G. (eds). *Acts of Religion.* New York: Routledge, 228–299.

Disability Discrimination Act. 2005. London: HMSO.

Dyck, I. 1998. Women With Disabilities and Everyday Geographies: Home Space and the Contested Body. In: Kearns, R and Gesler, W. (eds)*Putting Health Into Place: Landscape Identity and Wellbeing.* New York: Syracuse University Press, 102–109.

Foucault, M. 1972. *The Archaeology of Knowledge.* London: Travistock Publications.

Funakoshi, M. 2009 Taking Duncan Kennedy Seriously: Ironical Liberal Legalism. *Widener Law Review,* 15, 231–287.

Golledge, R. 1993 Geography and the Disabled: A Survey with Special Reference to Vision Impaired and Blind Populations. *Transactions of the Institute of British Geographers,* 18 (1), 63–85.

Harvey, D. 1996 *Justice, Nature & the Geography of Difference.* Oxford: Blackwell.

Hyde, A. 1997 *Bodies of Law.* New Jersey: Princeton University Press.

Imrie, R and Edwards, C. 2007 The Geographies of Disability: Reflections on the Development of a Sub-Discipline. *Geography Compass,* 1 (3), 623–640.

Kitchin, R.M. and Hubbard, P.J. 1999 Editorial: Research, Action and 'Critical' Geographies. *Area,* 31 (3), 195–98.

————. and Wilton, R. 2003. Disability Activism and the Politics of Scale. *The Canadian Geographer,* 47 (2), 97–115.

Lakoff, G and Johnson, M. 1980. *Metaphors We Live By.* Chicago: University of Chicago Press.

Leavitt, R.L. 1992. *Disability and Rehabilitation in Rural Jamaica: An Ethnographic Study.* New Jersey: Fairleigh Dickinson University Press.

Linley, R. 2007. Public Libraries, Disability and Social Exclusion,' *Working Paper 11,* available at; http://www.seapn.org.uk/content_files/files/vol3wp11.pdf; accessed 01/11/2010

Löfgren, A. 2006. Your Little Doorstep is My Wall: A Personal Experience of Living in a Disabling Society. *Norsk Geografisk Tidsskrift,* 60 (3), 267–271.

Martin, N. 2011. Hate Crimes Against Britain's Disabled On The Rise. *VOICE UK.* Available at; http://www.voiceuk.org.uk/News/hate-crimes-against-britains-disabled-on-the-rise/7f28110e-f87b-48b4-b897-67a7da47ed29; accessed 20/11/2010.

Office for National Statistics. 2009. Labour Force Survey, Jan – March 2009. Available at; http://www.ons.gov.uk/ons/index.html; accessed 01/11/2010.

Prosser, D. 2010. Going Nowhere: My Life In A Wheelchair. *The Independent.* Available at; http://www.independent.co.uk/life-style/health-and-families/features/going-nowhere-my-life-in-a-wheelchair-1761724.html; accessed 03/12/2010.

Quarmby, K. 2008. *Getting Away With Murder.* SCOPE: London.

Saussure, F.de. 1959. *Course in General Linguistics.* New York: Philosophical Library.

Schneider, C. 2010. Ready for Work: Feeling Rules, Emotion Work and Emotional Labour for People with Disabilities, *Interactions,* 4, 1–12.

Shakespeare, T. 2006 *Disability Rights and Wrongs.* London: Taylor and Francis.

Soja, E. 1996. *Thirdsapce.* Oxford: Blackwell Publishing.

Steventon, A and Sanchez, C. 2008. *The Under-Pensioned: Disabled People and People from Ethnic Minorities.* Manchester: Pensions Policy Institute.

Thompson, J.B. 1991. Editors Introduction. In: Bourdieu, P and Thompson, J.B. *Language and Symbolic Power.* Oxford: Polity Press. pp. 1–32.

Trailblazers Employment Report. 2010. Right to Work: Report 4 of the Inclusion Now Series. Available at; www.mdctrailblazers.org/Trailblazers_Right_to_work_webcopy.pdf; accessed 02/09/2010.

Vayda, A.P. 2009. *Explaining Human Actions and Environmental Changes.* Rownman Altamira: Lanham.

Wolbring, G. 2006. Disabled People: A Social Group with Cultural Identities? Available at; http://www.waccglobal.org/en/20061-celebrating-cultural-diversity/568-Disabled-people-A-social-group-with-cultural-identities.html; accessed 01/12/2010.

Chapter 10

Unruly Bodies (Standing Against Apartheid)

Gavin Brown

Introduction

For nearly four years from 19 April 1986 the members and supporters of the City of London Anti-Apartheid Group [hereafter City Group, as they referred to themselves] maintained a Non-Stop Picket on the pavement outside the South African Embassy in Trafalgar Square calling for the release of Nelson Mandela. They stayed on that pavement twenty four hours a day, 365 days a year until he was released from jail (and then some – the Non-Stop Picket did not actually end until two weeks after Mandela's release). For most of that time, as a teenager, I was part of that protest. This chapter describes the distinctive culture of solidarity created by the material space of the Picket and the practices that sustained it (Brown and Yaffe 2012). It examines how the cosmopolitan friendship networks created amongst Picketers enabled them to see beyond their own life experiences and extend their understanding of solidarity in important ways. City Group and the Non-Stop Picket had a culture of direct action against the representatives of the apartheid regime (and their supporters) in Britain. Through this non-violent, but confrontational political stance, the young Picketers learned to think and act against the (British) state, using their bodies in unruly ways. In the pages that follow, I examine both the positive, empowering aspects of holding this stance, but also consider the understandable, but less positive, paranoia that this could lead to. In doing so, I highlight the uneven terrain of this unruliness, demonstrating how some picketers could take (and get away with) the risks associated with being unruly more safely than others; whilst some found themselves positioned as 'unruly' in relation to the Picket's own culture.

Standing in Solidarity

City Group was formed by Norma Kitson (an exiled African National Congress [ANC] member), her children, friends and supporters in 1982 (Kitson 1987). City Group's unconditional solidarity with all liberation movements in South Africa (not just the ANC) and its principled linking of the struggle against apartheid with anti-racism in Britain led to group's eventual expulsion in 1985 from the national Anti-Apartheid Movement which viewed the ANC as the only legitimate liberation movement in South Africa (Fieldhouse 2005; Thörn 2006; Trewala 1995). City

Group deployed diverse tactics, including direct action, to express its solidarity with those opposed to apartheid. Due to the national Anti-Apartheid Movement's close allegiance to the exiled leadership of the ANC and South African Communist Party, it refused to extend solidarity to activists from other political traditions in South Africa, such as the Pan-Africanist Congress, Black Consciousness Movement of Azania or the imprisoned trade union leader Moses Mayekiso. In contrast, City Group took up their causes. Its support for those sidelined by the exiled leadership of the ANC was valued by activists in South Africa (Bozzoli 2004, Maaba 2001). The Picket played a key role as a 'convergence space' (Routledge 2003) through which transnational activist discourses and practices addressing the politics of race were articulated – fostering dialogue and the exchange of ideas not just between British and South African activists, but wider networks of activists from diverse nations who passed through London and engaged with the Picket.

The Picket was a highly visible protest against apartheid. Through its constant presence, the Picket developed a distinctive appearance, culture and sense of community. Bright hand-sewn banners (often in black, green and gold, the colours of the ANC) provided a backdrop to the Picket, declaring its raison d'etre; additionally picketers carried placards which declared their solidarity and commented on topical events and campaigns in South Africa. Members of the picket would leaflet and petition passers-by, whilst others made impromptu speeches on a megaphone or sang South African freedom songs. This petitioning served both as an opportunity for political debate with the public and also as a means of collecting donations to sustain the Picket's campaigning (and to send as material aid to the families of political prisoners in South Africa). Larger themed rallies were held on Friday evenings, and on Thursdays the Picket's numbers swelled as supporters danced to the music of a group of street musicians, the Horns of Jericho.

The culture of the Picket not only conveyed its political message of solidarity, but helped individual participants define their personal identities (Thörn 2009). For many picketers, but particularly the young, the opportunity to stand on a pavement in the centre of London singing, shouting and pushing the limits of legality with the police was powerful and empowering. This is not to throw their commitment to the struggle against apartheid into question, or accuse them of apolitical delinquency, but to recognise that the act of standing in solidarity, against the policies of the Thatcher and Botha governments, unleashed powerful emotions (including rage, fear, despair, pride, righteousness and joy, amongst others) that exceed easy political categorisations. To be on the picket was to bend or break the rules of appropriate behaviour in public space. The social and political life of the Picket had a particular emotional geography through which individuals overcame social isolation, transformed their sense of self, and enjoyed being 'unruly' in public space (Roseneil 2000).

The geography of the Non-Stop Picket extended beyond its location and its relationship with the struggle in South Africa. The combination of the Picket's central location and its expression of solidarity through confrontation with the representatives of apartheid attracted a broad and diverse group of mostly young activists from the UK and beyond (including participants from many European countries, Australia, Brazil and the USA). Some of these 'international' picketers were studying in London at the time, some were migrant workers and some, having first encountered the Picket whilst on holiday, moved to London to be part of it. The Picket provided 'uncommon ground' through which friendship networks developed that crossed boundaries of nationality, ethnicity and social difference (Chatterton 2006). Brought together by their common opposition to apartheid, young picketers protested alongside, and socialised with, people from very different backgrounds to their own. Although their activism entailed extending solidarity with distant others, the everyday life of the Picket fostered more immediate experiences of subaltern cosmopolitanism and enabled participants to see beyond their own positionality and (often limited) prior life experiences. The Picket provided a safe and supportive milieu in which to experiment with different identities and ways of being. This was not, of course, without its problems or limits. For example, at times the Picket became something of a haven for young street homeless people living in the West End, although their involvement was often short-lived and marked by the reassertion of social hierarchies by more settled and privileged members of the Picket.

Transnational solidarity connects people across territories where often there was no obvious prior 'connection' between them except a shared critique of existing power relations (Massey 2008; Olesen 2005). Such solidarity frequently seeks to reconfigure spatial relations between (and within) nations. Real and imagined connections forged through the international anti-apartheid movement (which was active in more than 100 different countries) contributed to creating contemporary global civil society and addressing global political concerns in new ways (Sapire 2009; Thörn 2006). Solidarity is a practice of taking responsibility for geographical inequalities (Massey 2004; Thörn 2009), but solidarity activists can still themselves be complicit in reproducing uneven geometries of power within their movements and colonial power relations towards those distant others that they seek to support (Koopman 2008; Sundberg 2007). White activists on the Non-Stop Picket were not immune from accusations of racism and these unleashed many tense political debates amongst the group. Similarly, class privilege could sometimes be reproduced on the Picket – particularly in the ways homeless youth were treated with suspicion by some picketers, discouraged from interacting with the public and relegated to the role of 'klingon' (holding the banner for extended periods of time). This does not negate the potential for grassroots cosmopolitan connections to be forged through the contacts provided by transnational solidarity. As Thörn (2009) has articulated, transnational anti-apartheid activism transcended some borders (of race and nation), but it also (re)produced others (between different liberation movements and solidarity groups; as well as reinforcing a 'them' and 'us' attitude towards most white South Africans). Such complex power relations further complicate the emotional geographies of activism that are the internal life of movement politics (Bosco 2007; Brown and Pickerill 2009; Goodwin *et al* 2001) and which inspire, sustain and, at times, curtail on-going political involvement.

Learning to Be Against the State

Positioned on the pavement directly outside South Africa House, the picket was strategically placed (Bosco 2006) to draw attention to apartheid and bring pressure to bear on the regime's representatives and allies in the UK. The Picket did not just stand outside the Embassy bearing witness to apartheid's crimes it took direct action against apartheid's representatives. This inevitably brought picketers into conflict with the police, courts and other representatives of the British state. These experiences of arrest, harassment, surveillance and, at times, police violence led many young activists to question the role of the state. Through the Picket, many picketers learned how to act against the state (although this did not necessarily produce anti-state perspectives or challenge state-like thinking-behaviours within the group). Standing in solidarity provoked picketers to critically reflect on the functioning of the state and the exercise of political power 'at home'. In this way, transnational solidarity became a reciprocal process with knowledge and learning flowing in more than one direction (not just from Britain to resisting distant others). Here, I consider how this happened.

Over the years, several attempts were made to surround the Embassy. This was achieved on 16 June 1988 at a rally to commemorate the 22nd anniversary of the massacre of protesting schoolchildren in Soweto in 1976. On this weekday evening, over 1500 people joined the protest and the Embassy was completely surrounded, hundreds of commemorative black balloons were released and, as frequently happened at rallies both large and small, flowers were laid on the Embassy gates. This audacious protest provoked a violent response from the Metropolitan Police who attacked the Picket and physically threw many picketers over the (largely ineffective) crowd-control barriers. Five picketers were arrested. At 10.30pm that evening there were still over three hundred protestors on Picket.

The 'Surround the Embassy' protest was characteristic of the high profile, spectacular actions City Group could mobilise and the direct action approach that they favoured. On 6 September 1989, the day of what turned out to be the last whites-only election in South Africa, the best part of a thousand protestors took direct action blocking the road directly outside the Embassy for over two hours. To block the road, protestors used their bodies in unruly ways – darting through lines of police to enter the road, risking their safety by lying in front of cars and buses, linking arms and going 'limp' to hamper police efforts to remove them from the roadway (and then jumping straight back in again). Despite the significant disruption caused to the evening rush hour traffic in central London, the police were more restrained on this occasion – undoubtedly on political orders, as hundreds of arrests outside the Embassy on that day would have been politically embarrassing to de Klerk's government and his supporters in the British Parliament. The state's response to this event highlights the relational nature of policing and protest on the Picket – picketers would try out new forms of protest, using their bodies in new ways to confound established police tactics, but they could never fully anticipate how the police would respond to their unruliness.

Actions on the Picket were undertaken for a number of reasons. Sometimes they sought to directly disrupt the functioning of apartheid's representatives in Britain, sometimes they were designed to produce photo opportunities or significant arrests that could generate press coverage for the Picket and its message; and, at yet other times they were more symbolic. For example, in August 1988, a group of women activists marked Azanian Women's Day by taking scrubbing brushes to the fabric of the Embassy to wash off the bloody taint of apartheid and draw attention to the double oppression of women under apartheid. These actions embodied the Picket's spirit of unruliness – part of the challenge (and fun) of even the most low key action was to see how far the police could be pushed. The unruly presence of the Picket was often performed through small acts of defiance that sought to assert and expand the space controlled by the protestors outside the embassy. Whether active participants in these actions, or witnesses to them, picketers learned to take an unruly stance in relation to the police, the courts and other representatives of the British state.

The Embassy repeatedly complained to the British Government about the Picket's presence:

> You are well aware of the numerous fruitless attempts to terminate or contain the City of London Anti-Apartheid Group picket outside South Africa House which to our mind constitutes harassment and impairment of the dignity of the Embassy. [Extract from a letter a letter from a South African Embassy official to the Foreign and Commonwealth Office dated 10 December 1987] (FCO *n.d*).

The Embassy encouraged the British government to restrict and ban the protest, and for nearly two months (6 May-2 July) in 1987, the Picket was removed from outside the Embassy by the Metropolitan Police (following an action in which three City Group activists threw several gallons of red paint over the entrance to the Embassy to protest the whites-only election taking place in South Africa on that day). During this period, the Picket relocated to the steps of nearby St. Martin-in-the-Fields Church and activists repeatedly risked arrest to break the police ban on their protest and defend the right to protest outside the Embassy. The police used an arcane Victorian bylaw, "Commissioner's Directions", which allowed the Metropolitan Police Commissioner to curtail public gatherings within a mile of Parliament, to allow MPs free movement to go about their business, to ban the Picket during this period. Prior to the paint-throwing action on 6 May, the Metropolitan Police had briefly moved the Picket under Commissioner's Directions on 30 April 1987. Clearly, under pressure from the Embassy, they were looking for an excuse to relocate and restrict the protest. This bylaw, designed to facilitate the movement of those bodies essential to the functioning of the liberal democratic state, was used to limit the presence of those bodies that challenged its policies, authority and legitimacy. Eventually, the ban was broken when four MPs protested outside the Embassy alongside other picketers and the police were unable to justify the ban any longer (Bailey and Taylor 2009: 318). In total 173 people were arrested during City Group's campaign to break the police ban and defend the right to protest. All charges were eventually thrown out of court. During the period of the ban on the Picket, City Group supporters acted in an unruly manner, breaking the law in order to defend their right to protest and thereby defend a space in which to be unruly. The irony of both the manner in which the Picket was restored to its place in front of the Embassy and picketers' subsequent legal victories in court was that the Metropolitan Police were exposed as bending legal 'rules' in order to curtail unruliness.

City Group's activism was not restricted to Trafalgar Square: picketers took direct action against apartheid across the UK and toured the country mobilising solidarity. These extended campaigns of direct action away from the Non-Stop Picket included 'trolley protests' against the sale of South African goods in supermarkets across London, where activists filled trolleys with South African produce, took them to the checkout and then refused to pay for them. At their most effective, these protests could tie up the majority of checkouts in a targeted supermarket simultaneously. In October 1986 City Group coordinated simultaneous trolley protests at seven supermarkets across ethnically diverse areas of inner London. In a similar vein, City Group organised frequent occupations of the South African Airways (SAA) offices in Oxford Circus through their "No Rights? No Flights!" campaign. These offices were frequently closed through successive occupations several times in a day. As the security staff at the SAA offices increasingly recognised repeat 'offenders', activists needed to utilise more and more imaginative disguises to enable their initial access to the premises. During one protest on South African Women's Day in 1988 a large party of women, varying in age from their mid-teens to their seventies, successfully entered the SAA offices dressed as nuns and a class of convent girls. Finally, City Group activists took direct action at sporting venues around the UK, including pitch invasions at various rugby and cricket grounds, in protest at sportsmen and women who had broken the sports boycott of South Africa (Maaba 2001). For these actions to be successful, activists used their bodies in particular ways to occupy space or block certain activities from taking place. They relied on their bodies' potential for intense speed (or slowness) to get into place to protest, evading capture by police officers or security guards, or to hamper their removal from the South African Airways offices or the cricket crease at Lords'. Frequently they would disguise their bodies or mask their identities in order not to appear unruly or out of place, thereby enabling their planned unruliness. Very often, as I have noted, these disguises could take absurd forms – so much so that it is a wonder they were not spotted and caught out more frequently. Timing was everything – protestors waited patiently for the optimum moment to act, and coordinated their arrival at an action carefully (to arrive too early could draw attention to oneself, but being late could leave others exposed and vulnerable). As should be clear, to create the potential to use their bodies in unruly ways, picketers exercised a high degree of calculation and control over their bodies.

Paranoid Stances

I turn now to an examination of how City Group established and applied its own rules and consider how certain bodies were positioned as unruly in relation to the political culture of the Picket. Unlike the functional anarchism of some of other long-term protests in 1980s Britain, such as the Greenham Common Women's Peace Camp (Roseneil 2000), the Non-Stop Picket was highly organised and City Group operated through a hierarchical leadership structure. Political leadership was provided by the Group's Convenor, Deputy Convenor and Secretary; a committee met weekly to plan and organise the Group's campaigning, and a volunteer Picket Organiser worked to ensure that shifts on the Picket's rota were adequately covered. On each shift (of either three or six hours), one picketer acted as the Picket's Chief Steward. For the most part, this responsibility was taken by an experienced and trusted (but not necessarily older) picketer, but a competent and committed activist could quickly find themselves in this role (especially on those shifts that were harder to cover on the rota). The role of the steward was, first and foremost, a political one. As an internal 'user guide' to the Picket, circulated in the final few months of the Picket in early 1990 stated,

> "The rules and policies of the picket are established at democratic meetings of City of London Anti-Apartheid Group. These rules and policies obtain despite the disposition of the picket at any given time. It is the responsibility of the Chief Steward to defend what City Group stands for. There is a political duty to ensure that the message gets through. The Chief Steward is the 'custodian' of the picket's political message." (City of London Anti-Apartheid Group 1990: 1)

The rules referred to here were simple, few in number and stood throughout the duration of the Picket. These rules served to ensure the political integrity of the protest and the safety of its participants. They banned the use drugs and alcohol on the Picket, and stated that no-one under the influence of either was allowed to be present there. Participants were encouraged to fully participate in the political work of the Picket and to ensure that it was tidy and presentable. The rules expressly forbade picketers from engaging in conversations with the police (or responding to taunts and abuse from racists).

Despite how the Non-Stop Picket fostered unruly stances in relation to the state, the group did not tolerate unruliness in relation to its own standards of conduct. The Chief Steward was empowered as the sole conduit for impromptu negotiations with the police. The same user guide advised,

> "In all tactical decisions consider:
> I. What do we stand to gain?
> II. What do we stand to lose?
> Discuss situations as they develop. Let the whole picket know what the problem is. Consider whether to stand firm or make a tactical withdrawal. Always look at a

decision in terms of what is to be achieved and what is to be lost. If in doubt, consult [the Convenor]," (City of London Anti-Apartheid Group 1990: 1).

This level of organisation certainly enabled the Picket to continue as long as it did with a clear political message and, to an extent, to minimize avoidable arrests and conflict with the police. Some picketers benefited more from this framework than others. Participating in the Picket, and particularly in direct actions, was riskier for some picketers than others.

In the autumn of 1986, six months into the Non-Stop Picket, City Group led a campaign against police harassment of women picketers, several of whom had been strip searched in front of male police officers, groped and assaulted, and subjected to lewd and abusive remarks following arrests on the Picket. Around this time, and throughout the four years of the Picket, high profile Black activists were also targeted for repeated arrest by the police. City Group took the defence of its supporters seriously, arranging for people to wait outside police stations until arrestees were released, organising and funding their legal defence, and supporting them in court. In the case of the sexual harassment of women picketers in 1986, a writ was even issued against the Commissioner of the Metropolitan Police and civil action taken in the courts. This level of organisation, support and solidarity was effective as, of the more than 500 arrests made during the first two years of the Picket, City Group secured a 92% acquittal rate. City Group may have stood against the state, but it was very effective at using the courts as a political platform when necessary.

City Group did not just experience arrests and harassment at the hands of the Metropolitan Police, they were the subject of 'dirty tricks' by agents of the apartheid regime. On at least two occasions bogus leaflets were distributed in an attempt to smear City Group and cause further divisions between the Picket and the mainstream anti-apartheid movement. These leaflets carefully mimicked the house style of City Group's publicity material, contained correct contact details for the group, and even promoted the group's regular weekly meetings.

In this context of police harassment and dirty tricks, City Group activists were aware that they and their activities were under surveillance not just by the Metropolitan Police and British Special Branch, but also by the South African state's intelligence services. They were aware that the group was probably infiltrated by the police and South African agents. Although no such agents were ever identified with any certainty, this suspicion was justified – after all, the ANC's Chief Representative in London throughout the 1980s Solly Smith (real name Samuel Khanyile) was later revealed as a long-term agent for the apartheid regime. He was a key player in engineering City Group's expulsion from the national Anti-Apartheid Movement.

That City Group managed to operate so effectively, and its activists were able to pull off so many clandestine direct actions over the years, was in large part a measure of how seriously they took security. In this regard, Norma and David Kitson, drawing on their experiences of operating underground in South Africa in the early 1960s, were fine mentors for many young activists. This regard for security infused many of the practices through which the Picket (and the broader work of the group) were constituted. One of the reasons for directing conversations with the police on the Picket through the serving Chief Steward was to minimize 'careless talk'. Similarly, picketers were discouraged from having personal discussions on the Picket, and from bringing personal diaries or address books with them there. All key activists took care over what they discussed on the phone. Great care was taken to maintain the security of the Group's office and new activists often had to wait quite some time before they were trusted with knowledge of its exact location. Again, given that the London offices of the ANC were bombed by South African agents in March 1982, this concern was not exaggerated. By following these precautionary security practices, activists enabled the success of many direct actions, and undermined the efforts of the police to successfully prosecute activists on conspiracy charges that could have resulted in lengthy custodial sentences.

This regard for the security of the Group's actions at times fostered paranoia in many activists. Although City Group operated in an open and democratic manner, and the Picket survived for so long because the Group was pro-active in encouraging the participation and inclusion of new members and supporters, it was easy for individuals to find themselves the object of suspicion. If the act of standing in solidarity on the Picket produced unruly bodies prepared to break the law to demonstrate their opposition to apartheid and to take on the state to defend their right to protest, then at times the internal life of City Group could produce state-like relations between people in response to events that were perceived to jeopardise the integrity of the Picket. Over the years, a number of activists were investigated by the group, called to disciplinary hearings with the Committee, with several expelled from the Group and banned from the Picket. Within City Group, the *most* unruly bodies were those that were suspected of stealing from the Group or acting as police informers.

Conclusion

Throughout this chapter I have outlined the distinctive culture of solidarity created on and by the Non-Stop Picket of the South African Embassy in London in the late 1980s. In examining (and remembering) life on and around the Non-Stop Picket, this chapter makes three important contributions to debate. First it offers a deeper understanding of the embodied nature of activism and direct action. Second, it offers new insights into the emotional geographies of activism and resistance – examining both how protest spaces can foster the empowerment of their participants, but also the limits of this that result from paranoid cultures of security (reproducing certain forms of state-like social relations). Third, I have articulated the reciprocal nature of transnational solidarity, arguing that the Non-Stop Picket did not just extend solidarity to those resisting apartheid in South Africa, but that in doing so it also created a space to think critically about racism in Britain and the role of the British state. In this regard, the cosmopolitan friendship networks created amongst picketers enabled them to see beyond their prior life experiences to question accepted political wisdom and experiment with the boundaries of social conventions. These grassroots cosmopolitan networks cohered as a result of shared opposition to apartheid, but through their quotidian reproduction contributed to extending and deepening cultures of (transnational) solidarity.

A study of the Non-Stop Picket's culture of direct action against the representatives of the apartheid regime has been central to this chapter. I have argued that through this non-violent, but confrontational political stance, the young picketers learned to think and act against the (British) state, using their bodies in (sometimes mundane, but often extraordinary) unruly ways. The space occupied by the Picket, on that pavement in Trafalgar Square, and the vibrant noisy culture of the protest, allowed teenage protestors and others the opportunity and freedom to express themselves in ways that they found constrained in other areas of their lives. More spectacularly, picketers used their bodies on and off the Picket to physically block the normal functioning of apartheid's representatives in Britain, trade with South Africa and those who sought to break the international sanctions against apartheid. In these ways, individuals not only learned how to use their own bodies in unruly ways, but through repeated joint actions with other picketers developed tacit knowledge of how other bodies would respond in particular circumstances. These embodied memories of (one's own and others') unruliness are persistent – more than ten years after the Picket ended, I had chance encounter with some former picketers on another protest. Frustrated by the timidity of other protestors when faced with the private security guards employed to protect the object of our protest, it took little more than a few exchanged glances for the three of us to click back into action, work our bodies together and anticipate what each other was about to do next. A new younger generation of protestors followed our lead, with one asking me with admiration "where did you learn to do *that*?" Twenty years on, although many current activists have never heard of the Non-Stop Picket, its legacy ripples through contemporary protests around Britain and beyond.

Note

Azania was the preferred, decolonized, name for 'South Africa' used by the Pan-Africanist Congress and groups working in the Black Consciousness tradition developed by Steve Biko and others.

References

Bailey, S and Taylor, N (2009), *Civil Liberties Cases, Materials and Commentary* 6th edition, Oxford: Oxford University Press.

Bosco, F.J. 2006. The Madres De Plaza De Mayo And Three Decades Of Human Rights' Activism: Embeddedness, Emotions, And Social Movements. *Annals of the Association of American Geographers*, 96(2): 342–365.

———. 2007. Emotions that Build Networks: Geographies of Human Rights Movements in Argentina and Beyond, *Tijdschrift voor Econmomische en Sociale Geografie*, 98(5): 545-563.

Bozzoli, B. 2004. *Theatres of Struggle and the End of Apartheid*. Athens, OH: Ohio University Press.

Brown, G. and Pickerill, J. 2009. Space For Emotion In The Spaces Of Activism. *Emotion, Space and Society*, 2 (1): 24–35.

Brown, G. and Yaffe, H. (2012), "Non-Stop Against Apartheid: practicing solidarity outside the South African Embassy," *Social Movement Studies.*

Chatterton, P. 2006. 'Give Up Activism' And Change The World In Unknown Ways: Or, Learning To Walk With Others On Uncommon Ground. *Antipode*, 38(2): 259–281.

City of London Anti-Apartheid Group. 1990. *The Non-Stop Picket: A User Friendly Guide*. Unpublished internal document.

Foreign and Commonwealth Office. *n.d.* City of London Anti-Apartheid Group (CLAAG) – Activities/ Non-Stop Picket of South African Embassy, London 1985–1991. Response to FOI Data Access Request.

Fieldhouse, R. (2005), *Anti-Apartheid. A history of the movement in Britain*, London: Merlin Press.

Goodwin, J., Jasper, JM. and Polletta, F. (eds.) 2001. *Passionate Politics: Emotions and Social Movements*. Chicago: University of Chicago Press.

Kitson, N. 1987. *Where Sixpence Lives*. London: Hogarth Press.

Koopman, S. 2008. Imperialism Within: Can The Master's Tools Bring Down Empire? *Acme: An International EJournal for Critical Geographies,* 7(2): 283–307.

Maaba, B.B. 2001. The Archives of the Pan-Africanist Congress and the Black Consciousness-Orientated Movements. *History in Africa*, 28: 417–438.

Massey, D. 2004. Geographies of Responsibility. *Geografiska Annaler* B, 86(1): 5–18.

———. 2008. Geographies of Solidarities. In Clark, N., Massey, D. and Sarre, P. (eds). *Material Geographies: A World In The Making*. London: Sage and Open University Press.

Olesen, T. 2005. *International Zapatismo: The Construction Of Solidarity In The Age Of Globalization*. London: Zed Books.

Roseneil, S. 2000. *Common Women, Uncommon Practices: The Queer Feminisms of Greenham*, London: Cassell.

Routledge, P. 2003. Convergence Space: Process Geographies Of Grassroots Globalisation Networks. *Transactions of the Institute of British Geographers,* 28 (3): 333-349.

Sapire, H. 2009. Liberation Movements, Exile, and International Solidarity: An Introduction, *Journal of Southern African Studies,* 35 (2): 271–286.

Sundberg, J. 2007. Reconfiguring North-South Solidarity: Critical Reflections on Experiences of Transnational Resistance. *Antipode*, 39 (1): 144–166.

Thörn, H. 2006. *Anti-Apartheid and the Emergence of a Global Civil Society*. Basingstoke: PalgraveMacmillan.

———. 2009. The Meaning(S) Of Solidarity: Narratives Of Anti-Apartheid Activism. *Journal of Southern African Studies*, 35 (2): 417–436.

Trewala, P. 1995. State Espionage and the ANC London Office. *Searchlight South Africa*, 3 (4): 42–51.

Chapter 11

Moments of Withdrawal: Homeschooling Mothers' Experiences of Taking Their Children Out of Mainstream Education

Peter Kraftl

Introduction

This chapter is about a moment. For some families, this is one of the most critical moments in their lives. It is a moment when the nature of the relationship between body and State is held under intense scrutiny; when the decision is taken to sever one of the most longstanding associations between body and State: to withdraw one's children from mainstream, State-sponsored education (henceforth: 'school'). This chapter focuses upon the events, decisions and emotions leading up to, during and immediately after families withdraw their children from school, in order to begin educating their children at home.

Home education, or homeschooling, has been a subject for intense debate in several geographical contexts. In some countries, like Germany, the practice is illegal, because it is deemed a contravention of Basic State Laws that tie individual citizens to the State (Spiegler 2009). In the United States, where around two million children are homeschooled, it has been legalised in most states after intense campaigning by parents and religious groups (Collom and Mitchell 2005). There, the gradual state-by-state legalisation of homeschooling has typically been won through recourse to the US constitution: in other words, the 'freedom' to homeschool one's children has been deemed a basic parental *right* afforded by the foundational principles of US law (Cooper and Sureau 2007).

In the United Kingdom (where the research for this chapter was based), homeschooling is legal. It is *parents'* (not the State's) duty to ensure the education of their children. In the vast majority of cases, this simply means that parents send their children to a State school. However, estimates show that somewhere between 50–150,000 children are homeschooled in the UK (Conroy 2010). As a function of UK law, parents only have to declare that they are homeschooling if they *withdraw* their children from school, but not if they never attend school. There is therefore no accurate figure to indicate how many homeschooled children there are in the UK. In addition, parents may elect to undergo State-sanctioned inspections of their teaching methods, but are not legally compelled to do so. In 2009, a review by Graham Badman (HMSO 2009) proposed that homeschooled families be subject to a far greater degree of scrutiny and surveillance, principally over fears that the practice was being used as a cover for domestic child abuse. The report itself found no evidence to support these fears, which, as Conroy (2010) suggests, speaks more of the anxieties of contemporary neoliberal governments over their efficacy to govern subjects 'out of the system' than it does child safeguarding.

Since the change of UK Government in May 2010, homeschooling has remained unaffected by the recommendations of the Badman Report. Hence, it remains – at least by default – a practice *outside* of State provision, scrutiny and control. I want to be careful to clarify here that the majority of homeschooling parents do not wish to divorce themselves or their children from the State *per se*. Ideologically, most parents are not necessarily anti-State – whether for education or other functions – and in a pragmatic sense may well remain tied to the State in all other senses (taxation, healthcare, welfare and so on). Whilst some parents do harbour more radical, anarchist or 'alternative' political convictions, the motivations for homeschooling are so diverse that it is in most cases inaccurate to speak of a complete withdrawal from the State following the decision to home educate (Green and Hoover-Dempsey 2007). Indeed, in research based in the United States (where the majority of research on homeschooling has taken place), the principal reasons for homeschooling are: religious (for politically right-leaning Christian parents fearful of secular forces in society); dissatisfaction with State schooling and its academic content or methods; anxieties about the school environment (for instance where a child is being bullied); and a raft of reasons linked to the intricacies of particular families' lives (Collom and Mitchell 2005).

Notwithstanding the above observations, it should be noted that in the UK (as in many contexts), school is the principal space in which children engage with the State. At school, children are exposed both to the immediate educational concerns of contemporary Governments and in-vogue pedagogical practices, as well as to the longer-term values that will enable them to become fully-functioning, 'autonomous' citizens in a liberal democratic system. Being educated at home, neither of these learning goals can be assured. Again, it is for this reason that in countries like Germany, homeschooling is illegal; and that in the UK, considerable anxieties surround the potential political and cultural alterity posed by homeschooled children not formally 'schooled' to become autonomous, responsible subjects (or, at least, not the kind required by neoliberal governments and economies).

It is with these contexts in mind that this chapter explores the moment when parents decide to withdraw their children from the UK schooling system. This chapter is based on in-depth, life-history interviews undertaken with over thirty homeschooling parents (predominantly mothers) in 2010. The next three sections of the chapter proceed through analysis of some relatively lengthy excerpts from these interviews, in order to illuminate the diverse bodily and emotional energies involved in the process of un-tethering children's bodies from State schooling.

Conceptually, my key contribution to this volume is to centre analysis of bodies/States around the *moment of withdrawal* from the State. As I draw out in my concluding discussion, the moment of withdrawal is a critical event whereby the relationship between body and State is *punctualised* (Munro 2004) and, thereby, heightened, even as that relationship itself is diminished. In the next part of the chapter, drawing on extracts from interviews, the 'moment' is broken down into three kinds of narrative through which the body/State relationship is questioned.

The Moment of Withdrawal: Three Narratives

The core of this chapter focuses on the moment at which parents withdrew their children from school. It is organised around three kinds of narrative produced by interviewees when discussing this moment. Each narrative marks a *punctuation* in the relationship between children's bodies and the State, as follows. First, that one of the key justifications for removing children from school is to cite the bodily effects of being at school before withdrawal. In other words, the decision to home educate is one designed to un-do the purportedly deleterious *bodily* consequences of being State-schooled (and, if only by implication, being subject to the curricula and surveillance techniques of the State). Second, that, in the face of societal (mis) perceptions and fears, many parents feel that they require robust narratives for why and how they homeschool (Lois 2009). Thus 'the moment' when they removed their children from school – and especially the immediate and ongoing bodily/ emotional changes that ensued *after* that time – is a key punctuation point in the construction of parental narratives and identities around homeschooling. Third, as will become obvious, the majority of homeschooling parents are *mothers*. Thus, it is a highly gendered practice that tends – for a variety of reasons – to reinforce spatial divisions of labour between men and women in the course of family life. Thus, the moment of withdrawal is a key punctuation in the lives of these women and, specifically, in their exposition of the particular style of mothering they had adopted.

'He Was Becoming So Physically Ill at School': Embodied (Learning) Practices at School

Parents homeschool their children for a variety of reasons. It would be misleading to suggest that a troubled experience of school is the only (or indeed principal) reason for parents to withdraw their children from school. In addition, a significant proportion of parents (around a third in my study) *never* send their children to school in the first place. Nevertheless, for those parents who do initially send their children to school, the school is a space where their child's body was subject to a range of problematic performative regimes and learning behaviours. These regimes can be schematised into two overlapping narrative categories: school as 'inappropriate', whether for a particular child or for a particular age group; and, school as 'dangerous', usually for an individual child.

Several mothers in my study felt that the school their children attended was *inappropriate*. Many felt that State schools in the UK operate with too much rigidity, asking children to appropriate 'formal' behaviours, styles of learning and ways of relating before they are ready to do so. There was widespread belief that the State-sanctioned behavioural regimes of school would compromise their children's right to a 'childhood'.

> I absolutely struggled with my daughter being in mainstream school at not even four and a half. I hated taking her to school. I hated the formality of the system. She was full-time before she was four and a half. And I felt the State was actually taking my children away from me. And, you know, I was the mother that after every school holiday I cried at the end. So I hated the process anyway. I am an older Mum. So I was forever taking on the teachers and questioning them. You cannot be teaching my five-year-old daughter that! (Donna, mother of two girls, eight and ten).

Donna's experience was a common one. Her notion that the State was 'taking her children away' can be interpreted in several ways. Not only did she have to literally leave her children at school but felt *compelled* – despite UK law allowing otherwise – to send them to school. Moreover, this process was one of a difficult emotional detachment and bodily separation of a mother from her children. As the above quote suggests, Donna struggled particularly with the emotional consequences of this detachment; yet this experience is far from unique and would likely characterise the experiences of many mothers, whether they had subsequently decided to home educate their children or not. The decision to homeschool, then, was not simply a function of the formality of the system or its local expression in Donna's neighbourhood school. Rather, it was the very process of *taking back* her children that mattered. Donna yearned to reinstate (symbolically and emotionally) the bodily proximity to which she had grown accustomed in their earlier years.

Another interviewee, Danielle, was also concerned with the kinds of behavioural codes that children learned in school. Again – implicitly – these codes asked children to acquire bodily skills that would, slowly, begin to divorce them from an unquestioning relationship with their parents and into one with the school (and thereby the State). Danielle suggested that her daughter's school was at least trying to reprogram, at most attempting to undermine, her relationship with her daughter by encouraging the children to keep a secret:

> [T]he children were making father's day ties. And the children were told not to tell anyone, for obvious reasons I suppose, it was supposed to be a surprise. But when they were making them, my daughter piped up in class, 'my Mummy has told me that teachers are not allowed to make me keep secrets'. The teaching staff apologised to me. And I said to them you should *never* ask a child of five to keep a secret from their parents, no matter how well-intentioned. So for me it was an absolute no-no. That was where I was at with *the school system*. I hated

the fact that at just over four she was being taught cursive hand-writing, you know, grown-up hand writing, when she could barely say please and thank you (Danielle, mother of two girls, seven and nine, speaker's emphasis).

Danielle interpreted that this episode was symptomatic of 'the school system'. This feeling is redolent of recent academic critiques that question the role of the State in not only dispensing education (as 'public service') but, increasingly, in intervening in intimate parent-child relationships (Conroy 2010) and even re-wiring individual subjects' neurological networks in the production of governable neoliberal citizens (Jones et al. 2011). Most tellingly, in the latter part of this discussion, Danielle specifically linked her critique of the ideological *approach* adopted in schools (gradual separation from parents and increased reliance on State-sanctioned institutions) with the kinds of bodily skills that her children were learning at that time (cursive handwriting). For Danielle, the two critiques went hand-in-hand. Thus, as in Donna's case, school was a place where children learned inappropriate behaviours and skills – inappropriate for their age, and inappropriate for the kinds of (proximate, bodily) relationship that their mothers would like to preserve with their children.

A second major concern was that school was *dangerous*. Several stories in this category were profoundly affecting – if not outright disturbing – and it felt as if interviewees had (had) to repeat these narratives many times before. Jenny's story is representative of several parents in this study who felt that the material spaces, institutional structures and bodily norms of a school were causing their children bodily and emotional harm.

We took [autistic son] out of school when he was five. That was mainly because he was becoming so physically ill at school. He was having nosebleeds, asthmas attacks, panic attacks – and, he had depression. He had a sick-note from out GP to actually keep away from school because he was so stressed by it. And we thought, if he's getting a sick-note at five then there's something very wrong. The special needs coordinator refused to accept that he had any special needs at all. She thought he was just a precious, precocious child. When he came home he would just melt down. He became suicidal. He would write notes saying he wanted to die, he wished he hadn't been born. They weren't dramatic. They were very logical. He had a very rational argument for why he wasn't happy being in the world.

The decision to take him out wasn't something we would have chosen. We wanted him to be in schools and we tried lots of things to keep him in mainstream [education]. But [son] has sensitivity to touch and smell. So for one hour he was taken out of the classroom to work with a support worker. And for the entire time she sat putting her acrylic nails on. For the whole hour. And she didn't say a word to him. And when he came home [son] said it was awful. He couldn't stand the smell. And his teacher said, oh, I didn't realise he was verbal. So she didn't even know she spoke. And he's really articulate. So we thought if we're fighting so hard for this then we might as well home education. So the decision was *easy* (Jenny, mother of one boy, twelve).

Princiotta and Bielick's (2006) United States-based survey of homeschooling parents found that nearly fourteen per cent of respondents cited special educational needs or disabilities as their principal reason for choosing home education. Thus, whilst the experiences of Jenny's son may not be common amongst broader populations without emotional, behavioural or other disabilities, this group makes up a more significant proportion of those being educated at home. Jenny's case is – whilst sounding extreme – illustrative of a broader feeling about school already articulated in this chapter: that it is inappropriate for the physiological and psychological capacities of a child. Indeed, US-based studies have shown that problems with the 'school environment' are the most frequently-cited reason of all (for more than 30% of parents) for homeschooling (Collom and Mitchell 2005). Moreover, there has been a considerable groundswell of polemical debate about the negative effects upon children of 'disappearing' or 'toxic' childhoods with State school-systems garnering a good proportion of the blame (Postman 1994, Palmer 2006). It should be iterated here that Jenny's experience is of an individual school and probably only three or four teachers at most; yet her experience does reflect these wider debates about the impact of contemporary approaches to State schooling (although not necessarily State provision of schooling *per se*) upon children.

Notwithstanding this distinction between schooling practice and school-as-idea, another common reason for withdrawing children from school was bullying. It was for this reason that Philippa and several other parents were not merely distrusting of State schools but of schooling *per se*.

We didn't so much [have] inspiration for doing home ed[ucation] as desperation. She was bullied extremely badly at the school we had her in. We had to pull her out. Because she was physically abused. It was getting dangerous. We had found her a place in a private school. The headmistress there suggested that we home educate her just for two months. To give her a chance to heal. And just rebuild her trust in people. Just for two months. But once we saw what was available, and how far she could go with this, er, it was her decision [daughter's] and ours not to send her back (Philippa, mother of one girl, 11).

Philippa and Jenny shared relatively extreme experiences of their children's attendance at school. In both cases, school was a place that was somehow bad for children's bodies. In different measures, however, this was a view held by many homeschooling parents who were critical of the UK school system. For, in Philippa's case we once again witness the imperative 'to pull her [daughter] out' of school. The physical act of severing the connection with school – of dis-placing a child back into the home – was one which in many cases becomes either an imperative (for safeguarding a child) or a natural instinct (for reinstated bodily proximity) – or, indeed, both. To 'pull out' is also to 'take back' – to regain full(er) responsibility and control and, as Philippa starkly put it, to allow children's bodily scars to 'heal' so that they can become children again.

Whilst most parents would not frame their decision to homeschool in such emotive terms, it would be fair to generalise that most parents *do* seek to regain a measure of what might have been lost when their children began school. I want to note in closing this section, though, that in the above extracts and in other interviews, parents tended to view their own experiences as somehow symptomatic of State schooling – and the State's treatment of children more generally. Donna felt that the 'State was taking her children' from her; Danielle that cursive handwriting was symbolic of the inelegance and age-inappropriateness of a universal system of education; Jenny that she was 'fighting' more than just a school but an entire system, and so on. But in all cases, the *solution* was expressed as a clear and *positive* one, and not merely a negative reaction: homeschooling. The next section of the chapter examines some of the positive justifications articulated by parents for homeschooling.

'It's A Very Freeing Experience': The Discursive Construction Of Robust Narratives for Homeschooling ater the Moment of Withdrawal

Many parents began their stories of homeschooling by outlining ostensibly *negative* experiences of school, as indicated in the previous section. However, the decision was as much (if not more so) a *positive* one. Specifically, in the narratives constructed by many parents, the move from State-provided, mainstream schooling to homeschooling was figured as a spatial and temporal move from negative to positive. This move was, superficially, a literal one – from the problematic spaces of school to the more fitting spaces of homeschooling (the home, the park, the museum, the library). The very physicality of this move was also symbolic: the moment of withdrawal marking a punctuation point in family life. It was, in some cases, a highly politicised statement of discontent with the State's ability to educate (and care for) children. In others, the moment of withdrawal was symbolic of sheer desperation or exasperation, as indicated by Philippa's and Jenny's stories in the previous section. In all cases, though, to withdraw from the State in such a resolute fashion was to take a brave and difficult step, wrought with uncertainty and angst, hope and relief.

> Initially it was relief it was getting her away from school. But then very worryingly I didn't have the faith in myself. I didn't want to stuff up her life because I couldn't teach her all she needed to do. But then if you do far more research into it, what other families achieve and all the other approaches. Then you get a lot more confidence. It's a very freeing experience. I'm very *glad* she's out of school (Susanne, mother of one girl, 14)

I was so relieved. I remember we wrote the letter, deregistering them from
school. Then we walked to the postbox. And we all cried on the way home. I
was so – glad, to see the back of you lot. I felt it really was them and us. I felt
it was just distant. Leave your child at the door, because I'm [school teacher] a
far better-qualified person to look after your child. And forgive me, I don't agree
that you're necessarily the best person overall. And I think they were glad to see
the back of me as well you (Danielle, mother of two girls, seven and nine)

Susanne and Danielle (above) recalled that the moment they withdrew their child
from school was one highly charged with contradictory emotions. In both cases, the
experience was a visceral one, at least for these two mothers: intense relief mixed
with uncertainty and anxiety. This was a moment that punctuated their lives in literal,
symbolic and emotional terms. It represented the instant at which the bodily stresses
of being 'at school' were replaced by the sudden, sheer weight of responsibility
entailed, as expressed above, in 'taking back' one's offspring. Susanne and Danielle
had – although not irreversibly – become homeschooling mothers; they were only
beginning to reconcile what that meant to their lives and their identities.

Without detracting from the visceral, emotive energy of these life-changing
moments, it is vital to understand how these moments were narrated by parents.
For, the intense emotions therein were attached to at least two broader imperatives,
evident in both Susanne's and Danielle's quotations. First, that the moment of
withdrawal was figured by as a key point of articulation for how and why they
came to homeschool. The move from negative to positive (for Susanne, to a
'freeing experience') allowed parents to set up a duality or opposition between
school and home. As I have already indicated, clear and often profound embodied-
emotional sensations were associated with each space. This was an important
discursive move that had been refined over years of being challenged by cynical
family, friends and strangers over the wisdom of homeschooling. In her wonderful
account of the emotionally layered accounts constructed by homeschooling
mothers In the face of such reproachments, Lois (2009: 203) argues that, '[w]hen
people engage in behaviours that conflict with situational norms, their identity
is called into question [..] violators often feel the need to repair their damaged
identities by explaining their "untoward behaviour"'. Lois (2009) demonstrates
how mothers do so by providing 'excuses' and forwarding 'justifications' for their
choices to homeschool. In my study, mothers' accounts of their reasons – centring
around the emotional duality of school/home – were narratives that, they told
me, had been refined and rendered more robust over time in the face of constant
scrutiny. Thus, the *moment* of withdrawal was not only a punctuation point in
the lifecourse of these mothers, but a key discursive punctuation in the stories
they felt compelled to construct about their lives. As I demonstrate in the third
section of my analysis, this imperative was also tied into discursive constructions
of homeschooling as a (new) identity for mothers.

Reading some of the earlier experiences of mothers, one might quite
legitimately question why they would require any further justification for removing

their children from school. Yet many deployed a second discursive device – a second imperative – to provide a yet-more-robust and contextualised rationale for their decisions to homeschool. This was displayed especially by Danielle(above), who to tied the localised embodied and emotional contingencies of the moment of withdrawal to a broader narrative justification that questioned the role of the State in providing any level of *care* for children. Several other interviewees also made this link, exemplified by Louise.

> At the time [of withdrawal], it was very much about them being children. I wanted them to *be* children. Not about having the latest trainers or whatever. It can be, not always, but it can be quite pressurised in school. My idea was that. I feel that you can't get your childhood back. And if you spend a lot of your time sitting, and writing, and putting your hand up, and being quiet. *I'm not anti-school*. I want to say that now. But I felt I wanted them to have a freedom, that I had in my childhood they would have an Enid Blyton childhood. And they did. And I think, hopefully, it's made them quite independent people. Which they are. They're quite self-sufficient (Louise, mother of two children, twenty and eighteen; emphasis added by author).

Louise articulated several broader discourses apparent not only in the homeschooling movement but in broader (Western) understandings of childhood and children's citizenship (see also James and James 2004, Kraftl 2008). In his ethnography of homeschooling families, Stevens (2001: 4) suggests that homeschooling advocates promote a view of the sanctity of childhood and 'have convinced [homeschooling] parents that their children's bodies are too fragile to be squeezed into desks all day, their needs too distinctive to be handed over to strangers, their minds too pliant to be subjected to secular teachers'. Albeit in a different geographical context – and, in the case of the mothers quoted above, outside the spiritual framework of right-wing Christianity – my study also revealed a strong imperative to link the embodied effects of schooling with broader critiques over the nature of contemporary childhoods in Britain. In particular, Louise suggested that she wanted to remove the *pressure* upon her children imposed by contemporary schooling practices.

Stevens's (2001) point notwithstanding, Louise made an important point in the middle of her discussion of childhood: that she is 'not anti-school'. This, as Suissa (2010, 101) indicates, is a key distinction: between what commentators on 'state schooling claim it *should* be doing – what it is *for* – from questions about what it is *actually* doing'. In Louise's case, it was the practices of schooling – sitting at desks, institutionalised behavioural and learning regimes – that compromise the quality of a childhood. She would not be 'anti-school' if it could offer more 'appropriate' childhood experiences (like those she provided her children after withdrawing them). Inevitably, though, this distinction is blurred in the negative/positive duality articulated above. It is hard to disentangle the spaces and bodily performances of schooling from the curricula and political philosophies with which the foundational principles of State schooling have become associated.

In the case of homeschooling mothers, the blurring of real and ideal presents considerable complexity when attempting to articulate robust justifications for their choice. However, this complexity actually affords a powerful narrative device nonetheless. The complexity is that in forging robust discursive connections between their embodied-emotional experiences of schooling and broader critiques of State schooling, many parents are critical of widely-held societal and political beliefs around school: in other words, that State-provided schooling is a common good. However, simultaneously, they are not, as Louise states, 'anti-school'; nor, indeed, are some parents against the State provision of schooling, if it were radically transformed in terms of *both* classroom practices and underlying pedagogies. More significantly still, Louise's view of childhood is similarly mainstream: it chimes perfectly with widespread Western understandings of childhood. Indeed, contra Lois (2009), the kinds of emotions that homeschooling mothers feel at the moment of withdrawal are perfectly *normal* – they are the kinds of feelings that a mother *should* display under societal assumptions about both mothering and childhood (Kraftl 2008). This seemingly contradictory association with mainstream views of childhood had the effect of bolstering the justificatory narratives articulated by homeschooling parents for their decision to homeschool.

My argument is, then, that the moment of withdrawal from school is a key punctuation point for homeschoolers. It literally punctuated the lifecourse of mothers and their children; but, symbolically and discursively it also provided a cipher wherein spatially and temporally localised emotions and bodily acts could be elided with more broadly rationalised (and therefore apparently more robust) critiques of State schooling. Evidently, in many cases, to simply *feel* that school is wrong is not enough. Furthermore, rather than couching their critiques in purely oppositional terms (i.e. 'anti-school'), some mothers also enrolled traditional, mainstream views of childhood into their accounts. In this way, their immediate emotional responses before, during and after withdrawal were narrated as symptomatic of how any 'normal' mother might feel towards their children. It is to this gendered aspect of homeschooling that I want to briefly turn in the next part of the chapter.

'Home education seemed a natural way to go on': homeschooling as an extension of mothering

In the United States, the work of homeschooling tends to fall disproportionately upon mothers in heterosexual, two-parent households where the father is the principal (or sole) wage-earner (Stevens 2001). The participants in my study indicated that the same is true for the UK. Here, though, I am less concerned with the inequalities and emotion work this involves. For one, these have been well-charted elsewhere (Lois 2010). Moreover, I want instead to focus upon how, despite punctuating their lives and identities in innumerable and profound ways, the moment of withdrawal from school was also framed as an inevitable (or at least 'natural') step in the way that women understood themselves *as mothers*.

I guess the way that we were parenting. I guess you'd term it an attachment style. Promoting the attachment between parent and child and putting that first – co-sleeping, long-term breastfeeding – it wasn't really compatible with the mainstream view, of separating parent and child quite early on. And that's when we came across home education. Which seemed to us a very natural progression (Emma, mother of two girls, nine and seven).

I had already known home educating parents. Partly through La Leche League. I guess it just became a normal part of that group of parents. It seems to be those that were taking the natural, nurturing kind of approach right from day 1, breastfeeding, listening to what the children needed. 99% in my breastfeeding group were like that. So home education seemed a natural way to go on. Listening to the baby and following their signals. Not having this regimented style of parenting (Sarah, mother of one girl, seven).

Significantly, the views of these mothers echoed Lois's (2009) findings with mothers in the United States. In her work, mothers also 'challenged cultural assumptions about the mother-child rhetoric' because developing a physically and emotionally proximate bond with children was simply 'good mothering' (Lois 2009: 222). Here, though, I want to make three further points. Firstly, that whilst homeschooling was deemed a 'natural' extension of mothering, this view was encountered and developed *socially*, at breastfeeding groups like *La Leche League*, for instance. That is not to say that something developed socially cannot also be 'natural'; rather, that the decision to homeschool was not simply part of mothers' individual biographies and was something that was nurtured with the support of other (like-minded) mothers. Secondly, I want to place the 'punctuation' point of withdrawal from school within the context of these longer-term biographies of mothering, whether collective and/or individual. The decision to homeschool was not simply characterised by the embodied and emotional 'shift' from negative to positive characterised above. Rather, the moment of withdrawal was also a punctuation point in the *ongoing* process of becoming a mother, which itself involves profound emotional and bodily changes (and not just before, during and immediately after giving birth). Nevertheless, within this often slow process, the moment of withdrawal was a critical disjuncture at which the 'natural' impulses associated with mothering were clearly articulated: a vital step in becoming a certain *type* of mother, to put it crudely.

Thirdly, however, some mothers drew on the idea of 'natural progression' to directly address the concerns of others about their decision to homeschool. Once again, they enrolled the emotional energies of mothering in order to produce robust justificatory narratives. Principally, mothers dealt with criticism by dismissing what they saw as problematic – and in some cases sexist – assumptions entailed in 'mainstream' mothering practices.

The two questions that everyone asked – that I asked at the beginning when we were deciding whether to do it – were what about time for housework, and what about time for me [mother]? And once I'd reconciled with myself that neither was going to happen, we were away then (Danielle, mother of two girls, seven and nine).

Some mothers who homeschool must, therefore, negotiate some difficult, and often constrained, *choices*. As Danielle indicates, homeschooling directly impacts upon the opportunities, lifestyles and identities available to a woman. It is difficult – if not impossible – to become a mother in paid-work who educates their children at home. Additionally, before visiting their homes, many mothers apologised to me that their houses would be very tidy and unkempt and that this was 'typical' for a homeschooling household. Thus, in Danielle's terms, it appears that homeschooling evokes a widespread fear – at least amongst some women – that more intense styles of mothering require a sense of loss of self or sacrifice. It also appears to simply add to the multiple roles and responsibilities that women in contexts like the UK are expected to fulfil. In several senses, then, this is a brave decision – not least because most mothers must actually decide to choose just *some* of these roles and not others. Indeed, ironically, they are choosing the less socially-acceptable, 'old-fashioned' route of ostensibly becoming stay-at-home mothers whilst not keeping immaculate houses.

For Danielle and other mothers, it was foremost in the conflicting emotions at the moment of withdrawing their children from school that this difficult decision punctuated the veneer of their lives. Even if homeschooling was a natural progression of particular styles of mothering, at the same time, mothers must justify what impact on *them* that decision to withdraw their children will have and how they will cope, both immediately and in the longer-term, with a massive change that will see them divert from the societal expectations that frame women's lives. Concurrently – and, perhaps, somewhat ironically – they drew on the rhetoric of 'natural mothering' to construct a robust counter-argument to those critics who charge them as being 'irresponsible' mothers for removing their children from school. It was not enough to embody natural mothering techniques and to extend them into homeschooling; rather, the decision to homeschool had to be *narrated* as such and framed as one of the sacrifices that women must make (if one that many would deem unusual). Thus, much like the complex ways in which they narrated their relationship with State schooling, women who homeschooled their children were both afflicted by, *and* turned to their advantage, their ambiguous identities as 'mothers'.

Conclusion

Writing on identity, Rolland Munro (2004) argues that the presentation of the self to the other – and its interpretation by that other – is a form of punctualised relation. For him, identities are neither the reflection or social structures (like class or gender); nor are they untethered to those realities, floating in a nihilistic space of unbridled opportunity; and, crucially, nor are they both of these things, as classic structurationist reconciliations of structure-agency would have us believe. Rather – in a move that echoes Emmanuel Levinas' writings on responsibility and Irving Goffman on the performance of the public self – Munro posits that a given identity is revealed in the here and now in response to a contingent situation. At its barest, a person reveals their identity when asked to by an-other. This is, for Munro (2004: 294):

> a 'punctualizing' of identity, the cutting of a specific 'figure' within the here and now. First, and already well established, there is a *positioning* effect, which requires the viewer to be in position to make a specific reading of identity.

> [..]. Second, if less well understood, there is a *timing* effect, in which the 'call' for a specific identity demands a display that annuls other 'calls' – principally by overtaking these within the here and now. [..] These demands over positioning and timing need distinguishing from previous tendencies to assume identity is mobile to context.

In this reading, identity is *called forth* by a social, spatial and temporal context. Identities may be ready, on call; they may be moulded in order to respond to any given situation. For identities to work in this way, we must keep them on-hold; but we cannot perform them all-at-once. Instead, identities are 'standing-reserve' until this or that given moment demands that an individual reveals the most appropriate one; or, 'the crux of such moments of climax is precisely a narrowing in the range of identities that are being ordered' (Munro 2004: 306).

I want to suggest that the *moment of withdrawal* from State schooling is such a moment of climax. That is, it is a moment of climax at the intersection of bodily praxes and feelings on the one hand, and some foundational principles governing the role of the State (specifically *qua* children) on the other. I mean this in four inter-related senses – and the point being that they must be inter-related for the logic of punctuation to fully take hold.

First, the moment of withdrawal itself is a key punctuation – perhaps *the* punctuation mark – within the material realities of life for families who homeschool. As a supplement to Munro's analysis, I have attended to the intense emotions and bodily changes that accompanied the moments before, during and after the withdrawal of a child from school. In fact, I have tried to demonstrate the emotional and bodily *demands* that the demanding relation of which Munro writes make upon (particularly) mothers. Whilst much of my analysis has tied such changes in bodily disposition and feeling *to* broader critiques of State-controlled schooling, I want to stress that it is the feeling of *separation* – of the lived reality of taking a child out of school, with all the responsibility, work and lifestyle changes that that entails – that constituted a key punctuation mark in many mothers' lives.

Second, I want to extend Munro's analysis by stressing how the narrative construction of 'being a homeschool mother' is a repetitive, iterative and anticipatory process that is undertaken over a longer time period than in/for the here and now. As I have repeatedly suggested – and as Lois (2009) has also observed– most mothers constructed highly articulate, well-argued and refined justifications for homeschooling. These narratives were afforded a particular robustness precisely *because* they were repeated so often – to a shop assistant, to a sceptical stranger on the bus, to family members, to police officers, and so on. For some people – like homeschooling mothers – a truly demanding relation is encountered far more frequently than for others. In fact, some mothers told me that they had a very limited repertoire of stories dependent upon the 'type' of person who had challenged them. The revealing of their identities occurred less in the here and now of a *specific* context, then (compare Munro 2004) and more in the well-rehearsed art of a making a value judgment as to whether a listener falls into one of perhaps three or four common categories. Furthermore, I have shown in this chapter that the demanding relation may – for some subjects – be highly specified and specialised. For homeschooling mothers, particular kinds of performance were required: namely, the ability to cope and justify in the face of an *accusation*.

Thirdly, I suggested that the punctuation instantiated by the moment of withdrawal should also be placed in the context of self-narratives that are *flowing* rather than fluid. That is, many mothers viewed the eventual decision to homeschool as an extension of longer-term mothering practices that they felt were right for their children. I argued that their depiction of mothering (of long-term attachment and a proximate bodily/emotive bond with their child) was articulated as a 'natural' bodily impulse that was suppressed by the assumptions inherent in going to school. In addition – again supplementing Munro's (2004) analysis – the process of becoming a 'natural' mother was a shared one developed through support groups rather than (only) in an individual's response to a time-place specific, situational demand.

Finally, taking the chapter as a whole, I have argued that mothers' narratives of homeschooling obtained their robustness because they placed the embodied-emotional contingencies of the *moment* of withdrawal within and at the heart of their reflections on State schooling and contemporary childhoods. The moment of withdrawal was a key punctuation point in the relationship between children's (and mothers') bodies and the State. If one is to analyse bodies and States together (as is the premise of this book), then I have begun to attend to why this kind of moment might matter to these analyses – not least to better understanding the bodily and emotional demands upon those children and mothers who homeschool. Bodies and States are combined in all kinds of (in)glorious concoctions and imbrications; yet, in practices like homeschooling, bodies/States are also decocted through the material realities of families' lives, in ways that throw into sharp relief the role of the State in its subjects' everyday lives. At the same time, in a rather complex and iterative process, justificatory *narratives* for those very moments of disengagement from the State combine the bodily exigencies of particular moments with widely-held, sometimes State-sanctioned discourses about mothering. Thus, the moment of withdrawal from school punctuates the relationships between body/State in many more ways than the mere articulation of identity.

Acknowledgments

Thanks to Jen, Angus and Nicola for asking me to contribute to this volume. I am sincerely grateful to the families who volunteered to take part in my research on Diverse Learning Spaces, and to Leslie Barson for starting the ball rolling.

References

Collom, E. and Mitchell, D. 2005. Home Schooling as a Social Movement: Identifying the Determinants of Homeschoolers' Perceptions. *Sociological Spectrum*, 25, 273–305.

Cooper, B. and Sureau, J. 2007. The Politics of Homeschooling: New Developments, New Challenges. *Educational Policy*, 21, 110–131.

Conroy, J. 2010 The State, Parenting, and The Populist Energies of Anxiety. *Educational Theory*, 60, 325–340.

Green, C. And Hoover-Dempsey, K. 2007. Why Do Parents Homeschool? A Systematic Examination of Parental Involvement. *Education and Urban Society*, 39, 264–285.

Her Majesty's Stationery Office [HMSO] 2009. *Review Of Elective Home Education In England*. London: HMSO.

Jones, R., Pykett, J. And Whitehead, M. In Press, 2011. Governing Temptation: Changing Behaviour in an Age of Libertarian Paternalism. *Progress in Human Geography*.

Kraftl, P. 2008. Young People, Hope And Childhood-Hope. *Space And Culture*, 11, 81–92.

Lois, J. 2009. Emotionally Layered Accounts: Homeschoolers' Justifications for Maternal Deviance. *Deviant Behavior*, 30, 201–234.

Lois, J. 2010 The Temporal Emotion Work Of Motherhood: Homeschoolers' Strategies For Managing Time Shortage. *Gender and Society*, 24, 421–446.

Munro, R. 2004. Punctualizing Identity: Time and The Demanding Relation. *Sociology*, 38, 293–311.

Palmer, S. 2006. *Toxic Childhood: How The Modern World Is Damaging Our Children And What We Can Do About It*. London: Orion.

Postman, N. 1994. *The Disappearance of Childhood*. London: Vintage.

Princiotta, D., & Bielick, S. 2006. *Homeschooling In The United States: 2003*. Washington: U.S. Department Of Education.

Spiegler, T. 2009. Why State Sanctions Fail To Deter Home Education: An Analysis Of Home Education In Germany And Its Implications For Home Education Policies. *Theory And Research In Education*, 7, 297–309.

Stevens, M. 2001. *Kingdom Of Children: Culture and Controversy In The Homeschooling Movement*. Princeton: Princeton Paperbacks.

Suissa, J. 2010. Should The State Control Education?, In *The Philosophy Of Education: An Introduction*, Edited By R. Bailey. London: Continuum, 99–112.

Chapter 12

Greatest Treasures of the Pacific: Multicultural Genders and HIV Prevention in Aotearoa/New Zealand

Matt Sothern

Our communities were an accepted part of Pacific life and culture prior to Western colonization, but have been subject to much stigma and discrimination in more recent times.. [it's] vitally important that we continue to educate mainstream populations in the Pacific on the importance of creating supportive environments... – Phylesha Acton-Brown, NZAF 2007.

To be oppressed you must first become intelligible – Judith Butler, 2004:30.

Introduction

Since the late 1990s those fortunate few who have had access to anti-retroviral treatments have proven that an HIV diagnosis no longer has to mean a death sentence. The World Health Organization insists that adherence to drug treatment regimes can almost halt the progression of HIV. Similar pronouncements about managing HIV infection as a chronic condition feature prominently in advice given by the US Centre for Disease Control and Britain's National Health System, among others. Much of the advice on how to live-with, rather than die-from, HIV is provided by "positive living campaigns" where the focus is on equipping new bio-social communities of people living with HIV (PLWH) to self-manage their diets, relationships to health professionals, advising them on how to comply with drug programs, as well as how to disclose their sero-status and negotiate safer sexual relationships.

Positive living campaigns are supposed to ensure that PLWH can manage their infection as a chronic condition *and* to ensure that they do not pass the virus onto others. Unfortunately these campaigns are not always successful. Indeed, as the number of PLWH has grown so too has the opportunity for diffusion of the virus: quite simply, because more people are living with HIV there is the increased chance of coming into contact with HIV especially if the behaviours with the virus do not change. Many rich countries, even those with comparatively low underlying prevalence rates, have witnessed dramatic growth in the number of people living

Figures 12.1 & 12.2
Images from "Greatest
Treasures of the Pacific"

with HIV since the turn of the millennium. For example, the annual number of new HIV infection in the UK is now twice the level it was in the 1990s. There has been similar growth in new HIV infections in Australia, Finland, and Denmark. While other rich countries have maintained relatively flat rates of new infection most have been unable to reduce the actual number of annual sero-conversions, the result is a growing population of people living with HIV in Germany, France, Japan, Canada, Singapore, the USA and many other places. Some commentators argue that the emergence of HIV as a chronic disease has contributed to these rises because, at least in these rich countries, we are not as scared of HIV as we once were.

Aotearoa/New Zealand is another country that has witnessed dramatic increases in HIV infection. In the eight years between 1996 and 2003 a total of 1027 people were infected with HIV; in the subsequent four years some 1030 people newly sero-converted. Just like the other rich countries mentioned above HIV is not evenly distributed throughout the population – of the 185 new infections diagnosed in 2010, for example, some 59% of were attributed to men-who-have-sex-with-men (MSM) whereas only 21% were the result of heterosexual transmission. Furthermore, it is estimated that 75% of all new heterosexual transmissions were acquired out-with the borders of New Zealand and that, by contrast, just 41% of MSM sero-conversion took place overseas. The result is that 86% of all new HIV infections attributed to sexual contact in New Zealand were the result of MSM practices. For this reason, HIV remains rhetorically figured as both a problem for – and indexes the problem of – the MSM "community". The prominence of MSM in HIV data helps to explain why the primary audience for safer sex messages in NZ remains MSM.

The connection between MSM and HIV is not new. What we now call HIV was first observed in Gay men in California and New York in early 1981 and was 'found' in Western Europe later that same year. Originally known as GRID, or Gay Related Immune Disorder, the HIV virus was finally isolated in 1983 but it took another year for the newly discovered virus be confirmed as the cause of the illnesses observed two years earlier. For the first years of the crisis, therefore, there was much ignorance, mis-information and panic about this new "gay-plague." By the mid-1980s it was clear that HIV could be spread by heterosexual contact, as well as blood products and contaminated needles, the association of HIV with gay men was firmly cemented in the public imaginary.

The New Zealand AIDS Foundation (Te Tuuaapapa Mate Aaraikore o Aotearoa, hereafter NZAF), like many other AIDs service organizations, can trace its roots to gay community organizing during this early period of the AIDS crisis. Early NZAF activities were aimed at providing support for those struggling with HIV/AIDS, fighting stigma, lobbing Government for better medical responses as well as for greater legal protection for those with HIV. Along side these efforts to support those who had been infected, the primary focus of NZAF activities has also been HIV prevention through the dissemination of safer sex messages, aimed largely at the MSM community. In the 25 years since NZAFs founding this focus on MSM community empowerment has become progressively integrated into the broader public-health infrastructure – almost 90% NZAF funding now comes directly from the Ministry of Health.

Over this same 25 year period New Zealand, and particularly Auckland, has witnessed dramatic demographic changes. The 2006 census, for instance, showed that there had been a 20% decline in the proportion of New Zealanders who self-identified as being of Pakeha/European descent. Moreover, while data showed a relatively static European population there was significant growth in Asian and Polynesian populations and clear evidence of their geographic clustering in South Auckland (where the Asian and Polynesian population was predicted to grow by up to 66% in the next decade). These rapid demographic shifts have been accompanied by a re-orientation of both political and economic imaginaries within New Zealand away from the old networks of the British empire and onto the broader Pacific Rim where trading and cultural links with Asia, Australia and the South Pacific are emphasized (see Larner 1998).

It is against this backdrop of rapid ethnic and cultural change as well as dramatic HIV increase that a new HIV prevention campaign was launched by NZAF's aimed at Polynesian MSM in the transnational spaces of South Auckland. "Greatest Treasures of the Pacific," as the campaign was known, involved the distribution of promotional materials such as postcards and posters (figs 1 and 2), workshops and public meetings; unlike previous campaigns that were able to assume a relatively unproblematic population of gay men "Greatest Treasures of the Pacific" was an attempt to recognize the cultural diversity of contemporary Auckland and to offer an explicitly multicultural HIV prevention program. At the heart of the campaign was the understanding that Polynesian formations of gender and sexuality were differently configured from their Pakeha/European counterparts (see NZAF 1996). The particular issue was that Polynesian MSM disidentified (to borrow a term from Jose Munoz 1999) with representations of Gay White Men that had traditionally formed the locus of NZAF prevention work; this was, in part, because "traditional" Polynesian gender categories did not exist in an exclusive binary structure. "Greatest Treasures of the Pacific," therefore, was organized around the explicit representation of Male Polynesian bodies, many of who were ambiguously gendered. The campaign offered spectacular displays of the bodies of *Fa'afafine* (Samoa), *Fakaleiti* (Tonga), *Vaka sa lewa lewa* (Fiji), *Rae rae* (Tahiti), *Akava'ine* (Cook Island) and *Fiafifine* (Niue) each of which was presented as "traditional" gender category. These "traditional" gender categories are commonly assumed to emerge from the highly gendered division of labour in Polynesian cultures where the work of social reproduction (cooking, cleaning, care for the elderly and sick) is only performed by women and thus extended families with an overrepresentation of men may choose to raise a biologically male child "in the way of a woman" from a very early age. These gender categories are therefore not understood as homosexuals, drag queens, transsexuals or transvestites – the Western categories they are sometimes held to approximate – but rather as something uniquely Polynesian. These bodies are neither male, nor female and therefore neither homosexual nor heterosexual, even as they do not exist outside but rather rework each of these categories.

For the sake of brevity I will use the term *Fa'afafine* (whose translation is usually given as "in the way of a woman") in place of each of the specific cultural formations: in choosing to subsume each of these Polynesian gender formations into this single term I obfuscate the different cultures, languages and histories which have given rise to these specific gender performances. In so doing this chapter necessarily repeats the error of squashing the difference within and between these "cultures" in to the anthropological category "Polynesian," a category which allows European to function in this chapter. This danger notwithstanding, I am not attempting to document *Fa'afafine* as an empirical group; nor does this short chapter examine the very real struggles of those New Zealanders who do not fit dominant racial and gender categories (but see Worth 2001). Instead, what I hope to do is raise (but not answer) questions about the way "Greatest Treasures of the Pacific" frames issues of gender and cultural difference as key to stemming the rise of HIV infection rates in Aotearoa/New Zealand.

A recent article in *Current Sociology* expresses something of the difficulty in translating the term *Fa'afafine* within the spaces of a contemporary multicultural Australasia; the definitive sounding opening sentence begins "Samoan *Fa'afafine* are biologically males who express feminine gender identities" (Schmidt 2003: 417) but this certainty quickly gives way to a broad range of oppositions between biological materiality from the cultural work of identity. The article also comments on the treacherous work of translation: while some *Fa'afafine* dress as women, not all do; while some *Fa'afafine* may have sex with "masculine" men, their "role" may be strictly "feminized" and thus cannot readily be described as homosexual; while some *Fa'afafine* may employ "body modifying practices," others do not and thus cannot be described as "transsexual." The oscillation between *Fa'afafine* being both recognizable within Western categories of gender and sexuality, and simultaneously disavowing the relevance of these selfsame categories turns on geographic metaphors of movement: *Fa'afafine* are from Polynesia but have moved to The West, either physically through diasporic networks to places like Auckland or Los Angeles or metaphorically in vehicles such as articles in *Current Sociology* or this chapter. But *Fa'afafine* are not simply from the "South Pacific"; importantly, we are told *Fa'afafine* are from a pre-colonial South Pacific even as they now inhabit a colonial present. The framework within which *Fa'afafine* are normally translated for "post"colonial audience, therefore, is also organized around the suggestion that authentic Polynesian formations of gender and sexuality are disfigured by the ongoing force of colonialization: as Phylesia Acton-Brown of NZAFs Pacific Health Project laments '[o]ur communities were an accepted part of Pacific life and culture prior to Western colonization.' *Fa'afafine* are thus liminal figures not only caught between the categories of male and female but also caught between a pre-colonial past and colonial present, between Polynesia and New Zealand.

It is against the backdrop both of increasing HIV rates and a growing Polynesian population that "Greatest Treasures of the Pacific" emerged. The campaign was an attempt to distance NZAF prevention work from the colonial logics that insist upon the binary distinction between male and female (and the concurrent hetero/homo divide this distinction engenders). This is necessary because HIV prevention campaigns aimed at gay men, for even "men" for that matter, will fail to interpolate *Fa'afafine* within their disciplinary narrative. "Greatest Treasures of the Pacific", in other words, was an attempt at providing a simultaneously multicultural and postcolonial public health intervention that was cognizant of the cultural specificity of sexual and gender identities.

"Identity" is a key term here, because as a contemporary practice of biopolitical regulation, public health campaigns often revolve around the interpellation of a self-identifying subject whose "identity" functions as the modality of their inscription into liberal health-care policy (Armstrong 1993). The aim of such interventions is to produce an educated subject who is thereby capable of adopting a relationship to a prescribed norm organized around the logic of risk (see Lupton 1995, Cruickshank 1999). Thus the billboard I pass daily on my way to work is designed not simply to advertise a growing obesity "epidemic" but to educate me into identifying as at risk of obesity and to eat a salad for lunch. Vulnerability is a key component of how we are supposed to identify ourselves. This "will to identity" is at the core of the disciplinary function of public health campaigns aimed at smoking, heart disease and a range communicable diseases as the recent panics over bird and swine flu demonstrate. Likewise, "Greatest Treasures of the Pacific" sought to encourage *Fa'afafine* to practice safer-sex by asking them to "Know the Risks" and "Stand up to HIV & AIDS": the imagery accompanying the campaign focused on the spectacular presentation of Polyneisan bodies – both of *Fa'afafine* and Polynesian *men*. It is in this visual imagery, an expression of a multicultural present, that *Fa'afafine* are asked to 'see themselves'.

However, reading these closely there is no reference to the kinds of complex urban spaces of contemporary Auckland; these are images of a vaguely Pacific nowhere of brooding volcanoes and blue lagoons, filled with bodies dressed in native/national costume they invoke nostalgia for a timeless Pacific, a place before the 'stigma and discrimination' that has been wrought by colonialism and. These are not so much images of multiculturalism as they are a camp reworking of familiar tropes of an exotic Pacific iconography that turns on temporal and spatial disavowal of the multicultural spaces they are supposed to invoke.

While these images are intended as an explicit response to a multicultural reality, their spatial logics undercut this by reproducing the distance between Polynesian bodies and the bodies of Pakeha/European Aucklanders. Rather than stress Auckland's multiculturalism "Greatest Treasures of the Pacific" confirms the strict divisions between cultures (a division that mirrors the institutional structures of NZAF more generally where various offices deal with Pakeha/ European, Pacific Island, and Maori 'communities'). No place is afforded in these representations for non-Polynesian men or for the relationships between *Fa'afafine* and non-Polynesian men.

Instead, the iconography of these images celebrates the pre-colonial South Pacific as a site of sexual possibility. Of course the South Pacific, and Polynesian culture in particular, as a site of sexual possibility is a trope well established in the archive of colonial encounter – and in this regard the centrality of the figure of the mermaid is perhaps unremarkable. Ever since the sailors on The Bounty decided the pleasures of Tahiti were preferable to life in the British Navy, the South Pacific has figured as a site of sexual pleasure centered on the bodies Polynesian women. Indeed, Captain Cook's legendary restraint when offered Hawaiian women underscored the distance between a sexually promiscuous Pacific the superiority of self-restrained (albeit class specific) European masculinity (see Wallace 2003, Edmond 1997). So saturated with sexuality, the projects of 18th and 19th century South Pacific colonialism were caught between two co-constitutive and hierarchically organized moments. The first, the production of a native Pacific as a site unbridled heterosexual gratification, and second the production of civilized, sexually restrained colonial Pacific modeled after the moral metropole that this image of the sexually excessive Pacific helped to produced and stabilize (see Wallace 2003, O'Brien 2006, Green 2002). The "civilizing" mission of colonialism was ostensibly bound to the inculcation of "proper" sexualities within the bodies of its brown subjects (McClintock 1995, Stoler 2002). Thus the archive of Pacific colonialism is one littered with stories of lost systems of Polynesian gender and sexuality. And so, as Wallace (2003: 1) insists, 'we have learned and learned to lament' as the force of colonialization transformed Pacific sexualities in their own image.

As the opening quote from Acton-Brown demonstrates, such narratives remain influential in accounts of the present-day (post)colonial South Pacific where the recovery of pre-colonial genders and sexualities is often linked explicitly to the epistemological and political-economic challenges facing Pacific postcolonialisms (Istar 1994). Within this narrative, however, a critical focus on the bodies of European men is elided. As Lee Wallace (2003) goes on to argue, the recession of both Polynesian and European male bodies within the colonial archive leaves unquestioned the impact of Pacific formations of male same-sex sexual activity as a site for 'sodomitical pleasure' had on the epistemic security of constructs of western masculinity.

Thus the spectacular representations of Pacific feminine excess within the archive of colonial encounter – and the heterosexual nirvana this excess is presumed to portend – may be seen as a defensive move to drown out the threat to Western masculinities posed by *Fa'afafine*. The South Pacific becomes a hyper-heterosexual space precisely to secure it from its own non-heterosexuality. Thus, for Wallace, the risk to Western sex and gender systems emerges not from European masculinities proximity to Polynesian women (the risk that gentlemen may indulge in the pleasures of brown flesh) but, rather, from the radically different configurations of same-sex activities between Polynesian "men." The threat, in other words, that the Western system of binary genders and the heteronormativities this assumption of gender dimorphism enables is potentially thrown into crisis by the figure of the *Fa'afafine*.

Does 'Greatest Treasures of the Pacific' unwittingly reproduce this same foreclosure by not explicitly allowing for relationships between these Polynesian bodies and the bodies of European New Zealanders? *Fa'afafine*, like other elements of Polynesian cultures in Aotearoa/New Zealand, remain on the order of the exceptional – their "place" in "Greatest Treasures of the Pacific" is found not in the contemporary spaces of a multicultural (whatever that is supposed to mean) and diverse country but instead in a placeless and timeless South Pacific that has been invoked under the signifier of multiculturalism (see Zizek 1997). In this way, is not this avowing of Polynesian presence also simultaneously a disavow of *Fa'afafine's* "hereness" and "nowness"? Moreover, do these spatial and temporal logics of displacing *Fa'afafine* not reinforce a disconnection between Pacific genders and their Atlantic transplant counterparts?

There is no representational space within "Greatest Treasures of the Pacific" to ask the kind of ethnographic questions about how identity is (re)made in the spaces of sexual encounter in a multicultural New Zealand: In what ways are *Fa'afafine* identities re-made in the spaces of a diasporic Polynesian community of a heterogeneous metropolis? To put this more simply, can *Fa'afafine* figure the same way in Auckland as it does in Apia? An equally urgent question is in what ways are Pakeha/European gender and sexual identities transformed in these selfsame multicultural spaces? To put it overly bluntly: what happens when the *Fa'afafine* and the white gay guy fuck? Is it possible that sex between *Fa'afafine* and European New Zealand men offers a moment where the strict epistemic boundaries between two radically different, yet highly interdependent, configurations of gender and sexuality break down? The spatial and temporal logics of "Greatest Treasures of the Pacific" foreclose these kinds of ethnographic questions about how genders and sexualities are currently being remade in Aotearoa/New Zealand. Instead this campaign confirms a kind of epistemic separation between cultures that reproduces the colonial insistence of difference between Europeans and Polynesians. That such a move is made in the name of stemming rising HIV infection rates seems ironic given that, for some time, key to the fight of the global AIDS pandemic has been the insistence that HIV respects no borders.

References

Armstrong, D. (1993) Public Health Spaces and the Fabrication of Identity, *Sociology*, 27(3): 393–410.

Butler, J. (2004) *Undoing Gender*, London and New York: Routledge.

Cruikshank, B. (1999) *The Will to Empower: Democratic Citizens and other Subjects*, Ithaca: Cornell University Press.

Edmond, R. (1997) *Representing the South Pacific: Colonial Discourse from Cook to Gauguin*. Cambridge: Cambridge UP.

Green, K. K. (2002) Colonialisms Daughters: Eighteenth- and Nineteenth-Century Perceptions of Hawaiian Women, in P. Spickard, J. L. Rondilla, and D. H. Wright, eds. *Pacific Diaspora: Island Peoples in the United States and Across the Pacific,* Honolulu: University of Hawaii Press. pp. 221–252.

Istar, Z. (1994) *Daughters of the Pacific*, Melbourne: Spinifek Press.

Larner, W. (1998) 'Hitching a ride on the tiger's back: globalization and spatial imaginaries in New Zealand' *Society and Space*, 16: 599–614.

Lupton, D. (1995) *The Imperative of Health: Public Health and the Regulated Body*, London: Sage.

McClintock, Ann (1995) *Imperial Leather: Race, Gender, and Sexuality in the Colonial Contest*, New York: Routledge.

Munoz, J. E. (1999) *Disidentifications: Queers of Color and the Performance of Politics*, Minneapolis: University of Minnesota Press.

NZAF (1996) *Needs Assessment: Pacific Island Men who have Sex with Men*, Report to North Health, Auckland.

O'Brien, P. (2006) *The Pacific Muse: Exotic Femininity and the Colonial Pacific*, Seattle: University of Washington Press.

Schmidt, J. (2001) 'Redefining *fa'afafine*: Western Discourses and the Construction of Transgenderism in Samoa' *Intersections*, No. 6.

Stoler, A. L. (2002) *Carnal Knowledge and Imperial Power: Race and The Imitate in Colonial Rule*, Berkley: University of California Press.

Wallace, L. (2003) *Sexual Encounters: Pacific Texts, Modern Sexualities*, Ithaca and London: Cornell UP.

Worth, H. (2001) 'Bad Assed Honeys with a Difference: South Auckland *fa'afafine* talk about identity' *Intersections*, Number 6.

Zizek, S. (1997) 'Multiculturalism, Or, the Cultural Logic of Multicultural Capitalism, *New Left Review*, 225: 28–51.

PART IV
Sovereignty and Surveillance

Chapter 13

Governing Mobile Bodies: Human Trafficking and (In)security States

Claudia Aradau

As the UK marks 200 years since the Parliamentary Act to abolish the slave trade, slavery goes on in another form. The slave trade, outlawed by legislation introduced in March 1807, saw people from Africa transported en masse to the Americas with the involvement of people from the UK and other European countries. Modern day victims of slavery are often young women from Eastern Europe, thinking they are coming to England to work as cleaners or au pairs, only to be forced into prostitution (BBC, 2007).

Introduction

As the description of human trafficking at the beginning of this chapter indicates, human trafficking evokes imaginaries of slavery, suffering and dehumanization. Modern slavery, victimhood and horrible suffering are the analogies most often deployed to render the plight of human trafficking to Western publics. Images of suffering bodies, bodies in pain accompany the stories of trafficking told by NGOs and the media. 'Sex Trafficking in the UK; one woman's horrific story of kidnap, rape, beatings and prostitution' titled an article in *The Observer,* for which its author, Mark Townsend was awarded the Human Trafficking Foundation Media Award (Townsend, 2011). At first sight, these are straightforward stories of victimhood and protection. The securitization of human trafficking would then entail the protection of victims of human trafficking by states, NGOs and international organizations. Yet, the story of human trafficking appears immediately less straightforward. Not only does human trafficking often go on undetected, but many of the anti-trafficking organizations point to the inadequacy or failure of protection.

This chapter argues that the failure of protection is not due to lack of awareness or insufficient training of authorities. Rather, the failure is intrinsic to the problematization of human trafficking as a security threat. I show that calls for protection are ultimately undermined by the imaginary of threat which posits victims of trafficking as modern slaves lacking agency, whose suffering gives rise to a 'politics of pity'. These calls for protection and emotional identification with bodies in pain obscure the fact that human trafficking is deeply entwined with fears of mobility. Mobile bodies are deeply caught in a 'politics of risk' which classifies victims of trafficking function of their vulnerability to re-trafficking and migration. The entwinement of victimhood and danger, of pity and risk can be understood by unpacking the continuities in the governance of human trafficking. Understood as a threat to potential victims around the world and to the fabric of states, human trafficking is made governable through attempts to prevent, reduce and eliminate the dangers it poses. The chapter will show how the governance of human trafficking insidiously transforms bodies in pain into psychological cases to be governed by risk technologies within a 'politics of risk'. Risk and pity are in no way mutually exclusive, but build upon each other to buttress governmental interventions.

To this end, the chapter proceeds in three stages. It first explores the 'politics of pity' deployed by anti-trafficking NGOs and European organisations to make sense of human trafficking and create emotional identification with victims of trafficking.[1] Second, I turn to the 'politics of risk' or how these actors engaged in counter-trafficking struggles also mobilise risk knowledge for the purposes of governing human trafficking. Finally, I analyse the continuities between pity and risk to reveal the danger of human trafficking as that of mobile bodies.

Emotions and the 'Politics of Pity'

From the war on terror to interventions in crisis situations (e.g. famine and natural catastrophes), political actions depend on and are limited by emotions. Emotions become thus a governing technology, they constitute intersubjective relations and steer the spectators' actions towards solidarity with victims, outrage with perpetrators or moral indifference.[2] We are to be emotionally affected and experience solidarity with victims of catastrophes or terrorist attacks, but to remain immune to the suffering of terrorists.

The 'politics of pity' (Arendt 1990: 59–114) is such an 'emotional' governmental model practised in relation to victims; the excluded and suffering others of international politics. Emotions can foster new commonalities in the face of diversity, creating solidarities beyond the traditional ones of the nation-state and common morality. In conditions of postmodernity, of fragmentary, discontinuity and inconsequentiality (Baumann 1995), suffering and emotions are at the heart of a new type of solidarity. Feminist scholars have also reclaimed emotions as grounds for progressive political action, challenging the equation of 'unhealthy' emotions with femininity. Emotional responses are viewed as important sources

---

1   This chapter focuses on anti-trafficking efforts in Europe and responses by the European Union and OSCE institutions.

2   Despite the role that emotions play in practices of international politics, their potential, challenges or inconsistencies have received scant scholarly attention in the discipline of international relations. For a discussion of the marginalization of discussions about emotions in international relations theory, see Crawford (2000).

of human values and ethics and as a proper basis for political action (Lupton 1998; Tronto 1995). The feminist literature has advocated an 'ethics of care' to replace the universalising assumptions of the 'ethics of justice'. Unlike justice, care is focused on concrete others and responds to specific situations. The ethics of care – feminists have argued – forces us to place moral and political concerns within the context of people's daily lives (Tronto 1995).

In these approaches, emotions can therefore ground new ways of radical politics, providing a bond for communities and creating solidarity in conditions of fragmentation or fragmented morality. Among emotions, pity as a response to suffering has a special position. In Cynthia Halpern's (2002: 10) formulation, '[w] hat we can do is the primal question that arises from the experience of suffering, either in ourselves or in relation to what we see at a distance'. Besides functioning as a crucible for empathy and intersubjective notions of the self, suffering is clearly linked with agency and action (Scarry 1985). Pity thus becomes directly linked with practical interventions, with actions which envisage a re-structuring of the existing situation. A politics of pity tackles the 'disordered situation' (Whitebrook 2002), the social context which has led to suffering by privileging particular others rather than 'objectively' the situation. In this sense it is meant to fulfil a double role that commends it to political theory: it can create new commonalities, while at the same time challenging existing social relations which have been conducive to suffering. Unlike fear or hate, pity can rather be said to function rather as an anti-governmental technology, concerned with emancipation from particular systems of power, or from the effects of the deployment of particular techniques of power (Hindess 1998).

Despite its emancipatory promise, pity also has harsh critics, who question this political potential. Wendy Brown (1995: 27) has insightfully warned that a politics of pity 'delimits a specific site of blame for suffering by constituting sovereign subjects and events as responsible'. Even one of the most astute defenders of politics of pity, Luc Boltanski (1999: 100), felt it necessary to formulate its downsides: 'emotions can be discredited as foundations and symptoms of a moral position due to their circumstantial character – bound as they are with a particular situation in which they are tethered to the real or imaginary presence of a particular unfortunate – which does not enable or construct a moral duty with general validity'.

Yet, all these objections can be thought to function merely as warnings about the efficacy of an (anti-)governmental intervention. In one of the most cogent theoretical treatments of pity, Boltanski engages with several of the tensions and criticisms of a politics of pity and translates such theoretical objections into practical injunctions to strategize pity. Boltanski acknowledges that suffering is socially constructed and that certain types of suffering have surfaced in various epochs, while others have passed unnoticed. He translates this insight into a practical task for those who convey suffering: to make it recognisable, to include it in a so-called repertoire of recognisable suffering. The politics of pity therefore needs to configure suffering as recognisable, something the spectators can identify and sympathize with. Suffering must be seen as undeserved, since pity cannot be experienced towards the culpable and the dangerous.

The elimination or alleviation of suffering is part of a process of governing, of social and political ordering, in which the causes of suffering are eradicated, dealt with or transformed. In governmental terms such an intervention has not only to represent and, in this sense, constitute a particular situation, but also to confer particular identities upon political subjects. As William Connolly (1999) has suggested, the subject of a politics of pity need be divorced from a construction of danger. The most important task for the politics of pity is therefore one of identifying victims of trafficking by dis-identifying them from such a dangerous subject. To activate the spectators' pity, trafficked women need to be specified as non-dangerous. Victims of trafficking are therefore dis-identified from illegal migrants whose mobility creates unease and raises fears about the policing of state boundaries. The requirement of identification/dis-identification becomes a request for knowledge about each individual.

Michel Foucault's (1999) analyses of the government of abnormals have shown how governmental interventions have become dependent upon the specification of the individual. Starting from the 18th century, punishment was no longer to be meted out according to the crime, but in close relation to the potential redemption and future danger of the individual. The invention of the 'dangerous individual', neither mad nor criminal, requires expert knowledge to decide on her identity. A governmental technology is therefore decided and depends upon an expert description of the subject. As the politics of pity can only operate for certain categories of individuals, i.e. the non-dangerous, the question 'who are you?' demands an urgent answer to make action possible.

Strategizing Pity: Trafficked Women and the Body in Pain

A politics of pity has been advocated and practised by various NGOs involved in anti-trafficking campaigns with the explicit purpose of challenging governmental practices that considered trafficked women as illegal migrants and foreign prostitutes involved in illicit affairs. Amnesty International, as many other NGOs involved in counter-trafficking campaigns, has argued that women are 'systematically subjected to torture, including rape and other forms of cruel, inhuman and degrading treatment' (Amnesty International 2004).

Pity and representations of victimhood aimed to challenge the threat representation of human trafficking, or what NGOs had called the 'law enforcement' approach, which considered trafficked women as illegal migrants and promptly deported them. As Jacqueline Berman (2003: 59) has shown, the particular combination of the movement, 'race', and gender of migrant East European sex workers turns them into an external and internal threat by 'disrupt[ing] the ability of the state to adjudicate membership in the political community'.

NGOs and anti-trafficking activists have argued that, besides being victimised by their traffickers, women were also subjected to increased suffering by the state. As a result of these practices of secondary victimisation, victims of trafficking were thought either to fall an easy prey to traffickers all over again or to experience suffering and stigma when returned to their countries of origin. 'The trafficking cycle cannot be broken without attention to the rights and needs of those who have been trafficked', states the UNODC Toolkit for Combating Trafficking in Women (UNODC, 2008). A politics of pity could thus disrupt the state repressive measures of treating victims of trafficking as dangerous illegal migrants, prostitutes and/or criminals; it was harnessed to a re-structuring of social relations in the sphere of trafficking and envisaged specific interventions, different from strategies embraced especially by those concerned with migration and organised crime.

To promote understanding and sympathy for the situation of victims of trafficking, the advocates of pity focus on the directly physical pain and suffering trafficking causes. The main purpose of these accounts is to promote identification with victims of trafficking in a way that overcomes any distinctions between genuine and bogus, innocent and guilty. Following Boltanski's (1999) analysis of pity, two strategies appear at work in representations of human trafficking to render all women equally innocent and deserving of pity.

One such strategy represents the suffering of trafficked women by directing it to a cause, the perpetrator of violence upon whom emotions and efforts will subsequently focus. This rather unproblematic *topic of denunciation* makes violence directly attributable to responsible agents. Emotional accounts of trafficking focus on portraying the evil traffickers who exploit and reduce women to an undignified state of slavery. The second strategy, focusing exclusively on women, is *the topic of sentiment.* Unlike the topic of denunciation, the topic of sentiment dispenses with accusation and the search for the victimiser or persecutor. It addresses the spectators who are to be moved by the victims' victims and attempts to create a community of 'visceral' reactions, which pre-exist their principled justification. The physical suffering of trafficked women is meant to trigger such visceral reactions, to function as a 'solidarity-inducing denominator' (Boutellier 2000: 68) and anti-trafficking campaigns have made extensive use of a symbolic of the body in pain: raped, beaten, and defenceless. In 2007, three of the most prominent NGOs in the anti-trafficking struggle in the UK – Amnesty International, Anti-Slavery International, Eaves UK and Unicef UK – organised an art exhibition 'Slave Britain: The 21st Century Trade in Human Lives' (Amnesty International et al. 2007). While the exhibition attempts to depict normal people, the images are accompanied by stories of suffering, pain and abuse. The exhibition is symptomatic of the representation of victims of trafficking.

And yet, not all trafficking victims have been redeemed by physical suffering. Despite these unifying representations of inflicted pain, not all victims have been physically abused, abducted and then repeatedly raped, beaten up, bodies burned with cigarettes ends. It is almost as if women need to be 'purified' through blood. Representations of 'innocent victims' versus 'guilty whores' insidiously infuse these images, as Jo Doezema has noted (2010). Moreover, Rutvica Andrijasevic (2007: 26) has remarked that 'this type of representation restages the familiar scenarios where female bodies are portrayed as passive objects of male violence and are positioned within the space of the home and the nation'. Just like the politics of pity more generally, the specific strategies that NGOs have devised for redefining and relocating the trafficking of women in a different narrative raises a series of problems by promoting a particular image of victims of trafficking as deprived of agency, rendered simply human by the power of suffering, passive and mouldable subjects who can be returned to their roles in the countries of origin.

However, the problem of identifying victims of trafficking as bodies in pain and advocating a politics of pity can never receive its final answer in visual representation or victim confessions. The governance of human trafficking requires knowledge of the individuals it is supposed to govern. Who are the women upon whom pity should be bestowed? The confessional answer the women themselves provide, or the NGOs' semi-confessional answers, need to be backed up by expert knowledge. The question 'who are you?' can never be completely answered by the incriminated individual. Although the 'psychiatrization' of criminal danger was based on procedures of confession, self-examination, and revelation, as Foucault has shown, it also involved an expert assessment of the future risk that the individual could pose. Such a doubling of confession by the knowledge of risk was linked to the shift from thinking that punishment should answer the crime, to thinking of it as a mechanism in the 'defence of society' (Foucault 2000). Thus, the question 'who are trafficked women?' needs a supplementary answer. This other answer, which is harnessed to the management and prevention of the phenomenon of trafficking, mobilises a politics of risk rather than a politics of pity.

Dangers and the 'Politics of Risk'

What is a politics of risk? From its beginnings in practices by the welfare state to insure against work accidents, risk has become one of the main technologies of neo-liberalism, which attempts to create prudential, autonomous and self-regulating citizens. The complex regime of risk management today owes to the various technologies of risk which have gradually developed over time in relation to the domains of insurance, work, and mental medicine (Greco 1993: 360). François Ewald (1993) has shown that for a long time the domain of risk has been co-extensive with the insurable. Risk as part of the insurable was an invention of the 19th century, which discovered the accident, something in-between nature and human will. Insurance risk therefore becomes social and is deployed as a 'technology of solidarity' which makes accidents, unemployment and other social problems collectively borne through insurance (Dean 1999: 140). This solidarity that insurance risk was supposed to foster in a collectivity, however, came to be opposed in another rationality of risk management; namely, prevention of social disorders. Formulated to deal with problems posed by 'dangerous individuals', delinquents, and criminals, this other rationality of risk has borrowed heavily from the expert knowledge provided by psychology and psychiatry. Such clinical rationality of risk was therefore initially focused on the likelihood of a person (in particular, a mentally ill person) committing a violent act. But if psychological *savoir* was initially taken out of the asylum and the clinic to govern the risk of dangerous behaviour of criminals, mental defectives, sexual perverts, and psychopaths, it has been gradually extended to more and more 'marginal' categories, such as alcoholics, drug addicts, and children with learning disorders. As the authors of *The Psychiatric Society* have aptly put it, psychology colonised social life (Castel et al. 1982).

Psychological knowledge of risk has increasingly transformed political, economic and social problems, and has made these problems thinkable in new ways and governable by different techniques (Rose 1989: ix). In her astute analysis of how the therapeutic paradigm functions in post-conflict societies, Vanessa Pupavac (2001: 359) starts from the premise that 'social psychology's perspectives have become central to Western domestic social policy, to how Western governments relate to their own citizens and also how individuals in the West understand themselves'. However, psychological knowledge itself is colonised in a particular way by the already existing technologies of risk.

The politics of risk refers to a specific combination of the various rationalities and technologies of risk. Robert Castel (1981) has documented a mutation of social technologies that minimise direct therapeutic intervention, supplanted by an increasing emphasis on a preventive administrative management of populations at risk. Strategies of prevention are based on the assumption that if prevention is necessary, a danger exists, even if only in a virtual state before being actualised. As these correlations remain arbitrary and can only be proven *a posteriori*, dangerousness becomes 'a quality immanent to a subject' (Ibid: 146). The virtuality of danger is related to specific individuals and groups who are to be categorized as 'high risk'. Risk practices therefore concern the qualitative assessment of people. Risk profiling is a privileged technique in the assessment of risk, based on 'procedures for the allocation of individuals to risk groups, on a genealogical basis, in terms of a family history of illness or pathology, and/or on a factorial basis, in terms of combinations of factors statistically linked to a condition' (Rose 2001: 8). Although linked with the risk management of populations, preventive risk also involves a therapeutic objective in the administration of individuals diagnosed as pathological (Weir 1996: 374).

This double aspect, individualizing and collectivising, of risk technologies appears most explicitly in clinical risk management. Clinical risk techniques, Weir has pointed out, 'breach the distinction between disciplinary governance that acts on individual bodies and security governance that acts on populations' (Ibid: 382). They implement population-based calculations, forming risk groups by applying risk categories to the bodies of persons who are then placed under surveillance or treatment. Some groups are to be defined as 'high risk', with risk being defined as internal, due to their behaviour or biography, rather than external. Those deemed a risk to the community are subjected to therapeutic (e.g. counselling, self-help groups, support groups) and disciplinary (training and re-training) interventions in an effort either to eliminate them completely from communal spaces (e.g. by various forms of confinement) or to lower the dangers posed by their risk (Dean 1999).

Technologizing Risk: Psychological Trauma(s)

If the 'politics of pity' relied upon confessional or semi-confessional answers to the question, 'who are the trafficked women?' (i.e. 'who are you?'), the politics of risk provides an expert answer. Victims of trafficking cannot remain pure presence; their identity needs to be further specified and assessed for the purposes of governing human trafficking by preventing its occurrence and limiting its dangers. Victims of trafficking need to be profiled for both identification and preventive purposes.[3] It is these specific profiles, developed in conjunction with psychological knowledge, that make possible their constitution as subjects to be governed. The governance of human trafficking relies on delimiting and categorising 'high risk' groups, which are at risk of being trafficked. This representation of vulnerability is at first sight consonant with the unifying representations of victims as suffering bodies, as the risk is taken to be the risk to the women's well-being. Yet, I will show that trafficked women also mutate into risky mobile bodies, just as groups at risk were thought to embody a permanent possible danger.

The identification and calculability of risk depend on the construction of risk profiles. Studies of risk practices have emphasised the construction of biographical profiles of human populations for risk management and security provision (Ericson and Haggerty 1997). Victim profiles have also become ubiquitous in trafficking reports and studies of the phenomenon. The Council Framework Decision on combating trafficking in human beings identifies trafficked women as victims of coercion, force or threats, including abduction, deceit or fraud, abuse of authority and vulnerability (EU Council 2002). In NGO analyses socio-economic conditions have been translated at the individual level as 'a strong desire to seek employment abroad', thus shifting the emphasis from questions of inequality to vulnerability factors (El-Cherkeh, Stirbu, Lazaroiu and Radu 2004). Psychological counselling counts as one of the most important methods for victim assistance and reintegration. A Report by the Regional Clearing Point (RCP) on Trafficking in South Eastern Europe (2004) cites medical care and psychological counselling

---

3   Identification of victims of trafficking has become one of the main elements in the fight against human trafficking. NGOs and organisations such as the EU, the Council of Europe and the UNODC deem the lack of identification or lack of proper identification as one of the reasons prevention has not been successful. Hence, these institutions have produced training manuals for judges, immigration officials and NGOs to help with the identification of victims of trafficking (see e.g. UNODC, 2008, Chapter 6).

as the first two strategies of integration, while expressing concern about the little emphasis placed on educational assistance and lack of vocational and training programmes in transit and destination countries.

In the general assemblage of risk factors used to govern specific groups, victims of trafficking become mostly an assemblage of psychological risk factors. From the NGOs perspective, this shift to psychological profiling is not surprising, given that they understand trafficking as a traumatic experience for women. For psychological expertise, a traumatic experience is also linked with specific factors in the victim's past. Animus, the main NGO involved with returned trafficked women in Bulgaria, warns that it is important to consider the predispositions that exist in the personal history of women and girls (Stateva and Kozhouharoya 2004: 110–16). Typical risk profiles of victims of trafficking will therefore include past biographical details deemed important by the experts. Animus also indicates that the groups most at risk of being trafficked are women and adolescents who have suffered traumatic experiences, e.g. victims of domestic violence, sexual assault, children from orphanages, and children with a large number of siblings and only one parent. 26% of the returned women at Animus had been victims of incest or childhood psychological abuse and all of them had untreated psychological trauma (Stateva and Kozhouharova 2004: 112).

In these reports, victims of trafficking appear as doubly traumatised, both by the experience of trafficking and by earlier/childhood experiences of abuse. The experience of trafficking is a repetition, an almost fateful reliving of earlier traumas. The past however, especially the location of a traumatic event in the victim's past (such as childhood abuse, dysfunctional family environment, domestic violence and institutional abuse) activates another scenario of psychotherapeutic practices. Victims of sexual abuse, psychological studies have shown us, are likely not only be re-victimised, but they might well become 'perpetrators' themselves. In cases of child abuse or violence, the necessity of abused children to defend themselves at an early stage in life might evolve into offending behaviour later on (Romano and De Luca 1997: 86). On a less extreme level, women who have been sexually abused as children and those who have been traumatised are more likely to engage in future risk-taking behaviour than those who have not experienced abuse (Zimmerman 2004). Even those who claim that survivors of childhood abuse for example are more likely to be victimised than to victimise other people cannot deny a connection with adult antisocial behaviour (Herman 1997).

These insights activate a politics of risk and calibrate the governance of human trafficking towards limiting the possibility of a risky offender to re-offend. The spectre of potential offences, whether understood as antisocial, risky or even criminal behaviour surreptitiously infuses the politics of pity. If the continuity of trauma could be thought as consonant with the politics of pity, which could still construe sexual exploitation as the undeserved surplus of earlier, also undeserved, abuse and violence, the risky-ness inscribed in the women's biographical profiles ends up by subverting pity. Strangely reminiscent of the governmentality of drug- and alcohol-addictions, 'rehabilitation' is the motto for victim assistance practices (see e.g. Tudorache 2004). The expert knowledge mobilised by NGOs with the purpose of helping trafficking women becomes 'hijacked' by a politics of risk which is based on risk minimisation and containment. The women 'at risk' insidiously metamorphose into 'high risk' groups and risk technologies are deployed under the banner of therapy not just to help victims of trafficking overcome their trauma and ease their suffering, but also to limit the possibility of 'potential dangerous irruptions' (Castel 1991: 288).

What is this dangerous irruption, what is the potential offending behaviour of trafficked women? EU documents are un-ambiguous on this point. If trafficked women are to re-offend, offence is to be understood as immigration, the undesirable mobility of strangers. The Council Proposal for a decision to combat human trafficking has explicitly stated that helping victims of trafficking or smuggling is a way of preventing them from lapsing into an illegal immigration situation (EU Council 2002). The joined EU-IOM-NGOs Brussels Declaration also harnesses victim reintegration to reducing the risk of re-trafficking (STOP Conference 2002). While trafficked women are involved in psychological therapy (together, for example, with victims of domestic violence and rape), these programmes are seen by the EU as part of prevention strategies and therefore need to be supplemented in most cases by return to the country of origin. A Commission discussion paper on granting a short-term residence permit can even unproblematically conceive of the fight against illegal migration as two-pronged: either through first dismantling the networks or through first helping victims get out of their illegal situation and avoid lapsing into it again (which would also be linked with psycho-social measures) (EC 2001). The 2011 EU directive on 'preventing and combating trafficking in human beings and protecting its victims' emphasises assistance and support for victims of trafficking 'before, during and for an appropriate period of time after the conclusion of criminal proceedings' and restricts protection ot the process of criminal investigation (European Parliament and EU Council, 2011). The distinction between 'assistance and support' on the one hand and 'protection' on the other carries connotations of illegitimacy or unjustifiability concerning lengthy assistance and legitimacy of protection in relation to prosecution of trafficking. These tensions and contradictions pass, however, unnoticed.

From the standpoint of women, protection is integrated with the risk management of illegal migration, which subverts and re-appropriates the non-judgemental concerns of a politics of pity. The potential risk of women's mobility is to be contained and prevented; mobile bodies are to be surveyed and disciplined, subjected to trauma therapy with the purpose of turning them into subjects able to monitor their own risk. Risk technologies have made possible the specification of the victim – previous object of pity – as inherently and continuously 'risky' and have modified the emotional promise of the politics of pity into an abstract suspicion of risk.

Conclusion

This chapter has shown that a politics of pity that represents human trafficking as a new form of modern slavery conducing to unspeakable suffering is reconciled with danger politics of risk that attempts to contain mobile bodies for the purposes of governing human trafficking. The insecure states in which victims of trafficking find themselves are subsumed under the strategies and technologies of securing the State-as-container against mobile bodies. By exploring how a politics of pity and a politics of risk are brought together in the governance of human trafficking, I have shown that the conjunction of pity and risk turns the vulnerable bodies of trafficked women into a site of potential dangerous irruptions of uncontained mobility.

Understood as interventions with the purpose of governing the threat of the phenomenon of human trafficking, the politics of pity and the politics of risk,, confer specific identities upon women: the politics of pity attempts to turn them into universal suffering bodies, while the politics of risk provides a scientific examination of their vulnerability. Victims of trafficking are specified as groups 'at risk', bearing the particularity of both social conditions and of biography. For the rationality of risk management, the 'discovery' of the victims' past traumas and abuse becomes an indicator of future risk. This particular construction of women's bodies turns women into 'risky' selves perpetuating a risk of illegal migration, of undesirable mobility to Western states. Consequently, victims of trafficking appear in need of being disciplined and monitored under the guise of protection. Risk management becomes the insidious, disavowed presence within the discourse of modern-day slavery and risky mobile bodies the threat that is effectively targeted by practices of governance.

Acknowledgements

An earlier version of this chapter was published in *Millennium: Journal of International Studies* 2004 33 (2): 251–277 under the title 'The Perverse Politics of Four-Letter Words: Risk and Pity in the Securitisation of Human Trafficking'.

References

Amnesty International, Anti-Slavery International, Eaves UK, Unicef UK. 2007, 'Slave Britain: The 21st Century Trade in Human Lives' [http://www.guardian.co.uk/slideshow/page/0,2013927,00.html] (accessed on 10 April 2012).

Andrijasevic, R. 2007. 'Beautiful Dead Bodies: Gender, Migration and Representation in Anti-Trafficking Campaigns', *Feminist Review* 86: 24–44.

Arendt, H. 1990. *On Revolution*. Harmondsworth: Penguin Books.

Bauman, Z. 1995. *Life in Fragments: Essays in Postmodern* Morality. Oxford: Blackwell Publishers.

BBC, 2007. 'Sex Slavery Widespread in England', available from http://news.bbc. co.uk/1/hi/england/6459369.stm (accessed 13 December 2011).

Berman, J. 2003. '(Un)Popular Strangers and Crises (Un)Bounded: Discourses of Sex Trafficking, the European Political Community and the Panicked State of the Modern State', *European Journal of International Relations* 9(1), 59.

Boltanski, L. 1995. *Distant Suffering, Morality, Media and Politics*, trans. Graham Burchell (Cambridge: Cambridge University Press, 1999)

Brown, W. 1995. *States of Injury, Power and Freedom in Late Modernity* (Princeton, N.J.: Princeton University Press), 27

Bruggeman, W. 2002. 'Illegal Immigration and Trafficking in Human Beings Seen As A Security Problem for Europe', Speech at the IOM-EU Conference on Combating Human Trafficking, 19 September 2002

Castel, R, Castel, F. and Lovell. A. 1982, *The Psychiatric Society,* trans. by Arthur Goldhammer (New York: Columbia University Press).

———. 1991. 'From Dangerousness to Risk', in *The Foucault Effect: Studies in Governmentality,* eds. Graham Burchell, Colin Gordon and Peter Miller (Chicago: University of Chicago Press: 281–298.

Centre for Prevention of Trafficking in Women/Centrul pentru prevenirea traficului de femei, 'Trafficking in Women in Moldova. Reality or Myth'/ 'Traficul de femei in Moldova. Realitate sau mit', 2002 [http://www.antitraffic.md/ materials/reports/cptf_2002_05/] (accessed 31 October 2004).

Connolly, W. 'Suffering, Justice and the Politics of Becoming', in *Moral Spaces. Rethinking Ethics and World Politics,* eds. David Campbell and Michael Shapiro (Minneapolis: University of Minnesota Press, 1999), 129.

Counter-Trafficking Regional Clearing Point (RCP), 'First Annual Report on Victims of Trafficking in South Eastern Europe', [http://www.iom.int// DOCUMENTS/PUBLICATION/EN/RCP_trafficking_southeastern_europe. pdf] (31 October 2004).

Crawford, N. C. 'The Passion of World Politics', *International Security* vol. 24 (4): 116–157.

Dean, M. *Governmentality: Power and Rule in Modern Society* (London: Sage, 1999).

——— . 'Risk, Calculable and Incalculable', in *Risk and Sociocultural Theory: New Directions and Perspectives,* ed. Deborah Lupton (Cambridge: Cambridge University Press, 1999), 67–84.

Doezema, J. (2010) *Sex Slaves and Discourse Masters: The Construction of Trafficking* (London : Zed Books).

El-Cherkeh, T., Stirbu, E., Lazaroiu, S., Radu, D. 'EU-Enlargement, Migration and Trafficking in Women: The Case of South Eastern Europe', Hamburgisches Welt-Wirtschafts-Archiv (HMWA) Report 247, Hamburg Institute of International Economics 200

Ericson, R. V. and Haggerty, K. D. 1997. *Policing the Risk Society* (Oxford: Clarendon Press).

European Commission (EC). 2001. 'Short-Term Permit to Stay Granted to Victims of Trafficking or Smuggling Who Cooperate in the Fight against Smugglers and Traffickers', Discussion Paper A/2/IGE D(2001), 23 October 2001.

European Parliament and EU Council. 2011. 'Directive 2011/36/EU on preventing and combating trafficking in human beigns and protecting its victims and replacing Council Framework Decision 2002/629/JHA', 5 April 2011 [http://eur-lex.europa.eu/LexUriServ/LexUriServ.do?uri=OJ:L:2011:101:0001:0011:EN:PDF] (accessed on 11 April 2012)

———. 2001. 'Report on the Proposal for a Council Framework Decision on Combating Trafficking in Human Beings', Rapporteur Eva Klamt, A5-0183/2001, 30 May 2001.

EU Council, 'Framework Decision on Combating Trafficking in Human Beings', 2002/629/JHA, 19 July 2002 [http://europa.eu.int/eur-lex/pri/en/oj/dat/2002/l_203/l_2032002080len00010004.pdf] (31 October 2004).

Ewald, F. 'Risk and insurance', and 'Two infinities of risk', in *The Politics of Everyday Fear,* ed. Brian Massumi (Minneapolis: University of Minnesota Press, 1993), 221–228.

Foucault, M. 1999. *Les Anormaux. Cours au Collège de France, 1974–1975* (Paris: Gallimard/Le Seuil).

Foucault, M. 2000. 'About the Concept of "Dangerous Individual" in Nineteenth Century Legal Psychiatry', in *Michel Foucault: Power,* ed. James D. Faubion (London: Penguin Books), 176–200.

Greco, M. 1993. 'Psychosomatic subjects and "the duty to be well": personal agency with medical rationality', *Economy and Society* 22(3): 357–372.

Halpern, C. 2002. *Suffering, Politics, Power: A Genealogy in Modern Political Theory*. New York: State University of New York.

Herman, J. L. 1997. *Trauma and Recovery. From Domestic Abuse to Political Terror*, 2nd edition (London: Pandora).

Hindess, B. 1998. 'Politics and Liberation', in *The Later Foucault,* ed. Jeremy Moss (London: Sage), 50–63.

La Strada, 'Who Are the Victims of Trafficking?' [http://free.ngo.pl/lastrada/page2.html] (26 October 2004).

Limanovska, B. 'Trafficking in Human Beings in South-Eastern Europe: Joint UN, OSCE and Unicef Report', 2002 [http://www.unhchr.ch/women/trafficking.pdf] (31 October 2004).

Lupton, D. 1998. *The Emotional Self.* London: Sage.

Romano, E. and De Luca, R. 1997. 'Exploring the Relationship Between Childhood Sexual Abuse and Adult Sexual Perpetration', *Journal of Family Violence* 12(1): 85–98.

Rose, N. 2001. 'The Politics of Life Itself', *Theory, Culture & Society* 28, no. 6: 1–30.

——— . 1989. *Governing the Soul: The Shaping of the Private Self* (Routledge: London).

Scarry, E. 1985. *The Body in Pain: the Making and Unmaking of the World.* Oxford: Oxford University Press.

Stateva, M. and Kozhouharova, N. 2004. 'Trafficking in Women in Bulgaria: a New Stage', *Feminist Review* 76: 110–116.

STOP Conference, 'Brussels Declaration on Preventing and Combating Trafficking in Human Beings: Draft Recommendations, Standards and Best Practices', 2002 [http://www.belgium.iom.int/STOPConference/Conference%20Papers/brudeclaration.pdf] (30 October 2004).

Townsend, M. 2011. 'Sex Trafficking in the UK: One's woman horrific story of kidnap, rape, beatings and prostitution', *The Observer* 6 February 2011 [http://www.guardian.co.uk/uk/2011/feb/06/sex-traffick-romania-britain] (accessed on 11 April 2012).

Tronto, J. C. 1995. 'Care as a Basis for Radical Political Judgements'. *Hypatia,* 10(2), 141–149.

Tudorache, Diana. 2004. General Considerations on the Psychological Aspect of the Trafficking Phenomenon. In *Psychosocial Support to Groups of Victims of Trafficking in Transit Situations. Psychosocial Notebooks*, ed. Schinina Gugliemo: 28–42: IOM.

UNODC. 2008. 'Toolkit to Combat Trafficking in Persons', Online Edition, Tool 8.3 [http://www.unodc.org/unodc/en/human-trafficking/2008/electronic-toolkit/electronic-toolkit-to-combat-trafficking-in-persons---index.html#8] (9 April 2012).

Weir, L. 1996. 'Recent developments in the government of pregnancy', *Economy and Society* 25(3): 373–392.

Whitebrook, M. 2002. 'Compassion as a Political Virtue'. *Political Studies,* 50(3), 530.

Zimmerman, C. 2004. 'The Health Risks and Consequences of Trafficking in Women and Adolescents: Findings from a European Study', 2003 [http://www.lshtm.ac.uk/hpu/docs/traffickingfinal.pdf], 34 (24 February 2004).

Chapter 14

The Smell of Power: A Contribution to the Critique of the Sniffer Dog

Mark Neocleous

Introduction

On 8 July, 2005, the day after the London bombings, the International Association of Chiefs of Police issued its new guidelines on the detection and prevention of suicide bombings. The IACP is the primary organization through which senior police executives across the globe try to co-ordinate their powers and practices, and it does this through a number of 'Training Keys'. The two 'Training Keys' issued in July 2005, numbers 581 and 582, were called *Suicide Bombers: Part I* and *Suicide Bombers: Part II*. Training Key 582 concerns the use of lethal force, emphasizing shooting at a suspect's head and thus shooting to kill. Training Key 581 instructs police officers in how to detect potential suicide bombers. It focuses on a set of behavioural and physical characteristics, including sudden changes in behaviour such as a religious person starting to visit sex clubs, the wearing of loose or bulky clothing in the summer, fidgeting or pacing, failure to make eye contact, mumbling, being overly concerned about their bags, strange hair colouring. Amongst this range of 'suspicious' things are also some indicators based on smell: 'is the individual wearing too much cologne or perfume, or does he or she smell of talcum powder or scented water?' To reinforce this point, the Training Key references the advice given to border officials by the Department of Homeland Security, to look out for individuals who 'may smell of herbal or flower water'. Smell is here treated, quite casually, as a technique of police power.

Aside from a few critics noting the racial profiling implicit in the instructions, such comments concerning smell have been largely overlooked. This oversight is symptomatic of a much wider focus within 'surveillance studies' on sight and vision. Extensive analyses of CCTV, spy cameras and technologies of global satellite tracking follow a long tradition which has honed in on the ocular as a locus of power. It is the gaze that has dominated critical discussions of surveillance. The ubiquity of the 'panopticon' as a theoretical tool for grappling with the powers of discipline and punishment captures this exactly, but there are a host of other critical analyses which have centred on the practice of 'seeing like a state'. After sight, it is mechanisms of aural surveillance such as eavesdropping, bugging, and phone-tapping which dominate the debate. Little is said about how the state smells, despite the obvious implications that arise when thinking about the powers of sight and sound in the body politic. The 'new surveillance' studies has failed to analyse smell as part of the state's sensory apparatus despite being founded on the 'extension of the senses' (Marx 2002: 16), and the literature on identity as surveillance has picked up on the eye, face, finger, hand or voice in its discussions of the body, but rarely the smell: a major and increasingly influential edited collection such as Jane Caplan and John Torpey's *Documenting Individual Identity*, for example, contains just one comment on smell, in an essay on 'body surveillance' by one leading surveillance studies thinker, and that is to dismiss the 'hype' surrounding any new technology in the field (Lyon 2001: 300).

Why is this? Why, with a critical intellectual culture saturated with analyses of biopolitics, biosecurity, biosurveillance and biometrics, has so little been said about the smell of power? Why is the even state's 'nosiness' still understood almost solely through the ocular and the aural?

One reason might be that 'olfaction is often deemed the least 'intellectual', or the least informative, of our senses'. Seemingly dealing with 'the airy, the insubstantial, and the formless', olfaction appears to be a very poor cousin to sight when it comes to power. Compared to sight, 'whose perceptions are so rational that they may be analyzed by the laws of geometry, olfaction rejects geometrical analysis' in much the same way that it rejects localization (Gonzalez-Crussi 1991: 65, 71). On this view, there seems to be little for the state to be doing with smell. 'Due to its marginal and repressed status in contemporary Western culture, smell is hardly ever considered as a political vehicle', notes one cultural history; 'power appears odourless' (Classen, Howes and Synnott 1994: 161).

Yet power's appearance of being odourless does not mean that smell is not also political. We know well enough that smell clearly has been a political vehicle, from the deodorization of the nineteenth century city as an exercise in class power through to its articulation as a means of delineating the otherness of the foreign, the state has long exercised a kind of olfactory police as part of its fabrication of order. But to really grasp this we need to understand how the state is now concerned less with merely eradicating the disgusting smell or mobilizing against the foreign smell, and much more with *using* it. Crucial to this process is the sniffer dog.

Critical theory has never really asked the question: what is the political meaning of a sniffer dog? As a sniffer *dog* it has an obvious range of uses, as witnessed by the snarling creatures confronting prisoners being tortured at Abu Ghraib and protestors being 'kettled' in London. But as a *sniffer* dog its meaning lies less in its ability to generate fear and more in its ability to enact a politics of smell; the use of the Chihuahua as a sniffer dog in Japan and the attempt to replace the sniffer dog with sniffer technologies are evidence of the fact that it is the power to smell rather than the power to scare that is important. Investigating this power situates the sniffer dog at the heart of the police power. As such, an investigation of the sniffer dog takes us past the banalities of surveillance studies and civil liberties discourse, and straight to the heart of the state's role in the permanent reinvention of bourgeois order.

Smell, Stop, Search

It is a little noted fact about the process of personal identity that before fingerprints were introduced as a primary means of police identification, Barruel had offered to the French police his 'discovery' concerning the odour of blood when, in 1829, he proposed 'smell prints' as a means of identifying criminals (Corbin 1996: 187; Cole, 2002: 12). Not much came of it then, and it would appear to have died out as a result of the growth of fingerprinting in the late-nineteenth century and advances in haematology which ruled out blood as the basis of smell prints. Yet regardless of his focus on blood, Barruel was indeed on to something with the idea of smell prints.

In 2007 it was revealed that German police had collected scent traces of activists prior to the G8 summit in Heiligendamm in June of that year. At the time, many thought this an unusual infringement of civil liberties and a new indication of how far the state is now willing to go in intelligence-gathering. But it was neither unusual nor new. In her analysis of 'Stasiland', Anna Funder reports visiting one room in the Stasi museum in Leipzig and seeing a cabinet containing glass jars. The woman who ran the museum explained that the jars were 'smell samples'.

> The Stasi had developed a quasi-scientific method, 'smell sampling', as a way to find criminals. The theory was that we all have our own identifying odour, which we leave on everything we touch. These smells can be captured and, with the help of trained sniffer dogs, compared to find a match .. The Stasi might break into someone's apartment and take a piece of clothing worn close to the skin, often underwear. Alternately, a 'suspect' would be brought in under some pretext for questioning, and the vinyl seat he or she had sat on would be wiped afterward with a cloth. The pieces of stolen clothing, or the cloth, would then be placed in a sealed jar. The containers looked like jam bottling jars. A label read 'Name: Herr [Name]. Time: 1 hour. Object: Worker's Underpants' (2003: 8).

Funder adds that the number of jars suggests that the Leipzig Stasi had smell samples of the entire political opposition in the area. The jars disappeared soon after the 1989 revolution, but then turned up in the office of the Leipzig police who thought they might still be of use after the revolution and thus kept them in a 'smell pantry'. So the collection of scent traces of political activists by German police may well be an 'unsavoury' reminder that German security agencies are 'using methods that the Stasi once practiced', as Hans-Christian Stroebelle, a Greens leader, put it (2007). But what if it can't be explained away as a relic of the Stasi period in German history? What if something else is at stake, something far more telling about liberal democratic regimes? What if the liberal state is more interested in smell than we realize?

In the early 1960s the CIA produced a fairly lengthy report called *Human Scent and Its Detection* (Tebrich no date [c1963]). The document spends a huge amount of time on the science of sweat production, including several paragraphs discussing the different functions of the eccrine, apocrine and sebaceous glands, and noting the different ways in which they produce smells. The political purpose of the scientific detail is to raise the possibility of estimating the amount of odour that a human body might produce and the distance that might enable a dog to smell a person. The document suggests that such research might have an important role in future intelligence work. More recently, the Defense Advanced Research Projects Agency (DARPA), the US state's key agency for military research, has developed a 'Unique Signature Detection Project', formerly known as the 'Odortype Detection Program', and has been working since 2007 on a system of Identification Based on Scent (IBIS). 'DARPA wants to be able to detect, track, and even positively identify them [criminals and terrorists] from a distance ... using nothing more than the heat and sweat that emanate from a person's pores', notes the Information Awareness Office report 'Detecting Sweaty, Smelly Security Threats' (IAO 2010). Both the Department of Homeland Security (2008) in the US and the Ministry of Defence (2006) in the UK fund research into smell, in the form of Remote Air Sampling Canine Olfaction (RASCO). Significantly, RASCO is said to be more accurate than, say, a retinal scan, because a person's smell is thought to be less controllable than their eyes, and dogs are trained to smell past the attempts to camouflage real smells with false ones. Such projects have been assisted by the chemical industries aiming to get in on the security bandwagon: the European Network of Excellence in Artificial Olfaction and the International Society for Olfaction and Chemical Sensing now list security politics as a major research interest.

In virtually all cases the focus of the research points to the sniffer dog as key to the politics of smell. Police forces work on the assumption that police dogs can detect a whole range of substances on a person. Note that this means that for the most part the dogs are used not to identify individuals, along the lines of a fingerprint or retinal scan, but to identify (or, more correctly, to *appear* to identify) substances. They are frequently employed in order to 'catch' a whiff of drugs on people as they go by and have therefore been a key weapon in the 'war on drugs'. Yet anyone who travels on public transport will have noticed a rather significant increase in the use of dogs around transport terminals in the last decade. This is often said to be about continuing the fight in the 'war on drugs', but it is also clear that the increased presence of police dogs in public spaces is an outcome of more generalized security measures in the 'war on terror'. 'Dogs are the public face of the war on terror', as one journalist puts it (Hind 2006). The use of dogs by the state has increased so much that they now have their own publication, the bi-monthly *K9 Cop Magazine*, launched in 2009.

As the public face of the 'war on terror' one of the main functions of the dogs has been identical to their role in the war on drugs: to justify 'stop and search' routines. Dogs sniff the air, the person, and their bags, and the police officer reacts accordingly. If it is the case that 'what smells good *is* good' and, conversely, that 'what smells bad *is* bad' (Synott 1993: 190), then from the police perspective what smells suspicious *is* suspicious. Yet it is also the case that anything appearing to the police officer to be 'suspicious behaviour' is grounds for a suspect to be stopped and searched, including trying to avoid the dogs or even looking like one might be trying to avoid them. Once this occurs the police have 'reasonable grounds' to engage in a stop and search routine. Thus one can be stopped without knowing whether one is caught up in the war on drugs, war on crime or war on terror at that precise moment in time. The sniffer dog is thus both an emblematic and symptomatic figure in the universal warfare of contemporary bourgeois order.

The standard civil liberties approach to this question is to point to the fact that sniffer dogs have been found to be wrong in their 'judgement' somewhere in as many as 3 out of 5 searches, or that the dogs can be influenced by the way their handlers hold their leads, and that the dogs are often overly trusted by handlers who think the dog is never wrong (an assumption reinforced by a wider such belief among the public) (NSWCCL 2004: 4; Grainger, 2004). But such arguments fail to address the ways in which the dog is, in effect, a technology of state power. A series of case laws across the Western world challenging the use of sniffer dogs reinforces this point. In New South Wales, the Council for Civil Liberties (CCL) challenged the use of police dogs through the case of a person stopped by a plain clothes police officer who had been working with a dog near a nightclub. As the defendant walked by the dog sniffed the air, flared its nostrils and then started sniffing the defendant. The police officer's search of the defendant then found cannabis. The CCL claimed that the use of dogs in such a way amounted to an illegal search, but the NSW Supreme Court held that the use of the dog was not unlawful. The basis of the judgment was that 'a police officer would have been entitled to walk in the vicinity of the appellant and, if he were to smell cannabis leaf in the appellant's possession, form a reasonable suspicion sufficient to entitle him to search the appellant'. The fact that a dog was being used to do this did not change the situation. In other words, as the Supreme Court made clear, it was 'treating a drug detection dog as an extension of the police officer, an aid to his olfactory senses' (Darby v Director of Public Prosecutions 2004: para. 62). More or less the same legal interpretation applies in all western societies, as Amber Marks research suggests (2007). Thus, legally, the dog is an extension of the police officer. If the police officer is the long arm of the law, the police dog is the nose of the state.

Note, however, that in contrast to the occasional use of smell by a police officer, dogs are always already sniffing something. In stark contrast to police officers and their far more limited olfactory powers having to deliberately move in close to check a smell, the police dog is permanently sniffing, and permanently sniffing a far wider area than might be sniffed by the human police figure. That is, this extension of police power means that when a dog is in the vicinity, a permanent and sweeping olfactory search of a wide and indefinable space is taking place. The presence of the dog means the state is engaged in a *de facto* search of an indefinable area and persons in the vicinity, creating the grounds for a *de jure* stop and search. A critical analysis of the sniffer dog, then, must deal with the nature of 'stop and search'; and this has to be understood not in terms of surveillance or civil liberties, but in terms of the violence of original accumulation.

Suspicion, Possession, Oppression

Writing about original accumulation in *Capital*, Marx outlines what he calls the 'police methods' used from the early sixteenth century to accelerate the accumulation of capital.

> Henry VIII, 1530: Beggars who are old and incapable of working receive a beggar's licence. On the other hand, whipping and imprisonment for sturdy vagabonds. They are to be tied to the cart-tail and whipped until the blood streams from their bodies, that they are to swear on oath to go back to their birthplace or to where they have lived the last three years and to 'put themselves to work"…

> James I: Anyone wandering about and begging is declared a rogue and a vagabond. Justices of the peace in Petty Sessions are authorized to have them publicly whipped and to imprison them for six months for the first offence.

And on it goes through a series of 'terroristic laws' (his term again) perfected through four centuries of capitalist development, through which the masterless men and women of the displaced peasantry were whipped into shape as the working class and bourgeois order was fabricated.

The laws in question were the various vagrancy acts passed throughout the western world. One of the features of such laws was their vague and incredibly broad scope, as they formed an all-encompassing discretionary power which could be used more or less at will by agents of the state. They allowed individuals to be stopped and searched purely on the grounds of suspicion; they were, in effect, the original 'sus' laws. The Vagrancy Act of 1824, for example, provided for 'the Punishment of idle and disorderly Persons, and Rogues and Vagabonds'. It was this Act which constituted the core police power exercised by the 'new' British police created in 1829 (and which explains why the Act creating the 'new police' was so thin: because the powers that were to be exercised by the new police already existed in the Vagrancy Act). The powers in question were consolidated with the Metropolitan Police Act 1839 which allowed the police to stop and search 'any Person who may be reasonably suspected of having or conveying in any Manner anything stolen or unlawfully obtained'.

The ambiguity built into the laws and the breadth of powers they offered means that they were 'sweep laws': they allowed individuals to be stopped on the grounds merely of *suspicion*, and even perhaps on the grounds of suspected criminal *intent*. Hence a huge range of acts or non-acts, forms of behaviour and inactivity, fell foul of the laws, such that a 'sweep' of any area would easily find guilty parties. In granting sweeping powers to target anything considered 'disorderly' or 'suspicious', the determining principle underpinning the vagrancy laws was not the liberty of the subject but the well-ordered society. Once we grasp that policing is about the fabrication of social order rather than 'law enforcement', the vagrancy laws can be seen as the police power par excellence; which is to say, they were a fundamental weapon in the class war.

Much as the heyday of vagrancy laws was the sixteenth through to the nineteenth century, the laws themselves remained in place until the second half of the twentieth century, at which point their vagueness, their criminalization of status without any particular criminal act being committed, and their overt class and race bias, came to be seen as problematic. Symptomatically, however, their abolition coincides with the birth of the quintessential social wars of the late-twentieth century: the wars on drugs and crime. The key operative law in these wars has been the law of possession. In such laws, possession qua possession becomes the crime itself, or can be used as evidence of intent to commit a crime. And so the law on possession has become what Markus Dubber (2001) calls the sweep offense of choice in modern policing, being used in exactly the same manner as the original vagrancy laws.

In offering sweeping powers, 'possession' shares the central advantages of 'vagrancy' as a policing tool: it is flexible and convenient, it relies heavily on the idea of suspicion, it panders to the law's belief that intent can be identified, and it continues the state's declared mandate to determine what constitutes a public threat and eliminate it accordingly. Moreover, in being focused on possession rather than vagrancy, possession law not only expands the scope of police powers into the home, thereby exploding the liberal myth of privacy, but also functions in a way that means millions of people commit some form of crime every day or could be suspected of being about to commit a crime. They often don't know this, until stopped and searched by a police after having been 'detected' as possibly possessing something suspicious. The list of items for which people have been found in possession is almost endless: drugs, drug paraphernalia, firearms and other weapons are obvious candidates for such a list. But it would also include imitation weapons, toy weapons, air pistols and rifles, any implement or instrument that might be used as a weapon, ammunition, body vests, equipment that might be used in burglary, stolen property, instruments that might be used for graffiti, counterfeit trademarks, unauthorized recordings of performances, public benefit cards, forgery devices, embossing machines, vehicle identification numbers, prison contraband, obscene material, eavesdropping devices, fireworks, noxious materials, slugs, and on it goes, right down to items deemed by the police to constitute a threat to 'security'. This list of items, compiled by Dubber from possession cases in just one US state, New York, could be extended to include those people held for possessing spearfishing equipment (in Florida) and undersized catfish (in Louisiana).

Now, the extent to which this police power permeates the social world can be seen in the fact that many possession offences begin with a simple traffic stop, a salutary reminder that traffic police are never just policing traffic. But it can also be seen in the fact that many possession offences *start from the nose of a sniffer dog*. The main law brought into action when sniffer dogs are thought to detect anything is the law on possession. Because of the more or less permanent 'sweep' mode that comes from the dogs sniffing everything and anything that passes by them or even near them, the 'sniff' very easily generates 'reasonable grounds' for an officer to stop and search; the sniff produces the suspect. The mythical reliability of the dog means that the initial sniff is virtually unchallengeable in the courts and thus the police officer has very simple and universal grounds for stopping and searching.

Note, however, that most uses of stop and search powers actually reveal very little 'crime', in the sense of leading to formal arrests and prosecutions. What stop and search powers do, rather, is open the possibility for the police to impose their authority as state officials on individuals and groups considered problematic, threatening, or, in the terms of that key concept of police power, 'disorderly'. The sniffer dog plays a crucial role in this process, thereby drastically extending the sensory reach of the technology of the state.

This is what explains the increased presence of dogs in public spaces since 2001, but also throughout the disciplinary apparatus of the modern state, in institutions such as schools, prisons and mental health institutions (visits to which are sold to us as exercises in 'community policing' but which are designed to nurture greater social acceptance of the dogs and to carry out searches – *de facto*, and thus *de jure* – while on the premises). The inflection of the war on vagrancy (that is, the class war) into the war on drugs, the war on drugs into the war on crime, and the war on crime into the war on terror, and then the war on terror back into the wars on drugs and crime, is a mechanism for articulating the enemy as existing anywhere and everywhere in a way that requires police infiltration of all space. The power of smell plays a crucial role in this infiltration. In the endless warfare of contemporary political order in which the complicated cultural practices surrounding drugs, the social dynamics surrounding crime and the political tactics surrounding terrorism are reduced to an amorphous and ubiquitous 'enemy' of good order, police discretion becomes a key to victory. And in this war, the sniffer dog is in the frontline.

Yet one of the crucial features of this war is precisely that there is no frontline in the traditional military sense of the term. This is why so much effort is being made to mechanize the sniffer dog. Much is made in the media of such new technologies: from the CIA's original attempt to create a 'mechanical dog' (who 'when he is born', the CIA report notes, 'should be much more unobtrusive than his natural ancestor, should be able to tell us just whom he has smelled, and should maintain a reliable permanent record of his visitors'); DARPA's spending in excess of $3 million a year since 2001 developing an E-Nose; the Commonwealth Scientific and Industrial Research Organization's 'cybernose project' (tagline: 'sniffing a better future with Cybernose') which prioritizes cheese, wine and biosecurity; the new flashlight called the Passive Alcohol Sensor which contains a new smell detection technology ('the sniffer', as the police call it, 'an extension of the police officer's nose'); right down to a new sensor called Scentinel to identity individual body odours, developed by a UK company called Mastiff Electronic Systems (note the dog reference in the name). Many of these developments imagine the technological sniffer as electronic filing system as well as the detector of the initial information, and re-connect the politics of olfaction back to the question of identification. But as I have been arguing, the real political issue is not the smell of identification, but how the smell of power functions in terms of the fabrication of order.

Thus far more telling is the attempt to develop technology that reinforces the obliteration of any frontline in the new universal war: the 'sniffer helicopter'. By radically extending the potential area to be sniffed, this technology makes possible a significant shift in the police of territory, extending the powers of olfaction from individual officers and their dogs in a relatively small amount of space to a much wider ground. If successful, such mechanization will overcome the limitations imposed on the state's use of real dogs – the training, maintenance and handling are expensive, time-consuming and cumbersome – and will be another tool in the technological armoury of the state. This move, from 'canine cop' to 'techno cop', will be one more step towards realizing the state's dream of exercising a permanent and ubiquitous police power to obliterate anything regarded as disorderly.

Acknowledgements

An earlier version of this paper appeared in *Radical Philosophy*, 2011 (May/June), 167, available at radicalphilosophy.com.

References

Classen, C., Howes, D. and Synnott, A. 1994. *Aroma: The Cultural History of Smell*. London: Routledge.

Cole, S. A. 2002. *Suspect Identities: A History of Fingerprinting and Criminal Identification*. Cambridge, MA: Harvard University Press.

Corbin, A. 1996. *The Foul and the Fragrant*. London: Papermac.

Gonzalez-Crussi, F. 1991. *The Five Senses*. New York: Vintage.

Darby v Director of Public Prosecutions. 2004. NSWCA 431 (26 November 2004).

Department of Homeland Security. 2008. *Five Year Research and Development Plan*, August 2008.

Dubber, M. D. 2001. Policing Possession: The War on Crime and the End of Criminal Law. *Journal of Criminal Law and Criminology*, 91(4), pp. 829-996.

Funder, A. 2003. *Stasiland: Stories from Behind the Berlin Wall*. London: Granta.

Grainger, D. 2004. Sit! Stay! Testify!, *Fortune Magazine*, 149(2), 26 Jan 2004.

Hind, J. 2006. You are Being Sniffed: Why Dogs are the Public Face of the War on Terror. *The Observer*, 5 March, 2006.

Ministry of Defence. 2006. Second Memorandum from the Ministry of Defence, to the House of Commons Select Committee on Defence. 29 September, 2006.

Information Awareness Office. 2010. Detecting Sweaty, Smelly Security Threats. 27 April, 2010 – http://www.information-awareness-office.org/IAO___DARPA_NEWS_PAGE2.html. – accessed 24 September 2010

Kirschbaum, E. 2007. Germans Outraged by 'Scent Profiling' Ahead of G8, *Reuters*, 23 May, 2007.

Lyon, D. 2001. Under My Skin: From Identification Papers to Body Surveillance. In Jane Caplan and John Torpey (eds), *Documenting Individual Identity: State Practices in the Modern World*. Princeton: Princeton University Press, Princeton.

Marks, A. 2007. Drug Detection Dogs and the Growth of Olfactory Surveillance: Beyond the Rule of Law?, *Surveillance and Society*, 4(3), 257-71.

Marx, G. T. 2002. What's New about the 'New Surveillance': Classifying for Change and Continuity, *Surveillance and Society*, 1(1), 9-29.

NSWCCL [New South Wales Council for Civil Liberties]. 2004. *Review of the Police Powers (Drugs Detection Dogs) Act*, August 2004.

Synnott, A. 1993. *The Body Social: Symbolism, Self, and Society*. London: Routledge.

Tebrich, S. no date [1963] *Human Scent and Its Detection*. CIA Historical Review Program [originally for official use only, released 22 September, 1993].

Chapter 15

The Faceless Map: Banning the Cartographic Body

Angus Cameron

Introduction

Scene 1. Nottingham, Castle Gate. From the raking angle of the light, the shuttered shops and the tubs of flowers, it seems to be early on a summer morning – about 8.30-ish, perhaps, just before everything gets going. A man in a high-visibility vest, blue overalls a cap and dusty work-boots leans casually against a wall and seems to watch as I pass. His face is blurred, so I cannot be sure. I spot someone else in the distance and try to follow him down the street. Although the buildings pass by fairly smoothly, the people around me, including my target, stretch and distort strangely and leap unpredictably around the scene before vanishing altogether.

Scene 2. London, St Paul's Cathedral, outside Cannon St. Underground Station. Here it is early afternoon, sunny and the streets are busy with tourists and a few city types. People still leap about but because of the greater numbers and, presumably, slowness of the traffic, they are easier to track for a few paces before they too vanish. They are occasionally captured with their hands half raised, about to point at us. Some are drawing their companions' attention to us; some seem about to remonstrate with us for photographing them unasked. A man standing on the steps of the cathedral waves at us. All faces are blurred.

Scene 3. A village in rural Leicestershire. Having (of course) visited my own house first, I move down the High Street. It is all very familiar, but strangely empty. At one point I encounter an elderly woman standing in the open doorway of a house talking to a younger man getting into a car. Although her face is blurred, I know her name – it is her house.

We are, of course, in the strange through-the-looking-glass world of Google's 'Street View', the controversial project that links street-level photographs of buildings to the powerful geo-locational software behind Google Earth, creating the appearance of a seamless three-dimensional landscape. Although still under development, Street View allows us to zoom in on an increasing number of places and, apparently, see them as though we were actually there. The project began with tourist sites and city centres, but as the strange cars with the panoramic digital cameras on the roof have ventured further and further afield, so ordinary dwellings in ordinary places are visible to any casual viewer with the right equipment and a fast Internet connection. Eventually, presumably, the aim is to have the entire world available to view at street level and, indeed, my ramble around Street View could be reproduced in and across many and diverse places already.

It is easy to forget that for all their sophisticated effects and apparently self-evident photographic 'realism', Street View and Google Earth are *maps*. Very complex maps opening up new representational and interactive possibilities certainly, but maps nevertheless – purposive and functional representations of physical and social landscapes that selectively include and exclude certain categories of data and particular aspects of the 'real' world they depict. I invoke them here because in addition to their intrinsic interest they do something that maps have never really done before. More accurately perhaps, they are unable to avoid doing something cartographers have for a long time shied away from. The mapped landscapes they present us with are populated with *bodies*.

This is not to suggest that maps have never contained bodies in the past – far from it. Rather, that the bodies in earlier maps have tended to be of particular kinds and that their inclusion has in any case diminished. Although depictions of bodies are common enough in earlier maps, since roughly the late 18 century – the period of mapping's most rapid development and proliferation – there have been fewer and fewer bodies of any kind represented cartographically, to the point where most modern mapping excludes them altogether. Indeed, were we to open a contemporary paper map and find ourselves, our neighbours or our homes plotted along with the coastlines, pylons, contours, railways and roads we would be, to say the least, a bit surprised. This partly explains why both Google Earth and especially Street View have been heavily criticised both by individuals who find their image included in the street scenes and citizens' groups concerned with anonymity and privacy[1].

My interest here is less to do with the rights and wrongs of Google's ever-expanding online empire, however, than with the evolving nature of the relationship between the map and the body. Put simply, and echoing Agamben's analysis of the 'structure of the ban' (1995, 111) over many years the body has been, in one way or another, 'banned' from the map. This exclusion of the body from the map is, I want to argue here an integral part of what Agamben (1995, 111) describes as, 'the originary spatialization that governs and makes possible every localization and every territorialization'. Just as maps – particularly cadastral and political maps – are active depictions of particular regimes of 'ban' articulated as systems of enclosing lines overlaying particular territories, so they also enact

---

1   Google's CEO, Eric Schmidt, has publicly stated that he believes anonymity is contrary to the future development of the Internet – cf. interview with CNBC (accessed 7 January 2011). http://www.cnbc.com/id/15840232?play=1&video=1559676491. Despite this, Google are extremely sensitive to privacy issues on Street View, removing or obscuring any object at the request of the public.

a form of representational ban. Until Street View, modern cartography has not 'seen' bodies-at least within the viewspace of the map. With Street View and other electronic maps, however, bodies have intruded upon mapped space. And this raises questions over the fundamental nature of the body's relationship to spatial representation and practice.

The Boot-Print and the Duck – The Curious Disappearance of the Mapped Body[2]

The ways in which bodies have appeared in and/or been eliminated from maps varies according both to the function of the map and to the time at which it was made. Broadly speaking, however, the more instrumental maps have become (for the state in the first instance, but now for many other organisations too), and the more widely they have proliferated through print and computer technologies, the less they populated by bodies they are. Although the process of their elimination has been gradual, by roughly the beginning of the nineteenth century, bodies had disappeared altogether from mapped space. To illustrate how complete this process has been, one need only examine a contemporary paper map. The closest things to representations of actual bodies that appear on the popular Ordnance Survey 'Landranger' maps in the UK, for example, are a boot-print ('Walk/Trail') and a duck ('Nature reserve'), and these are, of course, no more than symbolic abstractions.

Even when bodies did appear on maps, those included were rarely 'real' bodies. Rather they were various types of 'special' body – varying according to the predilections of the cartographer and their patron and/or the function of the map in question. Those that are populated only very rarely depict anything that could be described as 'real' people and then for particular reasons. Until recently, therefore, bodies have figured in the history of cartography in five main ways: as exotics or monsters, as metaphors, as ethnic, regional and/or metropolitan 'types', as monarchs and as graphic symbols.

Pierre Descaliers' *World Map* (c.1550) is one of the more heavily populated early maps: combining images of monsters with (for the time) up-to-date anthropological and ethnographic information about exotic peoples both pictorially and in dense textual cartouches (Barber & Harper 2010). The Desceliers map is not, however, evenly populated. Europe is almost devoid of figures, with the major urban centres depicted as stylised townscapes. The Americas are also relatively sparsely populated, though there are scenes of both Spanish soldiers and native populations. Africa and Asia, by contrast, are full of bodies, representing the full range of 'knowledge' of the regions and of recent European explorations of them.

---

2 For ease of reference most of the maps referred to specifically here are either reproduced in the widely available catalogue accompanying the British Library's 'Magnificent Maps' exhibition (Barber & Harper 2010) or are freely available at high definition on-line.

Thus, for example, we find traditional representations of the so-called 'plinian monsters' (dog-headed men, blemmye, skiapods, etc.), the land of Prester John (a legendary Christian priest-king with a huge and powerful domain in 'the East'), the Chinese Monkey King *Sun Wukong*, various ethnic and racial 'types' and the incursions of European explorers and soldiers among them all. Desceliers' map was not intended for navigational purposes (at over 2 meters wide and being painted on vellum, it was hardly practical), but was made for Henri II of France to represent the sum total of European (and therefore of course Eurocentric) 'global' geographical knowledge at the time. There is, therefore, a significant disparity between the depiction of the known (Europe) and the becoming known (Asia, Africa and the Americas) with the latter being communicated through the bodies of those involved. Although these bodies are roughly located in their appropriate place, geographic accuracy is of far less importance than the multiple embodiments of knowledge and practices. Desceliers' map is a collection of emplaced and embodied stories that together constitute an aggregated narrative of European superiority and exotic, orientalist otherness.

Although Desceliers' map is not unique in the way it deploys the body, it is indicative of the ways in which western cartography selectively employs and excludes bodies from its view. The 'ambulatory centrism' (Mignolo 1994) of the world map with Europe top and centre, is further exaggerated by the differentiation of depiction: the embodied stories of exoticism being reserved for those regions beyond the settled urban landscape of Europe. Bodies, this suggests, are indicative of difference, disorder and unpredictability.

Bodies as metaphors appear on many early maps signifying, variously, the winds, the gods, the seas and whatever other mythological elements the map-maker saw fit to include. Many early medieval *mappamundi* used an abstracted representation of the body of Christ as their basic structure – the world made in God's image. As Beckwith (1996:26), puts it.

> It is perhaps a commonplace of medieval political and social theory that the body is the image par excellence of human society. In an Aristotelian model that stresses the organic nature of society, medieval theorists commonly use the human body as an image which can accommodate difference within unity and give the metaphor the legitimation of the 'natural'.

For medieval cartographers and their viewers, the body was inherent to the meaning and function of the map. This was because, as Beckwith suggests, the whole of society was constituted as emanations of and/or in proximity to doubled real and divine bodies. In a similar vein, Daniel Birkholz (2004) demonstrates that the primary categories of what he calls 'The King's Two Maps' (world maps – *mappamundi* – and domain maps – *mapparegni*) were both thoroughly 'embodied' in relation to divine power in the form of both Christ and the divinely ordained monarch. As such, mapping practices echo and reproduce the complex construction of medieval sovereign bodies as beautifully described and analysed in Ernst Kantorowicz's (1997) *The King's Two Bodies*.

This mode of drawing a metaphorical analogy between territory and body persisted long after it fell out of cartographic practice. The frontispiece to Hobbes *Leviathan* (1651), for example, depicts the monarch made up of the multiple bodies of his citizens, looming proprietorially over the urban and rural landscape of the proto-nation state, the whole supported by pillars made up of symbols of civil and ecclesiastical power[3]. Around the same time, it became a fairly common literary fashion, to use the body as an analogy for the state and vice versa. So, for example, in John Donne's oft-quoted 'No man is an Island' (1624), each embodied person is presented as an integral element of the 'continent' – an interpersonal social landscape not dissimilar to that of Hobbes. The obverse, where the territorial state is metaphorised as a single human body, appears in Phineas Fletcher's extended poetical conceit, *The Purple Island, with the Piscatory Eclogues and Poeticall Miscellenie* (1633). Fletcher divides his bodily 'isle' into three 'Metropolises' conforming to the head, the heart and the gut, to which he attributes various characteristics as though they were cities variously competing and collaborating, but always part of the whole.

As European exploration reached further and further afield and as knowledge about the world 'out there' became increasingly systematised, monstrous and exotic bodies receded from the map. Metaphoric bodies persist, but they more and more occupy the margins and borders external to the map of territory – either as the winds blowing in from the edges, or as iconic, instructive figures in cartouches, keys and legends. Cartouches surrounding the titles of the map are often made up of hybrid landscapes combining 'real' features of the place depicted with contextualising (or propagandising) elements. Müller's 1722 map of Bohemia (Barber & Harper 2010: 70–73) for example, has scenes in each corner of the map, and thus outside the surveyed, 'scientific' space of the map proper, including both 'typical' aspects of the local landscape (forests, woodcutters, stonemasons, agriculture, viniculture), mythological figures (Fortune, Bacchus, cornucopii, putti, nymphs, fauns, etc.) and religious figures (St Wenceslas, patron saint of Bohemia and symbol of the counter-reformation) (Barber & Harper 2010). Like Descalier's image of the world, Müller's map presents us with a complex and purportedly totalising cosmography – a combination of chorological, political, religious and, increasingly, economic data represented by bodies. The map itself, however, already conforms to the abstracted and flattened conventions of the modern cartographic gaze – the 'satellite's eye' view of the distribution of landscape features represented by symbols.

The social function of the map is also evident when 'real' bodies replace the metaphoric bodies in the margins. A map such as John Speed's huge *Map of England, Wales and Ireland* from 1603–4 (Barber & Harper 2010:62–3) draws

---

3 Image available from: http://en.wikipedia.org/wiki/File:Leviathan_gr.jpg (accessed 29 November 2011)

together a detailed map of the territory of the British state with the complex paraphernalia of monarchic power in the form of elaborate royal lineages. Portraits of previous kings and queens, coats of arms, schematics of naval defences and warships entirely surround the mapped land. Speed's map is, therefore, thoroughly embodied, but as a *mappa regni* and thus only with the bodies of royalty and aristocracy – state bodies linked directly to the body of the state.

Perhaps the most thoroughly 'embodied' maps, however, are those depicting the *Leo Hollandicus* (sometimes *Leo Belgicus*) – the Dutch lion. Produced in various editions and by various cartographers and engravers in the late 16 and early 17 centuries[4], the image combines a detailed territorial map of the Netherlands overlaid with the form of a rampant lion and representations of social classes. The Dutch state incarnate in the form of the lion both articulates its new-found independence from Spanish occupation and its growing military and mercantile power. This is further underlined by images of the skylines of port towns in the margins to either side of the map (symbolising the embodied navigational knowledge necessary to a major maritime trading power) (Alpers 1984). Across the top of many of these maps are examples of 'typical' Dutch citizens arranged in couples (male and female) and representing both the political and mercantile hierarchies of the emergent state. Such maps extend and to a large extent secularise the Hobbesian vision of the embodied monarchic state, by portraying a territorial power driven by mobile, trading (and increasingly capitalist) bodies.

The 'Social Body' and the Distributed Human

Whilst the growing power of the modern state prompted cartographers to symbolise the emerging 'nation' in the form of representational bodies, the same dynamic led to their subsequent elimination from mapped space. The gradual reduction of the mapped body to a few abstract symbols and its effective elimination from map-space ran parallel to other processes of bodily representation. Specifically, over the past two centuries or so, individual bodies have gradually been interpolated into the ordering process of the bureaucratic state. The emergent 'nation-state' drew together the earlier metaphoric relationships drawn between bodies and territories (such as Donne and Fletcher's 17 century renditions above) and brought them together – the body represented as a unitary element in a complex, digital whole. Individual bodies were increasingly redefined as the flesh and blood capital of an emergent 'national' economy with responsibilities for hygiene, health and consumption (Ross 1995, Perelman 2000, Neocleous 2004). These newly minted individual bodies were then *incorporated* into the state, itself conceived of as a 'social body' – a more rigorous, 'scientific', 'economistic' and secular version of Hobbes *Leviathan*. As Mary Poovey (1995:29) puts it:

---

4   Various versions can be accessed through: http://en.wikipedia.org/wiki/Leo_Belgicus (accessed 24 November 2011).

From the geometric lineage of early social analysis, we can identify one set of features that eventually came to characterize abstract space. Like Hobbes's image of the individual, modern space was conceptualized as isotropic (as everywhere the same) and as reducible (or already reduced) to a formal (that is, empty) schema or grid. Partly as a consequence, abstract space was symbolically and materially associated with homologies: seriality; repetitious actions; reproducible products; interchangeable places, behaviors and activities.

This process of reductive incorporation of the body into the moral-disciplinary space of the state brings with it a particular understanding of the spatiality of the 'social body'. The process by which the actual body is normatively evacuated in pursuit of the virtuality of the social body in part explains the ways in which cartographic representations 'banned' bodies of all kinds from the viewspace of the map. The process of forging this abstract social body coincides closely with the systematisation of modern state cartographic functions through such organisations as the Ordnance Survey, established in 1791 (Pickles 2003).

That bodies of all kinds were henceforward excluded from the cartographic gaze does not mean that maps were no longer *about* bodies. Modern mapping operates a normative and powerfully asymmetric separation between the mapped space and the embodied user. Maps became socially functional tools used, variously, to transport, regulate, tax, fight, enclose and except bodies of all kinds reduced to the status of digital elements in a complex, machinic whole. In viewing aspects if this socio-space through a map, the map-user is accorded a single ocular perspective on the landscape (external and perpendicular) from which they are then expected to 'read', depending on the data represented and their purpose in using it, the spatial possibilities available to them. This, by extension, also entails a reading of the many restrictions to movement and access they also confront. Maps are about 'knowing one's place' in more than one sense (Sparke 2006).

Given the absence of direct reference to the body in cartographic representation, perhaps it should not be surprising that, as Denis Wood argued persuasively some years ago, that the 'semiological system' on which it is based should be 'invisible' (1992:104–5, cf. also Cameron 2011). As embodied subjects we look *through* the map to the imagined, analogous space beyond as though it were already real. The last thing we'd expect to see in it, paradoxically, is ourselves. Does, therefore, our sudden reappearance in StreetView and other digital mapping products mark the beginning of another change?

Brian Rotman has argued that emergent technologies, including those associated with digital cartography, are leading to what he calls the 'distributed human being'. As he argues, with respect to the advent of Geographical Information Systems (or Science – GIS) of the kind Google Earth and StreetView are built upon (2008: 99):

> GIS maps evade the fixity of the viewing subject by bypassing the demands of perspectival viewing. They promote a dynamic viewing body, one that 'sees'

precisely by refusing the stationary outlook of a single cartographic projection
and with it a claim to capture the 'truth' of a single visual scene.

This multiplication of the map's 'outlook' is undoubtedly a very important aspect
of what GIS technologies permit. By overlaying different types of geolocated
information and by incorporating dynamically updated data (from satellites,
sensors, webcams, etc.), GIS applications are greatly increasing the informational
power of mapping. One consequence of this, as Rotman argues, is the capacity of
people and organisations to break free from the restrictive and restricted nature
of conventional cartography and to manipulate and, to some extent challenge, the
singularity of the 'social body'. Organisations such as *MapAction*, for example,
have made important use of open-access 'wiki-maps' to provide information in
areas of natural disaster[5].

Exciting though many of these developments are, some caution is needed
about the extent of their novelty. First, as seen in the early 'embodied' maps
outlined briefly above, the ability to capture multiple viewpoints and outlooks
through mapping is not unique to GIS applications. Desceliers' map may only
have incorporated a range of viewpoints relevant to a Eurocentric monarch, but it
nevertheless successfully overlays multiple data sources and types (real, mythical,
military, anthropological, architectural, political, etc.). A significant part of the
way that Desceliers manages this complexity is through his differential treatment
of bodies – the selective 'banning' of some bodies *from* the image and others *within*
it as part of a complex and (for the time) dynamic spatialisation of knowledge. GIS
applications are, clearly, able to incorporate far more varied informational elements
(including bodies) and to manipulate them far more flexibly than conventional
maps, but in doing so they are reintroducing the multiple cartographic viewpoint
rather than inventing it. As this suggests, it is perhaps the period during which
bodies were most thoroughly banned from cartographic representation – that of
the modern nation state and its associated cartographic projects – that emerges as
the historical exception.

Caution is also needed with respect to the ways in which, for all their
flexibility GIS technologies incorporate and in many ways reinforce the evacuated
cartographic semiotics of the mapped 'social body'. GIS and GPS systems work
because both are based on the arithmetical, gridded, digital representation of
space first developed as part of the 'banning' of state space (Blomley, 2003).
GIS technologies may allow the incorporation of many different forms of data,
but these are then incorporated into a mode of cartographic representation that
remains fundamentally unchanged. Whilst some cartographers and artists have
sought to highlight this (cf. for example, the digital 'maps' produced by French art

---

5   Cf. www.mapaction.org. Other editable wiki-maps are used for less immediately
humanitarian purposes – cf. www.openstreetmap.org, www.mapquest.org (all three
accessed 5 December 2011).

collective 'Bureau d'Études' that often incorporate or are about bodies[6]), for the most part GIS applications for computers and mobile devices, massively deepen the representational power of the grid. The more such technologies come to be incorporated into daily life, the more closely our bodies come to conform to the grid. We may have the possibility of greater access to and control over the map, but for the most part it continues to gaze past us. Maps may no longer be the sole preserve of the governments, but they have not stopped, as James C Scott (1998) put it some years ago, 'seeing like a state'.

Conclusion

In 2007 Chinese artist Pak Sheung Chuen carried out a series of performance 'walks' in Tokyo (Chuen 2008). His 'Mountain Trip/Tokyo/1' involved spending four days physically tracing the lines that would be produced were the folds in a street atlas of the city transposed onto the ground. Similarly, 'Valleys Trip/Tokyo/1' entailed spending five days tracing the lines formed by the white spaces formed at the edges of the atlas pages. In both cases, Chuen's tracing of these arbitrary lines – artefacts of the physical production of the atlas as a book – were conducted on foot irrespective (as far as was possible) of the boundaries (concrete, cultural or institutional) encountered on the way. Chuen's performances (and similar projects by a group of predominantly Beijing-based artists who all explore the power relations of space – cf. Tan 2008), address many issues both locally (urbanism, spatial restriction) and more generally (artistic conservatism and censorship), but most importantly for my purposes here involve a specific reinsertion of a culturally and politically active body into the (paper) viewspace of the map. The folds and gaps on the atlas page produce lines that were wholly irrelevant to the cartographic function of the map, but nevertheless provided another abstract linear element that could, in theory at least, be physically and ironically recreated on the ground. One of the main things that Chuen's cartographic 'walks' illustrate is the extent to which the exclusion of the body from the map, leads to profound constraints for the actual body in space.

The absence of bodies from most modern maps is, at one level of course, unremarkable. It is partly a practical issue related to *scale*. A map of any useable scale simply cannot represent the many and varied bodies that actually occupy the landscape down upon which it gazes – it would be illegible. It would also be unusable, because the necessary omission of bodies is also a matter of *time*. Even very sophisticated maps based on satellite imagery are *static* – whatever they depict they do so at a particular point in time and cannot effectively capture motion[7]. There are historical exceptions to this even on paper maps – particularly,

---

6   http://bureaudetudes.org/ (accessed 5 December 2011)

7   Google themselves use this aspect of mapping in defense of Street View – noting that all the visual information in the 'map' is always out of date – often by years – cf. http://

for example, 'itinerary' maps of journeys or the narrative charts of historical battle scenes where the same map-image simultaneously contains the forces arrayed at various stages in some famous victory. Although real-time mapping is becoming possible if sufficient streamed data is available, mapping each individual in real-time remains a distant prospect[8]. Combinations of mobile telephony, GPS tracking, RFID technologies and wiki-maps are, however, rapidly opening up these possibilities. To the extent that we have access to these things, and choose to use them, we are in one sense radically changing the relationship between the map and the body. By allowing ourselves to be tracked and plotted we are – in a very different sense to Chuen above – inserting ourselves bodily into the map. Indeed, in the form of smartphones and GPS devices of various kinds we continuously place ourselves at the centre of a panoptic map-space that moves with us everywhere we go and, increasingly, monitors our behaviour. In a few cases such devices have even been voluntarily implanted into the body itself (Graafstra 2004), generating considerable opposition from those fearing the potential extension of state, military and corporate surveillance capabilities.[9]

Even without going to these extremes, the 'logical' extension of the sorts of technologies underpinning Street View might be the further incorporation of the body into the map, but it is far from self-evident that this is an extension many would welcome given the choice[10]. But as we have seen, even when (perhaps *particularly when*) bodies are 'banned' from its representational viewspace, the map is always centrally concerned with the body – the body as actual or potential subject, consumer, citizen or threat. The material body, this is to say, is the foundational 'originary spatialisation' that any process of territorialisation and its representation has to deal with (cf. Bruff, this volume). 'Sacred Life', in Agamben's terms, pervades the map, however determinedly we try to remove it. The question, therefore, is less concerned with whether or not bodies are present in the map, but with the nature and meaning of their (in-) visibility and, beyond that, who decides how they are to be represented.

References

Agamben, G. 1995. *Homo Sacer: Sovereign Power and Bare Life*. Stanford: Stanford University Press.

---

maps.google.co.uk/intl/en/help/maps/streetview/privacy.html (accessed 18 January 2011).

8   Cf., for example, the real-time map of London Underground trains at: http://traintimes.org.uk/map/tube/ (accessed 4 January 2011).

9   Cf. www.antichips.com (accessed 5 December 2011).

10   Cf. for example, the controversies surrounding the 'foursquare' social networking tool that uses mobile phones and other devices to geo-locate users (Hickman 2010) and the news that Apple's iPhones keep detailed records of their owners movements (Arthur 2011).

Alpers, S. 1984, *The Art of Describing: Dutch Art in the Seventeenth Century*, Chicago, University of Chicago Press.

Arthur, C. 2011. iPhone keeps record of everywhere you go. *The Guardian*. April 20 .

Barber, P. & Harper, T. 2010. *Magnificent Maps: Power, Propaganda and Art.* London: British Library.

Beckwith, S. 1996. *Christ's Body: Identity, Culture and Society in Late Medieval Writings.* London: Routledge.

Blomley, N. 2003. Law, Property, and the Geography of Violence: The Frontier, the Survey, and the Grid, *Annals of the Association of American Geographers.* 93(1), 121–141

Birkholz, D. 2004. *The King's Two Maps: Cartography and Culture in Thirteenth Century England.* London: Routledge.

Cameron, A. 2011. Ground Zero – The Semiotics of The Boundary Line. *Social Semiotics*, 21(3), 417–434.

Chuen, Pak Sheung. 2008. *Odd One In II: Invisible Travel.* Hong Kong: MCCM Creations.

Graafstra, A. 2004. *RFID Toys: 11 Cool Projects for Home, Office and Entertainment (4th ed.).* New York: Ziff Davis

Hickman, L. 2010. How I Became A Foursquare Cyberstalker, *The Guardian*, July 23 .

Hobbes, T. 1651. *Leviathan*, various editions.

Kantorowicz, EH. 1997 [1957], *The King's Two Bodies: A Study in Mediaeval Political Theology*, Princeton University Press.

Mignolo, W. 1994. The Moveable Center: Geographical Discourses and Territoriality During the Expansion of the Spanish Empire, in, Cevallos-Candau, FJ, Cole, JA, Scott, NM & Suárez-Araúz, N (eds). *Coded Encounters: Writing, Gender, and Ethnicity in Colonial Latin America.* Amhesrt: University of Massachusetts Press, 15–45.

Neocleous, M. 2004. 'Bloody Capital and Dead Labour: Cultural Studies or the Critique of Political Economy?', *Cultural Political Economy Working Paper Series: Working Paper No. 5*, Institute for Advanced Studies in Social and Management Sciences, University of Lancaster. Available from: http://www.lancs.ac.uk/fss/centres/ias/researchgroups/polecon/index.htm. (Accessed 25 November 2011)

Perelman, M. 2000. *The Invention of Capitalism: Classical Political Economy and the Secret History of Primitive Accumulation.* Durham: Duke University Press.

Pickles, J. 2004. *A History of Spaces: Cartographic Reason, Mapping and the Geo-Coded World.* London: Routledge.

Poovey, M. 1995, *Making a Social Body: British Cultural Formation 1830–1864*, Chicago, University of Chicago Press.

Ross, K. 1995. *Fast Cars, Clean Bodies: Decolonization and the Reordering of French Culture.* Minneapolis: MIT Press.

Rotman, B. 2008. *Becoming Beside Ourselves: The Alphabet, Ghosts and Distributed Human Being.* Durham: Duke University Press.

Scott, J.C. 1998, *Seeing Like a State: How certain scheme to improve the human condition have failed*, New Haven, Yale University Press.

Sparke, M. 2006. *In the Space of Theory Postfoundational Geographies of the Nation-State*. Minneapolis: Minnesota University Press.

Tan, A. 2008. 'A Small MAP PIECE of Performance Art in China', *Live Art Development Agency: Study Room*, available as a PDF from: http://www.thisisliveart.co.uk/resources/Study_Room/study_room.html (accessed 23 November 2011)

Wood, D. 1992. *The Power of Maps*. New York: Guilford Press.

PART V
The Body Virtual

Chapter 16
Placing the Virtual Body: Avatar, Chora, Cypherg

Tom Boellstorff

Introduction

What does it mean to have a body? How might virtual worlds transform understandings of the body, online but also offline? How might these virtual worlds also recall us to enduring conceptualizations and experiences of embodiment?

Bringing together my ethnographic research in the virtual world Second Life, anthropological work on embodiment, and a range of philosophical insights, my objective is to think toward a theory of the virtual body that responds to these questions. I push myself in this chapter to risk significant claims, but my argument is intentionally incomplete; I mean to contribute to a conversation rather than work in anything remotely resembling a mode of definitive closure. With this goal of setting up a provisional conceptual framework, vulnerable to ethnographic contextualization, I will emphasize that avatars are not merely representations of bodies but forms of embodiment, centered on constitutive emplacement within a world.

Thus, the key point I seek to advance is that virtual embodiment is always embodiment in a virtual place; as a result, the pluralization of place that virtual worlds entail holds foundational implications for online corporeality. (For the sake of synonyms, I will treat "virtual" and "online" as equivalent, as well as "embodiment" and "corporeality," though of course one could also develop rubrics in which these terms differed in meaning.) In working to make strange the Western cultural logics that have dominated the development and dissemination of virtual worlds, I seek an analytic of defamiliarization internal to that Western tradition. As I discuss briefly in the conclusion, by historicizing and analytically unpacking the Western cultural logics that strongly shape contemporary virtual worlds I hope to contribute to analyses of how various forms of cybersociality further or undermine colonial, patriarchal, heterosexist, and capitalist hegemony. Rather than pursue the stubbornly elusive goal of transcending the binarisms of mind/body and culture/nature so embedded in this tradition, we can redirect the conversation by refracting these binarisms through a third binarism, virtual/actual. To advance my analysis of how this pivotal refraction pluralizes being-in-the-world, I will set forth three new concepts that I see as naming key aspects of dominant understandings of virtual embodiment: virtual chora, being-inworld, and the cypherg. By the latter part of this chapter, I will suggest that this theory of virtual embodiment implies a new understanding of the "digital" itself.

Avatar's Avatar

Given the time in which I write this chapter, almost any imaginable opening to the discussion must address the motion picture *Avatar*. Written and directed by James Cameron and employing groundbreaking visual effects, this film, first released in December 2009, had by April 2010 already become the highest-grossing work of artistic production in human history, having earned more than 2½ billion dollars. *Avatar's* plot, for which Cameron insisted on sole credit, recalls (a less generous verb would be "is derivative of") the storylines of films from *Pocahontas* to *Dances with Wolves* in its tale of a "native" race threatened by a technologically advanced colonizer, saved only when the protagonist Jake Sully, a member of the colonizers, turns against them.

Cameron allegorized this colonial conflict, setting *Avatar* in the year 2154 and locating its humanoid "natives," the Na'vi, on Pandora, a jungle-like moon in the Alpha Centauri star system. In place of settler colonialism or missionizing, the narrative centers on corporate capitalism: humans have come to Pandora seeking a rare metal, and the Na'vi present little more than an ethical irritation, since mining the metal necessitates relocating them. The irritation is significant enough that the corporation has created "avatars," artificially grown bodies that look "native" but are in fact Na'vi/human hybrids. Each can be controlled only by the human whose DNA has been used to create a particular avatar (or by an identical twin of that person, as in the case of Jake Sully). These matched humans control their avatars by lying inside sensory deprivation chambers, outfitted with electronic equipment that allows them to remotely control the avatar bodies. Because Pandora's atmosphere is toxic to humans, they can live there only by using these avatars on the one hand, or by wearing gas masks or robotic exoskeletons on the other (these mutually exclusive possibilities will prove theoretically significant).

In three ways *Avatar* is surprisingly conservative in its portrayal of virtual corporeality. First, the film assumes a strict isomorphism between the virtual body and what I term the "actual" or "physical" body. (I never oppose "virtual" to "real;" such an opposition wrongly encodes presumptions that the online is not real, and that the real is technology-free.) Never in the film do we see Jake Sully operating an avatar other than his own, nor is there a plot twist revealing that some other person is controlling Jake Sully's avatar. Second, in the world of the film the destruction of an avatar does not kill the human with which it is paired; fears of death apply only to human bodies. This is one of the strongest contrasts between *Avatar* and the best-known filmic representations of the virtual body that appeared before it, the *Matrix* trilogy (the first of which was released in 1999). In these movies, humans also go into sensory deprivation to control avatar bodies, but the death of an avatar body while under human control causes that human's death as well. Third, in *Avatar* the avatars are not online entities and are thus "virtual" only in a limited sense. In fact, the dénouement of the film occurs when the Na'vi are able to successfully transfer Jake Sully's consciousness into his (physical) avatar body, leaving his human body to die—the ultimate act of "going native" in the actual world, and one linked to fantasies of settler colonialism.

Virtual Embodiment in Practice

To understand how *Avatar*'s understanding of embodiment differs from virtual corporeality, consider the meaning of "avatar" in the virtual world Second Life. At the time I write this chapter you can join Second Life for free, without providing any actual-world information about yourself; you create an account by making up a first name and choosing a last name from a predefined list. You then download and run the Second Life program (usually known as a "viewer" or "client") to enter the virtual world. In the language now standard across a range of virtual worlds, you are now "inworld," a term probably coined by Bruce Damer (Damer 1998). Once inside Second Life you find yourself in a virtual landscape built primarily by other residents and which can thus include anything from private homes to parks, from abandoned factories to glittering temples. These landscapes often have a rural feel to them—newcomers to Second Life often say it seems empty or abandoned. One reason for this is that to distribute server load, only a certain number of objects can be created or "rezzed" on a parcel of land. But as I discuss later, the predominant feel of Second Life as a countryside reveals something crucial about virtual embodiment.

Of course, a key aspect of virtual corporeality is the "avatar." Avatars in Second Life are almost limitlessly customizable. You can appear as any ethnicity or gender, and by rendering parts of your avatar body invisible, folding your avatar body upon itself, and attaching virtual objects, almost any imaginable embodiment is possible. Second Life residents have appeared as hundred-foot-tall dragons, two-foot tall baby animals, glowing balls of light, robots, enormous noses, walking trees, mermaids inside of fish tanks. Additionally, in Second Life (like many virtual worlds) it is possible to have more than one avatar (additional avatars are often known as "alternates," or "alts"). You can log off of one avatar's account and then log back in using a different account. By running two simultaneous instances of a Second Life viewer, being embodied by two avatars at once is feasible, as is having multiple actual-world people be embodied by a single avatar, either by taking turns or by collaboratively controlling the single avatar. The actual-world isomorphism between single person and single body can be transgressed in either direction, with significant consequences for virtual embodiment.

Residents do not always make use of these possibilities: most people, most of the time, have singular virtual embodiments that they see as resembling their actual-world embodiment, or that reflect dominant actual-world ideals of beauty and status. This often means light-skinned avatars, female avatars with large breasts, male avatars with bulging biceps, and so on. However, even in such cases our critical impulse should not foreclose examining how such ostensibly normative embodiments may have different meanings and consequences online—not least because, for instance, the male avatar with bulging biceps may be female in the actual world.

Regardless of the form an avatar takes, a fundamental way in which it constitutes a kind of embodiment is as an anchor for subjectivity. It is common in Second Life (and a range of other virtual worlds and online games) to view one's avatar in a "third-person" perspective, such that you see your avatar from a slight remove, glancing over its shoulder so to speak. But it would be incorrect to construe such a perspective with being disembodied, for regardless of whether or not one is using a first-person perspective, a third-person perspective, or switches between them, the avatar is the locus of perception and sociality.

To succinctly illustrate some consequences of virtual embodiment, I will recount two stories chronicled by the Second Life journalist Wagner James Au. In the first, Au describes the story of CyFishy Traveler, a Second Life resident who created an female avatar, "Beginning Thursday," after a difficult romantic breakup in the actual world. CyFishy would sometimes run two instances of the Second Life viewer so he could embody the two avatars simultaneously. One day, feeling despondent about his lost romance, CyFishy moved the Beginning avatar up to his CyFishy avatar and "offered myself a hug."

> At that point, "Something shifted," as he puts it… Something moved him about that moment, so CyFishy did the next logical thing.
> "We started dating"…
> Their romance continued in Instant Message. "I would talk to myself, tell myself the things that I secretly wished a lover would say to me, assure myself that I am beautiful and loved… it's become a means to explore how to give myself the kind of love I was constantly seeking from outside of myself."
> But one last thing to note before you go: In [the physical world], CyFishy Traveler's owner is actually not male. "I'd shifted genders as an experiment and discovered the joys of having a hot guy to stare at any time I wanted to," explains CyFishy, who as it turns out, is just another woman imagining herself as a man imagining himself partnered to another woman who's really herself. (Au 2008a)

Another story Au recounts is that of Eshi Otawara, a Second Life resident whose actual-world husband, Glenn, died unexpectedly in 2006. In the wake of that tragedy:

> "I felt so powerless and alone," as she recalls, "that I told myself, 'You know, it might be a sick thing to do, a pathetic thing to do, whatever—but if I cannot have this guy in real life, I will MAKE him in Second Life"…
> …His widow re-created him as best she could — rather, Eshi Otawara remade herself, transforming her avatar to look like her husband. And when she was done remaking him, she took Glenn on a tour through Second Life….

..."I get to do things with his pixel body that he'd be doing if he were alive," as she puts it. She even gave him a flat belly, something she'd known he'd wanted for some time. "I am sure he was cracking up in whatever form he exists now," she says...

...I ask Eshi if she'd ever thought of turning Glenn into an "alt," a secondary avatar she could control from another computer, while Eshi remained in-world, as herself. That way, in a certain sense, they could be in Second Life together.

"Yes I did," she tells me, then tears up. "It is a scary thought. It wouldn't be him and me.. it would be me and me." (Au 2008b)

Both of these fascinating stories are, like *Avatar*, not completely indicative of everyday virtual-world embodiment. As a journalist, Au understandably focuses on the newsworthy, the exceptional, which can of course reveal broader cultural logics. The most atypical aspect of these stories is that they hinge on knowing about the actual-world lives of the persons in question, though Au did not attempt to independently verify these details. People CyFishy and Beginning would encounter during their Second Life dates would not know they were simultaneous embodiments of the same actual-world person unless CyFishy or Beginning volunteered that information. Nor would most residents know what when Eshi transformed her avatar into the form of an older (if flat-bellied) man, this virtual corporeality was meant to invoke Eshi's deceased husband.

At first glance these two stories appear opposed. The experiences of CyFishy and Beginning are predicated on a plural personhood experienced through simultaneous multiple virtual embodiment, but Eshi rejects this possibility: for her, this would be "just me and me." It would foreclose the alternating selfhood invoked by the term "alt" itself. Yet these two stories share a sense that in virtual worlds, the body becomes a multiplicity, a supernumerary site of subject-formation, a zone of possibility that lies across a distinct gap from actual-world embodiment. A shared agreement behind debate can also be seen in the following excerpt from one of many discussions about virtual embodiment I encountered during my ethnographic work in Second Life. I was sitting around one day with several other residents when someone asked if being inworld in Second Life constituted an "out-of-body experience." The following exchange ensued between persons I will name John, Susan, Roger, and Amy:

John: I don't think it is an out of body experience per say. Since we are still "in our bodies" while looking at a monitor

Susan: John, I agree at one level, but do you never feel "embodied" in your avie [avatar]?

John: no, I feel my avie is an extension of myself, but I see how it can happen for others

Roger: I think people do feel embodied - hence all the sexual activity with add on genitals

John: my avie is an extension of my brain, but I don't feel embodied

Amy: we do a certain suspension of disbelief—that lets us shift into our Second Life looks

It is not surprising that Eshi and CyFishy disagree on the meaning of multiple virtual bodies—or that my Second Life interlocutors disagree on virtual corporeality more generally, understanding such embodiment in terms ranging from "an extension of myself" or "an extension of my brain" to "our Second Life looks" or "feeling embodied" (thus showing that for some residents at least, "embodiment" is an emic term). No culture is ever univocal, and foundational cultural logics often appear in the background assumptions against which disagreement is intelligible as such. These stories and conversations exemplify how aspects of virtual-world embodiment sometimes distill or even concretize what it means to be embodied in the actual world—recalling, for instance, how physical-world sociality is predicated on "the inherent multiplicity and indeterminacy of the body we have and are" (Van Wolputte 2004:259). I cannot overemphasize the importance of understanding that the very real existence of a gap between virtual and actual does not mean they are sealed off from one another and should not inaugurate an asymptotic analysis where they end up "blurring." The ethnographic evidence indicates that the theoretical framework needed is not teleological but indexical. For virtual embodiment, but for all aspects of virtual culture as well, the gap between virtual and actual is constitutive of bidirectional meaning-making, value production, subjectivation, and social praxis.

Theorizations of Embodiment

While even a remotely comprehensive review of literatures on embodiment is obviously beyond the scope of this chapter, questions of the body have certainly been central to human thought, harking back to the earliest written records and even prehistoric archaeological data, particularly in regard to death and burial. It is not coincidental that "avatar," first used to refer to online bodies in the 1980s, is a Sanskrit term referring to the incarnation of a Hindu deity (Boellstorff 2008:128). Despite the centrality of the body to biological anthropology and archaeology (see Joyce 2005), in cultural anthropology it has held a rather odd position. On one hand, many paradigms have deemphasized or downplayed the centrality of embodiment to culture, indicative of an "intellectualist tendency to regard body praxis as secondary to verbal praxis" (Jackson 1989:122). A result of these trends is that for many cultural anthropologists "the body, despite its ubiquity, has [been]… in effect simply 'bracketed' as a black box and set… aside" (Lock 1993:133). Yet cultural anthropologists have also built up a broad literature on embodiment stretching back to the beginnings of the discipline (for overviews see Farnell 1999; Lock 1993; Reischer and Koo 2004; Scheper-Hughes and Lock 1987; Van Wolputte 2004). This scholarship has shown how the body is produced, reproduced, and disciplined though contexts of culture and power (Martin 1992; Reischer and Koo 2004), and that as a result "the fact of our embodiment can be a valuable starting point for rethinking the nature of culture and our existential situation as cultural beings" (Csordas 1994:6).

Embodiment has also been a longstanding concern in work on virtual worlds and internet-mediated sociality, even in the early days of non-graphical virtual worlds and their textual avatars (e.g., Argyle and Shields 1996; Balsamo 1996; Doyle 2009; Gee 2008; Heim 1995; Hillis 1999; Ihde 2002; Ito 1997; McRae 1997; Mitchell and Thurtle 2004; Nakamura 2007; Reid 1996; Stone 1991; Sundén 2003; Taylor 2002; Van Gelder 1991; White 2006; Yee and Bailenson 2007). Embodiment even inspired the first virtual world in the contemporary sense. In 1970, Myron Krueger and a colleague were working in different rooms but collaborating using cameras trained on their respective monitors, so that their hands appeared superimposed:

> As I moved my hand to point to the data my friend had just sent, the image of my hand briefly overlapped the image of his. He moved his hand.... I was struck with the thought that he was uncomfortable about the image of my hand touching the image of his... Without saying anything, I subtly tested my hypothesis. Sure enough, as I moved the image of my hand towards his, he repeatedly, but unconsciously, moved the image of his hand to avoid contact. (Krueger 1983:125–127)

For Krueger, then, the pivotal moment in realizing virtual worlds were possible was a moment of virtual embodiment. Significantly for my later discussion, this moment of embodiment was a moment of two hands pointing toward each other (see Boellstorff 2008:43–44 for further discussion of this historical period and an image of these pointing virtual hands nearly touching).

Feminist and queer work (among other communities of scholarship) has shown how white, male, heterosexual bodies often stand as paradigms for embodiment (e.g. Bordo 1993; Burlein 1995; Prosser 1998; Salamon 2006). In only an apparent paradox, such scholarship has also shown how in many cultural contexts "the body has been and still is closely associated with women and the feminine, whereas the mind remains associatively and implicitly connected to men and the masculine" (Grosz 1995:32; see also Bigwood 1991; Probyn 1991). This attention to gender, race, and sexuality is crucial and I have addressed these topics in my work on virtual worlds as well as on sexuality and national belonging (e.g., Boellstorff 2005, 2007), but I have come to realize that the question of place must be central to any theory of the virtual body. I contend that virtual embodiment is always embodiment in a virtual place, and that this place-ness of virtual worlds holds foundational implications for online corporeality.

Virtual Chora

In previous research I have emphasized that virtual worlds are places (see Boellstorff 2008, chapter 4), as encapsulated in a telling prepositional distinction: in English you typically go "on" a website but "in" a virtual world. Richard Bartle, a pioneer in the design of virtual worlds, noted succinctly that "virtual worlds are not games. Even the ones written to *be* games aren't games. People can play games *in* them, sure, and they can be set up to that end, but this merely makes them venues. The Pasadena Rose Bowl is a stadium, not a game" (Bartle 2004:475; emphasis in all quotations is in the original). In this sense it is "wrong to conceive of the virtual as a kind of indetermination, as a formless reservoir of possibilities that only actual beings identify" Badiou 2000:50; see Deleuze 2004).

I have also emphasized the importance of *techne* to virtual worlds. Briefly, Greek thought differentiated *episteme*, or knowledge, from techne, the root of "technology." Most translations of *techne* interpret it as meaning something like "art" or "craft;" Heidegger frames it as meaning as "to make something appear, within what is present, as this or that, in this way or that way" (Heidegger 2001 [1971]:157). Heidegger's emphasis on "this or that," on what linguists would term an indexical relationship, underscores how techne introduces a gap between the way the world was before and after its application—in the way that, for instance, a simple tube made from a reed allows a person to breathe underwater, an ability the person would not have prior to the techne in question (this example is from Beniger 1986:9; see Boellstorff 2008:55). What makes virtual worlds distinctive— for despite their antecedents, they cannot be reduced to that which came before them—is that for the first time techne works not on the actual world, but upon a virtual world that is already the product of techne. Techne turns wood and ideas into a chair, but techne does not just turn ideas and silicon into a virtual world: techne becomes recursive and can also take place "inworld." This has consequences for how we theorize labor and value online, and offline as well (Ulmer 1994:66).

To push further on this relationship between place and the virtual body, I will now link techne with another concept from ancient Greek philosophy: *chora*, a term best known from its centrality in *Timaeus*, one of Plato's late dialogues. Although philosophers have debated this term for two millennia, most would agree that in Plato's view chora is the basis of being, such that "forms come to be *in* it without ever being *of* it" (Sallis 1999:109). Analogies Plato uses to illustrate chora include the wax upon which an image is stamped, the odorless oil used to make a perfume, and a mass of gold:

> That is modeled into all possible figures or shapes [for instance, a triangle..] if someone were to point to one of the figures and ask what it *is*, the safest answer would be that it is gold; but as for the triangle and other figures formed from the gold, one should avoid speaking of them as being, since they are changing even while one is thus speaking [..] The gold is an image of that which receives all the fleeting images, an image of what Timaeus has called [chora]. (Sallis 1999:107–108)

One way to think about this triple relation between idea, chora, and thing is that of father, mother, and child (Ulmer 1994:63–64), and indeed chora can connote receptacle, or even "the image of the nurse, a kind of surrogate mother who holds, aids, and succors the newly born child" (Sallis 1999:99; see also Derrida 1990; Derrida and Eisenman 1997). A range of feminist thinkers have drawn upon this meaning of chora to develop feminist theories of embodiment (Bianchi 2006; Braziel 2006; Burchill 2006; Grosz 1995; Kristeva 1984; Margaroni 2005).

These theories are immensely valuable, but as Grosz admits, they sideline another set of meanings for chora (Grosz 1995:112). Elsewhere in Plato's dialogues—and in ancient Greek society more generally—"chora" appears in statements like "Crete is not a level chora," or in debates over adapting the sport of horse racing to the nature of the chora (Sallis 1999:116). In these contexts, the antonym of chora is *polis*, the city—and chora clearly means something like landscape, land, country, or simply "place," for "Plato never seems to abandon the reference to country or land expressed in ordinary uses of the term *chora*. Rather, he extrapolates from those meanings to form a technical usage in which *chora* expressed *shared space or common visual field*" (Ashbaugh 1988:103). In fact, "*chora* stands out as the oldest Greek word for place, appearing in Homer and Hesiod" (Walter 1988:120). Recall that Second Life and many other virtual worlds have a rural feel to them: with chora in mind, we might ask if there could be more to this sense of virtual world as countryside than the mere need to reduce server load.

If we go back even further, to the first written records in the *Iliad* of "choron" and "choros," which are linked to chora, we find that these terms "refer to both a dance and a dancing floor... we see here an emerging recognition that a precondition for activity is a place for it to occur, as dancing requires a dancing floor... the growing realization that place and making are conjoined" (Rickert 2007:254). Chora was distinguished from *topos*, also often translated as "place," in that chora is place made meaningful through the embodied human engagement of techne. For instance:

> At the opening of Sophocles' *Oedipus at Colonus*... [Antigone] tells Theseus that he will show him the *choros* where Oedipus must die, but warns Theseus not to reveal the *topoi* in which it lies. Here, *topos* stands for the mere location... of the sacred *choros*, the grave. (Walter 1988:120)

Virtual worlds are thus chora recursively constituted through the work of techne itself, as if dancing bought a dancing-floor into being. Virtual worlds show the value in conceptualizing chora not in terms of topography, but in terms of chorography (see Ulmer 1994), or even a "choreography" of techne with chora. In an eerie anticipation of virtual worlds, Sallis summarized the effect of chora as follows:

> [Chora] grants, furnishes, supplies an *abode* to all things... [chora], in which the phantoms come and go, is that other that secures the image in whatever trace of being it has.... One could call it... a ghost scene that, enshrouding precisely in

letting appear, endows the fleeting specters with whatever trace of being they might enjoy. (Sallis 1999:122)

In 1985, Richard Mohr emphasized that Plato's analogy of gold was inadequate because gold is a thing of the actual world—physicality—while in contrast the notion of chora does not entail:

> ...viewing space as a material constituent out of which substances are created. Rather space is a medium or field *in which* phenomena appear as (non-substantial) images. If Plato had lived into [the twentieth] century, he might very well have chosen, not gold, but a movie screen or television screen as his analogue to a field across which ceaselessly changing non-substantial images may flicker. (Mohr 1985:94)

Writing 25 years after this statement, I contend that had Plato lived into the twenty-first century, he might very well have chosen, not a movie screen, but a virtual world as analogue and exemplar of chora. Virtual worlds underscore how chora is not place per se, but place-making or worlding (Zhan 2009), the embodied "dance" of techne making possible "being-in-the-world." As this last term suggests, this reframing of chora links it to a phenomenology of the virtual body.

Being-Inworld: The Digital Relation

Pivotal to my theoretical framework is the phenomenological insight that embodiment, as part of being, is always "being-in-the-world," like a dancer on a dance floor. Embodiment is always emplacement, suggesting that there is more to the virtual body than avatars: as in the actual world, the virtual body is always a "'spatial body'... produced and... the production of space... [and] immediately subject to the determinants of that space" (Lefebvre 1991:195). Virtual body and virtual world constitute each other, recalling the broader phenomenological conclusion that "the body can no longer be regarded as an entity to be examined in its own right but has to be placed in the context of a world" (Macaan 1993:174). The notion of being-in-the-world has been used to examine human-computer interaction in the actual world (e.g., Dourish 2004), and its productive utility extends to virtual contexts. It may not be coincidental that going back to "Videoplace" and "Habitat," and continuing through "World of Warcraft," "There," and "Free Realms," the names of many virtual worlds have emphasized place rather than avatars: we can transform the idea of "being-in-the-world" to "being-in-the-virtual-world" or just "being-inworld." This crucial pluralization of worlding underscores how virtual embodiment cannot be understood apart from its manifestation in specific virtual worlds, though of course we will discover commonalities between virtual worlds as well as differences.

The centrality of world to embodiment has been a common theme of phenomenological thinking. Husserl's notion of the "life-world," for instance, highlights "the intersubjective, mundane world of background understandings and experiences of the world" (Dourish 2004:106), which can now include a set of background understandings and experiences about virtual worlds. Merleau-Ponty approached this question of co-constitution of body and world though his notion of "flesh," through which distinctions like body versus world were "redefined as relational, intertwined and reversible aspects of a single fabric. [He] uses the term the flesh to designate this fabric. And he refers to both the flesh of the body... and the flesh of the world.. The perceiving subject, from this point of view, forms part of the visible world" (Crossley 1995:47; see also Leder 1990). We may thus think of virtual flesh as the intertwined fabric, emerging from virtual chora, that forms a shared fabric of virtual embodiment and virtual world.

Indeed, the key way that *Avatar* accurately represented virtual corporeality was its identification of emplacement as essential to embodiment. As noted earlier, this took one of two mutually exclusive modalities on Pandora: humans had to embody using either Na'vi avatars or some combination of masks and robotic exoskeletons. This neatly sums up the difference between the avatar and the "cyborg," a now-classic future in science and technology studies (Haraway 1991). In distinction to the still-earlier figure of the android (a robotic approximation of the human body), the cyborg is part human and part machine—predicated on relationships of interpenetration and attachment, as in the prosthetic relationship between artificial hand and severed arm. In contrast, the avatar is based upon a gap—there is a clear and ontologically foundational gap between Jake Sully's avatar body and Jake Sully's actual-world body in a control pod, just as there is a clear and ontologically foundational gap between an avatar and an actual-world person, and between any virtual world and the actual world. Ideas, metaphors, power relations, and even forms of materiality routinely move across this gap between the virtual and actual, but it is the gap and attendant movements across it—works of techne—that make the virtual possible at all. It is instructive to consider the prosthetic relationship between artificial hand and severed arm in light of Merleau-Ponty's ruminations on phantom limbs:

> To have a phantom arm is to remain open to all the actions of which the arm alone is capable; it is to retain the practical field which one enjoyed before mutilation. The body is the vehicle of being in the world, and having a body is, for a living creature, to be intervolved in a definite environment, to identify oneself with certain projects and be continually committed to them. (Merleau-Ponty 1962:81–82)

Merleau-Ponty here emphasized how embodiment involves "action" in a "practical field." The body is constitutive of being-in-the-world, a "definite environment" of projects, of techne, and a changed body can retain a memory of the "definite environment" before the change (for instance, via the phenomenon of a phantom limb). We do not know how Merleau-Ponty might have revised his understanding of phantom limbs were the idea of avatar limbs available to him. However, it seems possible that his rethinking would include how virtual bodies, limbs and all, make possible human action in the "definite environment" of a virtual world, and how being-inworld thus enables new possibilities for corporeality.

Embodiment as emplacement involves what Heidegger termed "dwelling." For Heidegger—for whom only one world, the earth, was thinkable—"to be a human being means to be on the earth as a mortal. It means to dwell" (Heidegger 2001 [1971]:145). Heidegger noted that the Old German and Old English term *buan*, meaning "to build or dwell" and still discernable in the modern English term "neighbor" (near-dweller), is also the root of the modern German copula: *Ich bin*, I am, I exist. To exist is to dwell in a place and to draw upon techne in order to participate in the building of that place: "being-in-the-world... has to be understood in terms of tasks, actions to be accomplished, a free space which outlines in advance the possibilities available to the body at any time" (Macaan 1993:174). This is why Merleau-Ponty regarded embodiment not as "a thing in objective space, but as a system of possible actions, a virtual body with its phenomenal 'place' defined by its task and situation. My body is wherever there is something to be done" (Merleau-Ponty 1962:250). Until January 2005, in Second Life the amount of time an avatar spent in a location was in fact termed "dwell" (Boellstorff 2008:95), and notions of dwelling remain central to notions of virtual embodiment in Second Life and beyond.

It is helpful to think about this dwelling-relationship between embodiment and place in terms of indexicality. When Heidegger referred to techne as making something appear "as this or that, in this way or that way," he emphasized an indexicality, a relation of pointing, which lies behind the mutually constitutive being of body and world. This indexical relation of making something appear "as this or that" is predicated on chora: it links chora to techne. In this regard Plato's analogy of chora to gold is telling because:

> that analogy tells us that whenever we observe objects regularly exchanging their look or their shape, we cannot call those things *this* or *that* if we wish to remain close to the truth. But if... something remains constant throughout the change, we can rightly say that the enduring item deserves both the fixed reference of the definite indicative pronouns and a specific name [chora]. (Ashbaugh 1988:115).

This indexical relation is emergent in the relation between actual bodies and their emplacement in landscapes of perception and sociality: "the forms of the landscape—like the identities and capacities of its human inhabitants—are not imposed upon a material substrate but rather emerge as condensations or crystallizations of activity within a relational field" (Ingold 2004:333).

In my prior work, I have noted that oftentimes "digital" (as in some uses of "digital media") does little more than stand in for "computational" or "electronic" (Boellstorff 2008:18). However, a very different approach would begin by noting that the etymologies of digit as "finger" and index as "forefinger" converge on a relation of pointing that draws together "digit-al" and "index-ical." Invoking Heidegger's indexical understanding of techne, the digital might be said to "point to" virtual embodiment as being-inworld—as made possible by the "digit-al" gap. This recalls the gap between 0 and 1 in digital binary code, or the gap between the fingers of God and Adam that in Michelangelo's famous Sistine Chapel painting marks the moment of the human body's creation.

Because virtual worlds allow techne to become recursive, virtual embodiment is digital in the sense that it enables indexicality within virtual worlds: it allows the digital to "point at" itself. Indeed, there is a striking difference between the Sistine Chapel image and Krueger's drawing of his virtual hand pointing at his colleague's virtual hand in 1970. Both images feature a constitutive gap between two pointing hands, but in comparison to a creator/created hierarchy, with God above and Adam sitting below, Krueger's image shows an act of recursive creation—the fingers point at each other in a mutually constitutive circle—recalling not Michelangelo so much as the famous Escher drawing of two hands drawing each other into being. Indexicality provides a different way of understanding the digital relation with regard to the virtual body.

In developing this line of analysis, I have found it illuminating to turn to the phenomenologist Karl Jaspers's notion of the cypher, an "objectivity which is permeated by subjectivity and in such a way that Being becomes present in the whole" (Jaspers 1959:35). Derived from the Arabic word for "zero"—the binary "0" to the pointing "1" of the digit—the originary meaning of "cypher" is "an arithmetical symbol or character of no value by itself, but which increases or decreases the value of other figures according to its position" (OED 2010). In other words, its value is not symbolic—predicated on signifying meaning—but indexical, predicated on positionality and pointing. Extended meanings include "a person who fills a place, but is of no importance or worth, a nonentity, a 'mere nothing'," and "an intertexture of letters, esp. the initials of a name, engraved or stamped on plate, linen" (OED 2010). Recall how one image of chora provided by Plato is "a mass of wax or other soft material on which the imprint of a seal can be made" (Sallis 1999:108). In a virtual-world context, to "fill a place" is the effect of a virtual body's being-inworld. If virtual worlds can be considered instances of "the world of the cyphers" (Jaspers 1959:49), then the avatarized subject of that being-inworld would be not the cyborg, but the "cypherg." The cypherg is virtual corporeality through which "a *participation* in Being takes place" (Jaspers 1959:61), a participation through techne that makes possible the conditions for emplaced being itself. A recursive indexicality, made possible by the pluralization of being-inworld, is quite literally the "point" of the virtual body.

Conclusions: Politics of Virtual Embodiment

In this chapter, I have sought to develop a theory of the virtual body that links (1) ethnographic insights from prior work by myself and other scholars with (2) a theoretical architecture drawing from a range of philosophical perspectives and (3) introducing three new concepts: virtual chora, being-inworld, and the cypherg. Given limits of space and scope, my argument is clearly provisional and heuristic, intended to suggest directions for ethnographic inquiry. A blockbuster movie like *Avatar* may grab headlines for a few years, but it is through everyday online practices that new virtual embodiments will emerge.

Over a hundred million persons already participate in virtual worlds: future research will be crucial to understand differing and shared ways that these virtual worlds effect actual-world socialities, as they increasingly imbricate with them in a staggering range of indexical relationships. One fascinating issue involves the question of how the pluralization of worlding offered by being-inworld might act as a form of internal destabilization, challenging the Western cultural logics of place and embodiment that I have worked to trace and defamiliarize in this chapter.

In addition, the growth of virtual worlds raises new possibilities for non-Western critiques and transformations of virtual embodiment. As the notion of "avatar" suggests, non-Western genealogies of embodiment have shaped virtual worlds since their beginnings, but these are clearly minor influences in the context of a dominant Western (indeed, American and even Californian) ideology of the virtual (Barbrook and Cameron 2001). In analyzing how indigenous persons of North and South America have understood embodiment, Viveiros de Castro notes that "the Amerindian emphasis on the social construction of the body cannot be taken as the culturalization of a natural substrate but rather as the production of a distinctly human body, meaning *naturally* human" (Viveiros de Castro 1998:480). Such a notion of the human body as a production of nature through social engagement would offer just one of many possible alternative genealogies of virtual embodiment.

Developing our ethnographic and theoretical understandings of the virtual body can thus provide powerful new ways of apprehending not just virtual worlds, but also how "the computer and the worlds it generates reveal that the world in which we live, the [actual] world, has always been a space of virtuality" (Grosz 2001:78). The virtual body can teach us about actual-world embodiment. For instance, for Merleau-Ponty bodily movement "superimposes upon physical space a virtual or human space" (Merleau-Ponty 1962:111). But when virtual bodies and virtual worlds enter the picture, the verb "superimpose" becomes inadequate for capturing reconfigurations of "world" and thus of ethnographic fieldsite. Might some anthropologists find treating virtual worlds as fieldsites unsettling not so much because of their virtuality, but because of their corollary ability to destabilize notions of physical place, radically demonstrating the cultural constitution of the "fieldsite" (Gupta and Ferguson 1997)? In this sense "it is interesting that at just about the time the last of the untouched 'real-world' anthropological field sites are disappearing, a new and unexpected kind of 'field' is opening up incontrovertibly social spaces in which people still meet face-to-face, but under new definitions of both 'meet' and 'face'" (Stone 1991:85).

For anthropologists and others interested in culture, the great advantage of a phenomenological approach to the virtual body is that it highlights how new possibilities exist for embodiment when it is not just culture that can be multiple, but the world as well, for "the notion of the virtual... provid[es] a new way of thinking *multiplicity*" (Ansell Pearson 2002:4). This opens up new possibilities for forms of multinaturalism (Viveiros de Castro 1998:472) that can reconfigure the multiculturalist logics of inclusion and belonging that typify much contemporary anthropological thinking. Where Merleau-Ponty stated that "consciousness projects itself into a physical world and has a body, as it projects itself into a cultural world and has its habits" (Merleau-Ponty 1962:137), I would argue that being-inworld productively reframes this distinction between physical and cultural worlds. It does so by making acts of projection constitutive of worlds as well as bodies: the virtual body provides crucial clues to cultural practices of worlding. Too often, only the first term of the phrase "virtual world" receives theoretical and ethnographic attention; only by deepening our understanding of "world" can we truly understand virtual embodiment and virtual worlds more generally.

This has political consequences, because it suggests that an attention to the politics of placemaking may have crucial consequences for virtual embodiment. My theoretically-informed hunch is that what might at first seem to be marginally relevant topics like virtual terraforming, property, building, and commodities are crucial to the politics of the virtual body. Many critics of Heidegger, particularly Levinas, emphasized how "thinking in terms of visualizable totalities necessarily leads to totalitarian ways of acting" (Keyes 1972:122). In other words, the idea of being-in-a-singular-world shapes a totalitarian understanding of selfhood and society. In contrast, virtual worlds pluralize being-in-the-world. Since no one lives twenty-four hours a day in a single virtual world without any form of actual-world sociality, and few persons participate in only one virtual world (many of which take the form of online games), being-inworld is always a form of being-in-multiplicity. This opens possibilities for internal and external reconfigurations of Western ontologies of place, body, and the social (and thus new deconstructions of the internal/external dichotomy itself).

Any truly anthropological approach to embodiment "begins from the methodological postulate that the body is not an *object* to be studied in relation to culture, but is to be considered as the *subject* of culture, or in other words as the existential ground of culture" (Csordas 1988:5). The fascinating, possibly revolutionary potential of virtual worlds for embodiment lies in how virtual corporeality co-grounds culture with a being-inworld founded in new pluralizations of place and sociality. From virtual chora emerges the cypherg, a figure of online corporeality, a figure whose recursively indexical being-inworld stands to fundamentally reconfigure what it means to be human—even while drawing upon and even concretizing longstanding notions of the human. To what new possibilities does placing the virtual body "point?" At stake is nothing less than the "the digital" itself.

Acknowledgments

I thank Fran Mascia-Lees for her encouragement in writing this chapter. I thank as well my interlocutors and colleagues in Second Life and at the University of California, Irvine for their inspiration and support. Early versions of this article were presented at the Institute for Advanced Study, University of Minnesota (March 2010), the Department of Anthropology, University of Toronto (April 2010), and the Society for Cultural Anthropology Conference (May 2010). I thank the organizers and attendees of those events for their helpful comments.

This piece is also forthcoming in Companion to the Anthropology of Bodies/ Embodiments. Frances E. Mascia-Lees, Editor. New York: Wiley-Blackwell

References

Ansell Pearson, K. 2002. *Philosophy and the Adventure of the Virtual: Bergson and the Time of Life.* London: Routledge.

Argyle, Katie, and Rob Shields. 1996. Is there a Body on the Net? In *Cultures of Internet: Virtual Spaces, Real Histories, Living Bodies.* Rob Shields, ed. Pp. 58–69. London: Sage.

Ashbaugh, A.F. 1988. *Plato's Theory of Explanation: A Study of the Cosmological Account in the Timaeus.* Albany, NY: State University of New York Press.

Au, W.J. 2008a. Friday's Traveler: The Avatar Who Loved Himself. New World Notes, <http://nwn.blogs.com/nwn/2008/06/thursdays-trave.html>, accessed February 28, 2010.

———. 2008b.The Husband That Eshi Made. New World Notes <http://nwn. blogs.com/nwn/2008/05/the-husband-tha.html>, accessed February 28, 2010.

Badiou, A. 2000. *Deleuze: The Clamor of Being.* Minneapolis: University of Minnesota Press.

Balsamo, A. 1996. *Technologies of the Gendered Body: Reading Cyborg Women.* Durham: Duke University Press.

Barbrook, R., and A. Cameron. 2001. Californian Ideology. *In Crypto Anarchy, Cyberstates, and Pirate Utopias.* (ed) Peter Ludlow. Cambridge, MA: MIT Press, 363–387.

Bartle, R. A. 2004. *Designing Virtual Worlds.* Indianapolis: New Riders.

Beniger, J. R. 1986. *The Control Revolution: Technological and Economic Origins of the Information Society.* Cambridge, MA: Harvard University Press.

Bianchi, E. 2006. Receptacle/Chora: Figuring the Errant Feminine in Plato's Timaeus. *Hypatia* 21(4):124–146.

Bigwood, C. 1991. Renaturalizing the Body (With the Help of Merleau-Ponty). *Hypatia* 6(3):54–73.

Boellstorff, T. 2005. *The Gay Archipelago: Sexuality and Nation in Indonesia.* Princeton: Princeton University Press.

———. 2007. *A Coincidence of Desires: Anthropology, Queer Studies, Indonesia.* Durham: Duke University Press.

———. 2008. *Coming of Age in Second Life: An Anthropologist Explores the Virtually Human.* Princeton: Princeton University Press.

Bordo, S. 1993. *Unbearable Weight: Feminism, Western Culture, and the Body.* Berkeley: University of California Press.

Braziel, J.E. 2006. Being and Time, Non-Being and Space.. (Introductory Notes Toward an Ontological Study of "Woman" and Chora). In *Belief, Bodies, and Being: Feminist Reflections on Embodiment.* (ed) Deborah Orr, Linda López Mcallister, Eileen Kahl, and Kathleen Earle. Oxford: Rowan & Littlefield, 103–125.

Burchill, L.2006. Resituating the Feminine in Contemporary French Philosophy. In *Belief, Bodies, and Being: Feminist Reflections on Embodiment.* (ed) Deborah Orr, Linda López Mcallister, Eileen Kahl, And Kathleen Earle. Oxford: Rowan & Littlefield, 81–102.

Burlein, A. 2005. The Productive Power of Ambiguity: Rethinking Homosexuality through the Virtual and Developmental Systems Theory. *Hypatia*: A Journal of Feminist Philosophy 20(1):21–53.

Crossley, N. 1995. Merleau-Ponty, the Elusive Body and Carnal Sociology. *Body & Society* 1(1):43–63.

Csordas, T. J. 1988. Embodiment as a Paradigm for Anthropology. *Ethos* 18(1):5–47.

Csordas, T. J. 1994. Introduction: the Body as Representation and Being-in-the-world. In *Embodiment and Experience: The Existential Ground of Culture and Self.* (ed) Thomas J. Csordas. Cambridge: Cambridge University Press, 1–24.

Damer, B. 1998. *Avatars!: Exploring and Building Virtual Worlds on the Internet.* Berkeley: Peachpit Press.

Deleuze, G. 2004. *Difference and Repetition.* London: Continuum.

Derrida, J. 1990. A Letter to Peter Eisenman. *Assemblage* 12:6–13.

———. and P. Eisenman. 1997. *Chora L Works.* New York: The Monacelli Press.

Dourish, P. 2001. *Where the Action Is: The Foundations of Embodied Interaction.* Cambridge, MA: MIT Press.

Doyle, D. 2009. The Body of the Avatar: Rethinking the Mind-body Relationship in Virtual Worlds. *Journal of Gaming & Virtual Worlds* 1(2):131–141.

Farnell, B. 1999. *Moving Bodies, Acting Selves.* Annual Review of Anthropology 28:341–73.

Gee, J.P. 2008. Video Games and Embodiment. *Games and Culture* 3(3/4):253–263.

Grosz, E. 1995. Women, Chora, Dwelling. In her *Space, Time and Perversion: Essays on the Politics of Bodies.* London: Routledge, 111–124.

————. 2001.*Architecture from the Outside: Essays on Virtual and Real Space*. Cambridge, MA: MIT Press.

Gupta, A. and J. Ferguson. 1997. Discipline and Practice: "The Field" as Site, Method, and Location in Anthropology." In *Anthropological Locations: Boundaries and Grounds of a Field Science*. Akhil Gupta and James Ferguson, (ed) Berkeley: University of California Press, 1–46.

Haraway, D. 1991. A Cyborg Manifesto: Science, Technology, and Socialist-feminism in the Late Twentieth Century. In her *Simians, Cyborgs, and Women: The Reinvention of Nature*. London: Routledge, 149–82.

Heidegger, M. 2001 [1971] Building Dwelling Thinking. In his *Poetry, Language, Thought*. New York: Harper Perennial Modern Classics, 143–159.

Heim, M. 1995 The Design of Virtual Reality. In *Cyberspace/Cyberbodies/ Cyberpunk: Cultures of Technological Embodiment*. M. Featherstone and R. Burrows, (ed) 65–77. London: Sage.

Hillis, K. 1999. *Digital Sensations: Space, Identity, and Embodiment in Virtual Reality*. Minneapolis: University of Minnesota Press.

Ihde, D. 2002.*Bodies in Technology*. Minneapolis: University of Minnesota Press.

Ingold, T. 2004. Culture on the Ground: The World Perceived Through the Feet. *Journal of Material Culture* 9(3):315–340.

Ito, M. 1997. Virtually Embodied: The Reality of Fantasy in a Multi-User Dungeon. In *Internet Culture*. David Porter, (ed) New York: Routledge, 87–109.

Jackson, M. 1989. *Paths toward a Clearing: Radical Empiricism and Ethnographic Inquiry*. Bloomington: Indiana University Press.

Jaspers, K. 1959. *Truth and Symbol*. Translated and With An Introduction by Jean T. Wilde, William Kluback, and William Kimmel. Albany, NY: NCUP, Inc.

Joyce, R. 2005. Archaeology of the Body. *Annual Review of Anthropology* 34:139–158.

Keyes, C. D. 1972. An Evaluation of Levinas' Critique of Heidegger. *Research in Phenomenology* 2:121–142.

Kristeva, J. 1984. *Revolution in Poetic Language*. New York: Columbia University Press.

Leder, D. 1990. Flesh and Blood: A Proposed Supplement to Merleau-Ponty. *Human Studies* 13: 209–219.

Lefebvre, H. 1991. *The Production of Space*. Translated By Donald Nicholson-Smith. Oxford: Blackwell.

Lock, M. 1993. Cultivating the Body: Anthropology and Epistemologies of Bodily Practice and Knowledge. *Annual Review of Anthropology* 22:133–155.

Macaan, C. 1993. *Four Phenomenological Philosophers: Husserl, Heidegger, Sartre, Merleau-Ponty*. London: Routledge.

Margaroni, M. 2005."The Lost Foundation": Kristeva's Semiotic *Chora* and Its Ambiguous Legacy. *Hypatia* 20(1):78–98.

Martin, E. 1992. The End of the Body? *American Ethnologist* 19(1):121–140.

McRae, S. 1997. Flesh Made Word: Sex, Text, and the Virtual Body. In *Internet Culture*. David Porter, (ed) New York: Routledge, 73–86.

Merleau-Ponty. 1962. *Phenomenology of Perception.* New York: Humanities Press.

Mitchell, R. and P. Thurtle, (ed) 2004. *Data Made Flesh: Embodying Information.* New York: Routledge.

Mohr, R. 1985. *The Platonic Cosmology.* Leiden: E. J. Brill.

Nakamura, L. 2007. *Digitizing Race: Visual Cultures of the Internet.* Minneapolis: University Of Minnesota Press.

Oxford English Dictionary online. 2010. "Cypher." <http://dictionary.oed.com/ cgi/entry/50040044?single=1&query_type=word&queryword=cypher&first= 1&max_to_show=10>, accessed March 15, 2010.

Probyn, E. 1991. This Body Which Is Not One: Speaking an Embodied Self. *Hypatia* 6(3):111–124.

Prosser, J. 1998. *Second Skins: The Body Narratives of Transsexuality.* New York: Columbia University Press.

Reid, E. M. 1996. Text-based Virtual Realities: Identity and the Cyborg Body. In *High Noon on the Electronic Frontier: Conceptual Issues in Cyberspace.* Peter Ludlow, (ed) Cambridge, MA: MIT Press, 327–345.

Reischer, E. and K. S. Koo. 2004. The Body Beautiful: Symbolism and Agency in the Social World. *Annual Review of Anthropology* 33:297–317.

Rickert, T. 2007. Toward the *Chōra*: Kristeva, Derrida, and Ulmer on Emplaced Invention. *Philosophy and Rhetoric* 40(3):251–273.

Salamon, G. 2006. Boys of the Lex: Transgenderism and Rhetorics of Materiality. *GLQ: A Journal of Lesbian and Gay Studies* 12(4):575–97.

Sallis, J. 1999.*Chorology: On Beginning in Plato's* Timaeus. Bloomington: Indiana University Press.

Scheper-Hughes, N. and M. Lock. 1987. The Mindful Body: A Prolegomenon to Future Work in Medical Anthropology. *Medical Anthropology Quarterly* 1(1):6–41.

Stone, A. R. 1991. Will the Real Body Please Stand Up? In *Cyberspace: First Steps,* Michael Benedikt (ed), 81–118.

Sundén, J. 2003. *Material Virtualities: Approaching Online Textual Embodiment.* New York: Peter Lang.

Taylor, T. L. 2002. Living Digitally: Embodiment in Virtual Worlds. In *The Social Life of Avatars: Presence and Interaction in Shared Virtual Environments,* Ralph Schroeder, (ed). London: Springer-Verlag, 40–62

Ulmer, G. 1994. *Heuretics: The Logic of Invention.* Baltimore: Johns Hopkins University Press.

Van Gelder, L. 1991 [1985]. "The Strange Case of the Electronic Lover." In *Computerization and Controversy: Value Conflicts and Social Choices.* (ed) Charles Dunlop and Rob Kling. Boston: Academic Press, 364–375.

Van Wolputte, S. 2004. Hang On to Your Self: Of Bodies, Embodiment, and Selves. *Annual Review of Anthropology* 33:251–69.

Viveiros de Castro, E. 1998. Cosmological Deixis and Amerindian Perspectivism. *Journal of the Royal Anthropological Institute* 4(3):469–488.

Walter, E. V. 1988. *Placeways: A Theory of the Human Environment*. Chapel Hill: University of North Carolina Press.

White, M. 2006. *The Body and the Screen: Theories of Internet Spectatorship*. Cambridge, MA: MIT Press.

Yee, N. and J. Bailenson. 2007. The Proteus Effect: The Effect of Transformed Self-Representation on Behavior. *Human Communication Research* 33:271–290.

Zhan, M. 2009. *Other-Worldly: Making Chinese Medicine through Transnational Frames*. Durham: Duke University Press.

Chapter 17

The Story of the 'I'

Heather Palmer

The following chapter is a discursive response to Joel Peter Witkin's photographic image, *Man without a Head* (toned gelatin silver print, 93 x 73 cm, edition of 12, 1993, Mexico). The image, not included herein, can be accessed at http:// a4rizm.tumblr.com/post/1102759076/joel-peter-witkin-man-without-a-head-1993-via (2012) or within the pages of The Bone House (Witkin 1998). The photograph portrays an anonymous decapitated male nude.

I will start at the foot. My eyes find consolation in his socks. They provide a humanising quality, a comforting, visceral point of reference. The image is monochrome, they are black; had they have been white the blood would have muddied their appearance and darkened them anyway but their weight and opacity provides the image with proportional stability, rooting the subject, the story's *'I'*. The backdrop is bereft of the rich and opulent baroque setting seen in a lot of Witkin's imagery; the floor is a bloody mess, the wall covering splattered, grubby, dated. The velvety sensual drapes frequently seen in Witkin's work here are stark and creased. They are however, only present in the simplest and most functional of forms; to hide a corner and perhaps the props which lend stability to the deceased *'I'*. It is not in Witkin's nature to give anything away to chance – Witkin wanted to create a seedy, denigrated vista. The sheer corporeal humiliation of the subject's naked body with incongruously clothed feet is a calculated disgrace. The shrivelled penis, the heavy girth, the slack chest that seems uncomfortably relaxed, the right arm that appears to have given way while the left pleads to God or perhaps the viewer, begging, in anticipation… of very little, in weakened cupping. The *'I'* is the antithesis of *The Thinker*, (bronze and marble 1902, Musée Rodin, Paris) whose closed, complete hard body gestures toward the head, the site of 'self' and enlightened reason. Witkin's open, incomplete, slack, low subject holds no such sentient dynamism. Indeed, Witkin suggests that the arms have been simply posed through necessity to balance the subject, the *'I'* who kept toppling from his pedestal.

The hospital staff are often too heavy handed, Witkin complains (Wilson 2000). They frequently allow the dead to fall and break their noses, damaging their otherwise photogenic faces. This man, this *'I'* would not have suffered in this particular way despite frequently overbalancing and having to be hauled back up onto the stool. Witkin had ordered a heavy, headless corpse this time. No face to bloody, no nose to break. The image is as Witkin had planned.

The gaping hole at the throat is ragged, betraying the recent post-mortem inflicted violence. There is an acute feeling of the incomplete being of the *'I'*. The awful absence forces the eye to check and check again before taking solace in the table covering, the flash reflected in the frosted window panes, the blood splattered floor, the ugly yet familiar socks.

Dissecting a Witkin image necessitates slicing and peeling away each layer of application, inference and staging. Beginning with the outermost layer, or epidermis, I will examine the treatment of the negative and the processed print alike which provide the scratched conduit lens through which we see. Beneath this veil lies the naked *flesh made word*; textual discourse evoked as justification for the non-sequitur of intellectualised 'unreason'. The *true* story of the *'I'* lies somewhere still yet beneath. The bones, the skeletal structure of the socio-political context which has allowed a man to be beheaded post-mortem without outcry, to be depicted for high-cultural satiation, lie buried beneath claims to a post-modern cultural epoch.

Epidermis

The print appears grubby, a dirty secret well touched, fingered, kept hidden. The scratched and aged, yellowing image produced conceals its naissance. To create the work minimal lighting has been employed which assists in the evocation of the baroque aesthetic. The preferred north lighting allows highlights and tonal distributions to be modified later in the printing process. From the resulting filmstrip, one negative is chosen, scratched and cut into. After the negative has been brought to size, tissue is placed, over the warm toned photographic paper; another dermal layer which acts as a light refracting membrane. Piercing and tearing this intermediate skin can sharpen or soften parts of the image. The negative has been altered once more by violent demarcation of the dermis during this part of the process. The ensuing weather-beaten, yellow-brown, aged effect gives the work an appearance of an old master, divorced from our contemporaneous culture; the resultant image alludes to an historical fantasy. The reality of the *'I'*, the *Man without a Head* has been buried in historicity to deaden the atrocity of his present, fractured being.

The epidermal layer of the processed print's skin which now appears like a cloaked peephole is added to by the fine brushwork of Witkin's lover, tattoo artist Cynthia Bency. Subsequently, applying a layer of beeswax and polishing the prints she humbly calls herself, 'Joel's extra eyes and extra hands.' (Vile Bodies 1998)

Many of Witkin's images pay homage to the photography of E J Bellocq, discovered by Larry Borenstein and preserved by Lee Friedlander. Bellocq's 1912 images of the Storyville whorehouses are, for the most part, touching intimate portraits, perhaps made for the brothel Blue Books, perhaps for personal use. We will never know for sure as the plates were discovered posthumously during a house clearance; hidden in a drawer. Time has left its indelible mark in the form of scratches, cracking and water damage from Hurricane Betsy (1965) but most disturbing are the few images in which identity has been erased through violent scratching of the glass negatives. Various theories have attempted to explain the metaphorical misogyny. Maybe his Jesuit priest brother was responsible? Perhaps Bellocq was attempting to protect someone's modesty? Maybe a sitter was acting to deny the intimacy of their previous engagement? However it may have come about, Witkin has appropriated both the look of incidental time-ravaging and purposeful post-negative violence to re-create a vision that Bellocq himself had never fully realised.

But *Man without a Head* is a step further still in identity eradication. Plunging the *'I'* further still into the mists of historicity, the post-mortem aesthetic in photography is not a new phenomenon. The finished image, alongside other Witkin works, pays homage to the Daguerreotype (invented by Louis-Jacques-Mande Daguerre in 1838) and the very earliest forms of photographic technology. The vivid illusions of reality created have much in common with the backdrops often created by Witkin. Nineteenth century 'memento mori' daguerreotypes such as those presented by Stanley Burns MD in *Sleeping Beauty, Memorial Photography in America* (Burns 1990) were fairly common, as were untimely deaths in a society not benefitting from modern medical knowledge. After commissioning such images, patrons would often reject the final works due to their horrific nature (Hobson 1996: 26) but the fact remains that an element of consent on the behalf of the loved ones did exist in such cases and the finished works were originally intended for a purely private sphere. Although *Man without a Head* has a similar '*epidermal*', surface aesthetic it differs entirely in terms of the reality of the *'I'* portrayed and for whom the image has been created.

The notion of desire is heightened by the presence of drapery and the resultant contemporary allusion to erotica and tease. They evoke the contemporaneously symbiotic notion of artistic elevation of classical, Greek statuary and denigration and the desire and otherness of G De Cerambault's studies on drapery (Doy 2002: 104). The fabric here does not conceal but lays bare the sensual absence of concealment. In 'erotica' something is seen and something is inferred but remains unseen; something is promised and something is withheld. Erotica tantalises and teases.

For Bataille, the half-dressed eroticised body was deliciously 'more nude than nude.' (Bataille 1993: 178) Since the *'I'*'s socks have been left on in *Man without a Head* can they be seen as pertaining to this stricture? It would be difficult to argue that socks on an otherwise naked body are unquestionably erotic (whatever floats your boat...) however in the image they do mask, screen, and withhold a degree of knowledge. Can they therefore be seen as erotic? Socks on the lumpen male subject perhaps do not bear comparative equivalence to stockings on the lithe female form. Witkin proposes instead that the image without the socks would have been 'too raw and punishing,' (Celant 1995: 38) and although it is doubtful that the socks are left on is in anyway redemptive they do connote some kind of humanity in an entirely inhuman circumstance. Acting in a similar way to the ridiculous footwear and watch in Bellocq's image of an unnamed naked lady (Bellocq in Szarkowski, J and Friedlander, L. 1970: plate 22) they unite the subject with the absurdly commonplace. Witkin also says that leaving the socks on pertains to some kind of Mediterranean custom but as I can find no mention of such practise I cannot verify this notion, (and surely a Mexican corpse would not normally be thus indulged anyway.)

Not that there is anything new in the use of the human cadaver by artists. The *Spectacular Body* exhibition at the Hayward Gallery (2000–2001) documented the use of human material for medical and artistic research in the field of anatomy and in the pursuit of divine knowledge. This is apparent in the *De Humani Corpois Fabrica* of 1543 by Andreas Vesalius and illustrated by Jan Stephan van Calcar, an artist from the Netherlands who had worked in Titian's Venetian studio. In such times dissections were macabre theatrical events performed in medical buildings but attended by specialists and curious non-specialists like, sanctioned by the pursuit of medical wisdom. Traditionally artists sought to inform their images of the living through knowledge of the dead. Leonardo's painstakingly detailed *Study of the Tendons and Muscles of the Foot, Ankle and Lower Leg* or *Muscles of the Shoulders and the Spine* (both c1510) betray this functional preoccupation. Such images were not for public consumption. Often when images of the body torn were intended for a wider audience they would hint at the justification for such violence as in *Muscle Man* (Vesalius, *De humani corporis fabrica*, 1543) where the flayed corpse is shown still hanging from the gallows. Or else the body would be fictionally preserved in lifelike animation as in *Dissection of a Woman* (Charles Estienne, *De dissection partium corporis humani* 1545) as if to defy death's finality, projecting liminal flesh into the realms of a tragic continuum. When bodies were displayed in frightful, rotting, contemporary truthfulness as in Géricault's *Raft of the Medusa* (oil on canvas, 491 x 716cm, 1818–1819, Musée du Louvre, Paris) the initial reaction was one of sheer horror despite the fact that artists had been obsessing over the fragmented corpse already for hundreds of years. Géricault broke with tradition when he chose to show the subject of time specific, contemporary[1] dead bodies, 'dead' *and putrefying* rather than the ageless classical dead body, 'living' or at least dead for a just cause. Witkin chooses to continue in the traditional representation of historicised death to deflect attention away from the currency of the *'I'*. However both Witkin's and Géricault's dead alike hail from the ranks of the abject, the poor and the unloved. Géricault found his flesh in asylums, prisons and hospitals of the poor. Similar institutions had been supplying to dissection theatres for years.

For the ritual of public dissection bodies would be washed, shaven and de-personalised. *Man without a Head's* socks separate him from this tradition as his partially clothed state perhaps pertains more to the intimate crime scene reportage forensic photography of Alphonse Bertillon (1853–1915) an example of which appears in *Harm's Way* (Witkin 1994). Bodies are discovered in shockingly

---

1   The Medusa sank on the 5 July 1816 off the coast of Africa leaving over 140 people adrift on a hastily built raft. 13 days later when a passing vessel came to the rescue only 15 men were still alive; the rest had died of starvation, jumped overboard or been killed and eaten by their comrades.

familiar settings yet portrayed in an unfamiliarly violated state. Once hidden from view crime scenes have exploded into cultural currency and are present in fictitious representation in television series' such as *Waking the Dead* (2000–), films such as *Se7en* (David Fincher 1995, influenced in no small part by Witkin's scratched imagery) and are also present in textual form in the work/tat of Patricia Cornwell (who incredulously 'theorised' that the painter, Walter Sickert, was Jack the Ripper.) Forensic scene-of-crime-porn is everywhere and in some way similar to dissecting the body for medical knowledge' sake we are viewing the fragmented body from the vantage point of the righteous investigator. But of Witkin's work no such investigation is spurred.

The image of *Man without a Head,* though scratched and dirtied, is elevated to artistic, ostensibly 'antiqued', status, fictionalising its corpo-real subject. Aesthetically and *dermatologically,* the story of the *'I'* is denied. Rather than a forensic document are we actually accomplices in the 'crime' by the very fact of our associated viewing thereof – are we complicit in its production? To slice deeper into the subcutaneous membrane will lay bare the heresy of flesh made word.

Flesh Made Word

On beholding the sullied vision of *Man without a Head*, the corpo-reality of the *'I'* demands explanation. The dissolution of interdiction deserves clarification. But the image portrays dead, naked flesh and 'nods', its headless incarnation in the general direction of erotic 'unreason'. Segue to Bataillean discourse. Flick through the pages of Bataille's, 'Tears of Eros'... flick, flick, flick... Witkin's fractured bodies are *so* current, *so* post-modern, *so* now. The link has been inevitably made by art theorists but they need not have looked too far for the tip-off. Witkin, sovereign master of all he portrays, would never leave anything even the generation of art theory to chance. His book *The Bone House* could easily be seen as alluding to *The Story of the Eye by Lord Auch – 'The Shithouse'.* But if that is not enough to ensure that Witkin and Bataille are inextricably linked on the pages of art historical discourse, Witkin has published his own thesis alongside his work. This is how he wants to be known, this is the link he wishes to be made.

Following his first degree in sculpture at Cooper Union, NY, Joel was drafted into the US army to serve in Vietnam. As a part-time student he had little alternative but he saw his opportunity to train as a combat photographer and enlisted for three years. During this time he was to document the deaths of fellow soldiers resulting from both accidents and suicides. According to Witkin however this was not his first experience of life's frailty. For as Witkin writes of an experience apparently from his early childhood: 'we heard a crash... I could see something rolling from one of the over-turned cars. It stopped at the curb where I stood. It was the head of a little girl. I reached down to touch the face, to ask it – but before I did – someone carried me away' (Witkin 1998)

Bataille's *Story of the Eye* reads:

we crashed into, an apparently very young and very pretty young girl. Her head
was almost ripped off by the wheels. For a long time, we were parked a few
yards beyond without getting out, fully absorbed in the sight of the corpse.
The horror and despair at so much flesh, nauseating in part, and in part very
beautiful, was fairly equivalent to our usual impression on seeing one another.
(Bataille 1982: 10–11)

Both incidents involve the monograph of the beheaded corpse and both events are
probably equally fictional. Both Witkin's mother and brother attest to his overactive
imagination and his penchant for creativity in autobiographical narrative.
However the link is far less than tenuous in theory. On viewing *Man without a
Head* there is a simultaneity of compulsion to see and repulsion at the sight of the
fragmented *'I'* which easily finds its ally in Bataille's theories of the Erotic. In fact
throughout the history of art and literature death has been intellectually eroticised
and never more so than in the works of Bataille, whose theory of Eroticism and
base materialism goes further than most in explaining the driving forces behind
the desire to look despite the horror which is beheld. Crowds of onlookers will be
transfixed by the gore of both the car crash (such as Princess Diana's death beheld
through the paparazzi's lens,) or indeed in recent times 'car crash' television which
includes such programmes as channel 4's *Bodyshock* series (2003–) and so on.
People desire to see. Aristotle suggested that this was a purely cerebral urge as
both philosophers and lay-people alike 'enjoy getting to understand something.'
(Aristotle from *Poetics* as quoted in Aperture 1997: 3) But Bataille sees it as a
powerful erotic drive to experience life at the very limits of existence or to observe
life being pushed to the limit, even to the point of death. The prominence and
popularity of such discourse goes some way to explaining how the dismembered
corpse can be portrayed without outcry. If we are horrified in beholding yet first
desired to see are we in some way complicit; does this process buy our silence?

Whereas the writings of Bataille usually involved the translation of 'phantasy'
into discourse and text, *Man without a Head* is a step further along in terms
of transgressing the taboo. Whilst the image can be seen as the incarnation of
intellectualised unreason and 'phantasy' its production is dependent on the
disruption of bodily singularity in the most real terms. The *'I'* of *Man without
a Head* sits in subservient re-enactment of the Bataillean vision of his sovereign
master; as the word made flesh, Witkin ensures that the production of documented
retelling reflexively reconverts the flesh to word. Flesh is denied its corpo-reality;
the flesh becomes part of the fiction of theoretical discourse. The *Man without a
Head* is the apocalyptic post-modern vision of a vogue for fractured bodies and a
base drive and desire to see.

Another compelling commonality between Bataille and *Man without a Head*
is the very theme of 'headlessness' itself. From 1936–1939 Bataille edited a
public review known as 'Acéphale' which is translated from the Greek ἀκέφαλος
akephalos, as 'headless'. At the same time Bataille had formed a secret society
of the same name about which very little is known except that the members had

each agreed to their own beheading although in the end no executioner could be found. This has become the legendary inauguration which apparently never was. Perhaps Witkin's *Man without a Head* has arisen from the original context of this Acéphalean discourse; could he be seen as the ultimate invention which Bataille had failed to exact in the days of those clandestine gatherings?

Emancipatory 'headlessness' crops up as a recurrent theme whether metaphorically, materially, politically or physically speaking, throughout Bataille's works. Members of the secret Acéphale society also celebrated the decapitation of Louis XVI as it anticipated political 'headlessness'. However, metaphorical 'headlessness' is portrayed as the pursuit of unreason or what Bataille calls 'unknowingness' (Bataille 1993: 208) and is often explained as an act of supreme 'sovereignty'. Witkin's *Man without a Head* embodies an 'unknowingness' which when juxtaposed to Rodin's *Thinker* represents a similar rejection of reason as Masson's (cover for the first issue of Acéphale, 1936) reworking of Leonardo's *Vitruvian Man* (pen and ink with wash over metal point on paper, 34.4 x 25.5cm, 1487, Gallerie dell'Accademia, Venice) embodying the visualised wilful pursuit of 'unreason'. Nevertheless, the material contextualisation of such eroticised bodily fragmentation is problematic to say the least, particularly when practiced on an unwilling subject[2]. The materiality of the *'I'* separates him from theoretical 'headless' discourse. But then if his own textual discourse and theory were so easily materialised Bataille would not have lived past the days of Acéphale as long as he did, dying of natural causes in 1962.

The reality of the *'I's* bodily fragmentation has been enabled because of his lack of sovereignty, because of the sociological, economic and political context which has rendered him not only headless but powerless even before his death and beheading. The *'I'* has been beheaded; his photograph has been taken by an artist. How did this come to be?

Skeletal Superstructure

It may or may not be interesting to note at this point that following a fairly recent string of operations *'I'* myself have become host to donor tissue. Does tissue have memory? Is the *'I'* purely cited in the head, the body, the unified or fractured body? Am I not *'I'* 'but *'we'*? I still refer to myself as *'I'* and feel *'I'* and were *'I'* not *'I'*, I would not have escaped from the chains of our normalised existence but would probably be sectioned[3]. It is a blind cul-de-sac not worthy of over-introverted inspection. It is a fact, nevertheless, that causes me a great deal of unease at times;

---

2   Perhaps this is why Bataille seeks to find more than just opiates behind the transfixed gaze of the Leng ch'e victim Fou Tcho-Li in The Tears of Eros (Bataille 1989: 205)

3   There are material consequences to transcending the boundaries of normalcy that post-modern theorists such as Deleuze and Guattari choose to edit out.

although my benefactor had consented whilst living, the tissue was 'harvested' from their dead body. It is non-traceable. I cannot know who lives within me.

How much of the body must remain for the flesh to remain *'I'*? The much quoted Cartesian hypothesis 'I think therefore I am' (Descartes 1968: 53) was not well received in its author's lifetime and has been rejected in post-modern theory but nevertheless remains highly influential. René Descartes (1596–1650) French philosopher and mathematician saw the 'self' as individual and absolute, located in the capacity for conscious thought. Whilst the body was seen as secondary to the disembodied rational thought process, the *'I'* of Cartesian discourse was superior. For Descartes therefore, the *'I'* of *Man without a Head* would be seen as absent, the physical shell having already given up the ghost of intellect even before the act of beheading.

Foucault, Derrida and others have argued that the self is fragmentary, destabilised and constructed through a proliferation of 'knowingness' and discourse. For the purpose of tracing inference and signification this seems entirely reasonable, however the *materiality of self* is once more denied. From this position the *'I'* in *Man without a Head* either never existed in any kind of complete sense at all, or there were a multiplicity of selves, *'I'*'s created through shifting context and inference, continuously created and extinguished. For Bataille the *'I'* has become the object of eroticism through the extrapolation of reason and Witkin alike sees the raw material for *Man without a Head* as entirely objectified and inanimate.(Witkin in Marler 2001) He calls the body 'it' because he contends that the absence of head constitutes the denial of 'selfhood'. For Bataille such objectification is ultimately demanded of the 'erotic' (Bataille 1997: 137.) The *'I'* of *Man without a Head* has been obliterated in the act of beheading; selfhood is necessarily disavowed.

Only an approach which seeks to dialectically situate this self in relation to a political, geographical, social and economic context can explain the ideological conspiracy that has resulted in a North American artist rummaging around in an unclaimed bodies department in Mexico to find the raw material for his tableaux. The fact is that at one time the *'I'* of Witkin's *Man without a Head* once had a corpo-reality that was known to himself at least as *'I'* – was known by his father, mother, friends and acquaintances. The *'I'* had a material reality, a material existence commonly denied by readings of Witkin's work. For me however, the image absolutely refers to this previous existence and the horrific disunity of his reality post-demise. I do not argue for the censorship of such images like perhaps the American Christian Right Wing pressure group Christian Action Network (CAN) has done of the work of Mapplethorpe and Serrano (Lambert 2000a) for example. Instead I wonder why even in the face of the fashionable bodily fragmentation questions relating to the asymmetry of power structures which allow such image production have not been adequately addressed.

One of the most obvious reasons for the anonymity of the *'I'* of *Man without a Head* is precisely because he has no head. Opportunity for recognition is masked through decapitation rather than through the motif of the mask that we see in Witkin's images of living 'otherness' such as *The Three Graces* (gelatin silver print hand-coated with encaustic, 73.7 x 73.7cm, 1988), or *Woman in a Blue Hat* (gelatin silver print, 37.3 x 37.3cm, edition of 15, 1985). Instead these living masked subjects have their identity collectively removed to unite them in the Nietschean portrayal of tragic continuum adopting what Nietzsche has called the 'mystery doctrine of tragedy' (Nietzche 1993:51.) Whereas Witkin's dead are quite different in portrayal.

Witkin has not always sought to conceal the face of the deceased he portrays. *Le Baiser* (gelatin silver print, 34.6 x 33 cm, edition of 15, 1982) is perhaps Witkin's most famous or infamous work. The concurrent compulsion and repulsion felt when viewing the work pertains to the feeling of disbelief at the impossible reality of the image. An aging dead man's severed head has been split from the bridge of the nose up, across the crown and down. The incision cannot be seen, as the head is face on. Instead both halves are twisted outwards along the horizontal plane so that the closed eyelids and parted lips contort to display the narcissistic illusion of self-embrace. The nose and chin intertwine to give the effect of impassioned symbiosis. The similarity of each half betrays the horrible fact of singularity over plurality; the two halves are one. Sinuous tissues, muscles and veins are displayed from the chin down. For all the canonical references to such as Brancusi's statue of the same name (1940–1945), *Le Baiser* portrays the severed head of a singular person, just like you or I. And since the identity was not adequately concealed on this occasion, it was discovered. The *'I'* of *Le Baiser* was recognised by a relative visiting an exhibition of Witkin's work. Information regarding the event is difficult to come by but an anti-censorship publication states that when the relative contacted Witkin he promptly destroyed the negative (Lambert 2000b) but retained the prints of the image (Woodward 1993). Due to its rarity and exiting provenance *Le Baiser* quickly became his most valuable picture. It sold recently at Christie's for $43,700, a sizeable increase on its estimate of $25,000 – $35, 000. (Park Ave. New York, 1997)

Andres Serrano's answer to the question of how to conceal the identity of the deceased corporeal subject was harsh cropping, which revealed tantalising clues but no answers (*Morgue Series* 1992).

Witkin's more brutal response was rather than to crop the image, crop the corpse. Or choose a subject who no-one will recognise or about whom no-one will care. Invigorate your sense of divine mastery by choosing the vagrant, the abject, the unloved, and picture them in the moment of ecstatic transfiguration (*Glassman*, gelatin silver print, 80 x 54.1cm, 1994, Mexico City) or have them decapitated.

Which body is allowed to be portrayed in such horrific post-mortem brutality? In England the artist Anthony Noel-Kelly was jailed in 1998 for nine months for theft of body parts from the Royal College of Surgeons in 1991–1994. The infamous Burke and Hare murdered their victims 1827–1828 to provide corpses for dissection by Dr Robert Knox, a private anatomy lecturer at the Edinburgh Medical College. Witkin would find it hard to source the meat for his design in modern England. Instead Witkin travelled to Mexico to source bodies for his work.

There is no mention of money changing hands between Witkin and the medical authorities but even if he did not compensate the hospital for their assistance there is every chance that the bodies had been unclaimed for economic reasons. A 1999 Report on Human Rights Practices focusing on Mexico (six years after *Man without a Head*) averages the Gross Domestic Product per person in that year at approximately $4 600. However the distribution of wealth is desperately uneven, meaning that the top 20 percent of the population receive approximately 60 percent of the total income, whereas the bottom 20 percent earned less than five percent (US Department of State 2000). The World Bank reports that in 1992 the income share held by the lowest 20 percent of the population was 3.9 percent and 55.6 percent for the highest 20 percent (World Bank Development Research Group 2010). Crude estimations would make this roughly $1000 US dollars per head for the lowest 20 percent of earners and 14 times higher for the highest 20 percent of earners. It is important to remember that these figures are averages which do not show the full range which would encompass far higher and lower earners in both brackets.

Chomsky quotes a World Bank study from 1982 (eleven years before *Man without a Head*) highlighting that '..twenty percent of all [Mexican] households live in destitution, meaning they lack the means of buying food that would provide them with a minimally adequate diet.' (Chomsky 1991)

When I first began to think about Witkin's work in an art historical context I was warned that death in Mexico has an altogether different meaning than death in England or North America. For Westernised cultures death is avoided at all costs, is done behind closed doors, is presided over by medical staff and is not spoken of amongst the bereaved. Nevertheless I have some experience of death 'up-close' accumulated in various positions I occupied at residential care homes to support my academic work. I have witnessed, touched and held death. While I was researching Witkin, when a close relative passed on, I held hands with the living until the point of dying – when it arrived I kissed death goodbye. No doubt this has coloured my view of Witkin but for me, death has not been an unspoken secret; it has been a fact of everyday life. I can only read Witkin from my own Westernised perspective but surely despite our cultural differences the pain of death in Mexico cannot be so inconsequential that it allows the empty shell to be butchered for artistic satiation?

Mexican 'deathways' have been discussed at length by Claudio Lomnitz in his book *Death and the Idea of Mexico.* (Lomnitz 2008) Lomnitz suggests that in Mexico familiarity with death has become a national sign. Beginning with the sixteenth century Spanish invasion and subsequent indigenous holocaust the colonial society would use visible signs of bodily fragmentation to dominate, oppress and spread fear. Missionaries were decapitated and the heads, arms and hands of criminals were displayed on spikes. In post-Mexican Revolution (1910–1920) days the fiestas and feasts of the Mexican Days of the Dead (November 1st and 2nd) have become more highly politicised. A time for communities to revisit their dead, honour and celebrate their lives, give and receive gifts of sugar skulls and construct *ofrenda* (altars to commemorate their dead), naturally emphasises what Lomnitz calls 'the unequal and unjust distribution of death..' (Lomnitz 2008: 463) Also, while the rich can afford to bury their dead on hallowed ground the belief still persists in rural communities that the souls of the poor return in ghostly re-visitations or have their corpses possessed to demand that their bodies receive a proper burial. (Lomnitz 2008: 258) The popular western belief that Mexico laughs in the face of death is simplistic at best as there is still a culturally tangible 'horror of the unholy death: suicide, sudden death, death before baptism…' (Lomnitz 2008: 277)

Witkin's abject 'I' is probably a citizen from the lower income bracket. If he had any loved ones would they be able to claim his body? Would they be able to bury him? How do they celebrate their loss on the Days of the Dead?

Poverty is only one of the many problems faced by many Mexican citizens. The Human Rights report (US Department of State 2000) presents a huge list of serious abuses such as killings, torture, police corruption, arbitrary arrest and detention, violence, sex discrimination and discrimination against sexual preference, limits on worker rights, person trafficking and so on… In a country of institutionalised abuse it appears that an artist who frequents the Mexico City Hospital Morgue to photograph the destitute raft of unclaimed bodies is the least of their troubles. The health service itself is accused of corruption in the same report where allegations state that the forced sterilization of men and women is known to be a problem although victims have been reluctant to file complaints. In 1997 the state health service workers encouraged men with financial benefits for surgical sterilization procedures but failed to pay the men following the procedures.

Lomnitz remarks that when visiting the National University back in the early 1970s he was, 'dismayed by the sight of the corpses, untagged and naked, stocked and piled without a modicum of care or respect. In short the degradation of corpses of the paupers and derelicts has a long history.' (Lomnitz 2008: 481)

This may have been twenty-four years before *Man without a Head* but even only taking into account Chomsky's research it would appear that the rights of the patient both before and after death matter little to the Mexican authorities, within which corruption is widespread. Witkin is making use of the relaxed rules of a chaotic society. The *'I'* testifies to a system which has devalued certain lives whilst protecting the concerns of others. Projecting the *'I'* into the realms of theoretical discourse 'deadens' the reality of the death, softens the blade which strips the *'I'* of identity and selfhood and allows us to embrace the intellectualised eroticised flesh of fear of unknowing whilst rejecting the skeletal framework of its corpo-reality. The Bataillean theory of 'excess' in *The Accursed Share* finds horrific poignancy through the use of this corpulent abundance.

It is interesting to note that the Christian right protestors, CAN, in North America, while demonstrating outside an exhibition of the work of Serrano, Witkin and Mapplethorpe chose to campaign against images of homosexuality and those of a pornographic nature (Redmond 2000: 10). The origins of Witkin's dead did not seem to matter to them. Would they change their tune if Witkin used U.S. hospital morgues for his raw material? Who cares about the Mexicans anyway? It is important to re-evaluate the work within the context in which it was produced in order to recognise the difference between a corrupt, desperate society and a society of excess. According to Bataille the erotic can only exist in the state of excess whereas he perceives the state of servitude to equate to alienation and objectification (Bataille 1993: 214). The *'I'* has been eroticised for the consumption of artistic excess. In fact art itself is sovereign; beyond utility. (Bataille 1993: 198) 'What distinguishes sovereignty is the consumption of wealth, as against *labour* and servitude.'

Conclusion

Throughout my writing I have attempted to materialise the signified selfhood of the *'I'* in *Man without a Head* by recognising its place within an inferred *epidermal* canon of art history. This canonical historicity serves to remove the currency of the *crime* whilst replacing it with the currency of fashionable eroticised fragmentation, masking the reality of the *'I'*'s dismembered being.

Reference to the works of Georges Bataille has already been made by the *'I'*'s post-mortem re-creator but is most prescient in terms of Eroticism and the simultaneity of horror and desire which pervades post-modern society. The proposed Acéphalean corpse of the secretive groups musings escapes the problem of erotic 'headlessness', sovereignty and servitude in that it would have been compliant in 'headlessness'. But Witkin's corpse is non-compliant, he is an unclaimed body and though Mexico accepts death in a way that the West may not, his treatment post-mortem cannot have come about except in a desperately unequal society.

For now, truth sits debased, dis-unified and fractured, in the corner. This is the result of North American ideological 'sovereignty' over South American economic decapitation. The *'I'* cannot be known but the *'truth'* is laid bare despite the fact that, at this point in the story of the *'I'* – *'truth'* is *'headless'*.

References

Books

Bataille, G. 1989. *The Tears of Eros*. San Francisco: City Lights Books.
———— . 1987. *Eroticism*. England: Calder and Boyars.
———— . 1993. *The Accursed Share Vol. II and III*, translated by Robert Huxley. New York: Zone Books.
————. 1982. *The Story of the Eye by Lord Auch*. London: Penguin.
————. et al. 1995. *Encyclopaedia Acephalica*. London: Atlas Press.
Burns, Stanley. 1990. *Sleeping Beauty: Memorial Photography in America*. New Mexico: Twelvetrees Press.
Celant, Germano. 1995. *Witkin: A retrospective*. New York: Scalo.

Coke, V D. 1985. *Joel-Peter Witkin: Forty Photographs* exhibition catalogue. San Francisco: San Francisco Museum of Modern Art.

Descartes, R. 1968. *Discourse on Method and the Meditations*, translated by F.E. Sutcliffe. London: Penguin.

Doy, G. 2002. *Drapery*. London, New York: I. B. Tauris.

Hobson, Greg and Williams. 1995. *The Dead* exhibition catalogue. Bradford: National Film Museum.

Laviessiere, S and Michel, R. 1991. *Gericault* exhibition catalogue. Paris: Editions de la Réunion des musées nationaux.

Lomnitz, Claudio. 2008. *Death and the Idea of Mexico*. New York: Zone Books.

Nietzsche, Friedrich. 1993. *The Birth of Tragedy*. London: Penguin.

Szarkowski, J and Friedlander, L. 1970. *EJ Bellocq: Storyville Portraits, photographs from the New Orleans Red-Light District, Crica 1912*. New York: Museum of Modern Art.

Sobieszek, R A. 1999 *Ghost in the Shell*. Cambridge, Massachusetts and London: MIT Press.

Witkin, JP. 1994. *Harm's Way*. New Mexico: Twin Palms Publishers.

————. 1998. *The Bone House*. New Mexico: Twin Palms Publishers.

Journals

Badger, G. 1986. Towards a moral pornography. *Creative Camera*, (6), 33–6

Baptie, D. 1996. Kodak from the grave. *Headpress*, (12), 52–3

Dermer, R. 1999. Joel-Peter Witkin and Dr Stanley Burns: a language of body parts. *The History of Photography*. 23 (3), 245–53

Durden, M. 1993. The word. *Creative Camera*. 321, 34–7.

Harris, Roalf and Stoll. 1997. Dark days: mystery, murder, mayhem. *Aperture* 149(3).

Koch, S. 1986. Guilt, grace and Robert Mapplethorpe. *Art in America*. (11), 144–51.

MacKenzie, A. 1992. Joel-Peter Witkin: the art of seduction. *Divinity*. 28–33.

Saltz. J. 1993. Andres Serrano at Paula Cooper. *Art in America*. 81(5), 124.

Seward, K. 1993. Joel-Peter Witkin. *Art Forum*. 31(6), 107–8.

Levi-Strauss, D. 1996. Joel-Peter Witkin. *Art Forum*. 34(3), 34.

Woodward, RB. 1993. An eye for the forbidden. *Vanity Fair*. 56(4).

Electronic Sources

Chomsky, N. 1991. The victors part II. *ZMagazine*. Available at: http://books. zcommunications.org/chomsky/articles/z9101-victors-2.html [accessed 11.12.10].

Goldin, N. 1997. Bellocq epoque – photographer EJ Belloqc. *ArtForum*. 35(3). Available at: http://findarticles.com/p/articles/mi_m0268/is_n9_v35ai_19587 070/?tag=content;col1 [accessed 11.12.10].

Lambert, K. 2000a. *Degenerate Art: The Christian Action Network Art Protest.* Available at: www.postfun.com/pfpfeatures/98/aug/entartete.html [accessed 13.11.2000].

———. 2000b. *Image information for Witkin's Kiss.* Available at: www. dailyimage.com/show.cfm?FuseClaender_ID=88 [accessed 13.11.2000].

Marler, C. *New Pope of Photography,* [Online May 2001]. Available at: http://www.cindymarlerphotography.com/Witkin%20text.html [accessed 11.12.10].

Redmond, B. 2000. *Bingaman: Turning his Back on New Mexico.* Available at: www.billredmond.com/BingamanBook3/3-1.asp [accessed 13.11.2000].

Wilson, C. 2000 Joel-Peter Witkin. *Salon* [Online, Tuesday May 9, 2000]. Available at: http://www.salon.com/people/bc/2000/05/09/witkin/ [accessed 11.12.10].

World Bank, Development Research Group. World Development Indicators [Online September 2010] Available at: http://data.worldbank.org/data-catalog/world-development-indicators [accessed 11.12.10].

1999 Country Reports on Human Rights Practices Released by the Bureau of Democracy, Human Rights, and Labor US Department of State, [Online: February 25, 2000]. Available at: http://www.state.gov/www/global/human_rights/1999_hrp_report/mexico.html [accessed 11.12.10].

Audio Visual Source Material

Vile Bodies (Blast! Films for Channel Four, 1998).
Waking the Dead (dir. Keith Gordon 2000–).
Se7en (dir. David Fincher, 1995).
Bodyshock (dir. Monica Garnsey, Channel Four 2003–).

Chapter 18

Act 3, Chapter 12, Authority

goldin+senneby

With an introduction by Angus Cameron

goldin+senneby's 'Act 3, Chapter 12, Authority' is what it seems - it is the 12th and final chapter of a detective novel called *Looking for Headless* by the 'fictional author' K.D. The British author John Barlow may or may not also be involved in its production. Whatever its authorship, in this final chapter a British academic by the name of Angus Cameron loses what little remains of his sanity after a long and peculiar collaboration with two Swedish performance artists – goldin+senneby – in the course of a public lecture in front of the macaque enclosure at London Zoo. A lecture by a real British academic, also called Angus Cameron (and co-editor of the current volume), entitled, 'Each thing seen is the parody of another, or is the same thing in deceptive form: on monkeys, organ grinders and sovereignty', did in fact take place in front of the macaque enclosure at London Zoo in October 2010[1]. This lecture addressed the complex and possibly entirely spurious relationship between money, Georges Bataille, goldin+senneby, decapitation, imperialism, Gibraltar, offshore finance and monkeys. It also contained sections read from 'Act 3, Chapter 12, Authority' that had been sent to Cameron by British novelist John Barlow immediately prior to the lecture.

goldin+senneby's ongoing performance, *Headless*, which began in 2007, is an international, multimedia, multi-authored investigation into possible connections between Georges Bataille's secret society *Acéphale* (that existed briefly from 1937 until the outbreak of war) (cf. Palmer, this volume) and the offshore-registered International Business Company *Headless Ltd.*, registered in the Bahamas in 2007. Many people have been drawn into the search for these connections and indeed for *Headless Ltd.* itself: some real, some fictional, some willing, some hostile, some knowing, others not. goldin+senneby's own participation in their project consists of what they describe as an 'act of withdrawal'. Since 2008, Angus Cameron has acted as a 'spokesperson/emissary' for *Headless*, appearing in various forms at the project's public manifestations.

Angus Cameron
University of Leicester School of Management
October 2012

---

1 A short section of this event can be seen here: http://www.youtube.com/watch?v=0yyZDjXvCyc (accessed 7/12/2011).

ACT THREE
Chapter Twelve
Authority

Art Discovery Ltd
'Paris Concorde'
4, rue Saint Florentin
75001 Paris
France

Dear Dr Cameron

We write to you with regard to the Headless project of artists goldin+senneby. We are aware that you have contributed in a variety of ways to goldin+senneby's work, and that you are scheduled to deliver another talk for them shortly, to be staged in London Zoo, a typically theatrical flourish from messrs. Senneby and Goldin.

What you might not know is that the writer John Barlow has recently withdrawn from their project, leaving an unfinished novel about off-shore companies, sovereignty, and French surrealism. The artists themselves are not in possession of the necessary funds to complete the work.

Our organization has a deep and compelling interest in Headless, and in light of this we have decided to step in and incorporate the project into our own activities. We would like to invite you to take on the task of working with us to finish Headless in a way which is acceptable to us, its new owners. Considerable funds will be made available for you for this purpose.

I am keen to discuss your involvement with us as soon as possible, and to explain our needs regarding this project. Perhaps your talk at London Zoo might be a good time to meet? I will, in any case, be attending the talk, and look forward to meeting you there.

A draft of the novel as it currently stands is enclosed. Pease do not hesitate to mail me with any questions.

With my very best wishes,
Leonardo Troya
Art Discovery Limited

Angus Cameron watches the verdant collage of eastern England slide past him and thinks about monkeys. The windows of his First Class carriage must be tinted because the fields seem almost unnaturally green. Stirring sugar into his mint tea he returns his attention to the small, slim Macintosh netbook in front of him. He is rather pleased with the text on the screen, although with the train almost three quarters of a hour out of Leicester, he has got no further than the first page, having made amendments to almost every line. Writing fiction, he has quickly discovered, never really ends; the author's final full stop signifies merely boredom, desperation, or a looming deadline.

It is now two weeks after the initial offer from Art Discovery Ltd. He hasn't waited to meet Mr Troya and receive his official instructions. On learning of the funds that were available to him, he immediately applied for a year's leave from work; his Department was promised a handsome compensation package for the loss of Dr Cameron's services, and his sabbatical had been approved quickly. Ahead of him now stretches a year free of faculty meetings and the daily search for a parking space, of bored students and niggling colleagues. His sole task will be to bring the orchestrated narrative ramblings and investigative leaps-in-the-dark of Headless to a satisfying end.

He has thrown himself into the work with his usual enthusiasm and energy, combing the existing chapters for possible ways to proceed. The real-life characters from the docu-novel, though, have been strangely unwilling to offer their help. Theatrical agent Jorge Mendes, in response to a polite enquiry as to the whereabouts of his client, mailed: *she is not in good health but will talk if subpoenaed under Brazilian law*. Other members of the cast have proved even less forthcoming. People either do not return calls, or they leave it to secretaries to make vague promises about speaking at a later date. As for the various experts that Cameron had met at the meeting in Tower 42, not a single one has replied to his polite approaches. There are always the monkeys, of course, both those in London Zoo this morning, and the ones in Gibraltar. The monkeys are not going to say no.

He takes a sip of mint tea, and looks down at the screen. A moment later he deletes a semi-colon, then, with a sigh of exasperation, re-inserts it. Are novels written like this? He considers how little he has written so far, and thinks of the great fictive doorstops he likes to devour on long-haul flights. Are *entire* novels written this way, he wonders? His sabbatical is only for *one* year.

Meanwhile, his train is drawn to the capital like a provincial yo-yo, then to be released northward again, all the way to Leicester, only to return later still, back and forth, up and down the country throughout the day. As über-green England moves past him, Dr Angus Cameron flips shut his slim new netbook, slides it into a bulky old leather briefcase, and takes out a bunch of papers, the notes for his talk this morning.

It is the fourth or fifth such performance he has given for goldin+senneby, and is to be staged in front of a monkey enclosure at London Zoo.

'Each thing seen is the parody of another, or is the same thing in deceptive form': on monkeys, organ grinders and sovereignty

The title had been suggested by the Swedes, not quite insisted upon, but urged, nudged toward him until he had simply agreed. It is the last thing he will do for them before he officially takes over the search for Headless, and the thought of that shift in authority makes it easier to accept one final commission. He feels like one of Louis XVI's trusted servants right at the end, there in prison, taking orders from the condemned king, the facade of monarchy reduced to a few shabby trappings of power, yet maintained nonetheless.

Art Discovery Limited, Google has informed him, hardly exists at all. A bespoke entity of some sort, no doubt, although an impressively well-funded one. goldin+senneby for their part have not mentioned it, and preparations for the talk have continued as normal, as if they do not know that a new author has been contracted. After reading about their working relationship with John Barlow, this comes as little surprise to Cameron, and he has made a point of not mentioning his sabbatical to them; they will find out in due course.

Neither will he mention the first class travel that he is currently enjoying. ADL's offer includes 'incidental expenses', the freedom to spend whatever he likes on extravagances large and small, for which he will be reimbursed monthly, no questions asked. These have so far included the new Macintosh netbook, which now sits inside his briefcase. The Mac contains all his work on Headless, secreted there, away from his old laptop and his PC at work, with no copies anywhere else. It is as if only on the new, pristine Mac can the project be safe, isolated and immunized on a single hard drive, the netbook itself, despite its name, having never been plugged into the internet nor linked to any other machine. Cameron has read the current draft of Headless carefully, and his own security measures are simple but absolute: no one is going to get their hands on his data, period.

From his jacket pocket he hears familiar digital plink of an sms alert. He pulls out his cell phone.

Something from the Department. Sabbatical! They can wait.
He closes the phone. Then, on a whim, he opens it again and composes a message:
Hi Pia
Do you like zoos..?

With the invitation to Pia Sarma sent, he returns to the notes in front of him. Too much information on Gibraltar, the Treaty of Utrecht, and the role of macaque monkeys in keeping the Rock British. He scans the page in front of him. Myth: the Rock of Gibraltar will revert to Spanish sovereignty if the small colony of macaque monkeys that live there ever disappears. How many are there, he asks himself, wondering what sort of infectious disease a small, land-locked group of macaques might be susceptible to? Would a modern country like Spain stoop to such baseless superstition? Who knows. In 1940 Winston Churchill was so alarmed at the falling numbers of monkeys on Gibraltar that he ordered another clan to be brought to the Rock from Africa and settled there.

There would not be time to discuss all this today. It would need simplifying, editing down. But he would return to the subject of Gibraltar at some stage. Kelly was there. Sovereign was there. So too was Headless, on the Rock.
His phone rings.
"Angus," he hears, a woman's voice, serious, unfriendly. "It's Pia. Where are you?"
"Oh, hi Pia, I didn't recognize your.."
"Where are you?"

"The 9.55 to London. Are you.."

But she's gone.

Twenty five minutes later and Dr Angus Cameron walks up the platform at St Pancras, still confused by Pia's phone call, yet trying to focus on today's talk. He has returned her call repeatedly, but she is not picking up.

He stops, trying to find a sign for the underground amid the dazzlingly modern glasswork of the station. There ahead of him is Pia Sarma.

"Angus," she says, not quite scowling, but nearly.

Her gray trouser suit is muted but smart. It seems to compliment the near-scowl. There is nothing welcoming about her, and she does not look as if she is about to visit a zoo.

"Hi Pia. What are you doing here?"

"Come on," she says, "walk me to the taxi rank."

They walk.

"Have you spoken to anyone else from the Tower 42 meeting recently?" she asks.

"No! None of you guys reply to my mails. Not a single one."

"A couple of weeks ago my firm received a message requesting that we have no further contact with anyone involved in the Headless project. Sound familiar?"

He stops short, confused.

"No, no. I mean, it doesn't, no. What..?"

"Signed ADL. Heard of it?" she asks, not stopping.

"Really? Yes, in fact I have. Art Discovery Limited."

"Well, there's a surprise. The email, unsigned, was addressed to the partners of the firm. A secretary opened it. There was what appeared to be a hyperlink. She clicked on it. It took us ten days to get our system up and running again."

"What? A virus?"

She stops walking.

"A trojan horse." It is not a joke. "Specially written, they think. And highly malicious. It deletes systems files, one by one, eats them up and shits them out until the machine just packs in."

"Jesus."

"We have back-up systems. Eventually we caught it, but it caused a lot of delay and expense. And it was my fault. I was the connection, the reason for the attack."

"You are sure this was from ADL?" he says, trying to ignore the growing anger in her voice.

"That's what the mail said." She begins walking again. "And that's not all."

This can't be G+S, he's telling himself, they wouldn't do this..

They emerge into the bright sunlight of a warm September morning.

"Gavin MacFadyen, you know, the journalist?"

"Yes."

"He got it. In fact quite a lot of the people who were at that Tower 42 meeting seem to have been targeted. Same mail, same problem. You know, busy people, doing three things at once, opening mails, easy to click without thinking.."

They arrive at the taxi rank.

"And," he says, "the mail asked you not to have.."

"Fuck what the message said. This is serious. Do not contact me or my firm again. Have your intellectual games with someone else. I'm sorry, I am, Angus, really. But that's it."

The door of the black cab closes with a thud.

This can't be G+S.

Or it can't be Leonardo Troya.

Cameron is milling around in front of a large, pyramid-shaped enclosure of Sulawesi crested macaque monkeys, the rendezvous point for today's outdoor lecture. He has decided to go ahead with the talk, and to confront Troya about the trojans afterwards.

What kind of name is that anyway?

He has not identified himself as the speaker, but those now gathering there cast glances at him and occasionally smile. Meanwhile, one of the better-groomed macaques has wandered up to the wire mesh at the front of the enclosure and seems to be watching him, occasionally baring its teeth as Cameron tries without much success to go over the opening sections of his talk.

He consults his watch. The talk should have started already. Twenty people are now there, mainly young. But they are not students. They seem less hesitant, and have the bearing of quiet anticipation. Many of them have turned their attention to the rather striking monkey before them. It seems to be a loner, and is sleek and subtly muscular, with an unusually elegant poise. There are several other macaques at the back of the enclosure, but only this one has ventured up front, tilting its head now and then, or examining a finger, waiting for the show to begin.

No one seems to be there to introduce Cameron. He decides that he should make a start before he loses his audience to a rather good-looking monkey. After a final scan of his notes he pushes them into his briefcase on the ground beside him. As he does so, he notices two macaques sitting high up at the top of the enclosure in a chaotic framework of old branches. They are in the shadows cast by overhanging tress, and remain for the most part motionless, looking down at the crowd. We'll call you two Goldin and Senneby, he mutters to himself, then clears his throat and, with the authoritative panache of an experienced academic performer, waits for everyone's attention.

I think we better begin. My name is Angus Cameron, and we are here in the slightly incongruous setting of London Zoo for a talk on fiction and sovereignty. I say incongruous, but in fact we will see that there are good reasons for being here rather than, say, in a stuffy lecture hall.

The title of my talk today comes from the first line of The Solar Anus by French sociologist and writer Georges Bataille. It was in fact the artists goldin+senneby who generously supplied me with the first part of the title. They like to call me their spokesperson, but I prefer to think of myself as an emissary: I speak on my own behalf, in goldin+senneby's stead. However, on this occasion I am happy to use their title.

Bataille's somewhat obscure version of personal sovereignty is of central significance to the Headless project, as I think anyone who has been following goldin+senneby's work will know. It also happens to be the case that Bataille developed these ideas right here in London Zoo while observing the monkeys.

I myself have been collaborating with goldin+senneby for a few years now. I know that some of you here will have read the novel as it currently stands, but for those who haven't, I 'entered' the narrative in chapter three, a fictionalized account of a colloquium of experts that took place in Tower 42, right in the heart of the City of London, just over there.

He gestures toward somewhere vaguely over his shoulder.

There was a fictitious description of me taking a particular interest in a young lawyer, plus quite a lot of real material from the discussion we had that afternoon. A trojan that eats your system files and shits them out. And what struck me, when I first read that chapter afterwards, was the idea that being an author of a multitext in which one is also a character would be an intriguing position.

A trojan?

Three more of the macaques have now ventured forward, attracted to the crowd that stands on the other side of the cage. They are less elegant than the first, more boisterous in their movements, their fur unkempt and bearing patches of dirt. The crowd, it seems, is not interested in monkeys but in a man standing with his back to the enclosure, talking; and this has begun to confuse some of the Sulawesi crested macaque monkeys of London Zoo, who are accustomed to a little more attention..

The reason why I am here today, speaking about monkeys, organ grinders and sovereignty, is a little more complex. Bataille noted, as he watched monkeys in this very zoo more than eighty years ago, that each thing seen is the parody of another, or is the same thing in deceptive form. Parody, and in particular the parody of sovereignty, is what I would like to discuss today.

Unlike a map, or a plan or a blue-print, a parody is an imitation or reflection or depiction of something that falls (usually humorously) far short of the real thing. The problem we have when thinking about parodies of sovereignty is that the 'real thing' does not exist. Arguably, it never has. The kind of parodies of sovereignty that we are confronted with every day – a confusing blend of state, supra-state, multi-state, corporate and personal sovereignties – all relate ultimately to each other, pale imitations of an ideal-typical sovereign power that exists nowhere.

A parody of a name? Troya?

National sovereignty in particular continues to be couched in traditional-absolutist terms, one nation under God, one national indivisible, my country right or wrong, and so on. Even if we reject the nastier nationalist and racist implications of this rhetoric, the practical necessity of believing in some kind of sovereignty is very important to us. We like to believe, for example, that the government has some kind of sovereign control over the 'national' economy; if we didn't, we probably wouldn't bother voting. The revelation that sovereignty is a rather rootless, vague parody does not make it go away as a problem. Rather, it makes the problem all the more urgent.

Let us turn for a moment to sovereignty in the context of Headless, which is a text without a head, one with its own strange and complicated kind of sovereignty. Headless is a novel, a fiction. And any fiction is about how the disparate parts of a story are drawn into a legible narrative, the writer juggling with as many story-strands as the plot demands until the whole thing has been told. The fictive art, then, is about manipulation. The writer controls the information, concealing or revealing as necessary, calling all the shots. Within his narrative he yields absolute power; indeed, he is the sovereign power of his own fictive realm.

Headless inverts this notion of authorial control. Its authors, at least thus far, have not been in control. People like me, for example, those of us who in other projects might offer expert opinion in the background, get written right into Headless, we get to stand here and talk, and in doing so become an integral part of the performance, 'authors' of the emerging multitext.

Yet the question of authorial control, of narratorial sovereignty, has been cloudy. This very talk, significantly, is not exactly under my control. Despite being the author of the words you are hearing now, I was not really in control of how they came about. goldin+senneby chose the topic and the title. So who is in charge here, who is the sovereign authority? Well, as far as this talk is concerned, probably goldin+senneby.

He pauses, resisting the temptation to add, but not for long.

Headless is a work of fiction about off-shore. The parody of sovereignty is a central theme in it, and as far as goldin+senneby are concerned, that includes the mimicking of off-shore's strategy of concealment, using agents (like me, and possibly you) to act on the artists' behalf. They describe this at various times as an act of withdrawal, an absent presence.

Up above, the two macaques that Cameron has named Goldin and Senneby sit patiently on their branches, looking on with benign interest, and occasionally picking fleas from their coats.

Offshore needs sovereignty to be both parody and 'reality' at the same time – it only functions because of the institutionalization of this profound ambiguity. We generally like our foundational socio-political and economic concepts to be simple, and sovereignty is far from simple once we start to unpick it. The way I want to approach that process of unpicking is to explore one of the component parts of off-shore.

He turns to find one of the dirtier, unkempt monkeys staring at him. It has moved right up close to the wire mesh of the enclosure. Resisting the urge to leap back, Cameron moves just a fraction further away from the wire, which is all that separates him from the animal.

I didn't actually realize they were so close! What I was going to say was that these monkeys also have stories. And just now their stories are interfering with mine..

He reaches down into his briefcase and extracts a glossy printout of an image:

This is an image of Sir John Mandeville. In 1367 a book appeared called *The Travels of Sir John Mandeville*, written in French, about an English knight of St Albans. It's a travel book. Mandeville travels to Jerusalem, which at the time was the center of the known world, before venturing further afield, both geographically and conceptually, the lands he describes becoming more fantastic as he goes. He travels, for example, to the land of Prester John, a mythical Christian priest-king said to have lived somewhere in the east, although no one was quite sure where. Mandeville actually gets stuck in the land of Prester John on his way to Paradise.

Leonardo = da Vinci. Art. Troya = Troy, trojan. Art Discovery, Leo the computer hacker??? Fuck, fuck..

The importance of this for us is that Mandeville's travels were fictional. These places did not exist. Mandeville himself did not exist, as far as we know. The book itself was compiled from at least twenty-seven different sources. Yet by 1450 there were translations into eight languages. It had become an incredibly important account of the world, and would remain so for several hundred years. The Dutch cartographer Ortelius produced a map of the land of Prester John some 250 years after Mandeville's text was published.

He puts the image of Mandeville down, leaning it up against the mesh wall of the enclosure, then takes a second image from his briefcase and holds it up.

The importance for me of this map is that it is a fairly accurate topographical map of north Africa, onto which has been imposed a completely mythical domain. Prester John never existed, yet the land of Prester John was a very important geographical *fact*.

He glances nervously over his shoulder. The monkey is still there, observant, patient, and apparently interested in Sir John Mandeville. Further off are several more, including the pretty one, who seems to be nodding in appreciation, her arms crossed.

This has some interesting parallels with off-shore, a similarly mythical space which has been with us since the 1950s, and in which we believe implicitly. And that, in part, is because we're very credulous when it comes to spatiality; we believed Mandeville was real for hundreds of years, just as today we believe in off-shore as a place. Also, just like Ortelius's map of the land of Prester John, off-shore masquerades as a real, geographically grounded place.

Off-shore, too, is often treated as a distinct place, an entirely legible space, especially by those who enjoy its fruits. In fact it is not. It is very illegible, or rather, it is legible only in particular ways. We are familiar with the popular conception of tax havens; Cayman Islands, the Bahamas, *off-shore*. But actually, the biggest off-shore centers on the planet are the city of London, Hong Kong, New York and so on. The majority of the world's off-shore centers are not physically off our shores. The whole off-shore topology is a myth, a fiction.

But what in fact is off-shore? Well, it's about concealing wealth, identity and ownership. There's a whole multiplicity of types of off-shore companies, but what they have in common is this notion of concealment, this function of agency at a distance. And this implies also that they develop a fictional spatiality. Off-shore, then, is a fiction. A real, legal fiction, if you want to get your head around that.

The meeting at Tower 42. Why?

The point about the Headless project, then, is not so much about whether a company called Headless exists, but the question of how you might look for it. The story, in this sense, is about exploring the possibilities of this strange place, this fictive realm, where things exist but also don't exist…

He senses that he has lost his audience. Looking up he sees that they are staring straight past him. The macaque standing close on the other side has poked his fingers through the mesh and is trying to pull the image of Sir John Mandeville into the cage. His fingers are surprisingly human-like, dark and agile, but they are unable to draw the print through. Cameron knows he should retrieve the picture, but cannot bring himself to risk getting scratched by those fingernails. The animal now uses his other hand to take hold of the lower edge of the picture, which soon tears, and a strip of the paper is pulled through the mesh. With both sets of fingers the monkey manages to make more small tears, each time depositing the new fragment of the picture at his feet inside the enclosure. Before long only a piece the size of a postcard is left, which, crumpled, he draws through with ease.

Let's have a quick break.

The group hovers for a few seconds, then spreads out, as people turn to chat, or to pull phones and blackberries from their pockets. Cameron scans their faces, the backs of their heads, wondering whether Mr Troya is among them.

"Hello," a young man says, extending a hand.

"Leonardo?" Cameron says. The young man is slight of build and perhaps five-six. His complexion is pale, and he is smiling. His suit hangs from the shoulders.

"No. I'm an emissary! He sends his apologies. I work for him."

"Ah," is all Cameron can think of to say, deflated yet relieved. He is in no mood for confrontation.

"Mr Troya will be in touch with you later today. Something cropped up at the last minute. But," and he turns to look into the monkey enclosure, "I'm really enjoying the talk. Very interesting indeed. And look at these fellas!"

He squats down and peers through the wire mesh. Five crested macaques are now sitting politely on the ground close to them, like story time at kindergarten. The sleek, elegant one stands behind them, looking out over their heads. Meanwhile, the scruffy one has now retreated with his fragments of the image of John Mandeville, and sits beneath the tree in which Goldin and Senneby are perched. He guards his spoils with an arm as he tries to reassemble the print. The fragments lie on the dusty ground before him and make little sense.

For a moment Cameron watches. He might be wrong, but the slender, elegant macaque seems to be keeping an eye on all this, both the animals sitting down in a row and the one under the tree trying in vain to arrange the pieces of paper. The scene is one of contentment, of calm, innocent curiosity. Yet it seems unnatural..

The young man stands, wiping the creases from his trousers.

"Anyway, nice to meet you. I think I'm getting in the way."

The two men shake hands again, and Cameron turns to face his (human) audience, which is now regrouping, along with several Japanese tourists who have also stopped to watch, and have no idea what is going on.

Bataille's secret society *Acéphale*, which may or may not be related to Headless Ltd, was, among other things, intended to both demonstrate and practice his particular understanding of sovereignty. Bataille's sovereignty had nothing to do with political or corporate power, but concerned the capacity of people to act beyond utility.

The extent to which an individual can articulate their 'sovereignty' derives, according to Bataille, from their capacity to consume that which is 'miraculous'. The sovereign individual lives entirely in the present, eschewing awareness of his or her inevitable death, and living to excess at all times. The sovereign man in a sense escapes death, in that he lives in the moment. He lives and dies like an animal. But he is a man nevertheless.

What Bataille tries to articulate is his envy for the capacity of animals – specifically the apes of London Zoo that inspired this insight – to live without the incapacitating fear of death. For Bataille, to live and die like an animal was not a matter of being bestial but of freeing oneself from the constraint on personal autonomy produced by the constant fear of death, decay, excrement and the body. The title of this talk comes from the very first line of *The Solar Anus*, in which he lays out a cosmology of excess, with sex, death, decomposition and interpenetration appearing gloriously and unavoidably at every scale of life from the planetary and geologic to the personal, incidental and ephemeral. Inspired by monkeys like the ones here today, Bataille's message is to live free of the constraints produced by a socialized and institutionalized fear of such aspects of the world.

If this seems distasteful or far-fetched, we might want to consider the degree to which the contemporary sovereign state seeks to instill a fear of death and disease in us all to curb our unhealthy pleasures. Not only should we not smoke, drink, overeat or neglect our daily exercise for our own sakes, if we do these things we are likely to become a burden on the state. In Bataille's terms we are forced to subordinate the freedoms of our sovereign selves in the name of the sovereign whole.

Bataille's sovereignty had, and still has, its adherents. I am thinking of the various movements resistant to the cultural norms of state and society in the 1960s, 1970s and beyond. Bataille was, in that sense, father to the hippies, the drop-outs and the anarchists, and possibly even the radical feminists and the deep greens. However, there is also no escaping the obverse side of overcoming the fear of death and destruction – something the sovereign state itself proved all too capable of orchestrating when it needed to reduce the lives of others to the status of the animal.

But what has any of this to do with the other major theme running through *Headless*, that of offshore finance? At one level, a central question posed by *Headless* is whether in addition to any organizational inheritance between Acéphale and Headless Ltd., there is also a philosophical one – albeit one that expresses the Marxian principle: 'first as tragedy, then as farce'. Is *Headless Ltd,* as a representative of the peculiar domain of offshore, the farcical inheritor of Bataille's notion of sovereignty?

At one level, clearly not. Offshore organizations like to think of themselves as professional, clean, dry and efficient and would hardly recognize themselves in Bataille's somewhat gruesome philosophy. Moreover, they tend to represent themselves as the very opposite of his dark imaginings. Offshore companies tend to use images of healthy, young fit bodies cavorting on sun kissed beaches. Of course, in doing so they also invoke an amoral eroticism and excess that Bataille might have recognized as a parody of aspects of his own version of sovereignty. Offshore does not directly reject the personal fear of death, but it undoubtedly utilizes, ironically, the principles of state sovereignty to overcome any restraint on the excesses of wealth. By placing money beyond sovereign space, through creating a sovereign space devised solely for the excessive consumption of money and all the miraculous stuff it can buy, offshore has created a parody of Bataille's universalistic personal sovereign freedom. The nature of its parody is especially exquisite, in that offshore is only available to a select few.

In the novel-in-progress *Headless*, we have also seen some representation of luxury and wealth, specifically in the Bahamas, and I reckon there'd be a lot more conspicuous excess and tropical sunsets before we get to the end! Another off-shore center of interest in the search for Headless is Gibraltar. As you probably know, Gibraltar is a sovereign British territory but is also claimed by Spain. Several themes inter-twine for us here. The company Headless was actually registered in the Bahamas via Gibraltar, through a company, conveniently enough, called Sovereign. British sovereignty in Gibraltar is said to depend on the survival of two clans of macaque monkeys that live on the rock. They are in fact Barbary macaques, smaller than these crested macaques here.

He turns his head to find the group has grown. Nine or ten monkeys have now gathered, some lying on the ground, their limbs loose and idle; others engage in slow, playful bouts of tugging and hugging, draped right across one another like big furry scarves. But it is all done very quietly, and with the implicit approval of their well-groomed leader, who stands behind them looking straight at Cameron, and occasionally glancing back at the scruffy monkey under the tree, who has made no progress at all with his fragments of picture, although he perseveres with a slow, docile determination.

This is why we are here, Cameron says. At least I think it is.

Trying to pick up the thread of his talk, he faces his human audience once more, only to realize that it too has been growing. There are perhaps forty people now watching him, or watching the monkeys watching him, or not quite knowing what they are watching, only that it is something you don't see in a zoo every day.

Once again he looks over his shoulder. Goldin and Senneby are still up high in the tree, two simian Buddhas looking peacefully on.

Squawking suddenly erupt down below. Several animals have attacked the one under the tree. They roll in the dust, a bundle of flailing arms and scratching hands, their shrieks visceral and unnerving, as in desperation he tries to protect his fragments of paper. Close by the sleek, elegant one stands. She does not participate, but looks on with what can only be described as satisfaction.

The fight stops abruptly, and the attackers return to their place close to the perimeter fence and sit back down. As they wait for Cameron to start talking again they chew, their mouths moving slowly and deliberately. From time to time they pick at their teeth with a finger. They are eating the picture of John Mandeville. Behind them, a lone monkey stands, sleek, pretty, her teeth half-bared in a grin.

There are now people standing right in front of him. The crowd is continuing to grow. The initial members of the audience greatly outnumbered by casual bystanders, who seem to be patiently waiting for the recommencement of his talk, while also taking the performance of the macaques very seriously. He prepares to continue speaking, but with a certain dread, because many of these bystanders no doubt think that the talk is zoological in nature, some sort of informative lecture programmed by the zoo. There are going to be some very confused tourists in the hotels of London this evening..

I now want to consider the long historical and metaphoric relationship between sovereign power and the monkey. The monkey or ape is neither the only nor necessarily the best metaphor for sovereignty, kingship or monarchy. Sovereigns are more normally metaphorized as lions, tigers, eagles, creature of absolute power and mastery, the masters of their natural domains. The monkey is a far more ambivalent creature, which does not mean that it cannot and is not used with respect to sovereignty, but that it tends to be used to communicate rather different aspects of sovereign power. That said, monkeys play a vital role in many cosmologies of sovereign power, from the monkey general Hanuman in the Ramayana and the Chinese Monkey King Sun Wukong, to *King* Kong scaling the Empire State Building, that iconic focal point of the modern commercial power of the west.

At the mention of King Kong there are murmurs of recognition from the crowd, as if only now has the true theme of the talk been touched upon. Cameron sighs to himself, and looks out at his audience, which is uncomfortably close; he is almost pinned against the mesh of the enclosure, people on both sides of him, with others leaning in behind them, straining to hear. A Leicester University lecture similarly overloaded with students eager to listen to his theories on geo-economics would be, he reflects, rather stimulating. And also pure fantasy.

He continues.

Perhaps the most striking feature of the monkey as a metaphor is its position as a creature of the boundary. The monkey is the trickster, the intermediary, the boundary setter and transgressor with a prehensile foot in both the domains of the human and the animal. We recognize ourselves in the monkey, particular in the 'higher' apes, partly for what they *are* (underdeveloped, primitive, pre-human versions of ourselves) and what they are *not* (they communicate but are non- or pre-linguistic, they are highly intelligent but pre-tool, they have simple rather than complex societal structures). To present monarchy in terms of the monkey is therefore a high risk business, if only for the person offering up the metaphor.

Where the figure of the monkey differs from other animal metaphors of absolute power is in that it is rarely applied to a living monarch. Rather, the metaphorical monkey stands for a metaphorical sovereignty, a reflection on the limits of man as monarch, the inability of the human to finally transcend its physical embodiment even (or possibly except) in the form of the divine monarch. Hence the role of the monkey in eastern pantheons is the god of disorder, of chaos, of motion, of transgression, but is also sacred. This sacredness is not 'holiness' in the dour western sense, but more akin to the figure of the *homo sacer* in Roman law, the person (or near-person in this instance) sacred by virtue of standing outside the social order completely. Where the *homo sacer* is cast out of the socio-legal order by force of law itself – an individualized state of exception – the monkey is already outside the social order of man, albeit recognizable as a close relation.

Despite this, it is what the monkey lacks that attracts Bataille and what makes it a suitable figure to represent his notion of the sovereign. It is precisely the monkey's lack of complex reflexive society, and particularly its lack of digital language, that makes it for Bataille the symbol of an unreflexive and unsocialized sovereign self-possession. Moreover, the monkey exhibits a sovereignty that cannot be represented by itself in the form of language. Simian sovereignty, this is to say, cannot be fictionalized. Human sovereignty, particularly that of the state, is always a product of fiction – narrative, performance, spectacle, law, institutions. Perhaps the most explicitly fictive aspect of the western conception of sovereignty (now essentially globalized but European in origin) is the figure of the sovereign himself (or herself). Of the two bodies of the king, one of these, the legally constituted fiction of the divine embodiment of monarchy, is considerably more important than the other, the human, physical monarch. Perhaps the most striking evidence for this lies in the fact that the fictive king outlives the physical one, even if there is no apparent immediate heir.

The great advantage of monarchy being fundamentally fictive, then, is that it exceeds even death.

He utters these final words slowly. About a hundred people stare at him, but most are oblivious to the fact that his talk has now ended.

The noise from the macaques suddenly increases. Cameron moves, trying to step away from the enclosure. But he's hemmed in. He looks down. His briefcase has gone. The noise intensifies, but rather than pull back, the crowd moves yet closer, pushing him into the mesh, eager not to miss the action inside the cage.

Then he sees it. The focus of the battle is now for possession of Cameron's old leather briefcase. Two of the larger macaques are yanking at it until it begins to come apart at the seams.

But this is impossible, Cameron tells himself, as behind him he feels shoulders and arms of the human crush that is slowly pushing him into the mesh. There is no way his briefcase could have been dragged through the small holes of the wire. He watches as papers and pens and his Leicester University Library card fall to the ground, to be greedily gathered up by hysterical monkeys and carried off. There must be twenty animals now, racing back and forth across the enclosure.

Papers and pens litter the ground in shreds and splintered fragments of their former selves, while several animals have retreated, jealously clutching their spoils close to their chests.

Then it hits him. It hits him (metaphorically) at the very moment that the object itself hits the ground with a (not-at-all metaphorical) bump. His netbook, thin and sleek. Despite the fact that all his work on Headless is stored only there, he breathes a small sigh of relief, knowing that a zoo keeper, attracted by the chaos, will soon be on the scene to retrieve the netbook, and that however badly damaged it is, the hard disk itself will remain intact, inside its robust, sealed aluminum casing.

The thin young man, he notices, has disappeared. When did he go? No time to think. The largest of the highly intelligent but pre-tool mammals in the enclosure hoists a large rock above his head, his bandy arms shaking with the strain of it, and with a gesture that closely resembles someone from a fully tool-using society, brings the stone down square onto the Mac, shattering its thin plastic casing, which detaches and flies off, to be scooped up and fought over by several other of the social but not complexly societal macaques, some of whom now stand around pointing and apparently offering instructions to their companion with the rock, who lifts and drops it again. And again. Each time it pounds the computer dead center, and the netbook soon begins to take the form of a large, misshapen waffle.

Desperate to call for a zoo keeper, but unable to escape the increasingly exited crowd, Cameron can do nothing. He takes out his cell phone and calls Pia, as if only the cold logic of the law can save him from the surreal and nauseating madness that he feels subsuming him. Call a lawyer: the action is instinctive.

But his call to Pia Sarma goes unanswered. As do three further calls to the same number, one right after the other, while inside the enclosure his netbook has begun to resemble a waffle that an elephant has chewed then spat out. He watches, cell phone in hand, as pieces of the Mac come away each time the rock drops, to be carried off quickly to innumerable macaque hiding places, up trees and inside old logs and car tires at the back of the enclosure. The hard disk casing has now split in two, and the disk itself, its shiny dark surface catching the sun and sending out a million rainbow flashes of light, sits on the ground right beneath the rock, getting pummeled relentlessly, as if a punishment for its hypnotic, every-changing colors.

Sweat has begun to run down his face, tickling his temples and the sides of his nose. He runs a hand across his forehead, then, after pausing somewhat dramatically, seems to have a change of heart.

What are you lot laughing about! he shouts at the monkeys.

He strains to think: the photographs of Jamie Wright were fakes. Or they were of another body. No one had died for Headless. Nothing at all had happened for sure. Nothing *is* anything with Headless. Acéphale had not been reconvened. Nothing. Headless has yielded up nothing, nothing more than its power to marginalize and isolate. John Barlow has been dragged down into the vortex of its secrecy almost to destruction.. And now?

Trojan horses!

He starts laughing, a guttural chuckle that grows exponentially until each cry is damning and ecstatic. Inside the enclosure the monkeys join in, working themselves up into a new frenzy, zipping about sideways and backwards, like circus performers, tumbling and cavorting until the dust from the ground rises slowly up like a curtain around them. Cameron looks on, his whole body shaking with hilarity, his breathing having degenerated into a series of phlegmy gasps to punctuate the laughter. As the curtain rises he sees the sleek, pretty one, her expression unchanged, her eyes still right on him, proud and satisfied. Then she turns, hoists her backside into the air, and walks away.

He can take no more. He slumps down onto the ground he cradles his head in his hands. Finally, when his breathing has calmed somewhat, he looks up, high into the shadows of the enclosure, and sees that Goldin and Senneby have disappeared.

Index

Gender in a Global/Local World

Also published in this series

Reshaping Gender and Class in Rural Spaces
Edited by Barbara Pini and Belinda Leach
ISBN 978-1-4094-0291-6

Federalism, Feminism and Multilevel Governance
Edited by Melissa Haussman, Marian Sawer and Jill Vickers
ISBN 978-0-7546-7717-8

Contours of Citizenship
Women, Diversity and Practices of Citizenship
Edited by Margaret Abraham, Esther Ngan-ling Chow,
Laura Maratou-Alipranti and Evangelia Tastsoglou
ISBN 978-0-7546-7779-6

Politicization of Sexual Violence
From Abolitionism to Peacekeeping
Carol Harrington
ISBN 978-0-7546-7458-0

Development in an Insecure and Gendered World
The Relevance of the Millennium Goals
Edited by Jacqueline Leckie
ISBN 978-0-7546-7691-1

Empowering Migrant Women
Why Agency and Rights are not Enough
Leah Briones
ISBN 978-0-7546-7532-7

Gendered Struggles against Globalisation in Mexico
Teresa Healy
ISBN 978-0-7546-3701-1

Encountering the Transnational
Women, Islam and the Politics of Interpretation
Meena Sharify-Funk
ISBN 978-0-7546-7123-7

The Gender Question in Globalization
Changing Perspectives and Practices
Edited by Tine Davids and Francien van Driel
ISBN 978-0-7546-3923-7 (hbk) / ISBN 978-0-7546-7322-4 (pbk)

(En)Gendering the War on Terror
War Stories and Camouflaged Politics
Edited by Krista Hunt and Kim Rygiel
ISBN 978-0-7546-4481-1 (hbk) / ISBN 978-0-7546-7323-1 (pbk)

The Price of Gender Equality
Member States and Governance in the European Union
Anna van der Vleuten
ISBN 978-0-7546-4636-5

Women, Migration and Citizenship
Making Local, National and Transnational Connections
Edited by Evangelia Tastsoglou and Alexandra Dobrowolsky
ISBN 978-0-7546-4379-1

Transnational Ruptures
Gender and Forced Migration
Catherine Nolin
ISBN 978-0-7546-3805-6

'Innocent Women and Children'
Gender, Norms and the Protection of Civilians
R. Charli Carpenter
ISBN 978-0-7546-4745-4

Turkey's Engagement with Global Women's Human Rights
Nüket Kardam
ISBN 978-0-7546-4168-1

(Un)thinking Citizenship
Feminist Debates in Contemporary South Africa
Edited by Amanda Gouws
ISBN 978-0-7546-3878-0

Vulnerable Bodies
Gender, the UN and the Global Refugee Crisis
Erin K. Baines
ISBN 978-0-7546-3734-9

Setting the Agenda for Global Peace
Conflict and Consensus Building
Anna C. Snyder
ISBN 978-0-7546-1933-8

For Product Safety Concerns and Information please contact our EU
representative GPSR@taylorandfrancis.com
Taylor & Francis Verlag GmbH, Kaufingerstraße 24, 80331 München, Germany